CORNELL STUDIES IN ENGLISH

EDITED BY

ROBERT CECIL BALD

DAVID DAICHES

CHARLES W. JONES

VOLUME XXXVII

SAMUEL RICHARDSON: MASTER PRINTER

BY WILLIAM M. SALE, JR.

Samuel Richardson: Master Printer

WILLIAM M. SALE, Jr.

Professor of English in Cornell University

CORNELL UNIVERSITY PRESS

Ithaca, New York, 1950

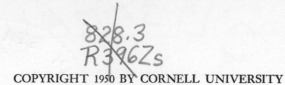
COPYRIGHT 1950 BY CORNELL UNIVERSITY

CORNELL UNIVERSITY PRESS

LONDON: GEOFFREY CUMBERLEGE

OXFORD UNIVERSITY PRESS

PRINTED IN THE UNITED STATES OF AMERICA BY THE

VAIL-BALLOU PRESS, INC., BINGHAMTON, NEW YORK

Prefatory Note

WHILE THIS BOOK was in press I received from Maggs Brothers, London booksellers, the kind permission to cite data from manuscripts owned by them and described in their catalogue (No. 773, Item 192) as "Two Accounts for the printing for Messrs. [John and James] Rivington by Richardson of various books. . . ." I have not examined these manuscripts, but from information supplied by Maggs Brothers I find that these accounts supplement the evidence that I have offered for Richardson's printing of editions of Chamberlayne's *Magnae Britanniae Notitia;* Church's *Vindication of the Miraculous Powers;* Delany's *Twenty Sermons on Social Duties;* Hervey's *Meditations and Contemplations;* Miller's *Gardeners Dictionary* and his *Gardeners Kalendar;* Richardson's *Aesop's Fables* and his *Letters Written to and from Particular Friends;* and Smith's *Select Manual of Divine Meditations.* I have no dates for these editions, but they undoubtedly fall between 1745 and 1756, the years in which John and James Rivington were in partnership.

The accounts enable me to add two books to my list:

John Dalton. *Remarks on XII. Historical Designs of Raphael,* 1752.

William Wogan. *An Essay on the Proper Lessons Appointed by the Liturgy of the Church of England to be Read on*

Sundays and Chief Festivals Throughout the Year, 4 vols., 1754.

There remain three books referred to in these accounts by titles that make identification difficult: "Description of Spain," "Bishop of Bristol's [John Conybeare's] sermon," and "Letters, and sermon by the Bishop of Oxford [Thomas Secker]."

My indebtedness to Maggs Brothers is matched by that I feel due to other booksellers both in America and in England, and in special degree to members of the staffs of libraries and repositories of manuscripts. I cannot refrain from specifically acknowledging the extraordinary demands I have made on the British Museum and the Yale University Library, or from expressing gratitude for the kindness shown me by the institutions whose books and manuscripts are cited in my notes. My colleague, Robert Cecil Bald, has allowed me continuously to profit by his wisdom. The editors of Cornell University Press have been gracious in their help with a difficult manuscript. Only one person, however, knows each step that was taken and was never lacking in understanding.

W. M. S., Jʀ.

Ithaca, New York
August 8, 1950

Contents

SAMUEL RICHARDSON: MASTER PRINTER

CHAPTER I

Introduction

SAMUEL RICHARDSON, master printer of Salisbury Court, began to emerge from the comparative obscurity of a successful London tradesman on Thursday, 6 November 1740, when, with the publication of *Pamela*, he started his career as an English novelist. Within the decade that followed the extraordinary success of *Pamela*, he wrote *Clarissa* and *Sir Charles Grandison*, and established himself as the most popular novelist of the century. Richardson had lived for fifty years before he sat down to write the story that was to become generally known as "the first English novel." The details of these fifty years are sparse indeed: they are recorded in summary chapters or in appendices to his biographies. The clues to the recovery of these details lie in Richardson's career as a printer; the pursuit of these clues leads to Salisbury Court, where he successfully met the conditions of the eighteenth-century book trade and found the way to prosperity and an established social position, from which he could observe the most vital social problem of his age—the interpenetration of the emergent middle class and the surviving aristocracy.

The biographer of the novelist must have a means of recovering the details of a half-century of Richardson's life if he is to find the pattern by which that life can be made comprehensible and humanly significant. Any critic, not time-bound within his own century, should have available such a body of information, that he may decide which facts are relevant in an interpretation of Richardson's fiction. This fiction shows his extraordinary awareness of class differences, his sensitiveness to human problems that arise from the interpenetration of classes. He realized for his generation the conditions of life that defined its hopes and that set limits to the fulfillment of those hopes. If we are ever to see more clearly the meaning that his fiction had for his own century and that it may have for ours, we must see more clearly how his fiction rendered the conflicts he saw in his own society. We cannot gain this knowledge, however, by divorcing the man from those activities that were the major preoccupation of his life.

Almost all the records of his career as printer have disappeared and in all likelihood have been destroyed. Perhaps the gravest disappointment of Richardson's life was the death of four sons and one nephew by whom he hoped to see his press perpetuated; and one of the sorrows of his last years came with the realization that a second nephew—one to whom he must entrust his plant or see it pass out of the family—was in his opinion an incompetent and irresponsible workman. When his press lost its master, it rapidly sank into unimportance. His surviving daughters and their husbands had no inclination or aptitude for carrying on the business. The account books of his press, which he kept with such meticulous accuracy, will probably never be found. To compensate in some manner for this loss the present study has been undertaken.

If we are to understand the character of the press and of its master, we must have a list of books that he printed. In the compilation of such a list, evidence provided by letters, accounts, occasional printing bills, and other similar documents has been used. But such evidence will not suffice. Hence the major portion of this study is based on the use of bibliographical evidence, and the argument for the validity of that evidence is set forth in detail in Chapter IX. I believe that a printer's work may be identified by the presence of his ornaments in books that he prints. I have therefore provided reproductions of many of Richardson's ornaments and, using these ornaments as evidence, have compiled a list of some five hundred books that came from his press.

From the list of books thus compiled and from other sources of information, I have acquired a body of facts that permits me to assert a threefold aim for this study. In the first place, this study provides a more complete story of an eighteenth-century printer and his press than any now available. In the second place, it provides a method by which the work of other presses may be studied and by which we may eventually learn who printed most of the books published in this century. In the third place, it traces the growth of a press under the direction of a man who so conducted his affairs as to become independent of the whims and favors of booksellers. From the outset of his career Richardson began to exercise choice over the books that he printed. As he became more and more independent, the exercise of this choice became more clearly a measure of his preferences and his prejudices. His press assumed a character that was in large part the character of its master. Consequently, in a list of books that he printed may be found clues that will lead to a fresh estimate of the social, political, and moral aspects of his life.

The only important part of his printing that I have neglected is the printing of his own novels. In the historical notes to my *Samuel Richardson: A Bibliographical Record of His Literary Career*, I have discussed in detail the printing and publication of these novels. Therefore I have chosen not to repeat here what is already available, though the choice was made with some reluctance. The lengths to which an eighteenth-century printer would go to save paper at the expense of labor, for example, is illustrated clearly in the printing of *Clarissa*. The difficulties that London printers encountered in meeting the threats of Dublin piracies is fully exemplified in Richardson's experiences with the publication of *Sir Charles Grandison*.

The materials of this book can be organized chronologically or they can be grouped so as to illustrate various aspects of the career of a printer. I finally elected to set forth in the second chapter the development of Richardson's plant and his rise to material prosperity and professional prominence from printer's apprentice to master of the Company of Stationers. In that chapter I have followed in part a chronological scheme, mentioning only briefly his relations with the periodical press, his government contracts, his changing relations with the trade, his printing for large bookselling congers, his ventures into publishing, his extensive printing "for the author," and his half-share in the patent of law printer to the King. In chapters following that one, I have treated at greater length these various aspects of his career, for I believe that they can be more readily comprehended if presented in an uninterrupted discussion than if considered as part of his activity in successive decades.

The present study is not a biography. Its aims are more modest than this. By presenting chapters in Richardson's life as a printer, I hope to add considerably to the data that we now have and to point the way by which our knowledge of Richardson may be materially increased. I have resisted the temptation to follow many of the clues offered by this study, for to try to write simultaneously the story of a printer and the life of a novelist seemed to bring into jeopardy any unity that this book might achieve. It has been apparent, however, that Richardson's activities during the first fifty years of his life were determined by the opportunities and the limitations of his trade, and by those alone. Nor did his success as a novelist divert his interest from the affairs of his press. Writing was always an avocation. Salisbury Square was to him a microcosm. From this small court he seldom strayed, and never without impatience to be back again. Here was his world, this small square with innumerable smaller courts opening into it, located just off Fleet Street at whose top stood what Richardson called "the bar of Temple Bar," separating the citizenry of London from the socially favored of Westminster. To his activities within the confines of this small world we must look if we hope to find the influences that shaped his mind and that finally made themselves felt in the nature and structure of his novels.

CHAPTER II

Master Printer

IN 1771 William Strahan, then one of the most prominent and prosperous of London printers, wrote to his friend in America, David Hall, describing in some detail the extent of his business. He pointed out that he owned a share of the copyright of many books that he printed. He held in partnership the patent for printing law books and the patent of King's printer. He had interested himself in the *London Chronicle*, a newspaper—in fact died possessed of a one-ninth share in this paper and a one-twentieth share in the *Public Advertiser*. He had been the printer of Ralph Griffiths' *Monthly Review*. Strahan wrote of this diversification with pride. "I quickly saw, that if I confined myself to mere *printing for Booksellers* I might be able to live, but very little more than live, I therefore soon determined to launch out into other Branches in Connection with my own, in which I have happily succeeded, to the Astonishment of the rest of the Trade here, who never dreamt of going out of the old beaten Track. Thus I have made the Name of *Printer* more respectable than ever it was before, and taught them to emancipate themselves from the Slavery in which the Booksellers held them." [1] Thus did one Scotsman seek to impress another, located in remote America.

Strahan was not exaggerating his success, but in his methods of achieving it he had been anticipated by a half-century. In the 1730's Samuel Richardson was well on his way toward securing the same kind of emancipation from the booksellers of which Strahan writes. Richardson had not only moved out of "the old beaten track," but he had moved out in precisely the same directions that Strahan had moved with such pride. He had foreseen that, with the rapid development in the physical facilities for making books, the printer would be overshadowed by the towering figures of the booksellers. His rise to prosperity was marked by his acquisition of shares in the copyright of books, by his partnerships in newspapers, by his securing of government contracts, by his printing of the *Philosophical Transactions* for the Royal Society, by his monopoly rights in the printing of law books.

This rise was gradual but continuous. It can in part be measured by the changes in his printing establishment and by his advance through the lower offices to the mastership of the Company of Stationers. These changes and this advance have never been fully recorded, nor have they been presented free of the minor inaccuracies that cling tenaciously to the story of his early years.[2] With as little repetition of well-known facts as is consistent with a continuous thread of discourse, I should like to set forth in this chapter the stages in the growth of his printing plant and an account of his relations first with his workmen and then with his fellow Stationers.

Richardson was bound apprentice to John Wilde on 1 July 1706,[3] and after serving seven years at Wilde's shop in Golden Lion Court, Aldersgate Street, under "a master who grudged every hour . . . that tended not to his profit," he left Wilde to become the "Overseer and Corrector of a Printing-Office," in a location that has not been identified. Septimus Rivington, writing in 1919, associates Richardson with a shop in Staining Lane, but I think incorrectly.[4] In the 1750's one of Rivington's ancestors, Charles Rivington, Jr., who served his apprenticeship with Richardson, became master of a plant in Staining Lane; [5] but his shop was part of the former residence of Sir Richard Levett, Lord Mayor of London, and could not have been the site of a printing plant before the death of Levett's son in 1740.[6] Richardson may have served as overseer in an unidentified shop in this little lane, or he may possibly have served with John Leake in Jewin Street, and thus first established relations with a family that he was to be intimately acquainted with until his death.

But wherever he went in 1713, we know that he did not remain with Wilde after he was out of his indentures and that, before he was able to start in business for himself, he served as overseer for five or six years, during which period—on 13 June 1715—he took up his freedom.[7] In these years he was making a guinea a week or more, and he was planning for the time when he could open his own shop. He saw that the center of the London book trade was shifting from the district in which he had served his apprenticeship, from Aldersgate Ward and Little Britain to the area of London dominated by St. Paul's Cathedral —Paternoster Row, Stationers' Court, Fleet Street, and the courts leading off Fleet Street. Consequently, when in 1719 or a little later he was ready to set up in business for himself, he took a house in the Salisbury Court district, just off Fleet Street. He always gave his address as Salisbury Court, but during his lifetime he lived in three different houses in this area. The first house can be readily located. At this period Dorset Street led off Fleet Street to the south into an open square from which led a number of small courts and alleys. The open square and the continuation of Dorset Street, leading down to the old playhouse and Dorset Stairs on the Thames, was frequently referred to as Salisbury Court. With good reason, then, Richardson could give as his address Salisbury Court. But actually his first printing plant was on the corner of Blue Ball Court and the continuation of Dorset Street, a house which formed the southeast corner of the open square.[8] This house—later the site of Bell's Buildings—could have been described as in Blue Ball Court or as in Salisbury Court, but the latter address would have been much more useful for a London tradesman.

To this house in 1721 Richardson brought his wife, Martha, the daughter of his old master, John Wilde, who had died in 1720.[9] He and his family lived in the same house in which he had set up his presses. It was not the one of "grand outward appearance" in which Laetitia Pilkington found the Richardsons in the 1740's.[10] That house was on the western side of the open square, located by one of his neighbors as "in the centre of Salisbury-square, or Salisbury-court, as it was then called." [11] When Richardson first moved to this district, the house on the western side of the square was rented by William Ventris, an auctioneer, who paid an annual rental of £57. Richardson paid but £26.[12]

Salisbury Court and its surroundings had been the property of the Sackville family for many years, and it was to the steward of Lionel Cranfield Sackville, first Duke of Dorset, that Richardson paid his rent. In November 1720, the Duke's steward entertained all the inhabitants at a "noble Feast" held in the Three Tuns, a public house in the court. He informed his guests that the Duke planned to hold court at the Three Tuns where all causes in case of debts would be heard and determined by twelve jurymen elected by the inhabitants of the district.[13] The jury was duly chosen and thus was constituted one of the last of the protests of these little pockets of population against the jurisdiction of the City.

The character of the inhabitants of Salisbury Court and its immediate environs had undergone a change between the seventeenth and the eighteenth centuries. Actors and men of letters who had made their residence in this section during the Restoration had given way to tradesmen and artisans. When the Duke's Theatre in Dorset Gardens was thriving, the locality had attracted such men as Betterton, Harris, Cave Underhill, and Sandford. Lady D'Avenant, widow of Sir William, had lived there after her husband's death. From Dorset Court John Locke dated his *Essay Concerning Human Understanding* in 1689—the essay that was to be Pamela's authority for the education of her children. Both Thomas Shadwell and John Dryden had lived in the neighborhood for a time; and at No. 13 Salisbury Court Samuel Pepys had been born. By the turn of the century, however, the neighborhood had attracted insolvent debtors, gamesters, petty thieves, and prostitutes because of its proximity to Whitefriars, the "Alsatia" of Shadwell's *Squire*.

These hangers-on in crime still consorted in the neighboring alleys when Richardson moved into the district, but Salisbury Court itself had become an island of respectability. Its inhabitants were innkeepers, clerks, doctors, attorneys, printers. John Senex was a bookseller at the Globe in Salisbury Court before he moved out into Fleet Street; Nicholas Blandford was a printer in the court in 1724; and in 1728 John Purser gave his address as Salisbury Court in the colophons of the *Daily Journal*. John Green, a clerk in the employ of the Carpenters and Joiners Company, lived in the court, because the company's timber yard was located near the riverbank. Dr. Robert Eaton in Dorset Street secured a paragraph in the *Daily Journal* when he died at the age of one hundred and seven. The doctor had been responsible for a medicine known as "Eaton's Balsamic Cordial Styptic," which had virtue enough to secure the recommendation of Richardson's friend and physician, Dr. George Cheyne. After Eaton's death its sale was entrusted to another neighborhood friend of Richardson's, the daughter of an attorney, Thomas Dutton. Miss Dutton, frequently referred to in Richardson's letters, died at his country house in Parson's Green many years later. Another of his correspondents, Francis Grainger, was the daughter of Thomas Grainger, proprietor of the Rose in Salisbury Court. Born in 1726, she grew up in the neighborhood, and when her family acquired a country place, she and Richardson exchanged a number of letters. William Ventris, a prosperous auctioneer, occupied the handsomest house in the court; and north of his house was the office of the corporation for the relief of clergymen's widows and children. Through the services of this organization, the son of a deceased clergyman was placed as an apprentice in Richardson's shop.[14] Thus it may clearly be seen that, despite the continued poverty and unsavory reputation of the smaller courts and alleys, Salisbury Court itself was acquiring a tone set by prospering middle-class Londoners.

At what date in his rise to prosperity Richardson moved from the house in Blue Ball Court to the western side of Salisbury Court cannot be accurately determined. All evidence, however, suggests that the move took place in the 1730's. Martha Richardson, his first wife, died in 1731 and in the following year he married Elizabeth Leake. Few memories of domestic happiness lingered about the house in Blue Ball Court. In the ten years of his married life with Martha, she had borne six children, five sons and one daughter. In a desperate attempt to perpetuate the name of Samuel, the Richardsons had named three of their infant boys after their father. The sixth child—the third Samuel—was the only one to survive his mother. He died in the following year.[15] Perhaps it was on his marriage with Elizabeth Leake that Richardson moved to the more spacious house across the square.

During the first five years of this decade Richardson had five apprentices living with him for most of the time, and after 1733 his business was considerably augmented by his contracts with the House of Commons. Furthermore, at least as early as 1736 Richardson was sharing in the lease of a country house, if I have properly interpreted Aaron Hill's expressed desire to become "a Witness of That friendly and agreeable Freedom where in you *divide and enjoy* a Retreat" in the country.[16] In December 1738, we know that he leased a country house in North-End Road, Fulham, for which—with two adjoining pieces of land—he paid an annual rental of £30.[17] It is not likely that Richardson would have leased a house outside London before improving his living conditions and expanding his plant in the city. Not until 1743, however, when Laetitia Pilkington visited him, do we have the first witness to his move to the western side of the square, to the house formerly occupied by Ventris. Two doors north was another house that Richardson soon rented as a storehouse and as lodgings for two families of his workmen. For this house he paid £15 rent, bringing his annual expenses for city and country houses to £102.[18]

Even after acquiring the new house in Salisbury Square, Richardson continued to house his family and his presses under the same roof. The ground floor and the attic of this house in the center of the square were used for business purposes, and the not inconsiderable upper floors, including the "little closet" where *Pamela* was written, were residence for himself, his wife, and the four children of Elizabeth Richardson who survived infancy. For fifteen or twenty years the house proved adequate, but it was an old house when the Richardsons moved in, it was damaged by fire in 1752, and by 1755 it had been rendered unsafe for occupancy by the weight and action of the presses in the attic.[19] Richardson thereupon planned a major change. The house in the northwest corner of the square, which had been occupied by his workmen, was remodeled to make a residence for his family. He converted it into a pleasant three-story brick house, with dormer windows across the front, opening into the attic. Solidly reconstructed, this house—known in the nineteenth century as No. 11 Salisbury Square—stood until torn down in 1896.[20]

Richardson decided not to combine residence and printing plant any longer. The new residence was forty-five feet in depth. Into its north wall at the rear Richardson opened a door leading into White Lion Court, which in turn led directly into Fleet Street. On the land on both sides of White Lion Court he took a sixty-year lease at £69 annual rent. He then tore down the old houses on both sides of this twelve-foot paved court and built two ranges of buildings, ninety-seven feet on one side and sixty feet on the other, joining the ranges by a bridge extending over the passage. The rent on his remodeled house was £80 and the cost of all alterations was £1400, but Richardson felt that he had secured a long lease on reasonable terms and that the investment would be turned to the good account of his family after his death.[21] In March 1756, they moved into the new residence, "less handsome and less roomy," as Richardson admitted, "but infinitely more convenient" than the old house. They might have moved in the autumn of 1755, but Mrs. Richardson insisted on remaining in the house they had occupied for so many years until the lease expired. She was never quite reconciled to the move. "Everybody," he said, "is more pleased with what I have done than my Wife."[22]

Richardson hoped that a change which he had made in his country residence in 1754 would compensate his wife for the inconvenience of a less commodious city residence. His landlord at North-End died, and the new owner of the property sought to increase the rent by £15 annually. Richardson refused, despite the fact that he had made improvements on the place, including the building of the summer house in which much of *Clarissa* was written.[23] He leased a house at Parson's Green, in the same parish but within the most aristocratic section of Fulham. After making alterations to the house and garden which cost him £300, he and his family moved on 30 October 1754.[24] The house, as Richardson described it, was an old monasterylike building, with a porch at the door, looking out upon the King's Road to Fulham, Putney, Kew, and Richmond.[25] Another summer house was built in the gardens to the rear, but the period of Richardson's authorship had come to an end with the writing of *Sir Charles Grandison* in 1753.

The steady improvement in his living conditions, the enlargement of his plant, and the increasing supply of available capital are all indexes to the profitable management of his business. Another index of his prosperity can be found in the number and in the character of the apprentices that he bound. In March 1722, within about three years after setting up as master printer, Richardson became a liveryman of the Stationers' Company,[26] and by August of that year he was ready to bind his first apprentices. He took over three young men who had originally been bound to members of the family of John Leake.[27]

In just what way Richardson made the acquaintance of the Leakes is not known. It is possible, as I have suggested, that he may have served as overseer for Leake in the latter's shop in Jewin Street. But the Leakes, like Richardson himself, recognized that the printing trade was shifting from the Aldersgate area toward St. Paul's. Near the close of the second decade, John Leake, the head of the family, decided to move his printing plant from Jewin Street to Old 'Change, just east of the cathedral; and James, his son, who had served his apprenticeship to a bookseller, established a bookshop in Stationers' Court, not far from his father's plant.[28] John Leake died in February 1720, leaving a wife and daughter, both named Elizabeth. For a short time his wife attempted to carry on the business; in fact, in August 1720, she bound a new apprentice. But her age and her failing health —she died in April 1721—made such an arrangement impractical.[29] Her son James seems to have had no disposition to take over a printing plant. He had his bookshop in Stationers' Court. After his mother's death he married the daughter of a bookseller at Bath, and at least as early as 1722, he had opened a shop at Bath in which he was to become one of the best known booksellers of the century.[30]

But in September 1720, James Leake became a liveryman of the Stationers' Company and in October he bound an apprentice, Thomas Gover, who was seeking to follow the trade of printer and indeed later became a master printer in Bridewell Precinct, Fleet Street.[31] At the time of Gover's binding Leake was described in the records of the Stationers' Company as a "Salisbury

Court Printer." This description is difficult to account for. It is possible that in the autumn of 1720, when Leake found himself about to inherit a printing plant that he did not want, he transferred his father's equipment and apprentices to Richardson's shop in Salisbury Court. If so, he may have had the intention of entering into some kind of partnership between printer and bookseller, or he may merely have hoped to dispose of property which he did not plan to use. Among the printers' ornaments used by Richardson in the early 1720's was at least one that I feel sure had been the property of John Leake;[32] and in August 1722, when Richardson was ready for his first apprentices, he took over from the Leakes three young men—Gover, who had been bound to James Leake, George Mitchell, bound to James' father, and Joseph Chrichley, bound to his mother.[33] It must have been at this time that Richardson became acquainted with James' sister, Elizabeth, for though she moved to Bath with her brother after their mother's death, she was to become, ten years later, Richardson's second wife. In the year before her marriage she presented to a friend a copy of one of the first volumes printed by Richardson, an edition of Jonathan Smedley's poems, printed "for the author" in 1721.[34]

Quite possibly, then, it was through his friendship with the Leakes that he was able to expand his plant on advantageous terms and to secure the services of partially trained apprentices. Three apprentices was a considerable number to house and to keep gainfully employed at one period, but during the decade of the 1720's Richardson continued to require this amount of assistance. When the three men whom he had taken over from the Leakes completed their terms, he promptly bound others, taking William Price and Samuel Jolley in 1727 and two years later binding Bethell Wellington, youngest son of the late Richard Wellington, a prominent bookseller in the first quarter of the century.[35]

All three of the apprentices that Richardson acquired from

the Leakes advanced far enough in the trade to take up their freedom in the Stationers' Company, and at least two of them became master printers. Thomas Gover, as I have noted, took up business for himself in Bridewell Precinct. An example of his printing, cited by Henry Plomer in his *Dictionary* as evidence of Gover's careful workmanship, looks so much like the printing of Richardson himself that at one time I thought it had come from the shop of Gover's master. Another of the three, Joseph Chrichley (or Crichley), had his shop in Charing Cross. He was one of the printers employed by Robert Dodsley. During part of the period in which Richardson was actively associated with William Webster's *Weekly Miscellany*, Chrichley's press was employed to print this periodical.

Richardson undoubtedly had one or more journeymen employees working for him from the start, but as Ellic Howe has pointed out in his *London Compositor*,[36] there is little or no information by which journeymen working in individual shops can be identified. We do know that for a short period Richardson employed Thomas Gent as a compositor, primarily to assist him with the part of Nathan Bailey's *Dictionary* that had been assigned to his shop by the bookselling conger that was sponsoring that work.[37] Undoubtedly some of his apprentices remained with him as journeymen. He and his apprentices could not have carried on the work that fell to his press during its first decade without some assistance, for during this period, as I shall describe in detail later, he began the printing of newspapers, made his first ventures into publishing, and attracted the attention of bookselling congers who were looking for capable printers and men responsible enough financially to take a share in the books that they were planning to publish.

Throughout his career Richardson continued to bind about a half-dozen apprentices during each decade, and there were periods when he had as many as four or five apprentices working for him at the same time. This number was considerably above the average, and not always equaled by the larger presses. If we follow the later careers of these young men, we find also that a far larger number of them than was usual made some advance in their profession after leaving Richardson's shop. Of Richardson's policy in the training and governing of his apprentices we have ample evidence. Undoubtedly he had just such an elaborate set of rules for his compositors, pressmen, and apprentices as is illustrated in Howe's *London Compositor*.[38] Such regulations seem to have been standard. But he was not content merely to set up rules with a corresponding system of fines for their infringement. He accepted the responsibility for the moral guidance of his apprentices and felt that he stood in the relation both of parent and of master to them.

His obligations and those of his apprentices he set forth in a letter to his nephew. In August 1732, when it seemed unlikely that Richardson was to have a son to succeed him, he bound his nephew, Thomas Verren Richardson. On this occasion he wrote the boy a long letter, setting forth in detail the professional duties and the moral obligations that he expected an apprentice to recognize. The original text of this letter was not published until 1804, but in a revised form it appeared as the second part of *The Apprentice's Vade Mecum*, a book of general instructions for an apprentice which Richardson wrote and published in 1734 and which has been fully described by Alan McKillop as the earliest known of Richardson's writings.[39] In briefer form this letter was later printed by the Company of Stationers, and a copy is still given to each apprentice along with the Bible and the Book of Common Prayer.[40]

The advice given in this letter is of the sort that might be expected, but it indicates a genuine concern with the career of his apprentices—a concern that bore fruit in later years. Of boys bound to the printer's trade, only about one in three advanced far enough to secure his freedom, and only a much smaller number advanced beyond the status of journeyman to become master of a press.[41] Of the twenty-four apprentices who served all or part of their seven years with Richardson, fourteen became freemen of the company. One of the ten who was not freed was Richardson's nephew, Thomas, who died within three months of being bound; another—Timothy Dicey—joined his father, a printer in Northampton, and for this reason probably did not take up his freedom in London.

Freedom was indispensable for those who looked forward to becoming master printers, but comparatively few achieved this status. In the eighteenth century no legislation limited the number of master printers, or the number of apprentices that any master printer might bind.[42] Such regulations as obtained in the seventeenth century had envisaged a permanent class of journeymen printers, and the freedom from regulation that characterized the trade in the eighteenth century did not alter this situation. Under this unrestricted competition, however, a dozen large presses did most of the printing, and at best many freemen set up for themselves only to face a struggle in which they were embarrassingly dependent upon the suffrage of booksellers. If a young man out of his indentures had insufficient confidence in his ability or slender prospects of success, he might well hesitate before taking up his freedom. Richardson himself completed his apprenticeship two years before he became free of the Company. For a man who had no intention of becoming a master printer, freedom qualified him only to partake of the Company's charity in old age or sickness. In consequence of this situation, we may infer that Richardson selected his apprentices carefully and trained them well, if only eight out of twenty-four failed to take up their freedom.

The number of apprentices bound by a master and the amount of premium paid to him on his accepting an apprentice are indexes of the size and importance of his press. Among the large presses were those of the Basketts, who bound nineteen apprentices between 1724 and 1753; of John Watts, who bound fifteen ap-

prentices between 1725 and 1749; of Henry Woodfall, who
bound seventeen apprentices between 1725 and 1747; of James
Bettenham, who bound seventeen apprentices between 1725 and
1755; and of the Bowyers, who bound twenty-four apprentices
between 1727 and 1765.[43] Obviously the number of apprentices
bound is not a precise measure of the size of the press: young men
may die, may become discouraged or prove incompetent; masters
may have available only limited space in which to house their
apprentices. But in general, the larger the press, the greater the
number of apprentices. In like manner, the size of the premium
paid is an index of the amount of inducement necessary to persuade a master printer to accept an apprentice. When a higher
premium than usual was paid, the parent or guardian had a right
to expect that his son would receive better and more extensive
instruction in order that he might be prepared eventually to rise
to the position of master printer. Richardson, in common with
other masters, occasionally accepted an apprentice without asking
any premium. Four of his twenty-four apprentices were turned
over to him by other masters. Of the twenty who were originally
bound to him, five were accepted without premiums. The fifteen
from whom premiums were asked paid amounts ranging from
£5 to £72, with an average payment of £39. This premium was
twice that of the average for the whole trade. Woodfall's and
Bettenham's premiums, for example, averaged £25, and Bowyer's averaged £20.[44] The size of the premium which he asked
increased steadily with the reputation of his press, though at all
periods he was prepared to accept boys whose fathers were unable to pay any premium.

Information about all of Richardson's apprentices, taken from
the manuscript records of the Stationers' Company, is provided in
Appendix C (pp. 350–352). The social position of their parents
represents many grades of English society. He bound the son of
a butcher, a mealman, a baker, a staymaker, a chairmaker, an upholder, a cutler. One was the son of a scrivener, one of a barber

surgeon; two were sons of the clergy; one was the son of a printer; five were sons of booksellers; four were sons of "gentlemen." Fifteen of the apprentices were from London or its immediate environs; eight were from the country, from Hertfordshire, Hampshire, Surrey, Lincolnshire, Northamptonshire, and Staffordshire; one from a locale that I have not discovered. Eight of Richardson's apprentices were fatherless when they began their terms.

Fourteen of Richardson's apprentices became freemen; at least nine of these became master printers. The subsequent careers of Gover and Chrichley have been briefly described. Charles Rivington, the son of the founder of the present firm of Rivington, set up for himself in Staining Lane and carried on an extensive business. In 1771 he was appointed City printer. In 1785—five years before his death—his address was 5 Noble Street, Foster Lane. Between 1753 and 1789 he bound twenty-nine apprentices.[45] William Richardson, Samuel's nephew, and Samuel Clark made some reputation for themselves, both as partners and independently. William Richardson's shop was in Castle Yard, Holborn, but he took over the direction of his uncle's business on the latter's death in 1761. He was the designer of a new printing type "in imitation of the Law-Hand." This type, called "Engrossing," was to be used as the proper character for leases, agreements, indentures, and so forth.[46] Halhed Garland went to Dublin after completing his apprenticeship and established a shop in Essex Street. He probably returned to London, for he took up his freedom in the London Company in 1752.

As late as 1785 Samuel Axtell was established as a master printer. In that year he was located at 17 Little New Street and had as his partner his son John, who had served his apprenticeship with Charles Rivington. Between 1769 and 1781 Samuel Axtell bound ten apprentices.[47] Richard Hett, son of a London bookseller, was associated with one of the most important printing houses in London, that of John Watts, who aided Caslon in starting his type foundry and with whom Benjamin Franklin was employed as compositor. Watts lived until 1763 and his name overshadowed that of his assistants. Hett, however, eventually succeeded to the business, and was still directing it in 1785.[48] Henry Campbell, when a boy of six, was staying with Aaron Hill and sat listening while Hill read *Pamela* to his daughters. "He is the son of an honest, poor soldier," Hill wrote Richardson, "quite unbefriended, and born to no prospect." Richardson later sent the boy a copy of his edition of Aesop's *Fables*.[49] In 1751 he accepted him as an apprentice without asking any monetary consideration. Campbell was one of the two witnesses to Richardson's will and the one member of his plant, besides his foreman, who received by that will a mourning ring. After securing his freedom in 1758, he set up in business for himself in Popping's Alley (Popingey Alley), which leads out of Fleet Street to the north opposite Richardson's plant in White Lion Court.[50]

Though some of Richardson's apprentices undoubtedly stayed on with him as journeymen after they had served their seven years, he needed in his expanding plant the services of more printers than he himself could train. The number of journeymen that he employed at any period is not known, but during the 1750's his weekly salaries for journeymen were between £30 and £40. This weekly payroll meant that he was then employing forty or more journeymen, for the wages of the best journeymen were a guinea a week, and many of them did not earn this much. This maximum wage varied but little throughout the century. Thomas Gent earned 20s. per week in 1719; Horace Walpole paid his pressmen a guinea a week in 1759; and Samuel Johnson, after placing a friend of his with William Strahan in 1774, wrote that he might, if he proved an able journeyman, "always get a guinea a week." [51] Such data as these are obviously not satisfactory, but it was not until 1785—the year in which an initial agreement between master printers and compositors was reached—that compositors' wage rates and the methods of charging for piecework can be accurately determined.[52]

Richardson's printing charges, however, do provide a means of determining fairly accurately, not only the amount of profit he made from a book, but also the amount per sheet that he paid a compositor, a pressman, and a reader for the press. His charges varied with the nature of the text, the amount of tabular material, the number of footnotes or marginal notes required, the amount of type to the page, and—when the price of paper was included —the quality of the paper. Upon such items as these he based his pay to his compositors. His charges also varied with the size of the edition, for upon the size of the edition depended the cost of work at the press—the wage of the pressmen. After 1785 both compositors and pressmen asked for an increase in base pay and for a specific definition of that pay in terms of the nature of the text and the size of the edition. Before 1785 the amount of increase in pay that was allowed as compensation for the increased difficulty of the job was at the discretion of the master of the press.

Among the better printers no significant difference in prices, and hence in wages, seems to have existed. An examination of the ledgers of William Strahan shows, for example, that his charges for a given kind of printing job were approximately the same as Richardson's.[53] In writing a detailed account to Alexander Gordon of his own method of determining prices, Richardson clearly implied that he was speaking not for himself alone but for other printers who might be employed to serve the society of which Gordon was then secretary, the Society for the Encouragement of Learning.[54] Not only does there seem to have been little difference in charges as between one competent printer and another, but there seems also to have been little difference as between one decade and the next. This fact is attested both by Strahan's ledgers and by the annual bills that Richardson submitted to the government for his printing for the House of Commons between 1733 and 1761.[55]

Richardson's ledgers, as I have said, have disappeared, but the letter to Gordon, referred to in the preceding paragraph, and a few printing bills, in addition to those submitted to the Treasury, provide the information for an adequate estimate of his practices.[56] The wages of the compositor were dependent upon the amount of type that he set and the number of interruptions in the operation of composing that were occasioned by stopping to make up a type page, to impose, to correct, and so forth. He could set more type per hour if he was working on a duodecimo with normal space between lines, for example, than if he was working on an octavo with the lines separated by an unusual number of leads. There is reason to believe that some masters paid compositors slightly less when they were working with smaller-size type, but whether or not Richardson followed this practice, his compositors made more money when working on duodecimos with smaller type than when working on octavos with type somewhat larger. When James Hervey wanted Richardson to reprint in duodecimo a work that had originally appeared in quarto, Richardson explained to Hervey that the bill would be larger. "Small Print is dearer than large." [57]

If Richardson's compositors were working on an octavo with reasonably normal text, they were paid at the rate of 8*s*. per sheet. If the typesetting required notes, the pay per sheet normally ranged between 9*s*. and 12*s*., depending upon the number of notes. For a book in quarto, Richardson paid the compositor 5*s*. 2*d*. per sheet; for a folio, 12*s*.; and for a duodecimo, 10*s*. 6*d*. The composing of a double-column folio page with marginal notes, such as that in the *Journals* of the House of Commons, seems to have been paid at the rate of 13*s*. 8*d*. per sheet, or thereabouts. A folio page with complicated tabular material might earn for the compositor as much as 17*s*. per sheet. If a good compositor made a guinea a week, then a week's work on an octavo with straight text consisted in his setting about two and a half sheets, or about forty pages of type.

The wages of his pressmen depended upon the number of sheets that were pulled. Richardson paid for presswork at the rate of 1s. 2d. per "token," that is per 250 sheets, printed on both sides. He does not seem to have varied his price according to the number of impressions required. The presswork for 500 copies was figured at 2s. 4d.; for 750 copies, at 3s. 6d.; for 1,000 copies, at 4s. 8d., per sheet. If there were two men at the press, one to ink and the other to pull the forme, a production of 125 sheets per hour, printed on both sides, might be accomplished.[58] Thus two pressmen, working ten hours a day, might print 1,250 sheets, for which they would be paid, between them, 5s. 10d. Each might earn about 3s. a day, or a little less per week than a good compositor.

For reading proof Richardson paid a workman 2d. to the shilling on the price paid to the compositor. If the compositor was working on copy for which he was paid 8s. per sheet, the proof-reader was paid 1s. 4d. for his job. To the sum of the amounts paid per sheet to the compositor, the pressmen, and the reader, Richardson added 50 percent for his own profit. If an edition of 1,000 copies of an octavo was to be printed, the composition would cost 8s. per sheet, the presswork 4s. 8d., and the proof-reading 1s. 4d.—a total of 14s. To this sum Richardson added 7s. as his profit, and billed the author or bookseller at the rate of a guinea a sheet. Consequently, if we have a printing bill of Richardson for 2,500 copies of a book in duodecimo at £1/16/0 per sheet, we know that Richardson claimed as his share 12s. per sheet; that the presswork was paid at the rate of 11s. 8d. per sheet; that the compositor earned 10s. 6d. per sheet; and the reader 1s. 10d.

The charges for paper were dependent upon the quality. In 1742, when Richardson appeared before the House of Commons to submit his estimate for printing the *Journals*, he said that good

English paper could be purchased at 12*s*. to 20*s*. a ream. When the printer included the charges for paper in his bill, he had, however, to base his charge on a ream made "perfect." The ream as it came from the manufacturer contained 20 quires, but two quires were "foul" and could be used only for pulling proof. Each quire had twenty-four sheets, but if the printer bought a ream of paper—480 sheets—he had only 432 usable sheets. To bring the ream to 500 sheets, Richardson figured that he must buy two additional quires with each ream, and an extra sheet to add to each of the twenty quires. Consequently when he quoted the paper charge as 15*s*. per ream, he meant that he was buying paper for which he paid the manufacturer about 13*s*. per ream.

To illustrate the whole procedure which Richardson used in keeping his accounts, a single book can be followed through the press. In 1738 he printed Sir William Keith's *History of the British Plantations in America*, in quarto, 1,000 copies, twenty-five and one-half sheets per copy. He needed 51 reams of paper, each ream made "perfect," that is, each ream containing 500 usable sheets. In his bill he entered a charge for 51 reams at 12*s*. per ream, for a total of £30/12. Since he got only 432 usable sheets per ream, he would have had to buy not 51 but 59 reams. Therefore, the kind of paper he actually used was bought at about 10*s*. 4*d*. per ream instead of 12*s*. His compositor would earn 5*s*. 2*d*. per sheet, or £6/11/9; his pressmen would be paid 4*s*. 8*d*. per sheet for 1,000 impressions, or £5/19/0; his reader, receiving 2*d*. in the shilling paid to the compositor, would be paid 10*d*. per sheet, or £1/1/3. Compositor, pressmen, and reader would thus receive 10*s*. 8*d*. per sheet, or £13/12/0 for the whole job. Richardson then added one half of £13/12/0 for his own profit, bringing the cost to the purchaser to 16*s*. per sheet, or to a total of £20/8/0. The paper charge for this book is three-fifths of the total charge.

Though we know in some detail the arrangements that Richardson made with his workmen, we know next to nothing about who these workmen were. The story still persists that Oliver Goldsmith worked for him for a short period, but I have no evidence to substantiate this. William Tewley of Whitefriars was the foreman of his press from a date at least as early as 1753 until Richardson's death.[59] Thomas Killingbeck was working for him as a compositor and Peter Bishop as a proofreader when Richardson discovered that piratical printers in Dublin had been supplied with sheets of *Sir Charles Grandison* before the English edition of this novel was published. He suspected these two men of being confederates in abetting the Dublin pirates and dismissed them both. Killingbeck, he said at the time, had worked for some years in Ireland before seeking employment in London.[60]

In August 1755, his nephew, William Richardson, completed his apprenticeship and was made a freeman of the Stationers' Company. At this date Richardson planned to entrust the management of his plant to his nephew. His old account books had been filled up, and he transcribed, as he said, "all that is to purpose in them, in new ones, and have taken great Pains in the doing them, for the Instruction of my Kinsman, my late Brother's Son, a worthy young Man, into whose Hands I shall commit them, and to whose Care consign the Managing Part of my Business, by Degrees, for the Sake of my Family hereafter." [61] This plan did not work out satisfactorily, however, and four years later William Richardson left his uncle to set up in business for himself in Castle Yard, Holborn.[62] In May 1759, Lady Bradshaigh wrote of a "good Mr. Bailey" who was serving as Richardson's deputy at the press while he was at Parson's Green.[63] This was undoubtedly the Mr. James Bailey of 9 St. John's Square, Clerkenwell, who, by a codicil to Richardson's will in 1760, was made coexecutor. It seems likely that he was the James Bailey who was master of the Stationers' Company in 1768.

In the main Richardson seems to have maintained good relations with his workmen. He was undoubtedly strict in his demands, and as his nervous disorders increased with age, he probably became more difficult. Yet two years before his death, when both his overseer and the corrector to his press resigned in order to go into business for themselves, he faced without complaint the tedious prospect of breaking two new men into the duties of these important jobs. "God prosper them in all their worthy Endeavours," he wrote.[64] His only serious difficulties came in the 1740's when journeymen in other trades, making demands for higher wages, were joined in this attempt by some journeyman printers. In November 1748, Richardson wrote: "At present we are but settling into a Calm with our Compositors, who have wanted to raise their Prices, and combined for that purpose, with as little Reason as Provocation—so that I, as well as others, have been forced to part with some of my Hands, and have not yet got them replaced to my Wish, and go but lamely on, with my Common Business." [65]

The journeymen had no alternative. Printers and booksellers in the Stationers' Company were in a position to make them come to terms. The compositor indeed might seem to have little cause for complaint when he could make between £50 and £60 a year, while an apprentice to a bookseller would be fortunate if he made £20 during the same period.[66] In a sense Richardson was right in saying that a compositor had little provocation for demanding an increase in wages. Workers in other trades fared much worse with respect to both wages and working conditions. But as the century progressed, the opportunities to escape from the permanent status of compositor became less. When the journeyman faced this fact, he naturally sought to improve his condition within the status to which he seemed permanently condemned.

Large presses like Richardson's absorbed most of the business. They were financially able to share in important publishing ventures; they could negotiate with the government for profitable contracts in which speed and accuracy were demanded; they were approached, as was Richardson, for the printing of such profitable work as the *Transactions* of the Royal Society, which, printed periodically, kept presses from standing idle; and they could, as Richardson did, amass £40,000 to £50,000 to buy a half-share in a monopoly right such as that of law printer to the King. The concentration of business under one roof, so well illustrated in Richardson's career, characterized the conditions of the trade in the eighteenth century. Such concentration was discouraging for the apprentice who, on completing his training, looked forward to starting in business for himself. It remained for William Strahan to secure the greatest concentration of monopoly rights in one printing establishment by acquiring a share in both the law patent and the King's printer's patent. But Richardson, more conspicuously than any other printer of the first half of the century, had shown the way that Strahan was to follow.

Richardson's steady improvement in his relations with the trade will be described in a later chapter. A brief statement of certain trends in these relations may serve, however, to mark the growth of his press. During the 1720's Richardson frequently accepted the job of printing only parts of books. He and Henry Woodfall, for example, shared the printing of Nathan Bailey's *Dictionary;* his press was assigned portions of the first edition of Defoe's *Tour Thro' Great Britain* and his *New Voyage Round the World;* he printed only a portion of the first volume and the whole of the third volume of a three-volume edition of Sidney's works; and to his press was allotted part of the second volume of the sixth edition of Thomas Burnet's *Sacred Theory of the Earth.* As his press grew in size, he seemed less disposed to accept the printing of parts of such comparatively small books, though he frequently accepted one or two volumes of large booksellers' projects like the folio editions of the *State Trials,* De Thou's *History,* and Harris' *Voyages;* and indeed the custom of turning over part of a printing job to another press continued throughout the first half of the century. After 1740, however, Richardson, as might be expected, was in the position of a printer seeking rather than rendering help. Volumes of the works of his friends, James Hervey and John Leland and Aaron Hill, were on occasions put out to other presses. Seven printers helped him with an edition of *Sir Charles Grandison* when he was threatened by Dublin pirates.

The printing of newspapers actively engaged his press during its first two decades, but as he became better established, he protected himself from slack periods by such steady printing as that of bills and reports of committees of the House of Commons, of the *Journals* of the House, and of the *Philosophical Transactions*. Near the close of his career, when he had at least nine presses to keep busy,[67] he acquired a share in the law patent and printed for himself and his partner all books protected by this patent. He made friends with certain prominent booksellers— Charles Rivington, John Osborn, Andrew Millar, among others —and these men kept his press supplied with manuscripts; he acquired a share in the copyright of books expensive enough as publishing ventures to require the co-operative effort of bookselling congers; and he extended his acquaintance among authors who continually returned to his press with new works or new editions of old works. He established the reputation of his press with certain authors in Ireland, and the reputation thus established brought him other work from Irishmen or Englishmen in Ireland. In this variety of ways the rise of his press can be traced.

With the growth in prominence of his press went his steady increase in prestige among his fellow stationers. Within two or three years after beginning in business, Richardson had prospered sufficiently to become a liveryman of the Stationers' Company and to pay the customary fine of £20 for the privilege of being clothed.[68] As a liveryman he could hold office in the Company and purchase larger shares of its stock than were available for the Company's yeomen. He was privileged to wear the Company's robes at public ceremonies, and a year after the payment

of his fine he could vote in the City elections, for both the higher
City officials and the members of Parliament for the City of
London.

In 1727, while still located at the shop in Blue Ball Court, Richardson's reputation was sufficiently advanced for him to be
marked as a potential officer of the Stationers' Company. In that
year he was elected renter-warden (or steward) of the Company,
with Nathaniel Mist, the notorious printer of *Mist's Weekly
Journal*, serving as his assistant.[69] The office of renter-warden in
London livery companies involved no important duties, but only
liverymen who had served or had paid the fine for not serving
in this office were eligible for election to higher offices. As Campbell pointed out in *The London Tradesman*, "a Youth, having
taken up his Freedom, if he is a popular Man, he may in two or
three Years have the Honour to be appointed Renter-Warden,
or Steward, which intitles him to the Privilege of treating Half
the Fraternity with an elegant and expensive Entertainment on
Lord-Mayor's Day, for the whole Company is treated by the two
Stewards on that Day, which may cost them, in some Companies,
thirty Pounds a-piece." [70] Renter-wardens of the Stationers'
Company contributed £24 each toward the banquet on Lord
Mayor's Day. Their only responsibility was the collection of the
four pence quarterage, due from all liverymen. By making an
investment only two pounds less than his annual rent, Richardson might in return acquire the prestige that went with holding
higher office, and upon his election to higher office might purchase, when they became available, higher denominations of the
Company's stock.

In 1730 he was voted a £40 share in the Company's stock; in
1736 an £80 share. In 1746 he secured one of the comparatively
few £160 shares, and five years later, as the senior member of
the court of assistants not then owning a share of the largest
denomination, he was voted a £320 share.[71] The dividends on
this stock—12½ percent, declared semiannually—were derived

from the monopoly rights that the Company held in the printing of almanacs, psalms, psalters, primers, and ABC's. The Stationers attempted to provide shares for as many liverymen as possible. From time to time they increased the size of the issue of shares of each denomination, and they required a liveryman to turn over to another member his share of lesser value when he was voted a share of larger denomination. Consequently no member could hold more than £320 of the stock. Even with these provisions, however, there was no period in Richardson's lifetime when all members of the livery were enabled to profit by the company's monopoly rights. The interest was considerable, even for a period accustomed to higher rates than ours. Maitland in his *History of London* (1756) could not record the fact that a £320 share paid interest of £40 without putting an exclamation point at the end of his statement.[72]

The administrative power of London livery companies was in the hands of a master, two wardens, and a court of assistants. The three highest officers were chosen from the members of the court of assistants, of whom there were twenty-seven in the Stationers' Company. In December 1741, Richardson became one of the twenty-seven assistants, and from that date until his death in 1761 he was an almost invariable attendant at the monthly meetings of the court.[73] In June 1750, he was elected under warden, but he chose to pay the fine of £10 for not serving.[74] A member of the court who had either served as under warden or who had paid his fine for not serving was eligible for election as upper warden; and in June 1753, Richardson was elected to and accepted the post of upper warden, with Thomas Longman, the founder of the house of Longman, as under warden.[75] On the 6th of July of the following year Richardson was elected master of the Company.[76] In this year the officers and court revived the custom, discontinued in 1731, of sitting on court days in the scarlet and brown-blue gowns of the Company's livery.

During Richardson's term as master, Stephen Theodore Janssen, a member of the Company, was elected Lord Mayor of London. Though the third Stationer to be elected to this office, Janssen was the first to retain his membership after election, the other two Stationers having been translated to one of the twelve great livery companies after receiving this honor.[77] Janssen was not a printer or a bookseller, but a paper dealer and apparently a large importer of Genoa, Dutch, and Irish paper.[78] Presumably he felt that membership in the Company was a valuable means of furthering his business, but in deciding to retain it, he confronted the Stationers for the first time with the need to prepare for extraordinary duties at his inauguration and in connection with the Lord Mayor's Procession.[79] In October Richardson headed a committee of sixteen Stationers who attended Janssen on his being sworn into office; and he designated a number of members who were near the Lord Mayor's age (forty-nine) to walk before Janssen in the procession, clothed in the gowns of the Company, carrying javelins and shields painted with the arms of the King, the Union, the City of London, the Lord Mayor, the master, and a number of members of the Company.[80]

While serving as master, Richardson made one important contribution to the organization of the Company. Its finances were being irregularly handled, because the treasurer, receiving no salary, devoted but little attention to the job. Upon the recommendation of Richardson and his committee, the Company created the position of treasurer as a post with an annual salary of £100, with certain perquisites, and with free house rent at Stationers' Hall. His duties included the registering of all books and the keeping of a store at which books printed for the Company were to be on sale.[81] Richard Hett, an elderly bookseller of some prominence and the father of a boy who served his apprenticeship with Richardson, was the first stationer to hold the newly created post.[82]

After completing his year as master, Richardson returned to

the court of assistants. The only extraordinary duty that he undertook after his mastership was to serve as a member of a committee appointed to consider the remodeling and enlarging of the courtroom. This committee's report, involving an expenditure of £450, was adopted in 1757.[83] Richardson faithfully attended the monthly meetings of the court until May 1761, two months before his death.

When we consider the fidelity with which Richardson dedicated himself to his press and to his profession and the steady though not spectacular rise to prosperity that accompanied this dedication, it is surprising to find him turning with such zeal and energy to the writing of three long novels. His business seemed to offer him sufficient and satisfactory outlet for his capabilities, and its minutest details were still a matter of concern to him up to the time of his death. Yet the number of hours in which he withdrew from it to write, revise, and excise the text of his novels must have been extraordinary. That his financial success should have brought a degree of complacency is to be expected, and some of that complacency is reflected in his fiction. But Richardson wrote his novels because he had not—and indeed could not—come completely to terms with his age, because in spite of the rewards that his age offered him, he did not share fully in what Saintsbury has so aptly called "the peace of the Augustans." His professional career gives little hint of what his novels so clearly show—his refusal to accept his age; his unwillingness to follow his contemporaries in finding a place into which to fit everything, and for everything a place into which it might be fitted.

CHAPTER III

Richardson and the

Periodical Press

I

THE advantages that an eighteenth-century printer derived from the printing of newspapers were considerable enough to justify the trouble entailed and the occasional risk of prosecution for libel. He could expand his plant sufficiently to meet extraordinary demands without having equipment lie idle during slack periods. To the extent that his plant was engaged in contractual printing, he was independent of the favor of booksellers, who might withdraw favor if disputes arose, if the printer's prices were undercut, of if he should try to exercise some choice over the kind of book that he printed. Emancipation from the booksellers was the desire of every printer, and periodical printing was the first step toward such emancipation. With the printing of the Duke of Wharton's *True Briton* in 1723–1724, Richardson entered the field of periodical printing. At his death forty years later he had not entirely abandoned it.

During Walpole's administration the printer and the publisher of newspapers could not escape the political implications of their contracts. Consequently a survey of Richardson's relations with newspapers is an index to his political thinking. Such a survey reveals nothing original in his political thought, but it shows the extent to which he identified himself with the citizenry of London, the extent to which he felt that London was a citadel within the kingdom. Like many of his fellow-citizens he at first opposed Robert Walpole; like many of these same citizens he grew to see that accommodation with Walpole was preferable to alliance with his somewhat irresponsible opponents. Richardson's sense of the position and power of Londoners is set forth in a passage that he retained in successive editions of Defoe's *Tour Thro' Great Britain:* "The *City* is indeed, and at all times must be, so necessary to the *Court,* that no prudent Administration will ever seek Occasions for Misunderstandings with it: but will, if not infatuated, do all in its Power to incourage and increase the Opulence of the *City,* which upon any Emergency will be able and willing, if not disobliged, to support the *Court,* and furnish Means to protect the Kingdom, against either Foreign or Domestick Enemies." [1] Had Richardson been able to identify himself completely with the London citizenry, however, his novels would have been strictly in the tradition of Puritan family literature. Had he, on the other hand, not felt a strong allegiance to his class, his novels would have been in the tradition of the romances. The conflict within him was always present and finally found fullest expression in the conflict between Clarissa and Lovelace in his greatest novel. A full development of this point is not appropriate in a study of this nature, but his association with both Tory and Whig periodicals is evidence of the attraction of two conflicting ways of life, neither of which he could completely adopt, and between the claims of which he could find no thoroughly satisfactory compromise. He could always be counted on to express his loyalty to the City, but he was never ready to accept unquestioningly the ethics of the countinghouse. In like manner, he was alternately attracted and repelled by the careers of such rakes as his early employer, the Duke of Wharton.

The newspapers that Richardson printed and those whose pol-

icy he in part controlled either supported the cause of the freemen
of London or refrained from actively attacking it. As long as
Walpole seemed to threaten the freedom of its citizenry, London
opposed him, and that opposition forced Walpole to certain in-
cautious measures for which he finally paid perhaps more heavily
than he deserved. But the later opposition to Walpole was not
so responsible as that which he first met, and the character of this
opposition, as much as the growing confidence in many of Walpole's measures, accounted for the gradual change in the attitude
toward his administration. If Londoners turned to Walpole only
as the lesser of evils, nevertheless they did turn to him, just as Richardson's press turned from the printing of Wharton's opposition
sheet to the printing of papers in the main favorably disposed toward him, or at least not disposed to favor his enemies.

Despite conflicting evidence, the statement that Richardson
printed Wharton's *True Briton* is probably true. The evidence
calls for careful examination, however, not merely in order to
affirm Richardson's relations with this newspaper but also to
throw what light this evidence sheds on the conditions of printing and publishing newspapers during the early years of Walpole's government. The reliability of witnesses needs testing; the
evidence afforded by his printers' ornaments needs to be considered; and the likelihood of Richardson's being associated with
an organ so clearly Tory in its sympathics must be placed in question. Before taking these steps, we need a brief description of the
newspaper and of the conditions that called it forth.

The *True Briton* was a semiweekly periodical, published from
3 June 1723 to 17 February 1724. Sponsored and probably largely
written by Philip, Duke of Wharton, this journal was one of the
four or five opposition papers to attract wide attention during
the years that saw Robert Walpole's rise to power. Its birth was
coincident with the demise of another Tory organ, the *Freeholder's Journal,* begun by the Jacobite Thomas Carte, who was
Bishop Atterbury's secretary and with whom Richardson was

later associated in the editing and publishing of the *Negotiations of Sir Thomas Roe.* The main contributor to the *Freeholder's Journal,* however, was a more moderate and politically impressive Tory, Archibald Hutcheson, the member for Hastings, whose economic writings in attack upon the South Sea Scheme had been printed by Richardson during the years 1719–1723. Hutcheson was an anti-Jacobite who repudiated any notion of divine right and based his opposition to the government upon the fraudulency of elections, upon the evils of the Septennial Act, and upon the weaknesses in Walpole's financial policy, of which he was one of the few competent critics.[2] Richardson's political position in the early 1720's accords closely with that of Hutcheson. Twenty-five years after he had printed Hutcheson's economic tracts, Richardson still remembered him favorably, for in *Clarissa* Lord M. quotes certain remarks of Hutcheson when advising Lovelace about a career in politics.[3]

Wharton was less politically responsible than Hutcheson, but from his seat in the Lords he joined with Hutcheson in the Commons to attack the proposal of the South Sea Company when that company sought to redeem the public debts by making them part of its capital stock. Hutcheson directed his speeches and pamphlets against this proposal. Wharton branded it as "a dangerous bait, which might decoy many unwary people to their ruin."[4] Despite opposition, the bill became law, and both Wharton and Hutcheson were on the popular side when the South Sea bubble burst.

Wharton started the *True Briton* when he was a young man of twenty-five with an immense amount of energy and undoubted personal charm. Though considered by the French attaché in London as one of the two "greatest fools in England," he was a difficult man to silence when he brought his money and his talents to the establishing of a newspaper.[5] In lending his name to the *True Briton,* he initiated an epoch in political journalism marked by the social importance of journalists and fulfilled in the career of the *Craftsman*. The young Duke, styling himself an Old Whig, set about to oppose Walpole at every point; he scattered broadcast hundreds of copies of his paper and he won an extraordinary popularity in the City by espousing the cause of the Common Council against Walpole's attempts to control London through increasing the prerogative of the Lord Mayor and Aldermen. He hoped to provoke Walpole into instituting proceedings against him, but Walpole shrewdly refused to be drawn and confined himself to answering Wharton's attacks in such Whig journals as *Pasquin* and the *Briton*, the latter launched in August 1723 as a direct counterthrust to the *True Briton*.[6] It was said that the government gave Wharton rope "supposing he'll at last hang himself." [7] Beyond replying to Wharton in the Whig press, Walpole contented himself with embarrassing the Duke through issuing warrants for the arrest of his publisher and printer.

In estimating the extent of Richardson's relations with Wharton, we must realize that the Duke, though opposing Walpole, was not at this time an avowed Jacobite. As the son of an Old Whig, he held himself bound by the principles of Old Whiggism that he had inherited from his father, Thomas Wharton, the first Marquis. Thomas Wharton's principles differed little from those of Shaftesbury, a man whom Richardson's father had supported and in whose cause he had been driven from a profitable London business to a form of exile in Derbyshire. The terms Whig and Tory were so variously used in this part of the eighteenth century that they lost all precise meaning. Even when Wharton emerged later in the decade as an avowed supporter of the Pretender, he said that what the Jacobite cause needed was "a Whig and a brisk one, too, and I am the man." [8]

From the vantage point of the twentieth century and in the light shed by the publication of the Stuart Papers, we can now see more clearly the details of the frustrated Jacobite plot of 1722 and understand the role played in this affair by Wharton and by

Atterbury. But eighteenth-century Londoners knew nothing of these details. Walpole continued from first to last to treat all his opponents as traitors, and he constantly applied the term Jacobite to them, regardless of their motives.[9] Consequently when Bishop Atterbury and his amanuensis, George Kelly, were brought to trial for complicity in the Jacobite plot of 1722, many Londoners were ready to believe in their innocence. When Wharton spoke in the Lords in defense of Atterbury and when Richardson printed his speech, there is no reason to believe that Richardson felt himself thereby implicated in a plot to bring James to the throne of England. After Atterbury had been deprived of his office and banished, Richardson printed the Bishop's *Maxims, Reflections, and Observations*. When George Kelly spoke in his own defense before the House of Lords, Richardson's press was ready to print this speech. Both Wharton's speech in defense of Atterbury and Kelly's speech in his own behalf were made in the months immediately preceding the first issue of the *True Briton*. When Kelly was convicted by both Houses, Wharton joined with thirty-seven other Lords in publishing a protest.[10] Kelly was committed to the Tower for life, but Richardson's relations with him were not to cease. While in the Tower Kelly translated Castelnau's *Memoirs*. In 1724 this work, advertised as "done into English by a Gentleman, and publish'd for his Benefit," was printed by Richardson and delivered to subscribers from his shop in Salisbury Court. All of this evidence does not mean that Richardson must have been the printer of the *True Briton*, but it certainly suggests that he would have had no scruples about accepting the contract.

To this evidence may be added testimony of another sort. We know something of the votes Richardson cast and of the political color of the candidates he supported. In 1722 three of the four members of Parliament for London were in opposition to Walpole: Sir John Barnard, an Opposition Whig, and Francis Child and Richard Lockwood, Tories. With Barnard, Richardson was later associated in publishing ventures.[11] Richard Lockwood was supported by the *True Briton* in his race for sheriff in 1723. When Lockwood was declared defeated after a scrutiny of the polling, the *True Briton* and many London citizens felt that the election had been unfairly decided by a puppet Court of Aldermen, responding to Walpole's string. In the following year the race for the shrievalty was also hotly contested. On the 6th of March Wharton organized at the Five Bells Tavern in the Strand a mass meeting of those Londoners who were supporting Sir John Williams, the Tory candidate for sheriff.[12] From the tavern all liverymen supporting Williams were to proceed to the Guildhall for the polling. Among these liverymen was Richardson, who cast his vote for Williams.[13] The race was close but the results of the polling showed that Williams was elected. After a scrutiny, however, his Whig opponent, Edward Bellamy, was declared to have received a majority.[14]

In the autumn of 1724 Peter Godfrey, Whig member for London, died, and the Tories sought to return Charles Goodfellow. He was opposed by the Whig candidate, Sir Richard Hopkins. The *True Briton* had ceased publication by this time, but the *Daily Post* accused Goodfellow of being supported by the ghost of Wharton's defunct paper.[15] Richardson voted for Goodfellow, as did James Leake, Thomas Woodward, Arthur Bettesworth, and John Walthoe—all Stationers with whom he was closely associated.[16] Hopkins was elected and in 1725 he was the only City member to vote for the famous "City Bill" of that year, a bill granting extensive veto power to the Mayor and Aldermen over the acts of the Common Council.[17] "The Bill seems as if it were particularly calculated to enable Twenty Six Citizens to lord it over all the rest of their Neighbors," wrote an indignant citizen.[18] Though the City Bill passed both Houses, it was strenuously opposed by Barnard, Child, and Lockwood in the Commons and by Wharton in the Lords.[19]

Wharton can thus be seen as spokesman for a spirit of opposi-

tion springing from many motives and including only on its luna-
tic fringe the avowed Jacobites. He gave effective expression in
the House of Lords and through the columns of his newspaper
to ideas that were in the minds of most of the citizens of London.
He has been accused of fomenting this opposition, but he might
be more accurately described as having capitalized on it. Only
when Walpole had effectively subdued the City did Wharton
openly ally himself with the cause of the Pretender. Richardson
was never ready to follow the Duke to these lengths, but he continued throughout this decade to support Tory candidates. In
1727 he voted in the parliamentary election for John Barnard,
for Humphrey Parsons, and for Richard Lockwood, the Tory
that Wharton had supported in the race for sheriff in 1723.[20]

From the evidence provided by Richardson's printing and by
his voting, we can see that his principles were not at odds with
the professed intentions of Wharton, nor was Wharton in 1723
the kind of employer whom Richardson would have sought to
avoid. This is not to suggest that the relations between the two
men were intimate, for perhaps much, if not all, of the copy for
Wharton's newspaper reached its printer through the hands of
an intermediary. Nor is it to suggest that Richardson would
have approved Wharton's alliance with James Stuart, even
though Edmund Curll, with some thought of being believed,
falsely accused Richardson before a committee of the House of
Commons of having printed a letter that Wharton had sent from
France in 1728, attacking the Hanoverian dynasty.[21] Immediately after the Duke died in 1731, however, Richardson did
print a sympathetically written memoir as introduction to a reprint of the essays that had originally appeared in the *True
Briton;* and many years later Richardson took special occasion to
describe Wharton as a man "remarkable for his great Abilities,
however misapplied." [22]

We come now to consider the only piece of direct evidence,
save Richardson's ornaments, that connects his name with Whar-

ton's paper. It is in the form of a note supplied to Nichols for his *Anecdotes of William Bowyer*. Nichols was born too late to have had much knowledge of Richardson. He therefore applied to John Duncombe (1729–1786), an intimate friend of Richardson during his later years. Duncombe's note reads:

Dissimilar as their geniuses may seem, when the witty and wicked Duke of *Wharton* (a kind of *Lovelace*) about the year 1723 fomented the spirit of opposition in the city, and became a member of the Wax Chandlers Company; Mr. *Richardson*, though his political principles were very different, was much connected with, and favoured by him, and printed his "True Briton," published twice a week. Yet he exercised his own judgment, in peremptorily refusing to be concerned in such papers as he apprehended might endanger his own safety, and which accordingly did occasion the imprisonment and prosecution of those who were induced to print and publish them. He printed for some time a news-paper called "The Daily Journal;" and afterwards "The Daily Gazetteer." [23]

Duncombe's friendship with Richardson began years after the latter had made his peace with the government and had become the official printer to the House of Commons. It dated from the period in which the memory of Wharton was strongly colored by his frenetic and abortive Jacobite gestures. Duncombe's interpretation of the facts set forth in this note is subject to modification, but the facts themselves are in the main corroborated by other evidence. John Duncombe's father, William Duncombe, a clerk in the Navy Office during the career of the *True Briton*, was part proprietor of the Whig newspaper, the *Whitehall Evening Post*. He, too, was a friend of Richardson and in a position to know of his relations with Wharton and with Wharton's journal. John Duncombe's unqualified statement that Richardson was Wharton's printer cannot be dismissed. To be set against his statement, however, is a considerable body of evidence that must be reviewed.

In the first place we must examine another note of Nichols'. "It appears," he wrote, "by the original edition of *The True*

Briton . . . that Richardson printed no more than *six numbers;* and it seems highly probable that the *sixth* (June 21, 1723) was written by himself, as it is much in *his* manner." [24] Nichols does not acknowledge the source of the information in this second note. Presumably he looked himself at a file of the *True Briton,* but in all the files that I have been able to examine there is nothing to suggest that a change of printers took place between the sixth and seventh numbers. The colophon is unchanged and the same factotums (ornamental blocks into which were inserted capital letters) are used in issues both before and after the sixth. One factotum, for example, appears in Nos. 1, 3, 7, and 8, and another factotum in Nos. 4 and 18. The sixth number is clearly not in Richardson's style. It is signed "A.B.," a signature appearing in later numbers, but probably only one of the several pseudonyms used by Wharton himself. Nichols' selection of issue No. 6 as marking a change in printers was based, I believe, on his discovery that Nos. 3, 4, 5, and 6 of the *True Briton* had been specifically cited in proceedings brought against the printer and publisher of this newspaper. These proceedings involved Thomas Payne, a small bookseller or pamphlet shopkeeper. Hence Nichols, apparently unwilling completely to discount Duncombe's statement, inferred that Richardson printed only the first six numbers and then abandoned the *True Briton* to Payne, who became both printer and publisher. Nichols made no attempt to find out anything about Payne or to follow the legal proceedings that were instituted against him. Later biographers of Richardson have been content to combine and rephrase the information in the two notes that Nichols supplied. [25]

Nichols' second note and the inferences he drew from it are highly questionable. It was Thomas Payne who was accused of printing Nos. 3, 4, 5, and 6 of Wharton's paper. It was Payne who was the subject of other proceedings against the *True Briton.* No one but Payne was fined or imprisoned in the attempts to stop Wharton. [26] Consequently we might reject in its entirety the statement made by Duncombe if two considerations did not need to be taken into account. In the first place, there is no evidence that Payne ever printed anything. In the second place, the presence of Richardson's ornaments in the *True Briton* itself and in other works printed for Wharton and his friends cannot be ignored.

Before weighing these considerations, however, we need to examine the government's policy in instituting such proceedings as those against Payne. We must remember that Walpole was moving cautiously, at times almost half-heartedly, in his attacks on the opposition press, and that he did not have the authorization of any specific law or regulation. Parliament had refused to re-enact the Licensing Act, and the government had to depend on the common law, which meant dependence on judges and juries. Furthermore, Walpole knew that Wharton himself wanted to become the target of the government's action, and he knew that for him to make Wharton such a target would be ill-advised. His own position was daily becoming stronger, while the Tories continued to wander in the wilderness, Jacobites contesting seats in the government with anti-Jacobite Tories. The Pretender's correspondence shows that his restoration was the idlest of dreams, and no method of propaganda could really make anything but a molehill out of English Jacobitism.[27] London finally saw that even the bursting of the South Sea bubble had only taken money out of one pocket to put it in another. Walpole realized that he could be more effective by first stifling London's opposition through the City Bill of 1725 and by then converting Londoners to his side through the general soundness of his financial policy.

Nevertheless Walpole did have his subsidized press and he did direct the Secretaries of State to employ, among other means for controlling the opposition press, the instrument of the warrant, calling for the arrest of printers and publishers. Less than a month after the *True Briton* had begun publication, passages from its columns were read at a meeting of the Lord Justices, and Walpole, then Chancellor of the Exchequer, issued, in the absence of Secretary Townshend, a warrant for the arrest of its printer and publisher.[28] Charles Delafaye, as Under-Secretary, wrote to Townshend on 6 August 1723:

Payne the printer and publisher of the True Briton has been pretty much visited of late, Last Fryday was sev'night I bound him in £500 with two sureties of £250 each to appear in the Court of King's Bench next term and to be of good behaviour. This day sev'night the Lord Mayor and Court of Aldermen sent him to Newgate, whence he was bailed out by Judge Powys on Friday. On Saturday he was taken up again by a messenger & this day I bound him over again in the same summs as before. He was before that under a like recognizance and if his papers are proved criminal and consequently breaches of the good behaviour there's £3,000 forfeited in recognizances, besides what the magistracy of the City have laid upon him. In the mean time these seizures and imprisonment cannot but be expensive to him.[29]

The government must have known that Payne could not pay fines in the amount here described. Even if the courts and juries assessed them, they would have to be paid by Wharton if they were to be paid at all. The government must also have recognized that the *True Briton* continued to appear regularly despite its proceedings against Payne. With no desire to proceed against Wharton himself and with a means of reaching Wharton's pocketbook, the government was probably content.

In the first charge cited by Delafaye, Numbers 3, 4, 5, and 6 of the *True Briton* were offered in evidence. Proceedings in King's Bench, however, were not actually started until 24 February 1724, eight months after No. 6 was issued and a week after the newspaper had ceased publication. On 18 May 1724 Payne was sentenced, with a fine of £400 and a year's imprisonment.[30] Boyer, in reporting the event in the *Political State*, described him as "Mr. Payne, the Publisher." He was likewise described as publisher in the press when he was examined and sent to Newgate on the second charge mentioned by Delafaye.[31] In the manuscript records of the Court of Aldermen for 30 July 1723, however, it is said that Payne "did own himself to be the Printer and Publisher" of Nos. 12 and 17 of the *True Briton,* issues held to be libels on the conduct of the Court of Aldermen with respect to that court's behavior in the election of sheriffs.[32] We must infer either that Payne actually printed this newspaper or that he was the man designated to accept the responsibility.

That Payne was a printer at all is, as I have said, a matter of grave doubt. Neither Timperley nor Plomer in their dictionaries of printers and booksellers even mentions him. The records of the Stationers' Company show no evidence that he bound an apprentice between 1689 and 1724. All other works that I have found with his name in the imprint are said to be printed for him and not by him. Edmund Curll, who knew Payne and was associated with him in publishing ventures, testified on one occasion that Payne was wholly ignorant of the contents of the *Freeholder's Journal,* for certain numbers of which he was then being examined. Curll said that Payne was merely its publisher, and that he had let Curll see each number before he offered it for sale.[33] Curll is not the most reliable of witnesses, but regardless of the truth of his statement, he is implying that Payne is a publisher and not a printer. Other newspapers always referred to him as a publisher. When the *True Briton* was discontinued, the *Daily Post,* for example, directed its correspondents to send their letters in the future to "the Author of the Universal Journal, at Mr. Payne's at the Crown near Stationers'-Hall, which will continue publishing this Paper every Wednesday."[34] Payne promptly replied to this notice in the *Post:* "Whereas an Advertisement was published last week relating to the Universal Journal, which has been understood by some Persons as if I meant to continue that Paper with the same Offence as the True Briton has given. To undeceive such Persons, this is to assure them, that . . . the said Universal Journal will be carry'd on with all becoming Decency to our Superiors, and to particular Persons, as well as with strict Regard to Truth and Justice, by T Payne." [35] The *Universal Journal* was not strictly a party organ, but it did on occasion reply to the Tory journals of Mist and Applebee, and even entered the lists against such a mild Tory periodical as Hill's *Plain Dealer*. Presumably Payne was quite willing to publish papers that stood on either side of the political fence.

Except in the law courts Payne only once acknowledged being a printer. The colophons of the earlier issues of the *True Briton* indicate that this paper was printed *for* T. Payne, but with issue No. 15 (22 July 1723) the paper was said to be printed *by* and *for* T. Payne. Identifiable factotums were used in the earlier issues, but when a lawsuit was threatened and the change in colophon took place, unidentifiable printers' "flowers" were used instead of factotums to enclose the large initial letters. Factotums again appear in December. The factotum used in Nos. 1, 3, 7, and 9 is the same as that used in Wharton's speech in defense of Atterbury and in Kelly's translation of Castelnau's *Memoirs*, a book that we know Richardson printed. Its damaged condition makes it easily recognizable.[36] Furthermore, some of Richardson's well-known ornaments are used in the fortnightly reprintings of the *True Briton*. Each fortnight four numbers were printed consecutively on six leaves for distribution to country subscribers. Tailpieces appropriately fill up blank spaces in these reprints. Many more of Richardson's ornaments were used in two collected editions of the essays under date of 1723 and of 1732.[37] These ornaments are known to have been part of his equipment both before and after 1723–1724.

The presence of Richardson's factotums in regular issues of the paper is adequate evidence that he printed some of the issues. The change in colophon and the removal of recognizable ornaments, coincident with court proceedings, does not necessarily argue a change in printers. Since ornaments were used and then withdrawn to be used again, we might more reasonably infer that

Richardson was proceeding with caution, but that he nevertheless continued to print all issues of the paper while Payne was being haled into court and getting himself into and out of prison.
With Payne waiting trial that might result in the forfeiture of
£3,000, the government may have felt that it had gone far
enough in embarrassing the Duke of Wharton. Prosecutions
were, after all, grist to Wharton's mill, and the zeal of Walpole's
agents was always greater than his own. As might be expected,
the *True Briton* raised the issue of the liberty of the press and was
ready to identify the defenders of that liberty with the Old or
Opposition Whigs: "I was not a little surpriz'd," wrote "Cavalier"
in the *True Briton* for 2 August 1723, "at the Information I
received lately in the Country, that the Printer of the *True
Briton* had so often been taken into Custody, and a Paper so
universally esteem'd, because universally read, shou'd give Offence to any, but a certain Magistrate and his *Ephori*, inspir'd by
a *vindictive Servant*. In vain have our *Whig Ancestors* so frequently, so strenuously, asserted the Usefulness of *Liberty to the
Press*, shou'd the Printers, on *Inuendos* . . . be subject to daily
Arrests." Such bait for Walpole was truly barbed.

Though Duncombe's unqualified statement that Richardson
printed Wharton's paper cannot be completely substantiated, I
think he was probably correct. But to decide the question of how
many issues Richardson printed is less important than to estab-
lish on a sound basis his connection with Wharton and to see
more clearly that such a connection would not have been unwel-
come. The men whom Wharton supported and who supported
him were not—despite Duncombe's later opinion—markedly different in their political outlook from Richardson himself.

II

Less conclusive is the evidence that connects Richardson with
the printing of Aaron Hill's *Plain Dealer*, the first issue of which
appeared in the month following the demise of Wharton's news-

paper. In the last number of the *True Briton* Wharton apologized for not having been able to print all the letters which he had received from numerous correspondents, and he added that "whenever a Subject of PLAIN-DEALING and *Gallantry* appears in the World, many things that were incongruous to this [the *True Briton's*] Design, may obtain proper Place therein." [38] Some correspondent, perhaps Wharton's protégé, Edward Young, had contributed to the issue of the 13th of December an essay in praise of Hill's version of *Henry the Fifth*, defending it against an attack that had appeared in *Pasquin*, one of the *True Briton's* rivals.[39] It is possible that letters of Hill himself were among those of the "numerous correspondents" whom Wharton acknowledged, and that plans for launching the *Plain Dealer* had been made by Hill and his coeditor, William Bond, when Wharton said that many letters, incongruous to the design of his newspaper, might find a place in a journal devoted to *plain-dealing* and *gallantry*. Hill never took an active interest in politics, and his *Plain Dealer* was not a party organ. But he would have been in the main sympathetic toward many of Wharton's professed ends; in fact, he was said at one time to have "plied at Cato's elbow, in the South Sea Days"—a remark which suggests that he assisted Trenchard and Gordon, who were responsible for the famous letters of Cato directed against the South Sea Company.[40] Through his early employer, the Earl of Peterborough, who certainly had cause to favor the Tories, Hill met Harley and Bolingbroke; and for the latter he never lost his admiration.[41]

That Richardson printed the original numbers of the *Plain Dealer* has been put forward as a strong probability by his recent biographers.[42] The evidence that has been presented, however, has been meager. Inconclusive this evidence must remain, but its bulk can be considerably increased. The most important source for such information, the voluminous correspondence between Richardson and Hill, unfortunately dates from 1735. In 1736, however, Hill wrote: "I have too long been acquainted with the extent of your spirit . . . to wonder at any thing that does new justice to your character." [43] It is clear from this letter that Hill has known Richardson for some time and on an intimate basis, but whether the friendship extends backward to 1724 is a matter of conjecture. In 1730 Richardson and his brother-in-law, Allington Wilde, printed the collected essays from the *Plain Dealer* in two volumes. The imprint of this edition—"for S. Richardson and A. Wilde"—suggests that the two men were publishing as well as printing these volumes, and that perhaps Hill had consigned to Richardson, as he often was to do later, the rights to the text of the essays, content himself merely to see his writings offered to the public. In 1730 Richardson also printed for Hill his *Progress of Wit*, a caveat for Alexander Pope. Between 1725 and 1730 no new work of Hill was published. In 1725, however, the death of Peter the Great was the occasion for publishing a new edition of Hill's poem *The Northern-Star*. This edition came from Richardson's press and of course was prominently advertised in the *Plain Dealer*.

Indeed the nature of all the advertising in the *Plain Dealer* is evidence that Richardson had a hand in its printing. Hill's paper was perhaps the best of the nonpartisan periodicals to appear between the *Tatler* and the *Rambler*, but it was not a popular medium for advertising and issues frequently carried no more than one advertisement. Hill sought no financial rewards from the venture; in fact, he was said to have started the paper as a charitable gesture "for the advantage of an unhappy gentleman (an old officer in the army)." [44] He used its columns to introduce new or neglected genius, and its advertising space to announce his work and that of his associates and protégés. Consequently it is not without significance to find that when Richardson was ready to deliver to subscribers Kelly's translation of Castelnau's *Memoirs*, he inserted an especially prominent advertisement in three issues of the *Plain Dealer*.[45] In these issues his was the only advertisement. On another occasion, when Richardson was acting as agent in the disposal of some printing equipment, he used advertising space in the *Plain Dealer;* and when he was assisting Morgan in the collection of materials for his *History of Algiers,* he announced in the *Plain Dealer* that "memoirs proper to illustrate this Work" might be left with him in Salisbury Court.[46]

The *Plain Dealer*'s colophons—"printed for J. Roberts"— neither affirm nor deny Richardson's printing. Roberts was the proprietor of a prominent pamphlet shop and acted for many years as publisher for books and pamphlets printed by Richardson for authors who held the copyrights and wanted an agent who would sell their works on commission. An arrangement of this sort undoubtedly existed between Hill and his printer and publisher.

No other evidence confirms Richardson's printing of Hill's periodical, unless we are willing to assume that his printing for many of the authors whom Hill sponsored in his essays was the outcome of an acquaintance between Hill and Richardson. The number of such works that found their way to Richardson's shop is not unimpressive. Joseph Mitchell, David Mallet, Richard Savage, and James Thomson were all praised by the *Plain Dealer* and to some extent owed their original hearing to Hill's efforts. The young Scots whom Hill sponsored were described by him as sharing a "friendship that knows no strife, but that of a generous emulation to excel in virtue, learning, and politeness." This literary coterie, as Dorothy Brewster pointed out, constituted a "little mutual admiration society over which Hill presided." [47] Despite the fact that these men later followed divergent paths, that Mallet later referred to Thomson as "that dull fellow whom Malcolm calls the jest of our club," and that Thomson called Mitchell a "Planet-blasted fool," each member of the original group did find something in common in the early days of their friendship and each sought out Richardson's press during the decade of the 1720's.[48] Richardson also printed for William Popple, John Dyer, and Thomas Cooke—all of whom were included

by Savage in his *Miscellanies*, designed to further the reputation
of Hill's group. John Dennis, for whom Richardson printed in
this decade and to whom he lent money apparently with no wish
to be repaid, was frequently cited with approval by the *Plain
Dealer*.[49] In two papers (Nos. 54 and 82) Hill made specific pleas
for practical support of the aging critic.

None of the evidence presented in this last paragraph is more
than corroboratory. If we are to accept the fact that Richardson
printed the *Plain Dealer*, the strongest evidence lies in his other
printing for Hill, in his publication of the collected essays from
this periodical, and in the advertisements, for they seem to have
been inserted either by editor or printer.

III

Richardson's connection with the *Daily Journal* has never been
challenged. John Duncombe, who was responsible for the
statement that Richardson printed the *True Briton*, said that
Richardson "printed for some time a news-paper called 'The
Daily Journal.' "[50] This remark, adequately enough corroborated, has not been questioned, but none of Richardson's biographers has determined when or for how long he printed this
paper. Nichols said that Richardson printed the *Daily Journal*
in 1736 and 1737, but he offers no evidence for the selection of
these two years.[51] Brian Downs in 1928 examined the colophons
for these years, said that they read "printed by T. Cooper," and
promptly dropped the whole question. Dottin selected 1735, a
new and totally inexplicable choice. Even Alan McKillop, in his
exceptionally thorough study of Richardson, seems content with
Nichols' statement. He quite rightly recognized that the correspondence of Hill and some verses of Edward Cave make it clear
that Richardson had some connection with this paper in 1736 and
1737, despite the evidence of the colophons; but he did not push his
investigations farther.[52] To decide this question with finality is
impossible, but the best approach to a solution lies in a brief re-

view of the history of the *Journal* and an examination of its files.

The career of the *Journal* reflects the general accommodation that London and Londoners made to the ministry of Walpole. Unofficially and in stages less clearly marked, the *Daily Journal*'s policy underwent changes similar to those which can be more definitely traced in the *London Journal*. The *London Journal* was vigorous in its attacks on the government during the early 1720's when its principal contributors were John Trenchard and Thomas Gordon, both at that time Independent Whigs. The *Daily Journal*, then printed by John Applebee, was described by Samuel Negus as a "high-flying" Tory organ.[53] The *London Journal*, more important and influential than the *Daily Journal*, had to be silenced, and in September 1722 it was acquired by the government. Gordon and Trenchard were no longer to find its columns open to their letters of Cato. Benjamin Norton De-Foe continued to do its hack work, but Benjamin Hoadly, Bishop of Bangor and a brilliant controversialist, was secured to defend the government's policies.[54]

During the process of silencing this opposition sheet, John Peele, its publisher, was examined by Charles Delafaye in the office of Lord Townshend.[55] I mention Peele, because he, like Richardson, was associated with the opposition press early in this decade; and he, like Richardson, made his peace with Walpole's government. Peele and Thomas Woodward were among the partners in the *London Journal* after it became a government organ; he, and probably Woodward also, were associated with Richardson in the publication of the *Daily Journal;* and he and Richardson, in association with John Walthoe, were to direct the celebrated government newspaper, the *Daily Gazetteer*, when the ministry decided in 1735 to combine all of its subsidy and all of its talent in a single journal.[56] But in 1721 Peele was in the opposition and without doubt jointly responsible for the article in the *London Journal* for which he was examined by Delafaye.

The *Daily Journal* does not seem to have been directly supported by government funds, but it is impossible to be certain how much money drawn from the Secret Service funds in the 1720's was diverted into the pockets of printers and publishers of the government's press. Though the *Journal* was reported by Negus in 1723 as a Tory paper, its columns during the second half of this decade were open to Whig contributors. Both Thomas Cooke and John Dennis, for whom Richardson printed in 1726, 1728, and 1729, were writing for the *Journal* after it was removed from Applebee's shop. James Moore Smythe was accused in an appendix to the *Dunciad* of having written several letters and notes against Pope that appeared in the *Journal* during March and April 1728. Jonathan Smedley, then Dean of Clogher, found the *Journal* hospitable to his scurrilous attacks on Pope and Swift, some of which were reprinted in *Gulliveriana*, a book of his that Richardson printed in 1728.

Before attempting to decide when Richardson's relations with the *Journal* began and how long they lasted, we may inquire into the implications of the apparent shift in Richardson's political position between the demise of the *True Briton* and his connections with a newspaper sympathetic to Walpole, or at least hostile to his enemies. Richardson's change of position was not merely a desire to serve best his own interests. London's citizenry slowly began to see that the commercial prosperity of England, threatened by the South Sea affair, was being effectively served by Walpole. Arthur Onslow, later an intimate friend of Richardson, was at first lukewarm in Walpole's support, but became Speaker of the House in 1728. Sir John Barnard, elected to Parliament in opposition to Walpole and still Richardson's choice in 1727, joined with Walpole against Pulteney on financial questions considered by the House in the years preceding his re-election.[57] Taxes were reduced, the interest rate was lowered, credit was on a firm basis, the South Sea Company was conducting its affairs in a seemly fashion, and any attempt to bring religious questions into politics by proposing to repeal the Test Act was effectively quieted.

Walpole had gained confidence. Jacobitism was the last resort of desperate men. The disparate elements that had constituted the early opposition were no longer dangerous, and the new opposition centering around the *Craftsman*, which was eventually to gather enough strength to overthrow Walpole, had no real desire to set aside the Hanoverian Succession. Walpole continued to call his opponents Jacobites, and they continued to attack both his financial and foreign policies. But they were hardly able to make a case for themselves, except as a group of politically disposed gentlemen who would like to get Walpole out of power and themselves into his place. The pot called the kettle black. Mist's Tory *Weekly* admitted that in the conduct of elections the "true patriot" had to use the same means "for the good of his country" that Walpole used to keep himself in power.[58] The opposition protested against Walpole's spending of public funds, but such protests came all too frequently from those who found more objection to the recipients of the sinecures and subsidies than they did to the practice of providing them. Richardson's comment on the whole conduct of the government and opposition press was written in 1739, but it undoubtedly represents an opinion that was slowly shaping during the preceding decade. The attitude toward Walpole expressed in this comment probably differs in no essential respect from that of hundreds of London tradesmen:

'Tis the business of *one set* of papers to *bespatter* and *throw dirt*, and of the other to follow after them, with a *scrubbing-brush* and a *dish-clout*: And after all—the one *bedawbs* so *plentifully*, and the other *wipes* off so *slovenly*, that let me be hang'd, Bob, if I'd appear on 'Change with the coat on my back that a certain great man stalks about in, without concern, when these *dawbers* and *scourers* have done their *worst* and their *best* upon it. But 'tis a great matter to be *used* to such a coat. And a great happiness, I'll warrant, your name-sake thinks it, that, with all this *rubbing* and *scrubbing*, it does not appear *threadbare* yet, after twenty years wear, and an hundred people trying to pick holes in it.[59]

Thomas Gordon, who had opposed the government when the *London Journal* was an opposition newspaper, joined forces with the ministry and from time to time wrote essays for the ministerial press, while exercising a general supervision over it.[60] Pope accused Gordon of having succumbed to bribery, protesting that there was no glory in opposing the government when it would only be thought that Walpole's opponents were those to whom "the great man never offered . . . a groat." If such cynicism was justified, its justification is based on the failure of the opposition clearly to differentiate themselves from the government except as a group of men who were out of power and who wanted to be in power.

Thomson dedicated his *Winter* to the Whig speaker of the House, Sir Spencer Compton; his *Summer* to George Doddington, then a ministerial adherent and a Lord of the Treasury. His poem to the memory of Sir Isaac Newton was dedicated to Walpole himself. Compton sent him the customary twenty pounds, and the other two men ignored him. But Walpole and his wife and brother subscribed to the edition of Thomson's *Seasons* which Richardson printed for Thomson in 1730. Though Thomson expressed himself privately in none too favorable a fashion of Walpole and his "blockhead laureate," Laurence Eusden, he accepted in 1733 a post from the Lord Chancellor, Charles Talbot, and did not join Prince Frederick's party until Talbot's death in 1737. Joseph Mitchell, whose poetry was patronized by Aaron Hill and printed by Richardson, professed himself totally indifferent to "the bubble of popular applause" in 1721, but became known as "Sir Robert Walpole's Poet" before the decade was out.[61] Both Young and Savage sought the favor of the court, though both overplayed their hands by venturing into rival camps at the same time. Of all of Hill's protégés whom he sponsored in the *Plain Dealer*, David Mallet alone seems to have secured no favors from Walpole.

Some of the motives behind such accommodation may well have been questionable, but they were undoubtedly mixed. Richardson grew to feel that it was as honest a policy to print the newspapers which consistently whitewashed Walpole as it was to print those which consistently blackguarded him. However complete a convert to Walpole he became, he certainly must have become a dubious spectator of the gesturings of the opposition. The later opposition to Walpole was not characterized by the spirit of disinterestedness that marked the early opposition of Archibald Hutcheson. Even the motives of Wharton were at worst the desire to start a lively scrap. No one could be said to have acted less in his own interests than Wharton, for he always turned to the losing cause just at the time when its fortunes were lowest. But the motives of the later opposition, of Bolingbroke and Pulteney, of Wyndham and Shippen, were as mixed as those of many of the men who made their peace with Walpole. To a Londoner the attacks upon Walpole in the *Craftsman* and in the *Occasional Writer* would not have seemed the lifted voices of "true patriots."

In the election of 1727 Richardson continued to cast his vote for Tory candidates, for Barnard and Humphrey Parsons, and for the Tory Richard Lockwood, who had been supported by the *True Briton* in his race for the shrievalty in 1723. Though Lockwood had been sent to Parliament in 1722 with the largest vote accorded to any of the four members elected, his seat in 1727 was filled by a Whig. The Whig Lord Mayor, Sir John Eyles, received the largest vote in 1727, followed by the Independent Whig, Sir John Barnard. On the other hand, the Whiggish Sir Richard Hopkins, against whom Richardson had voted in 1724, was completely repudiated by the City in 1727.[62] The election of 1727, therefore, represented in London no real clash between Whig and Tory, between Hanoverian and Jacobite. Richardson expressed the London liveryman's desire to reward Lockwood and Barnard for their attack on the City Bill of 1725, and to repudiate Hopkins for having supported legislation so threatening to the rights of the citizenry. It was not until 1734 that Richardson's vote shows him supporting the ministry. In March of that year Samuel Robinson, Chamberlain of the City of London, died, and the candidates for this post were John Bosworth, a Tory who had actively opposed Walpole's unfortunate Excise Bill, and William Selwin, a Whig, who was reported to have "solicited the ministerial party to oblige all their dependents to vote for him." The election, called by the *Weekly Miscellany* "the greatest Struggle that has been known in this City," was hotly contested and the result was very close. Not until May were the results of a final scrutiny announced, showing Bosworth with 3,212 votes and Selwin with 3,208. Whether or not Richardson considered himself a ministerial "dependent," he voted for Selwin.[63]

Because it seems to me likely that Richardson's relations with the *Journal* date from the 1720's, I have been at some pains to make clear that his turning from an antiministerial organ to a newspaper well-disposed toward the government did not represent an unscrupulous volte-face. If John Peele had found it possible to continue his connections with the *London Journal* after that paper had been converted to the government's cause, Richardson would have found it as easy, if not easier, to turn from the *True Briton* in 1724, to link himself with the nonpartisan *Plain Dealer* in 1724 and 1725, and to become the printer of the *Daily Journal* in 1725. With the issue of the *Journal* on 1 January 1725, the Tory Applebee's connection with it ceases. The colophons from that date until 14 March 1728 read "Printed for T. Warner." From 1725 to 1730 the *Journal* shows itself hospitable to Whig contributions, but it is against the *London Journal* as Walpole's avowed mouthpiece that most of the fury of the opposition press is turned. Quarrels between the *Daily Journal* and the *Grub-Street Journal* were apt to break out at any time, but these quarrels were not essentially political in their origin.

Beginning in 1725 and extending throughout the life of the *Journal* in the most complete file that has been preserved, advertisements containing Richardson's name can be found. These advertisements are of two sorts: the first are prominently displayed announcements of books for which Richardson served, or planned to serve, as publisher; the second are those in which the finders of lost articles are instructed to return them to "Mr. Richardson, Printer, in Salisbury-Court." Representative items of the first class are Castelnau's *Memoirs*, 1725; Morgan's *History of Algiers*, 1726; Acherley's *Britannic Constitution*, 1727; Salmon's *History of Hertfordshire*, 1728; an edition of Cicero's *Epistles to Atticus*, 1729; the collected essays of the *Plain Dealer*, 1730; and the *State Trials*, 1730. During these five years and continuing at least as late as 1736 readers of the *Journal* are asked to return to Richardson's printing shop such a miscellany of items as a hundredweight of raw coffee, five yards of cambric, two yards of muslin, a canvas bag, a fifty-pound bank note, an old blue grogram gown, and two ells of new Holland.[64] Those persons interested in the purchase of the materials of a complete printing house or in the renting of an elegant and well-accustomed pastry cook's and confectionery shop were directed to inquire of Mr. Richardson.[65] When Richardson's brother, William, had a new brick house to let, or was distributing catalogues for the sale of household goods, the *Journal* prominently displayed his announcements.[66] When the Czarina of Russia awarded Aaron Hill a medal for his poem, *The Northern-Star* (printed by Richardson), the *Journal* carried an account of the event and four days later repeated the account with additional details; when Aaron Hill's wife died, her interment in the cloister of Westminster Abbey was reported.[67] William Popple's play, *The Dou-*

ble Deceit, in which Richardson, John Walthoe, John Peele, and Thomas Woodward owned joint shares, was advertised in an unusually prominent fashion on the front page of the *Journal*. A fortnight before publication, the *Journal* carried a long article, explaining the postponement of its first performance and defending it against a charge of plagiarism. The same account was repeated verbatim on the following day.[68]

After the government centered all of its support in the *Daily Gazetteer*, the *Journal* frequently filled some of its space with extracts from the *Prompter*, another paper in which Richardson, Popple, and Hill were interested and whose career is briefly described below. This practice of reprinting brought forth an attack from the *Grub-Street Journal*, which pointed out that people bought the *Prompter* for twopence and the *Journal* for three halfpence only to discover that

> these twins of different name,
> Prompter and Daily Journal are the same.[69]

In 1736 when Richardson advertised Hill's works at a discount in the *Journal*, Hill wrote that he was "confounded at the unreasonable, as well as unexpected, Civility of that very handsom Action." [70] A year later the *Journal* printed Hill's verses to the editor of *Albania*.[71]

The foregoing evidence suggests that Richardson had some connection with the *Journal* from 1725 to 1737. If Richardson was advertising Hill's works at a discount in 1736, then he must have had some financial interest in the paper as late as that year. It is impossible, however, to determine exactly when he was doing the actual printing. In 1725 the paper was probably acquired by a group of men including Peele and possibly Richardson, who moved it from the shop of the Tory John Applebee to signify a change in its political color. From January 1725 to March 1728 the colophons read "printed for T. Warner." They then for a time read "printed by J. Purser," and later they sometimes read "printed by" but more often "printed for" Thomas Cooper. After Purser's name appeared, Thomas Warner, among others, continued to receive advertisements and to serve as publisher. All during this period as well as later, lost articles were advertised as reclaimable at Richardson's shop in Salisbury Court.

If I am right in suspecting that Richardson printed the *Journal* until Purser took over in March 1728, then Richardson was responsible for an interesting experiment in format conducted by this paper. The *Journal* had started as a single folio half-sheet in double columns. In January 1727, its make-up was changed to three 14½-pica columns. A year later the publishers planned to experiment with issuing a larger paper on days when the amount of news was greater than usual. Several issues in January 1728 were printed on a larger sheet, with the type area measuring 15 by 9⅘ inches, and with the news set up in four columns. Since the price of the larger-sized issues was not advanced, this change proved expensive; furthermore some readers found the larger size "inconvenient." The experiment was therefore abandoned and on 1 February 1728 the *Journal* returned to three columns.[72] The format—four pages, quarto—was retained for a short time, but after a few weeks this flurry of experimentation was over and the paper returned to folio format, with three columns.

Little is known about John Purser, who took over the printing in 1728.[73] Plomer in his *Dictionary* gives 1728 as the beginning of his career. He locates him first in Whitefriars and then in Shoe Lane, but his address in the *Journal* is Salisbury Court.[74] Purser may have been printing the *Journal* independently or under Richardson's supervision. Whatever the arrangement may have been, Richardson's name continues to appear in advertisements, and in 1732 when the name of Thomas Cooper, in Ivy Lane, first begins to appear in the colophons, notice is given that advertisements are taken in at the "usual place" in Salisbury Court.[75] Cooper seems to have done some printing, but his reputation rests on his prominence as a publisher. If Richardson ceased the actual printing of the paper in 1728, he may have resumed it in 1732, when Cooper replaced Warner as the paper's principal publisher.

In 1736 Richardson was printing at least two daily newspapers, if Edward Cave's doggerel lines mean what they seem to mean. Cave wrote:

> For you, I think, print Journals Daily,
> By names unknown to *Nathan Bailey*.

Bailey, the lexicographer, had defined *Courant* as "the Title of a News-paper," thus implying that a newspaper by any other name was unknown to him.[76] Cave's allusion thus corroborates Duncombe's statement that Richardson printed the *Journal* for some years and that afterwards he printed the *Daily Gazetteer*, the first issue of which appeared in June 1735. Regardless of what changes took place in its printer, Richardson's interest in the paper seems to have been maintained over a number of years and to have terminated only with the paper's demise.

The date of that demise, however, is uncertain. Crane and Kaye in their *Census of British Newspapers* and Stanley Morison in his *English Newspaper* maintain that the *Journal* continued until 1742.[77] On the other hand, the *Grub-Street Journal* triumphantly announced its death in April 1737, and I have found no copies after that year.[78] Yet in July 1738, Aaron Hill promised to send a contribution now and then for "either of the two [newspapers] which you, and Messrs. Peel, &c. are concerned in the success of."[79] One of these newspapers is the *Gazetteer* and one of the associates of Peele and Richardson is John Walthoe.[80] Was the second paper the *Journal* or a third and unidentified project with which Richardson and Peele were associated? Hill of course may have been in error. If he was right, then it is easier to believe that he was referring to the *Gazetteer* and the *Journal* than to the *Gazetteer* and an unidentified newspaper. The other newspapers with which we know Peele to have been associated had been left to die or to languish briefly when the government transferred all its subsidy to the *Gazetteer* in 1735.[81]

Despite the confusion created by these conflicting statements and despite the lack of evidence for dating Richardson's actual printing of the *Journal*, it is evident that he maintained some connection with this newspaper over a period of years, that at some point his interest was more than that of its printer, and that when the *Journal* advised advertisers that copy was receivable at the "usual place," the book trade and other advertisers knew that this place was Richardson's shop in Salisbury Court.

IV

The *Daily Journal* cannot properly be styled a government organ, but the *Daily Gazetteer*, first appearing on 30 June 1735, represented a concentration of all the government's efforts in one newspaper. An account of its founding is given by James Ralph, a journalist of some note, whose latent talent was not discovered by Walpole. "In the Year 1735," wrote the disgruntled Ralph, "it was thought proper to unite all the Strength of the [Whig] Party, in order to animate one Paper. . . . This mighty Performance came out under the name of the *Daily Gazetteer*, and was continued, at so small a Price as four or five thousand Pounds a Year, for writing, printing, and circulating, to the end of the late [Walpolean] Administration." [82]

The government withdrew its support from the *London Journal*, the *Free Briton*, and the *Daily Courant*. James Pitt, who directed the *London Journal* and contributed to it many of the essays signed "Francis Osborne," ("Old Mother Osborne," as the opposition press called him) was to write for the *Gazetteer* on Saturdays; William Arnall, the "Francis Walsingham" of the *Free Briton*, was to write on Thursdays. "For the rest," wrote Arnall in the first issue of the *Gazetteer*, "there are other Gentlemen, particularly those of the Daily Courant, who will choose for themselves, such Days as may be convenient." These gentlemen included Henry Bland, Dean of Durham, Francis Hare, Bishop of Chichester, and Robert Walpole's brother, Horatio.[83] "Mr. Osborne," wrote Ralph, "was to give solid Reason, Mr. Walsingham Wit, and the occasional Gentlemen Humour or secret History, as the Exigencies of the Patron might require." [84]

Pitt, however, soon withdrew from his regular duties and contributed only on infrequent occasions; and Arnall is said to have died in May 1736.[85] In any event, the *Gazetteer* soon became largely the responsibility of Ralph Courteville, who wrote under the name of R. Freeman.[86] To the opposition press he was known as "Court Evil, Esq." Fielding proposed in the *Champion* a subscription edition of an "Apology for the Life, Actions, and Writings of Ralph Freeman, alias, Court Evil, Esq.," promising the public an account of how Freeman turned political writer, though much to the surprise of his friends, who still believed him unable to spell.[87] At his death Richardson had in his possession two letters from Courteville, recording the latter's high praise of *Pamela* and incidentally providing some evidence of his inability to spell.[88] Courteville had learned the craft of political writing among the opposition, but by 1735 was a zealous supporter of Walpole. Within his limits he also displayed ability as a moral essayist; and when the *Gazetteer* fell to his charge, he proved agreeable to Richardson's suggestion that the paper might profit by varying its contents instead of confining itself strictly to political subjects.[89]

Courteville certainly attacked Fielding with virulence, however, and deserved to incur the latter's wrath. Many of Courteville's moral judgments of Fielding are in the same vein as those of Richardson, whose prejudice against Fielding may stem from his association with Courteville and the *Gazetteer,* even as his prejudice against Pope was first implanted by Dennis and Smedley in their contributions to the *Daily Journal.*

Under Courteville the *Gazetteer* was less vigorous than it had been at its inception. As late as 1739 Hill was writing to Pope to defend Richardson from the implications of the *Gazetteer*'s political policy.[90] But it had been the *Gazetteer* edited by Pitt and Arnall that the opposition hated. It was Pitt and Arnall that Pope chose to lash savagely in the *Dunciad*, for these journalists were men of considerable ability. When they retired from the paper, it began to play a more passive role, content in the main to reply to the *Craftsman* and to *Common Sense* and to pursue on its own part a somewhat timid policy. Walpole never had the confidence in other journalists that he had in Arnall. He seemed content to allow the *Gazetteer* in its later years to descend to personal abuse. Though he continued its subsidy, his interest waned after Pulteney died and Bolingbroke went to France. It had been Pulteney and Bolingbroke who had lent distinction to the opposition.

Here, then, is a brief account of the newspaper that Duncombe tells us Richardson printed and that Hill refers to in 1738 as one of the two in which Richardson and Peele, among others, were "concerned in the success of." John Walthoe was certainly another of the partners, and Thomas Woodward, formerly associated with Peele in the *London Journal*, may have been a fourth partner.[91] Walthoe at this time was drawing on the treasury for about £3,600 a year, and between 1735 and 1739 Peele received more than £2,500 for money spent in His Majesty's service.[92] Ralph had maintained that the *Gazetteer* cost the government between £4,000 and £5,000 annually. Walthoe and Peele between them were drawing about four-fifths of this sum, though it is impossible to ascertain exactly what services Peele was being paid for, and into whose pockets went the money collected by him and Walthoe. But when Walpole withdrew his support from all papers except the *Gazetteer*, he must have required about 3,000 copies of this paper. Many, perhaps all, of them were "double" *Gazetteers*, that is, issues in folio every other day of the daily single sheets. For "double" *Courants* the government paid about 2*d*. a copy.[93] If 3,000 copies of the double *Gazetteers* at 2*d*.

a copy were printed triweekly, the cost would be £75 a week, or approximately £900 a quarter. This sum represents the amount that Walthoe received. How it was divided and among how many partners, we do not know. The editors, however, were paid directly from the treasury. Presumably Richardson's share of the £900 quarterly payments included his costs plus a legitimate profit as printer and his portion as one of the three or four partners. Advertisements and sales of copies other than those taken by the government must have increased the profits. Richardson found it a lucrative business, for he continued his association with the *Gazetteer* for five years after the fall of Walpole's ministry, and only then withdrew because his partners had thrown it upon his sole "Charge and Hazard." [94]

Much misinformation about Richardson and the *Gazetteer* has appeared in print and has been perpetuated. Nichols is responsible for the statement that Richardson printed the paper in 1738, but the reason for his error is easy to trace. When Mrs. Barbauld published her edition of Richardson's correspondence in 1804, she printed a letter from Hill, dated 1738, and referring to Richardson as a partner in the newspaper. To Duncombe's statement that Richardson printed the paper, Nichols merely added the date 1738 from Hill's letter. Nichols' note is responsible for Brian Downs' flat statement that Richardson printed the *Gazetteer* in 1738 and for Dottin's curious elaboration: "En 1738, il sortit l'éphémère *Daily Gazetteer* qui faillit lui attirer une désagréable histoire avec Pope." [95]

Letters from Hill to Richardson make clear, however, that he was associated with the paper until 1746.[96] In 1743, for example, Hill offered Richardson some translations of Horace's Odes for the *Gazetteer* and asked that they be printed if Richardson thought fit. "But you, who know That best, shou'd be so good to set me right as to the Doubt I am in about it . . . . while I purpose a poor little Service to a Paper you are interested in the Success of, I may really be doing it a Prejudice . . . . let me

know, whether Things of any other kind wou'd be welcome." [97]
A few years later Hill submitted some "trifling Papers" on the
current drama. "I wou'd willingly persuade myself, that [they]
. . . may do Service, in your Gazetteer. . . . The first 3 Papers,
which I herewith send you, I cou'd wish your Goodness would
find Opportunities to let appear, on such 3 Days of next week as
you can best make Room for." [98] When Richardson withdrew
from the paper in 1746, Hill wrote: "As to the *Daily Gazetteer*,
since it had been thrown wholly upon your own Charge and
Hazard, and wou'd have always had a *Prejudice* to make way
against, from the original Partiality it was suppos'd to have *sett
out* with, I am not sorry you determin'd to drop it." [99]

Clearly Richardson did not terminate his connection with the
Gazetteer in 1738. Likewise, there is no reason to believe that he
began it in that year. As soon as the ministry launched the paper,
Walthoe, who had been drawing sums from the treasury for the
Daily Courant, began to receive payments for the *Gazetteer*.
He and Richardson had been previously associated in other ventures; in fact, Walthoe, Richardson, Peele, and Woodward appear in 1736 in the Stationers' Register as joint owners of the
copyright of a book that Richardson printed.[100] Nothing suggests that a change of printers took place between 1735 and 1738.
Beginning in 1735 advertisements may be found in the *Gazetteer*
similar to those that were appearing in the *Daily Journal*. Richardson's shop is designated as the place to recover lost articles; his
brother, William, is given preferred space for his advertisements
—on the front page, in at least one instance.[101] Hill's play, *Alzira*,
in which Richardson owned a share, was advertised on 17 August
1736, and extensively thereafter. Each issue of the *Prompter*, a
periodical over which Richardson exercised some editorial charge,
was advertised lavishly in the *Gazetteer*, and space in the news
columns was given to summarize the contents of the *Weekly Miscellany*, edited by Richardson's friend, William Webster, and
printed by him for a time. Books printed by him for his friends—

those, for example, of Stephen Duck, Mary Barber, William Popple, Philip Skelton, Patrick Delany—were advertised more extensively than their potential profits would justify.[102] After 1738
the same kind of evidence is available, but there is no question of
Richardson's connection with the paper from 1738 to 1746.

The printing of the *Journal* and in particular the printing of
the *Gazetteer* are not without political implications, but it is easy
to see that Richardson was using what influence he had as a partner in these two papers to diversify their content and to relieve
their columns from the monotonous burden of adulation and
defamation. However financially profitable he found these dailies,
his real interest was in periodicals in the tradition of the *Spectator*.
He undoubtedly encouraged Courteville in preparing occasional
moral essays for the *Gazetteer*, even as he welcomed Hill's
literary essays. He had done what he could to enliven the columns
of the *Journal* by reprinting essays from Hill's *Prompter*. But
it was the periodicals that we are now to consider, the *Prompter*
itself and Webster's *Weekly Miscellany*, that enlisted Richardson's lively interest.

V

During the decade of the 1730's Richardson not only printed
the two dailies, but was also engaged in printing the *Weekly Miscellany* and the semiweekly *Prompter*. He may also have printed
the short-lived *Citizen*, a weekly periodical edited by Sir William
Keith from February to July 1739.

Conflicting statements about Richardson's connection with
William Webster's *Miscellany* have been made. Brian Downs
says that it can "only have come from Richardson's press (if at
all) during the last fifteen months of its career, between March
1740 and June 1741." [103] Alan McKillop says: "The first printer
was presumably Richardson, whose active connection with the
paper may be dated 1733–1736." [104] McKillop is essentially correct. Webster wrote to Zachary Grey, 15 July 1738: "You know,

before the paper could be established, it brought me in debt to my printer [Mr. Richardson] 140 l.[,] ninety of which is still unpaid. To encourage my present printer to undertake and propagate it with industry, I insured to him all the profits." [105] Webster said that when he left London to take up his living at Ware, he was £90 in Richardson's debt, though he had cleared off £50 of the original debt by quarterly payments; "and when he saw that I liv'd as *frugally* as possible, he forgave me the whole Debt. I forbear to inlarge upon his Character, because I know not how to do it Justice." [106] Both of these statements tally; and an examination of the colophons of the *Weekly Miscellany* supports them. From 16 December 1732 until 28 January 1737, the paper was printed for J. Roberts, with several issues for J. Jackson. On the 28th of January the colophon reads "printed by C. Jephson." Jephson's name continues until the issue of 24 February 1738, when the paper is printed and sold by Henry Woodfall, Jr. Woodfall is the "present printer" to whom Webster refers in his letter to Grey of 15 July 1738.

I think we may safely assume that Richardson printed the *Miscellany* from its inception until December 1736, when he was succeeded in turn by Jephson and by Woodfall. This conclusion is further borne out by a reprint of the essays from this periodical in two volumes, 1736–1738. The first volume, printed for the author, was from Richardson's press. The second volume and a second edition of Vol. I, 1738, were from another press.

During the early months of 1733 letters and verses of Aaron Hill were printed in Webster's weekly. Among Richardson's papers are preserved manuscript copies of these contributions of Hill's.[107] In December 1734, George Cheyne, Richardson's friend and physician, wrote him from Bath, thanking him for copies of the *Miscellany* supplied by Richardson and promising that perhaps at some time he might contribute an article or so "to keep it full." [108] When Richardson raised the question of paying Cheyne's fee for medical advice, the doctor wrote him (9 August

1735): "You pay weekly by your Miscellany which, if I had not from you, I should most certainly purchase at any Price I could spare." [109] This evidence points to the fact that Richardson was more than the paper's printer. He was obviously assisting Webster by encouraging his friends to contribute to its columns. Even when Webster sought a printer "who was more at leisure rigorously to pursue the Interest of it," the friendship between him and Richardson did not cease.[110] The issue for 17 January 1741 called attention to Richardson's *Familiar Letters* a week before publication, and carried a slightly emended version of Letter CXLIV. On 11 October 1740 *Pamela* began to receive similar advance notice in Webster's periodical.

Despite Webster's financial difficulties, he kept the paper going. It even attracted some attention from the government. Webster said that Lord Palmerston (Henry Temple) came to him before the paper had been going a year and offered " £300 a year, besides Preferment," if he would put it at the service of the ministry.[111] Viscount Perceval urged Walpole to allow it to be sent post-free into the country.[112] Needless to say, Webster declined Palmerston's offer.

The *Prompter*, edited by Aaron Hill, William Popple, and others, ran from 12 November 1734 until 2 July 1736. During the first years of this decade Hill was to be found in and out of the theaters of London with a half-formed project for launching a new playhouse of his own, with an expressed desire to buy a share in one of the existing patents, and with a crusading impulse for the improvement of English acting and the taste of the theater-going public.[113] When his plans for securing an actual foothold in the theatrical world fell through, his desire to improve the stage found expression in the *Prompter*, which he was instrumental in launching and which Richardson printed for him. William Popple, a minor officeholder under Walpole's ministry and the author of a few plays and pamphlets, contributed regularly to the *Prompter*, though Hill, with his characteristic tact, wrote

Richardson that he thought Popple's "best strength of genius did not lie, at all, in that particular Turn of Writing." [114]

On the eve of Hill's second venture into periodical journalism, Richardson brought out a second issue of the essays from Hill's *Plain Dealer*, with a new dedication. He kept an interleaved file of the *Prompter* against the day when these essays might also be reprinted. That day never came, though Hill and Richardson were still discussing the project in 1746. In this discussion Hill refers to the file as "your Prompters (for I claim no Right in Any of 'em)." [115] This statement implies that Richardson had a greater interest in this periodical than that of printer. It is clear that his shop was known to be the place where contributors sent letters for publication. One such letter from Eustace Budgell was passed on by Richardson to Hill with his comment appended.[116] When Hill wanted to disclaim responsibility for some articles in the *Prompter* that had occasioned an attack upon him in the *Grub-Street Journal*, he wrote Richardson: "As You know, that I have nothing to answer for, on either of these Two Heads [on which I was attacked], having never seen any of those Papers, till I read them in the published Prompters, I should take it as a Favour, if you wou'd, immediately, find means to undeceive the gentlemen concern'd." [117] If Hill designed this letter, or its contents, to be passed on to the editors of the *Grub-Street Journal*, he makes evident, in choosing Richardson as intermediary, that the latter is acting in a more significant role than that of mere printer of the *Prompter*. In fact, one remark of Hill's suggests that Richardson was assisting in outlining the kind of policy that the paper should take. Hill wrote: "I have sent you the finishing Prompter, for Friday next: but you will always be sure of and [?] may command me, upon any Like, or different, Occasion." [118] Hill is here referring to the essay in the final issue of the *Prompter*, but he clearly implies that he will be at Richardson's command should Richardson want other essays of the type that the *Prompter* had published. After the *Prompter*'s demise, essays appeared in the

Daily Journal signed "Occasional Prompter." Richardson seems to have opened the columns of the *Journal* to Hill after the *Prompter* proved unable to maintain itself. As I have mentioned earlier, the *Daily Journal* reprinted extracts from the *Prompter* during the latter's lifetime.

Specifically designed as the voice of a prompter without doors, Hill's periodical concerned itself in large measure with the affairs of the stage. That the stage by proper regulation might be made a suitable and profitable amusement, Richardson himself had contended at some length in his *Apprentice's Vade Mecum*, published more than a year before the first issue of the *Prompter*, and Pamela echoes this sentiment with illustrations.[119] But the editors of the *Prompter*, with the avowed theory that all the men and women on the stage of the world needed prompting, varied the nature of their essays, prompting on occasions the wife or the virgin, the party man or the poet, the prison keeper or the masquerader. Richardson liked this diversification, exemplified in both the *Weekly Miscellany* and the *Prompter*. In the columns of all these papers there may well be unidentified—and perhaps unidentifiable—essays comparable to that which he contributed to Johnson's *Rambler* in 1751.[120]

The short-lived *Citizen* provided weekly conversations of an informal society of London merchants on trade and other public questions. That Richardson printed it is a matter of mere conjecture. Sir William Keith, its editor, had been governor of Pennsylvania from 1717 until 1726. In 1728 he returned to England, became involved in financial difficulties, was imprisoned for debt in the Fleet Street Prison in 1734, and finally died in the Old Bailey in 1749. In 1738 Richardson printed Keith's *History of the British Plantations in America*, a book sponsored by the Society for the Encouragement of Learning. In 1739, when Keith undertook the *Citizen*, he may well have turned to Richardson to help him. Unless Richardson was its printer, his interest in the periodical is hard to account for. He sent copies to Aaron Hill, urging him to contribute; and Hill felt under some obligation to account to Richardson for failing to do so. "I am asham'd to have been so lazy a correspondent with The Citizen—" Hill wrote on 12 April 1739, "Tho' it has not altogether proceeded from Laziness, but, chiefly, from a Desire to observe, from the Turn of a proper Number of Papers, in what *Manner*, and with what *Choice* of Subjects, Sir *Wm* wou'd incline to distinguish his Purpose." [121] Thomas Cooper, whose pamphlet shop served as distributing agent for other periodicals printed by Richardson, served as publisher for the *Citizen*. It is not unlikely that Richardson was coming to the assistance of the debt-plagued editor by contributing gratis the services of his press. He had been generous in this same fashion when William Webster's *Miscellany* encountered financial difficulties.

VI

Definite evidence that Richardson printed the *Philosophical Transactions* of the Royal Society is not available for any year before 1752. Before this date the printing of this periodical was entrusted to the secretary of the Society, but with Vol. XLVII in 1753 the supervision was placed in the hands of a committee. The number to be printed was fixed at 750 copies for the use of members, with an additional but unspecified number for public sale by the Society's booksellers.[122] Richardson printed this volume; his bill as presented to the Society was for £76/11.[123] From this date until his death Richardson held the contract for the printing. In 1758 a letter from Mark Akenside to Richardson refers to the proof of one of Akenside's articles in the *Transactions*, Vol. L (Part I, 1758), pp. 322–328. This letter is published in Charles Bucke's biography of Akenside, but the article is not identified.[124] In the Errata Richardson made the correction requested by Akenside. On the very day of Richardson's death,

William Bowyer wrote to request that he have the honor of printing for the Society if that office was to be removed from Richardson's plant to any other printing house.[125]

Whether Richardson's shop was chosen by the committee that the Royal Society appointed in 1752, or whether this committee found Richardson printing the *Transactions* and merely approved of his continuing to print them, is a question that must remain unanswered, since no official records of the printing for the Society were kept before 1752. Before this date the *Transactions* carried in the imprint the names of Thomas Woodward and Charles Davis (who were described as Royal Society Printers) until Woodward's retirement in 1743. After 1743 they were printed for Davis until his death in 1755. From 1756 until Richardson's death in 1761 they were printed for Lockyer Davis and Charles Reymer. None of these men except Reymer was a printer, and Richardson was certainly printing the *Transactions* when Reymer's name was being carried in the imprint. It can thus be seen that the phrases "Royal Society Printers," and "Printer[s] to the Royal Society," are of no use in determining the actual printer of the papers. Richardson, for example, printed in 1743 Charles Perry's *View of the Levant* for "T. Woodward and C. Davis, Printers to the Royal Society"; and the volume of the *Transactions* for which his printing bill was given (Vol. XLVII, 1753) was said in the imprint to be printed for C. Davis, "Printer to the Royal Society."

The reputation of Richardson's press was certainly well known to Fellows of the Royal Society as early as the 1730's. For many years he printed for Philip Miller, beginning in 1731 with a handsome folio edition of the first volume of Miller's *Gardeners Dictionary*, printed "for the author." In 1734 he printed Edward Hody's edition of Giffard's *Cases in Midwifry*. At least as early as 1738 his press was known to Thomas Birch, who later became secretary of the Royal Society. William Maitland's *History of London*, a fine folio volume of 1739, was printed by Richardson as a subscription edition, with Richardson himself subscribing for five copies. Many members of the Royal Society were also members of the Society for the Encouragement of Learning, established in May 1736 for the purpose of subsidizing books of a scholarly nature by advancing sums of money to authors and deducting the amount of the loan from the first profits of the books. Charles Lennox, Duke of Richmond, the first president of this organization, was a Fellow of the Royal Society. Thomas Birch was the treasurer. This society chose as its printers James Bettenham, William Bowyer, and Samuel Richardson, because their presses were thought equipped to produce books that were accurate in text and pleasing in typography. Richardson's press was responsible for four of the first six books chosen for subsidization by the Society.[126] One of them, *The Negotiations of Sir Thomas Roe,* he and Thomas Carte edited. Another of them was the Latin text of Alexander Stuart's *Dissertatio de Structura et Motu Musculari,* 1738.

If the Society's secretary chose its printer before 1752, there is no evidence to show whether or not the incumbent, Cromwell Mortimer, would have been likely to select Richardson. If the choice rested with the Society's booksellers, then there is good reason to believe that Thomas Woodward, the senior member of the firm that published the *Transactions,* would have been favorably disposed toward Richardson. The two men preserved the most friendly relations and both were partners in other publishing ventures.

Whenever he may have begun printing the *Transactions,* this is the only periodical printing that his press was engaged in after he severed his connection with the *Gazetteer* in 1746. Perhaps his printing for the House of Commons, to be discussed in the following chapter, led him to abandon contracts for printing where the deadline was so relentlessly exigent as that of a daily newspaper.

CHAPTER IV

Government Contracts

RICHARDSON'S withdrawal from the extensive printing of periodicals after 1740 may have been occasioned by the large contracts which he secured for government printing in connection with the bills and reports, and then with the *Journals*, of the House of Commons. He began his long period of service to the House of Commons in 1733. Each morning while the House was in session Richardson waited in what he chose to call his "personal out-doors' Attendance at Westminster," to receive from the clerk of the House the text of bills under consideration and of reports that were ordered to be printed.[1] The texts of these bills were to be printed for distribution to each member. On occasion they were printed on leaves with abnormally wide margins, with blank spaces left to be filled in later after agreement in the House on such questions as dates, numbers, scope of jurisdiction, or officers to be empowered to enforce a law. When necessary, these bills were returned to Richardson to be reprinted with the blanks filled up.[2] "Half a Day every Day obliged to be thrown away," Richardson wrote to Aaron Hill in 1749, describing his attendance at the House. Sixteen years earlier, however, he undoubtedly welcomed this addition to his annual income.[3]

Through the interest of the Clerk of the House and its Speaker, Arthur Onslow, Richardson was awarded this contract. A part of this printing had previously been done by William Bowyer. After 1733 Bowyer continued to print the votes of the House, but Richardson printed all the bills and reports of committees. Nothing is known of the personal relations between Richardson and the Clerk of the House, Nicholas Hardinge, before this contract was awarded; nor is there evidence at this time of the later intimate friendship that developed between Richardson and Arthur Onslow. Onslow and Richardson's friend in the House, Archibald Hutcheson, were both opponents of the early ministry of Walpole; and Onslow, like Wharton in the days of the *True Briton*, considered himself an Old Whig, defending Old Whig principles against the measures of Walpole and the court party. "I often voted with both parties as I thought them to be in the right," Onslow wrote. "I loved independency and pursued it." [4] Hutcheson echoed these sentiments, and Richardson quoted his remarks in *Clarissa*.[5] At the time when Richardson was printing Hutcheson's tracts against the fiscal policy of Walpole, Onslow had no more enthusiasm for Walpole's South Sea scheme than had Hutcheson, though he voted for Walpole's bill in default of a better plan. His unanimous election as Speaker in 1728 represented at best a working agreement with the ministry. Richardson's early relations with the opposition press would, therefore, not have prejudiced Onslow against him, but at what period Richardson first became a welcome guest at Onslow's house at Thames Ditton cannot be determined, since Richardson's preserved correspondence does not extend back into the decade of the 1730's. Though Richardson's friendship with Hardinge cooled after the latter became a member of Parliament in 1749, his relations with the Onslows became more intimate as the years passed. To Arthur and his son George, Richardson left mourning rings in his will. The Speaker said on one occasion that he would have given Richardson a "station at court" had he desired it.[6]

The listing of all the bills and reports printed by Richardson hardly seems warranted, but I have provided references for locating his itemized accounts and have indicated the annual payments which he received for this printing.[7] In the years in which long reports had to be printed, his income was considerably greater than it was when bills alone were referred to his shop. The largest annual payment was £587 in 1746, but in most years he earned far less than this sum. From 1733 to 1761 his base price remained the same. Normally he had to provide six hundred copies of the bills and reports. If the text was not especially difficult, if no table work or figures were required, and if a good quality of demy paper was acceptable, Richardson charged £2/5 a sheet, paper included. It is impossible to analyze this charge with exactness. Probably 600 sheets of paper of the quality required would have cost about 17s., that is, about 12s. per ream of 432 usable sheets. If this price was paid for paper, the printing charges would come to £1/8 per sheet, with Richardson taking 9s. 4d. for himself, and paying his compositor 13s. 6d., his pressmen, 2s. 11d., and his proofreader 2s. 3d.[8] When he printed a bill on fine Dutch Royal paper with a sheet large enough to contain twice the measure of the normal sheet, he charged six guineas a sheet.[9] For a bill on fine large demy paper, he charged £3/3 per sheet, 800 copies; for a broadsheet on normal paper, he charged £1/1; for a broadsheet on crown paper, £2/12/6.[10] From these figures it can readily be seen how much of an item the cost of paper proved in reckoning total printing costs.

Until 1741 the warrants for the payments were issued in Richardson's name. Beginning in 1741 they were issued in the name of the Clerk of the House, Nicholas Hardinge, until he resigned in February 1748, and then to Jeremiah Dyson, who succeeded him and was in office at Richardson's death.[11] To the Clerk of the House was paid 1s. per sheet for copying the bills and reports for the press, though this money was probably distributed among underclerks, who did most of the work. It was with John Grover, clerk of the committee of elections and clerk of the ingrossments, that Richardson had the most intimate contact. Until his death in 1749 Grover was paid for what was called "his extra care and pains in attending the service of the House of Commons," a duty which brought him into constant contact with the House's printer.[12] In 1739 Richardson gave Grover his power of attorney to collect a sum of £253/10/6 that was owed him by the government for printing from 1737 to 1739.[13] In the company of Grover, Richardson visited their mutual friends, Joseph Spence and Edward Young, when these men were living in the country; and when Grover died Richardson wrote Young that he would be missed by the whole House of Commons.[14] That Richardson was personally grieved by Grover's death is attested by the fact that he wrote of it to young Susanna Highmore and reproved her when she found his sentiments "sentimental." [15]

After Grover's death and following some changes in the organization of the underclerks of the House, Richardson's duties brought him into contact with Newdigate Poyntz and John Burman, who were clerks without doors, attending committees; with Osborn Barwell, clerk of the papers; and with Robert Yeates, one of the clerks of ingrossments. Several years before Richardson's death Yeates was promoted to a clerkship without doors, Osborn Barwell replaced him as clerk of ingrossments, and Edward Barwell became clerk of the papers. To each of these men, except Edward Barwell, and to Dyson, the chief clerk, Richardson left mourning rings at his death.[16]

Many of the bills printed by Richardson defined the social evils of his age and set forth the means that his society proposed for eliminating or obviating some of the effects of these evils. Measures were considered for preventing stockjobbing, for preventing clandestine marriages, for relieving and employing the industrious poor, for punishing rogues and vagabonds, for regulating the lives and conduct of actors and other theatrical folk. The famous Licensing Act of 1737 was introduced in the House in its first form as a measure to control playhouses, which were corrupting the youth, encouraging vice and debauchery, and proving prejudicial to industry and trade. The attempt to control the moral life of the country through legislation and to alleviate the evils of a social structure which no one really wanted to change is manifest in much of the legislation that passed through the hands of the House's printer.

In addition to bills of this sort were measures for improving highways, erecting public buildings, expediting river traffic, and aiding the conditions of trade throughout England. Upon the information provided in such legislation Richardson drew in large part when he periodically edited and brought up to date Defoe's *Tour Thro' Great Britain*. Four editions of this work were revised by Richardson, beginning with the third edition in 1742 and continuing with the fourth, fifth, and sixth in 1748, 1753, and 1761–1762. Constant references are made to legislation proposed in the House and eventuating in an act of Parliament. He cites, for example, an act confirming and enlarging the powers granted by royal charter to the Foundling's Hospital; he includes many of the provisions of an act for establishing a hospital for disabled seamen of the merchant marine and their widows and orphans; he mentions proposed legislation for the widening of certain London streets and the opening of new ones; he points out that several acts have been passed that may eventually lead to a new bridge over the Thames. Information from acts that applied to the counties of England was of especial assistance to him, for he seldom got away from London and then only on brief holidays to Bath or Tunbridge Wells.

Growing out of his contract for the printing of bills and reports was the large contract for the printing of the first edition of the *Journals* of the House. In May 1742, Sir Watkin Williams Wynne, reporting for a House committee, approved the printing of the *Journals* from 8 November 1547 through 1741, the last session of the preceding Parliament.[17] John Grover had calculated the number of words at 26,537,603; and Richardson, whom Hardinge recommended to the committee as "a Printer, in whose Skill and Integrity I can confide," had appeared before the committee to deliver an estimate of the cost of printing 1,000 copies. He estimated that the work would require 4,422 sheets. With 200 sheets to the volume, the entire text could be comprised within twenty-three volumes, allowing for indexes. He would do the printing at 30s. per sheet, or £300 per volume. Fine English demy paper could be bought for 15s. per ream, with the reams made perfect for printing, that is, with sixty-eight sheets added to each ream to replace the foul sheets that came with each ream from the paper dealer. Four hundred reams would be needed for each volume, bringing the price of paper to the same amount as that of the printing.

In addition to the costs for paper and printing would be charges for preparing copy for the press, for proofreading, and for drawing up the indexes. This was the first printing of the *Journals* and the text was of course in manuscript. Nicholas Hardinge was to exercise general supervision of the project, and the House asked that £5,000 be advanced to him in anticipation of immediate expenses in contracting for paper and preparing copy. It further ordered that the *Journals* "be printed by such Person as shall be licensed by Mr. Speaker: And that no other Person do presume to print the same."

The printing of these volumes extended over many years. In addition to the twenty-three volumes which Richardson originally undertook, three more were added to bring the printed *Journals* down to 1754.[18] Richardson was correct in his estimate of the number of volumes required to print the *Journals* through 25 April 1741, the close of the eighth Parliament of Great Britain. If his estimated cost was correct— £300 a volume for the printing—he received £6,900 for the twenty-three volumes. Hardinge was voted £5,000 in 1742 when the contract was let, another £5,000 in 1749, and a third £5,000 in 1752. In 1756 he advised the House that £15,000 would not be sufficient to pay for the twenty-three volumes and that body voted him "such further sum" as was necessary.[19] The sum that was necessary was £2,500, as can be seen in the treasury warrant issued to Hardinge, dated 24 June 1756.[20] Hardinge drew £17,500; Richardson estimated paper and printing at £13,800. The difference between these two sums is £3,700. It seems surprising that this amount of money was spent legitimately on the incidental expenses connected with printing the *Journals*, but Hardinge had originally estimated that these costs, including preparing copy for the press, would be £9,200.

Whatever may have been the difficulties encountered by Hardinge in getting adequate appropriations, he certainly withheld Richardson's payments far beyond the date when they were due. In January 1749, he owed Richardson £1,500.[21] Richardson wrote to Philip Skelton, an Irish clergyman, to help him collect the debt, because Hardinge, then a member of Parliament for Eye, Suffolk, was spending his time on the Isle of Man when the House was not in session. Skelton wrote in reply to Richardson's request, but Mrs. Barbauld in her edition of the correspondence has left the name blank. "As to——, he is still in very good circumstances, if a man can be said to be so, who hath a great deal of other men's effects in his hands. His privilege protects him in parliament time; and at all other times he skulks in the Isle of Mann, where nothing is to be come at, but such chattels as he may have with him in the island. . . . If it is thought expedient, I will make a trip to the island, and try what may be done through the bishop's [Thomas Wilson's] credit and authority there." [22] Richardson had printed Wilson's *Knowledge and Practice of Christianity Made Easy to the Meanest Capacities*, a book that the Bishop had published at his own expense. Whether Wilson actually intervened or whether Hardinge feared the possibility of a motion in the House, he seems eventually to have paid this bill. Seven years later, however, another £1,500 was due and unpaid. At this time Arthur Onslow agreed to expose Hardinge if necessary, and the former clerk gave him two notes for £500 each, payable in a month, and security for the remaining £500.[23]

In 1756 the House voted to print the *Journals* from the beginning of the ninth Parliament to the end of the current session. Jeremiah Dyson, then Clerk of the House, was voted £2,500 for this printing.[24] Richardson lived to print only three of the volumes covering this period. The last volume to come from his press is the twenty-sixth, carrying the *Journals* through 6 April 1754. When Richardson died in 1761, William Bowyer applied for the privilege of printing for the House, but the contract was awarded to John Hughs, one of Robert Dodsley's principal printers. Hughs began printing for the House in December 1761.[25]

Such printing as this constituted a form of monopoly right, but in the eighteenth century few moves were made effectively to disturb printers in the possession of such rights. In fact as late as 1832 when the House appointed a select committee to investigate the King's printer's patent, this committee took evidence from any number of printers who made clear that each was prepared to do the kind of printing protected by the patent at a considerably cheaper rate. Nothing seems to have come of the report of this committee. The House tabled it, and the King's printers continued to exercise their monopoly rights.[26] All sorts of such monopolies, some large, some small, were in existence. Perhaps because Richardson began to gather such rights and privileges in a more significant way than almost any other printer of his age, he has been said to have held more of them than he actually did. A note in the *Letters of Thomas Herring to William Duncombe* states that Duncombe's corrections to Tate's psalms were sent by the Archbishop to "Mr. Richardson (king's printer) for a new edition of Tate's psalms, then preparing." [27] This handsome patent, however, was held by Thomas Baskett. As late as 1928 Brian Downs repeats the statement of Septimus Rivington that Richardson was printer to the Lord Mayor. The records at the London Guildhall show no evidence that Richardson did any official printing for the City of London; and Charles Welch's article on the City printers makes clear that John Barber, George and Elizabeth James, and Henry Kent held the official appointment during Richardson's career.[28]

However difficult it was for other printers to challenge such monopoly rights, they did not hesitate to try, nor were they slow in seeking to obtain them for their own establishments when opportunity offered. As I have pointed out, William Bowyer wrote to the Earl of Macclesfield to secure the printing of the *Philosophical Transactions* before Richardson's body was in the grave. Three years before his death Richardson wrote a long account of an attempt of a fellow printer to invade a right that he thought was his. This account I shall include, for it reveals both the sense of security which Richardson felt that he was entitled to and the lengths to which a competitor would go. Richardson wrote:

A false and perfidious Scotchman [has been] pretending Friendship to me for Years, confessing all the time Obligation to me; constantly visiting me, tho' he had made secretly near a Year before he was detected, Offers of Circumvention and Underpricing, to one of my Friends in a principal Branch of my Business; Himself a prosper'd Man; a Friend he had never known, but for my Hospitality to him the Invader . . . This Man has already done me great Mischief; obliging me to lower Prices not too high for the Service; and goes on propagating the Mischief; And his View is, to interfere with my Family when I am no more; when I had so lately laid out great Sums of Money in Building for the better Convenience of carrying on this particular Branch of Business, improved and, as I may say, established in my Self and Family, by my honest Care and Industry. . . . This Attempt [of his], striking at the Welfare of my Family, all Women, when I shall be no more.[29]

This letter, designed by him for publication, does not contain the name of the Scotsman; nor, unfortunately, does he identify the branch of business which the Scot was seeking to secure for himself. The facts that he does provide suggest that the Scotsman was William Strahan, who had maintained a friendship of long standing with Richardson, and that the business that Strahan sought was his printing for the House of Commons. But whoever may have been threatening what right, Richardson reflects in this letter the attitude of a trade not disposed to accept willingly the principle of competitive bargaining.

In defense of his position, however, it can be argued that his charges for printing done for the government were in line with those of London printers of comparable ability. Such printing could not be satisfactorily handled by the provincial presses, though their prices were cheaper; nor could it be safely entrusted to smaller London presses, which were not prepared to furnish copies as promptly printed and as accurately proofread. If Richardson's charges were in any sense exorbitant, the cause lay not in his desire to milk the government but in the easygoing cost accounting of the eighteenth-century printing trade.

CHAPTER V

Richardson's Relations

with the Trade

THOUGH Richardson was primarily a printer, he, like other prominent printers, sometimes served as a publisher of books, and sometimes, when owning the copyright or part of the copyright in a book that he printed, served technically as a bookseller. Confusion still exists about the use of these terms in the eighteenth century, but ample evidence exists for clearing up this confusion. *Bookseller* and *publisher* were sometimes used interchangeably, but Richardson and the printing trade had a clear conception of the limits of these two terms.

Stated in its simplest terms, the difference between bookseller and publisher is not the difference between one man and another but the difference between the roles that one man is playing in getting books into the hands of the purchaser. If the proprietor of a bookshop owns the copyright of a book, seeks out a printer for it, and then manages the sale to the public, his role is that of *bookseller*. If, on the other hand, the author (or printer) owns the copyright and secures the services of the proprietor of a bookshop in selling a book, then that proprietor is in the role of *publisher*. Perhaps some proprietors played exclusively the role of bookseller, but in general they were at times acting as booksellers, at others acting as publishers. Pamphlet shopkeepers may have occasionally been serving as booksellers, but in general their role was that of publisher.

Richardson makes clear this difference in some of his letters to authors. Patrick Delany, for example, retained the copyright of his *Life of David* and sent the manuscript directly to Richardson's press. After printing it, Richardson made arrangements with John Osborn to serve as publisher. Osborn is referred to by Richardson as "my Publisher," for to him copies of the book were sent and from him Richardson received reports as to sales and passed these reports on to Delany.[1] Osborn in turn placed copies of the book with other booksellers, who either sold them on commission or bought them from him at a discount. All booksellers concerned with the sale of the *Life of David* were acting as publishers.

Richardson printed the first edition of Thomson's *Seasons* as a subscription edition "for the author." Andrew Millar and James Brindley, a bookbinder, agreed to deliver copies to subscribers and to sell for Thomson any remaining copies.[2] Brindley, serving as publisher, offered the poem in sheets at a guinea a copy. He hoped that those who purchased books from him in sheets or in boards ("half-bindings") would employ him to bind them. Brindley, thus drawn into publishing, finally emerged as a bookseller, the proprietor of what has been recently called "The Oldest London Bookshop."

In 1749 Aaron Hill was planning an edition of his collected works. Richardson recommended to him Andrew Millar who "has great Business, and is in a Way of promoting the Sale of what he engages in." [3] He goes on to say that had Hill's single poems and pamphlets which Richardson had previously printed been "of Bulk, and fitter for a Bookseller's than a mere Publisher's Management, I should have Desired his Name [Millar's] to them, preferably to any other Man's that I knew." Many of Hill's poems and plays had been sent directly to Richardson's press by the author. Whenever Richardson would accept the copyright,

Hill would thrust it upon him, but for the most part Richardson insisted that the copyright remain with the author. In 1746, for example, Hill's *Art of Acting* was printed by Richardson. The imprint reads: "Printed for J. Osborn." Hill had had no dealings with Osborn; he had been secured by Richardson as a "mere publisher." Osborn was a bookseller of considerable standing in the trade. That he agreed to publish a pamphlet of Hill's was probably due to his friendship with Richardson. Normally, the bulk of the publishing of small and ephemeral pieces was entrusted to the proprietors of pamphlet shops.

Reginald Griffith, Pope's bibliographer, found that in the first quarter of the century the names of recognized pamphlet shop-keepers could be used in the imprint of a book "with as little of negotiation as one may now stamp a letter and send it to the postoffice." [4] Undoubtedly certain printers engaged in this practice. At the outset of his career Richardson may have used the name of A. Moore, an obscure pamphlet shopkeeper, in this fashion. But after his press became established, he habitually turned to the more substantial shops and published through James Roberts, through Thomas Cooper and his wife, Mary, and through William Owen. When Edward Young proposed originally to publish his *Centaur Not Fabulous* in four separate letters, Richardson wrote him: "I presume you would not have the separate letters sell under twelve-pence each? And be put into a publisher's hands? Have you a wish for a particular publisher? Roberts or Owen, I think, would either of them do it justice. Yet Dodsley generally deals with Cooper, against whom there can be no objection." [5]

The words *published* and *publisher* begin to appear in imprints in the second quarter of the century. Andrew Hooke's *Essay on the National Debt*, for example, was "printed for W. Owen, Publisher," in 1750. In 1744, *Altamira's Ghost* was "printed and sold by Charles Corbett, Publisher." Thomas Gardner, who was both printer and occasional publisher, varied his imprints to indicate the capacity in which he was serving. Eliza Haywood's *Present for a Servant-Maid*, 1745, is "printed and publish'd by T. Gardner." In 1739 he published but did not print *An Examination of a Pamphlet entitled His Catholic Majesty's Manifesto;* in 1743 he printed for William Shropshire, a bookseller, *Old England's "Te Deum,"* but he did not publish this work. On occasion his imprints indicated that a book was to be sold at his "Printing Office at Cowley's Head."

Richardson never played the dual role of printer and publisher as conspicuously as did Thomas Gardner. In fact he was technically publishing only when he delivered to subscribers copies of subscription editions. When George Kelly, confined in the Tower for complicity in the Jacobite plot of 1722, translated Castelnau's *Memoirs of the Reigns of Francis II. and Charles IX. of France*, Richardson printed the book and delivered copies to subscribers at his shop. He received subscriptions for Roger Acherley's *Britannic Constitution*, 1727, and would have assisted in publishing this work, had it been published as a subscription edition, as first planned. In 1729 the first volume of Captain James Ogilvie's translation of Giannone's *Civil History of the Kingdom of Naples* was printed by Richardson to be sold by subscription. Advertisements indicated that subscribers might collect copies from several booksellers, from Andrew Johnston, an engraver, from Ogilvie at his house in Warwick-court, and from "Samuel Richardson, Printer." After printing Nathanael Salmon's *History of Hertfordshire* in 1728, Richardson entered the book in Salmon's name in the Stationers' Register and delivered copies to subscribers.[6]

More important than this role was the one that Richardson played in printing books for which he owned the copyrights, or a share in the copyrights. Technically he was neither publisher nor bookseller on such occasions, but I have elected to discuss this aspect of his business career in this chapter. Richardson had a considerable amount of money invested in copyrights. At the time that he made his will (1757), he said that his chief assets were his printing establishment, which he had rebuilt in an extensive fashion in 1755, and his copyrights.[7] These rights included a one-third share in the first two volumes of *Pamela* and in the *Familiar Letters*, and the sole copyrights to the third and fourth volumes of *Pamela*, to *Clarissa*, and to *Sir Charles Grandison*. The value of the copyrights to his novels may be approximately gauged by the price that fractions of them brought at a sale a few years after his death. A one-twenty-fourth share of *Clarissa* brought £25; a share of *Grandison* of the same size brought £20; and a one-sixteenth share of *Pamela* was sold for £18.[8] What share, if any, he owned in his edition of Aesop's *Fables* or of Defoe's *Tour Thro' Great Britain* cannot be determined. He presumably owned all the rights to his edition of the *Negotiations of Sir Thomas Roe*, which had been originally planned as a subscription edition. When subscribers failed to materialize, he offered the work to the Society for the Encouragement of Learning.[9] The Society accepted the book, Richardson printed it; but when some difficulties arose between the Society and its booksellers, the sale of the edition lagged. Richardson thereupon assumed all the expenses, took over the copies that remained unsold, and made his own arrangements for their sale. The profits must have been slight, for some of the 750 copies of the original edition were still being advertised in 1751, eleven years after first publication.

Equally slight must have been the profits from occasional volumes of his friends of which he owned the copyright or a share of it. In 1730 Richardson and his brother-in-law, Allington Wilde, each printed a volume of a collected edition of the essays from Aaron Hill's periodical, the *Plain Dealer*. Richardson shared with Wilde the financial responsibility for this publication, and the two men secured nine booksellers to publish for them the two-volume set. Richardson and Wilde either overestimated the demand for this work or entered upon its publication largely as a favor to Hill. Whatever may have been their original motive, they had copies of the first edition on hand in 1734. These copies they then reissued, with a new title page, proclaiming this issue a "second edition" and including a new dedication to Lord Hervey written by William Bond, who had assisted Hill in editing this periodical in 1724–1725. The year 1734 seemed a propitious time to dispose of unsold copies, for in that year Hill and Popple were to launch a new periodical, the *Prompter*. William Popple's play, *The Double Deceit*, was printed by Richardson while Popple was associated with Aaron Hill in editing the *Prompter*. The book's imprint indicates that it was printed for Walthoe and Woodward and sold for them by the publisher, Thomas Cooper. The Stationers' Register, however, shows that John Peele and Richardson, with Walthoe and Woodward, each owned a one-fourth share in the copyright.[10] Richardson also owned a share in Hill's *Alzira*, though he sought to turn all the profits back to the author. Hill agreed to accept half of them *"upon condition you give me your word*, to make no future opposition to the pleasures I shall seek to enjoy, from a proper disposal of whatever may lie in the power of . . . A. Hill."[11] He continually offered Richardson the copyright to his incidental pieces. His *Fanciad*, for example, was offered to Richardson as an Easter present.[12] In this same category belongs the small pamphlet of Sir John Barnard, *Considerations on the Proposal for Reducing the Interest on the National Debt*, which Richardson entered in his name in the Stationers' Register in 1750 and which John Osborn published for him.[13] More copyrights of such a nature may have been owned by Richardson, but the infrequent use of the Stationers' Register throughout Richardson's lifetime makes it difficult to identify them. None was perhaps of much real value to him.

It was in his association with bookselling congers, large and small, that Richardson made most of the profit that did not come to him as author or printer. The extent of such association is impossible to ascertain, but in the following pages are examples of the kinds of printing ventures in which Richardson had a financial stake. Bookselling congers, defined by Nathan Bailey as societies of booksellers who have a joint stock in trade, or agree to print books in copartnership, usually included one or more printers. "When a printer held a share of a copyright," wrote F. H. Rivington in the *Athenaeum*, "he usually printed the work for the proprietors, e.g. Sam. Richardson and the successor to his printing business and Woodfall printed most of the work of which they held shares." [14] Rivington was writing with access to the records of the eighteenth-century bookseller, Charles Rivington, an intimate associate of Richardson. Printing undertaken by the congers brought the combined judgment of a group of booksellers to the selection of a work and made available the combined energies of this group in furthering its sale.

Richardson may have begun his association with congers as early as 1724, when he printed part of a bookselling project of that year, Bailey's *Universal Etymological English Dictionary*. In 1726 when a conger proposed printing Roger Acherley's large folio volume, *The Britannic Constitution*, Richardson's name was among those receiving subscriptions. [15] The number of subscribers does not seem to have been sufficient to publish the work by subscription, but the conger proceeded with its publication in the following year. Though Richardson's name does not appear in the imprint, the advertisements state that it was printed by him for the conger. [16] This conger had overestimated the demand for Acherley's defense of the fundamental form of English government. A so-called second edition in 1741 was in reality only a second issue; and as late as 1759 sheets of the original edition were available for a third issue.

A larger and more successful project was the publishing by a conger of Salmon's *Complete Collection of State Trials* in six folio volumes, 1730. The idea of a series of state trials had been conceived a decade or so earlier by John Darby, Jr., a Whig printer. He collected most of the material for a first edition and entrusted the editorship, curiously enough, to an unreconciled Tory, Thomas Salmon. The first edition was published in four volumes in 1719.[17] The second edition of 1730, with which Richardson was concerned, was revised with considerable improvement by Sollom Emlyn. The size of the conger sponsoring this edition steadily increased, as may be seen by comparing the list of booksellers in the imprint with the lists announced in the *Proposals* in 1729 and in a preliminary announcement of the work in June 1730.[18] The imprint carries forty-two names. Richardson's name is not among them, but he was one of the group that signed the *Proposals* and he is listed as one of the "undertakers" of the project in the newspaper announcement of June. The conger included other printers besides Richardson; in fact, his press appears to have been responsible only for the fourth volume. The newspaper advertisement implies that John Darby, the original entrepreneur, printed the sixth volume. Included in the conger were Samuel Buckley and John Clarke, both printers and both undoubtedly responsible for printing portions of this work.

The edition required 1,446 folio sheets. The price was estimated at three halfpence a sheet for the regular edition, and at twopence halfpenny a sheet for an edition in large paper. This meant that the price for the six volumes in sheets was either £9/0/9 or £15/1/3.[19] In 1735 Vols. VII and VIII, also edited by Emlyn, were published, but Richardson does not appear to have had any part in these supplementary volumes. In 1742, however, when a third edition of the first six volumes was published, Richardson again shared in the printing. The principal shares, or perhaps all the shares in this work, had by 1742 been acquired by a much smaller group of booksellers and printers than those concerned in the second edition. Darby had died by this time, but the title page of the third edition indicates that it was printed for his heirs and four other principal "undertakers"—the Walthoes, father and son, Thomas Wotton, Charles Bathurst, and Jacob and Richard Tonson. A number of other booksellers whose names appear on the title page either held fractional shares or were serving as publishers for the third edition.

In 1732 appeared a handsome edition in six folio volumes of a *Collection of Voyages and Travels*, which has been ascribed in an article in the *Library* to Richardson's press.[20] Obviously the first four volumes cannot have been printed by Richardson, for they constitute the second issue of volumes first published in 1704. Awnsham Churchill, an exceptionally enterprising London bookseller, had collected the material for these four volumes, some of which were manuscripts in his library. When he issued the four volumes, he promised his subscribers that additional volumes would follow, but they were not forthcoming. On his death in 1728, a number of these sets remained unsold and his additional material had not been printed. These sets and the unprinted material were taken over by a conger, including Richardson's friend, John Walthoe. New title pages were printed for the first four volumes and two more volumes were printed to make a set of six. As early as December 1730, newspapers carried an announcement that this six-volume edition was being prepared for the press.[21] When it appeared two years later, its imprint stated that it was printed by assignment from Awnsham Churchill and his surviving brother, William. Richardson's ornaments appear in Vol. VI only.

It is manifest that Awnsham Churchill owned some of the manuscripts of Sir Thomas Roe, for his first volume contains "The Journal of Sir Thomas Roe . . .Taken from his own Original Manuscript." It is likely that he had in his possession at his death the manuscripts of Roe that Richardson finally published as *The Negotiations of Sir Thomas Roe*. In the same year that the six volumes of voyages were announced as being prepared for publication, Richardson and a group of booksellers issued proposals for printing by subscription a work called *The Negotia-*

tions and Embassies of Sir Thomas Roe.[22] As I have pointed out earlier, this subscription edition was never published.

As early as 1729 proposals for printing by subscription Jacques Auguste de Thou's *Historiarium sui Temporis* were circulated.[23] Samuel Buckley was the moving spirit in this venture. He was at this time an elderly bookseller and printer, a man of considerable learning and a linguist. A number of presses were engaged in printing the seven folio volumes in which the history finally appeared in 1733. Richardson printed Vol. II, which contains his name in the colophon. In 1734 a group of booksellers including Walthoe, Andrew Millar, and John Osborn decided to publish a new edition of *Eight Chirurgical Treatises* by the principal surgeon to Charles II, Edward Wiseman. Richardson printed the second volume. In 1735 another group secured him as printer for a reprint of John Banks' *Unhappy Favourite: or, The Earl of Essex;* and a year later for still another group he printed the English part of a new edition of William Nicolson's *English, Scotch, and Irish Historical Libraries.* Osborn and Millar were among the group of booksellers who published a second and revised edition of Defoe's *Tour Thro' Great Britain* in 1738. Richardson printed the first two volumes of this three-volume work. He may have been a copartner in the publication of these books, but I have found no evidence of this fact.

As Richardson became more and more involved in publishing, he became increasingly sensitive to the timing of a book's publication. He shared with the book trade a dislike of publishing before the sitting of Parliament in the autumn, or after the rising of Parliament and the emptying of the town in the spring.[24] With Hill's works he was especially particular, for few of them created their own demand. Only fear of a rival translation of *Alzira* led him to publish this play in August 1736, instead of waiting for the autumn. When the play was revived at Drury Lane in 1744, he finally decided that the revival was sufficient justification for a new edition.[25] The first edition of the essays from the *Plain*

Dealer was published at the height of the season, on 28 November 1729.[26] When publishing a book in the late autumn, Richardson usually followed the practice of the trade in dating the imprint a year ahead.

During the two decades from which examples have been drawn of Richardson's printing for groups of booksellers, there flourished two congers whose organization was permanent enough for them to be known by names—the so-called "Old Conger" and the "New Conger." They were joint stock associations in which membership changed only infrequently, though shares were sometimes bought and sold.[27] Copyrights held by members represented a considerable sum. A one-tenth share in the New Conger, for example, was bought in 1742 by James Hodges for £366/14/3.[28] These congers gained a certain amount of ill-repute, because they were thought to be powerful combines that could bring an author to terms. McKillop says that the Society for the Encouragement of Learning "evidently originated in more or less direct opposition to the control over publication exercised by the inner ring of booksellers known as the 'Conger.' " [29] Perhaps he is right, though I have found little evidence to suggest that the congers dealt unfairly with authors. It is true, however, that they were generally unwilling to publish books that were financial risks even though genuine contributions to knowledge.

Richardson does not seem to have printed for these two large congers, though he did business with individual members of the groups. His opinion of their practices is not known. He was, however, actively interested in the Society for the Encouragement of Learning, and when it became evident that this society was not to prove a success, he interested himself in another organization that had the same end in view—Thomas Osborne's Society of Booksellers for Promoting Learning.[30] Osborne's Society advertised its offer to buy manuscripts, either paying the author a price agreed upon by two competent judges or allowing him to share in the profits to the extent of 50 percent. In an early—perhaps the first—book to be published by this Society, Richardson was a partner.

This book was Robert James' *Medical Dictionary*. James was a schoolmate and friend of Samuel Johnson's. Boswell tells us that Johnson once observed that "no man brings more mind to his profession" than James. He continues: "Johnson, as I understood from him, had written, or assisted in writing, the proposals for this work; and being very fond of the study of physick, in which James was his master, he furnished some of the articles. He, however, certainly wrote for it the Dedication to Dr. [Richard] Mead, which is conceived with great address, to conciliate the patronage of that very eminent man." [31]

The *Dictionary* was published in parts, No. 1 consisting of five sheets appearing on 4 February 1742.[32] The parts were published fortnightly. The first volume, printed for Thomas Osborne and sold by Roberts, is dated 1743. Vols. II and III were not ready until 1745. No ornaments are used in these volumes, but documents and letters make clear that Richardson was a partner and hence, in all likelihood, the printer of the work. After the publication of the third volume, Osborne signed the following document: "Dec. 12th 1745. I acknowledge to be Indebted to the partners in Dr. James Dictionary in the sum of Fifty Nine Pounds fifteen shillings and two pence for Books Delivered to me by Mrs. James Roberts which I will acct for to the Partners when the Books are Divided. Tho: Osborne." This note is endorsed by Richardson: "25 Jan. 1750–51. Received of Mr. Thomas Osborne a Note of Hand for the within sum of 59:15:2; payable Twelve Months after Date; which Date is the 25th of Jan. 1750–51; which when paid is in full Discharge of the said within sum. Saml. Richardson. Witness Ja: Mendez." [33] Osborne presumably secured the services of Roberts as publisher for the *Dictionary*. In December 1745, Mrs. Roberts returned to him unsold copies. Because these books were the property of the partners, Osborne acknowledged his indebtedness to them, planned to sell the books himself, and bound himself to make payment at a later date. Richardson is clearly one of the partners. The transactions had not been completed by 1759, for on the 14th of February of that year Richardson wrote to Osborne, asking him to send all the letters, papers, books, and accounts relating to the *Medical Dictionary:* "and this for my ease of mind; I am expecting every day to be attacked." [34] The details of this dispute are unknown to me. That Richardson remained an undisclosed partner is thoroughly characteristic.

In a letter of Hill's, 30 June 1736, is a passage that suggests Richardson's undisclosed partnership in other books than those that I have reason to believe he printed. The lack of ornaments in one of these books makes identification uncertain; in one of them, Morgan's *History of Algiers,* the imprint states that the two volumes were printed by James Bettenham. Hill wrote: "I have now the further Favour to beg, of Perusing your—Chambers' (imperfect at Letter S.) [;] your—Breval, 1st and 2nd. [;] your—Morgan's Algiers:—which I noted from the Catalogue you were so good as to send me." [35] The "Breval" contains Richardson's ornaments. John Durant Breval's *Remarks on Several Parts of Europe* was published in two volumes, dated 1738. Breval had published an earlier series of *Remarks* in 1726. Proposals for this second series had been circulated as early as 1727; but it was not until 1736 that Hill finds what he calls Richardson's "Breval" in a catalogue that Richardson had sent him; and it was not until 12 December 1737 that Hill wrote to thank Richardson for "the 2 beautiful Volumes of Mr. Breval." [36] Morgan's two volumes of the *History of Algiers* were printed by Bettenham in 1728 and 1729. In 1726, however, proposals for printing this work by subscription had been circulated, with the request that anyone "possessed of Memoirs proper to illustrate this Work" should send them as soon as possible to Richardson.[37] Richardson's name is among the subscribers, where he is designated as "Mr. Samuel Richardson, Printer." The imprint in the first volume reads:

"Printed for the Author, by J. Bettenham, 1728. Sold by the several *Booksellers,* whose Names are in the List, as Subscribers." [38] That Hill refers to this work as "your Morgan's Algiers" implies that Richardson had some interest in it, even though he did not print it.

The book that Hill calls "your Chambers' (imperfect at Letter S.)" is undoubtedly Ephraim Chambers' *Cyclopaedia.* Richardson promptly sent Hill a copy, but not the imperfect one. "I am uneasy," Hill wrote, "in the Apprehension, that I have been more troublesom than I intended to be, when I desir'd the Perusal of Chambers. I only meant the Imperfect one, that I found noted in your Catalogue. But, I perceive, It is one of Mr. Richardson's Peculiarities, to appropriate what is Defective, to Himself, while He thinks nothing compleat enough, when he is to provide it, for Another." [39]

These references of Hill to Richardson's books and to Richardson's catalogue are puzzling. For a number of years Hill made similar requests. Many books were merely lent to Hill that he might read and return them; some that were requested as loans Richardson insisted that Hill accept as gifts. On one occasion Hill specified that he would like to read a certain book "if printed for Any of your particular Friends—but, not otherwise." [40] This stipulation is ambiguous: Hill does not say that he wants the books if printed *by Richardson* for one of his friends. With respect to Chambers' *Cyclopaedia* the request from Hill is especially difficult to interpret. Chambers had been an apprentice of John Senex, whose shop was in Salisbury Court when the first edition of the *Cyclopaedia* was published in 1727.[41] The second edition —in reality almost a new work—was planned for the winter of 1737 and more than twenty sheets were printed. Publication was delayed, however, for an act had been introduced into the House containing a clause requiring publishers of all improved editions to print the improvements separately. This bill passed the House but was finally rejected by the Lords. The second edition was published in 1738; hence, this could not have been the edition which Richardson sent to Hill in 1736.

A third edition was published in 1739, a fourth in 1741, a fifth in 1746. In 1753, thirteen years after Chambers' death, a *Supplement to Mr. Chambers' Cyclopaedia*, edited by George Lewis Scott, was published. McKillop says that Richardson owned a share in this *Supplement*.[42] It is possible that he owned a share in the encyclopaedia itself, but no ornaments were used and this means of identification is not available. From an examination of the two volumes of the *Supplement*, I cannot be sure that these folios—or portions of them—are from his press.

A similar problem is presented by a request from Hill that Richardson allow him "the Favour of a Second Inspection of the *Harris*, which you formerly sent me." [43] Considering Hill's interests, I think this book must be John Harris' *Navigantium atque Itinerantium Bibliotheca*, published in 1705. Hill's letter is of 1739. What interest, if any, Richardson owned in the book at this time, I do not know. He did print at least portions of a second and revised edition, which was first published in parts, beginning with No. 1 on 16 April 1744 and continued weekly. The work of editing and revising may have been undertaken, or at least contemplated, in 1739. John Campbell, the editor employed by the conger that published the second edition, had been associated with Richardson as one of the authors of the *Universal History*, a work that I shall consider in the latter part of this chapter. From one of Campbell's works in manuscript Richardson drew materials for a revision of an edition of Defoe's *Tour Thro' Great Britain*.[44] The conger sponsoring Campbell's revised edition secured the protection of a royal license for the work, and the first volume was published in 1744. Since the second volume was not ready for publication until 1748, we may infer that Campbell worked slowly and that he may well have begun his revision of the text of Vol. I four or five years before April 1744, when the first number was ready for publication.[45]

During the period 1740–1760 Richardson was undertaking less printing for bookselling congers than he had done in the preceding decades. Besides his possible share in Chambers' *Cyclopaedia* and his printing of Campbell's edition of Harris' *Voyages*, he printed for a conger a portion of the edition of Chamberlayne's *Magnae Britanniae Notitia* of 1755 and was continuously engaged in printing the ancient and modern parts of the *Universal History*, a gigantic publishing scheme. He subscribed for and may have printed an edition of the *Works* of Francis Bacon that was published in 1740 in four volumes, edited by Thomas Birch with a life of Bacon by David Mallet. No ornaments are used in this edition. He subscribed for two copies of John Ward's *Lives of the Professors of Gresham College*, printed by John Moore for the author in 1740. Ward, Professor of Rhetoric at Gresham College, had assisted Richardson with the dedication and preface of the latter's edition of Roe's *Negotiations*. There is no reason to believe that Richardson had any interest other than a personal one in Ward's *Lives*.

In the publication of *An Universal History, from the Earliest Account of Time to the Present* Richardson was concerned from 1736 until his death in 1761. Proposals for this work were distributed in 1729, but publication was delayed.[46] Beginning in 1736 and extending until 1750, the printing and publication of eight folio volumes was completed, with Vol. VII in two parts, and Vol. VIII called "Additions to the Universal History in Seven Volumes in folio." After the two parts of the seventh volume were published in 1744, the material in the folio edition was reprinted for an edition in octavo of twenty volumes. In 1758 Proposals for the "Modern Part" of the *Universal History* were issued and the earlier volumes were then generally referred to as the "Ancient Part." [47] The "Modern Part" required sixteen volumes, folio, and forty-five volumes, octavo, 1759–1765.

How early in this undertaking Richardson acquired a share cannot be exactly determined. The first volume in 1736 and the second in 1737 contain his ornaments. In succeeding volumes no ornaments are used, but in Vols. V and VI Richardson's name appears among the list of "Encouragers," and the imprint of the second part of Vol. VII reads: "Printed for S. Richardson, T. Osborne, J. Osborn, A. Millar, and J. Hinton." Advertisements for Vol. VII list Richardson as one of the proprietors.[48] Booksellers' names appeared and disappeared from the imprints as successive volumes were published. Two of the proprietors died between 1737 and 1741. When a royal license was secured for the work in 1739, it was granted in the names of Edward Symon (d. 1741), Thomas Osborne, John Wood, and James Crokatt.[49] Between 1739 and 1747 all shares were acquired by Richardson, John Osborn, Thomas Osborne, and Andrew Millar. The Stationers' Register on 2 January 1747 shows that Richardson and Osborn each owned a one-sixth share and that the remainder was held in thirds by Millar and Osborne.[50] Thomas Osborne had been associated with the history from the start; Millar and John Osborn came in with the publishing of Vol. VI in 1742. By 1747 these three substantial booksellers and Richardson had acquired all the rights. The four men registered each volume of the edition in octavo between 1747 and 1749; and in 1754 they registered a twenty-first volume, a chronological table to accompany the twenty volumes of the history itself. Though ornaments are not generally used in the octavo edition, these volumes were undoubtedly from his press. In fact, a vignette on the title pages— a tower underneath which is the motto "In Recto Decus"—is sometimes said to have been Richardson's "trade-mark." In the place of this vignette in Vol. II only is Richardson's ornament No. 78. In both the royal license for the octavo edition and the imprints for these volumes, only the names of Osborne, Osborn, and Millar appear. As customary, Richardson was an undisclosed partner.

The authors of the Ancient Part of the history were identified in a conversation between John Swinton and Samuel Johnson. Swinton told Johnson that the authors, including himself, were Archibald Bower, for whom Richardson printed a series of controversial pamphlets; John Campbell, the editor of Harris' *Voyages*; George Psalmanazar, who submitted to Richardson some material for his continuation of Pamela's story that Richardson dismissed as "ridiculous & improbable"; George Sale, the orientalist; and George Shelvocke.[51] The octavo edition was printed from a text revised by Archibald Bower, who is said by the *D.N.B.* to have received £300 for a slovenly performance.

Bower, on the other hand, said that Andrew Millar, whom he speaks of as manager of the *Universal History*, would have willingly engaged him for the Modern Part, but that, in order to devote himself to his *History of the Popes*, he declined and was in nowise concerned with the continuation.[52] There may be some truth in his statement, but in any event the proprietors employed Tobias Smollett to act as general editor for the Modern Part.[53] The letters of Smollett are the best source of information about the authorship of the Modern Part. Louis Martz has offered reasonable evidence to show that Smollett himself wrote nearly 3,000 folio pages, about one-third of the whole.[54] Psalmanazar and Campbell, authors for the Ancient Part, seem to have been re-employed, and a Mr. Shirley (William Shirley?) wrote some portions of Vols. XV and XVI which Richardson told Smollett showed a "barrenness both of style and compilation." [55] John Swinton does not seem to have been re-employed, though an undated letter of Richardson's (in the 1750's?) refers to a "warm Dispute" between Swinton and the proprietors of the *History* in which Richardson himself has neither "Leisure or Inclination to make himself a Principal." [56] Though the copyright of the Modern Part was divided among a larger number than that which finally shared in the Ancient Part, the editorial work seems to have been entrusted to a board consisting of Smollett, Millar, and

Richardson, with all contributions finally passed by Smollett. The latter, as editor of the *Critical Review*, used the columns of his periodical to advance the project.

Nine booksellers are listed in the *Proposals* for the Modern Part. They included Millar and Thomas Osborne from the Ancient Part, and Thomas Longman, whose father bought John Osborn's one-sixth share in 1751.[57] These proposals promised eight volumes in octavo and three volumes in folio by 1 January 1759, the former for £2 and the latter for £4/4. If desired, one volume in octavo could be purchased every month at 5s., in boards. An advertisement in the *London Evening Post*, 16–18 November 1758, announced that the work would be printed for Richardson and the nine firms of booksellers whose names had appeared in the *Proposals*. But when entry was made in the Stationers' Register, 1 January 1759, only seven firms of booksellers were joined with Richardson's name as owners of the copyright.[58] Osborne and Longman were listed, but through oversight Andrew Millar's name was not included until the entry for Vol. IX.

In the Stationers' Register no indication is given of the size of the shares held by individuals and by firms. Richardson, whose name continues to appear at each entry even after his death in July 1761, was one of eight owners. Some indication of the size of the whole venture may be gathered from the fact that in 1753 —nine years after the last volume of the Ancient Part had appeared—John and James Rivington purchased from Richardson a one-twelfth share in this part for £262/10/0.[59]

The size of shares held by Richardson in books other than those he wrote and the number of books in which he held such shares will probably never be accurately determined. The Stationers' Register in the eighteenth century contains relatively little information of this sort; and, as has been seen, Richardson was characteristically a hidden partner, or a partially hidden one. Fragmentary and inconclusive as some of the evidence is, enough of it exists to account for the fact that he was occasionally referred to by men in England and on the continent as a "book-seller." Enough evidence also exists to conclude that through sharing in the ownerships of copyrights, he had found another way to escape from the tyranny of the booksellers.

CHAPTER VI

Printing for the Author

A LOGICAL grouping of items can be achieved for a discussion of Richardson's printing of periodicals, for his printing of bills, reports, and journals for the House of Commons, and for his printing of books in which his interest was not solely that of printer. But important as this printing is in a description of his professional activities, it does not constitute the bulk of the work of his press, and we must turn to a consideration of the steady flow of miscellaneous items with which his press was occupied for forty years. Such consideration demands the establishing of categories, none of which is entirely logical or wholly useful. Furthermore, categories thus established cannot anticipate the interests of all readers, nor can an overlapping of categories be readily prevented.

Richardson printed plays of a dozen or more dramatists, and poems for more than twice as many poets, most of whom were slight in stature and meager in output. He printed surprisingly little fiction. Except for some of the work of Sarah Fielding and Charlotte Lennox, both of whom were in that circle of minor literary ladies that he gathered around him in his later years, he printed practically no novels, unless we include such questionable ones as Fénelon's *Adventures of Telemachus*, Ramsay's *Travels of Cyrus*, the sixth book of Sidney's *Arcadia*, and an abridged version of *Gulliver's Travels*. Among the plays that he printed were some that were the work of earlier dramatists like Lee and Banks but more that were the work of his contemporaries—plays that were published coincident with their performance or revival. With a few of these dramatists—men like Hill, Popple, Young, Jeffreys, Madden—he was more or less intimately acquainted. Others—Mrs. Centlivre, Eliza Haywood, Robert Drury, William Taverner—he probably did not know and would not in all cases have approved of. His interest in the drama was not inconsiderable. The characters in his novels discuss plays, and the fictitious letter writers of his *Familiar Letters* attend them. The characters of *Sir Charles Grandison* are listed as dramatis personae, and their conversation is occasionally presented as the dialogue of a dramatic scene. Even in such an unlikely place as his guide for apprentices is a section on the advantages and disadvantages of the English stage in the moral life of Londoners. But a discussion of Richardson's printing that arises from grouping books in this fashion leads us away from his activity as a printer into a study of literary influences, literary tastes, and judgments.

A category that keeps us more closely concerned with printer and author is that of works printed at the author's expense—works that Henry Woodfall described in his ledgers as "Gentlemen's work, and others not booksellers." Among the men and women with whom Richardson finally established some degree of friendship were many who had known him first as a printer. They sought out his press and to them he rendered an account of the printing costs. Either Richardson or the author then secured a publisher to handle the sale of the work. Other authors, dealing themselves with a bookseller, requested that the bookseller take their manuscripts to Richardson's press. In either case, author and printer became known to each other, and a list of such authors enables us to extend the range of Richardson's acquaintances. In Chapter VIII I have listed all the books that I have traced to

Richardson's press, first arranged alphabetically by authors and then chronologically by titles. From the first list can be seen the extent of his printing for any given author. Clues for the identification of some of this printing lie in Richardson's printed correspondence and in the manuscripts of letters between him and the authors who employed him. But even when letters have survived, the correspondence never indicates the exact amount of such printing, nor the date at which it began or terminated. A prolific author like Young, who was on the most intimate terms with Richardson, did not begin to employ his press until 1744, when he arranged for a change in printers between the publication of the sixth and seventh "Night" of his *Night-Thoughts*. The work of Aaron Hill, in large part printed by Richardson, had on occasions to be diverted to other presses.

During the lifetime of Richardson's press, publishing by subscription continued to be a popular method of providing sponsorship for books that in an earlier period might have found a patron's support. Illustrative of subscription editions that Richardson printed for the author are works of three sorts—books of a scholarly nature, editions of occasional poems, and writings of a miscellaneous sort, published to relieve the financial distress of an author or as a tribute from an author's friends to his minor talent.

The first of the scholarly books that Richardson printed for subscribers was Nathanael Salmon's *History of Hertfordshire*. Salmon had resigned a curacy early in the century to devote himself to the writing of antiquarian works. He had originally planned to have the Bowyers print his *History*, perhaps because young Bowyer was a fellow Cantabrigian.[1] But between the time of his issuing proposals and that at which subscribers were sufficiently numerous to encourage him to launch the work, he changed his plans and moved the printing to Richardson's shop. Richardson printed the book, entered it in the Stationers' Register for Salmon, delivered copies in London, and sent a supply to Salmon's home at Bishop's Stortford for delivery to subscribers living in his neighborhood.[2] So satisfied was Salmon with Richardson's work that he had him print his *New Survey of Great Britain*, published in eleven parts in 1728 and 1729.

In 1729 Richardson was engaged by Captain James Ogilvie to print and to assist in delivering to subscribers Ogilvie's translation of Pietro Giannone's *Civil History of the Kingdom of Naples*, Vol. I. Captain Ogilvie, then living in Warwick Court near Charing Cross, was probably the Captain James Ogilvie of the Earl of Orrery's Regiment of Scotch Fuziliers (Royal Scots Fuziliers), whose commission as captain was renewed in 1715 and who was mustered out in 1717.[3] Orrery had been arrested for conspiracy in connection with the Jacobite plot in which Bishop Atterbury and his amanuensis, George Kelly, had been involved. He had been associated with the Duke of Wharton in the early opposition to Walpole. Richardson's printing for Atterbury, Kelly, and Wharton may have led Orrery's retired captain to seek out his press. But whatever may have brought the men together, Ogilvie had Richardson print the first volume of his *Civil History* in 1729 and returned to have the second volume printed in 1731. George Strahan, who had assisted Richardson and Ogilvie in delivering to subscribers copies of the first volume, served as publisher for the second. Either Richardson or Ogilvie suggested securing Strahan again when in 1735 Ogilvie was ready to publish another work. This work was Robert Mentet's *History of the Troubles of Great Britain* and D. Riordan de Muscry's *True Causes . . . Which Contributed to the Restoration of King Charles II*, both translated by Ogilvie and printed by Richardson with separate title pages but with continuous pagination. The sale of this book was slow; sheets remained unsold in 1738. Richardson printed a new title page, labeled the work a "second edition," and reissued the unsold sheets of the edition of 1735.

Andrew Millar was secured as publisher for the second edition. This issue is said to be printed for and sold by Millar, but it was obviously not printed for him.

A third scholarly work printed by Richardson as a subscription edition was Philip Miller's *Gardeners Dictionary*. Miller was the head of the Chelsea Botanical Garden and Fellow of the Royal Society. His dictionary was published in two large folio volumes, 1731 and 1739. Richardson printed the work, subscribed for a copy, and secured Charles Rivington to act as publisher. The book met with immediate success and Rivington bought from Miller a share in the work.[4] Second and third editions of the first volume were printed in 1733 and 1737 before the first edition of Vol. II. In 1735 an abridged edition of Vol. I was published in two octavo volumes. Richardson also printed for Miller his *Gardeners Kalendar*, and this book likewise went at once into second and third editions. Richardson continued to reprint these works for Miller throughout the 1740's and 1750's, and probably printed a seventh edition of the *Dictionary* as late as 1759. Out of these transactions grew a friendship that was maintained until Richardson's death. When Philip Erasmus Reich visited Richardson in the 1750's, he found him at his country home, surrounded by "a large company, all people of merit; Mr. Miller, author of the Gardener's Dictionary, (which has been translated at Nurnburg, with such success), and Mr. Highmore, the famous painter." [5] Richardson paid tribute to Miller's professional skill in his edition of Defoe's *Tour Thro' Great Britain*, 1762: "At *Chelsea* also is the Physic-garden belonging to the Company of *Apothecaries of London;* which is and long has been in a very flourishing Condition, under the skillful Management of the ingenious Mr. *Philip Miller*, F.R.S." [6]

In an earlier edition of Defoe's *Tour* Richardson praised the author of another scholarly volume that he had printed as a subscription edition. This work was William Maitland's *History of London*, printed for the author in 1739. Richardson subscribed

for five copies. He cited it in the *Tour* as the best recent history
of London, and pointed out that it contained "many Things
needful to be known by the Curious, which are incompatible
with the Brevity to which our narrow Limits confine us." [7]

For the bluestocking, Elizabeth Carter, Richardson printed a
fine quarto subscription edition of *All the Works of Epictetus,
Which Are Now Extant*, 1758. The book went to press in June
1757, but was not published until April 1758. The number of
copies printed, 1,018, was insufficient for the subscribers, and 250
more copies were printed in July. The work sold for one guinea.
Richardson's charges for the first impression, including proposals
and receipts for subscribers, was £67/7. The profits for Elizabeth Carter were about £1,000. As it turned out, the interest
of many of the subscribers in Mrs. Carter exceeded their interest in Epictetus, for more copies were subscribed for than were
ever claimed. [8]

Poets as well as scholars found that publishing by subscription
was a convenient recourse, if not the only one available. The first
edition to contain all four of James Thomson's *Seasons* was printed
by Richardson for the author in 1730 and published in the main
by subscription. In the preceding year Richardson had printed
Thomson's *Britannia*. If we assume, as seems likely, that Thomson himself sought Richardson to print his first edition of the
Seasons, we can account for his choice by remembering that
Aaron Hill had recognized the "masterly" hand of Thomson in
No. 46 of the *Plain Dealer*, a periodical that Richardson probably
printed. At that time Thomson was still in Scotland, but six
months later he arrived in London and was introduced to the
little coterie of poets over which Hill presided. [9] Richardson
printed poems for Mitchell, Mallet, and Savage, each of whom
owed his original hearing in part to Hill's efforts. It is not surprising, therefore, to find him printing for Thomson. A fairly
close relationship between Thomson and Richardson was maintained up to the death of the poet. He was among those friends

of Richardson who tried to persuade him to give *Clarissa* a happy ending; and a poem addressed to Thomson by Thomas Morell, a country neighbor of Richardson's, was among the manuscripts that Richardson had preserved at his death.[10]

The subscription edition of the *Seasons* had been proposed as early as 1728, but the poem was not ready for delivery to subscribers until 8 June 1730.[11] Richardson printed it on royal paper and Kent executed engravings to be bound with the text. It sold for a guinea in sheets. The imprint reads simply "Printed in the Year M.DCC.XXX." Thomson seems to have acted as his own publisher, delivering copies to subscribers. Richardson had printed 457 copies, but Thomson, much to his disappointment, secured only 388 subscriptions. Andrew Millar and James Brindley, the bookseller and bookbinder, engaged themselves to sell for Thomson the copies not subscribed for. Many remained unsold in 1736 when they were reissued as Vol. I of a two-volume edition of Thomson's *Works*.[12]

A subscription edition of Stephen Duck's occasional verse was printed by Richardson in 1736. Duck was a friend and correspondent of Richardson. They may have met because of their mutual friendship with Joseph Spence, who, while holding the chair of poetry at Oxford, sought to secure an introduction for certain poets by writing biographical essays for editions of their work. Richardson printed an edition of Spence's *Essay on Mr. Pope's Odyssey* during the period when Spence was at Oxford. Samuel Wilmot, an Oxford bookseller, owned the copyright of this work. That Wilmot had the work printed in London by Richardson seems surprising, unless we assume that the printer was chosen by Spence.[13] When Spence left Oxford to retire to Richardson's ancestral home, Byfleet, he employed Richardson's press on several occasions and spoke of him as "in the little circle of my own most intimate Friends." [14] In one of Spence's letters to Richardson (3 May 1758), in the hands of a private collector, he mentions certain accounts with Richardson that he is planning to discharge. This remark indicates that Spence was publishing his work during the 1750's at his own expense. In 1759 when Spence published a book designed to elicit contributions for Robert Hill, a poor tailor at Buckingham, Walpole printed the first edition at Strawberry Hill and Richardson printed the London edition. His name heads the list of those who were prepared to receive donations for Hill and his family.[15] This evidence implies that Spence's acquaintance with Richardson was of long standing. It has led to my inference that Duck may have been introduced to Richardson by Spence, for Spence wrote the biographical account of Duck that serves as preface to the subscription edition of his poems. This edition, published in quarto in 1736, was followed by an edition in octavo in 1737. Richardson was among the subscribers and he made a present of a copy to Aaron Hill.[16] He continued to print Duck's poetry, and when the thresher poet drowned himself in a fit of depression, Richardson wrote: "Poor Stephen Duck . . . I had a Value for him, and am much concerned at his unhappy Exit." [17]

Another example of this sort of subscription edition is that of George Jeffreys' *Miscellanies, in Verse and Prose,* which was printed by Richardson at Jeffreys' expense in 1754.[18] The *Miscellanies* included Jeffreys' plays, *Edwin, Merope,* and *The Triumph of Truth,* as well as a collection of poems and translations. The author, the son and grandson of musicians, was an actor as well as a playwright and poet. He was probably introduced to Richardson's press by their mutual friend, Thomas Edwards. The edition of his *Miscellanies* was a handsome quarto, with some copies on royal paper. It was not exhausted by subscription, for two years after publication Richardson was advertising unsold copies.[19] The author himself, however, died in 1755.

For the sister of Henry Fielding, Richardson printed a subscription edition of *The Lives of Cleopatra and Octavia* in 1757. Richardson subscribed for four copies; his wife for two; and a gentleman, through Mr. Richardson, took ten copies. Sarah Fielding was one of Richardson's correspondents. Ten years earlier she had also published by subscription her *Familiar Letters between the Principal Characters in David Simple*, which Richardson subscribed for and read twice, but did not print.[20] He did print *The Governess* and *The History of the Countess of Dellwyn* for Miss Fielding, but these books were both printed for Millar, Henry Fielding's bookseller, and he probably had bought the copyright of both of them from the author. Millar certainly owned the rights to the second of these two books, for we know that he paid Sarah Fielding sixty guineas for an edition of 1,000 and promised her forty guineas more if the book went into a second edition. She advised Richardson of these details and asked him to watch over the printing and make any alterations in the text that he thought fit.[21] She had asked him to suggest emendations for the first of these two books, *The Governess*, and this he had done.[22]

A subscription edition of the poems of Thomas Blacklock, with an introduction by Joseph Spence, was sponsored by Spence, in part because of his genuine interest in Blacklock's poems and in part because of his desire to get some money for this blind Scottish poet. His poems had first been published in Glasgow in 1746. Six years later Spence arranged with Richardson for an English edition to be printed for the poet's benefit. Richardson subscribed for two copies. Again he followed a frequent practice by printing the first English edition in quarto and following it with another in octavo.

The poems of Blacklock possessed sufficient merit to justify this form of patronage, but the publication of the verse of Mary Barber and Mary Leapor required a strong appeal to the charitable and the sentimental instincts of subscribers. Mary Barber was the wife of a Dublin woolen draper. Swift befriended her and introduced her in England. His London booksellers, however, only infrequently employed Richardson's press. It was probably through the advice of another of her Irish friends that she found

her way to Salisbury Court. Patrick Delany, then Chancellor of
St. Patrick's, Dublin, had employed Richardson's press as early
as 1732, and in 1729 Richardson had printed a play for Samuel
Madden, Dublin clergyman and philanthropist. Either of these
men may have recommended Richardson to Mrs. Barber. In any
case, he printed an edition in quarto of her occasional poems in
1734 and reprinted them in octavo a year later. He subscribed for
both editions, and when he discovered that all copies of the octavo
edition were not taken by subscribers, he reissued it with a new
title page in 1736.

The publication of these two editions did not relieve all her
financial difficulties, however, for in November 1736 she sought
and obtained from Swift the rights to the English edition of his
Complete Collection of Genteel and Ingenious Conversations.
In April of the following year he sent her the manuscript through
the Earl of Orrery, who notified him in July that it was in her
possession.[23] In publishing this work Mary Barber needed the
services of a bookseller, who would guarantee the printing bill.
Benjamin Motte, then in partnership with Charles Bathurst, was
Swift's London bookseller. Through some arrangement arrived
at by Richardson, Motte, and Mrs. Barber, the book was printed
for Motte and Bathurst by Richardson. The rights given by Swift
to Mrs. Barber did not include those of the Irish edition, for on
8 March 1738 Swift wrote to George Faulkner, his Dublin bookseller, urging him to hurry the publication of the Irish edition
in order to get copies in the bookshops before the English edition
was published.[24] Mrs. Barber was said to have made enough on
the English edition, however, to place her in easy circumstances
for some years. The relationship between her and Richardson,
thus established, was maintained; and we find her in 1741 writing
to thank him for a copy of *Pamela* that he had sent to her daughter.[25]

Mary Leapor, the daughter of a gardener in Brackley, Northamptonshire, had died in 1746. A first volume of her poems was

published two years after her death. Three years later Isaac Hawkins Browne, the elder, undertook to put together a second volume, and Richardson and Thomas Edwards busied themselves in trying to get subscribers for the benefit of her father.[26] To Susanna Highmore Richardson wrote in June 1750: "I am afraid we shall want matter of Molly Leaper's [sic] works to make out the bulk of the new volume. We must try, if so, to get more of her letters." [27] When Miss Highmore offered one of her own sonnets to be prefixed to the volume, Richardson told her that he thought it would not be appropriate amidst the "sweetly easy poems" of Miss Leapor.[28] Presumably it was the completely unsophisticated quality of these verses of a gardener's daughter that attracted Richardson, though the idea of a second volume had probably originated with Edwards. The undertaking was not conspicuously successful; the number of subscribers for the second volume fell far short of that for the first. Edwards, writing to Richardson on 8 May 1751, said that "if we had but thought of *vamping* her with cuts [a phrase borrowed from Richardson], we had done the business." [29] Richardson subscribed for four copies.

The publication of a subscription edition of George Kelly's translation of Castelnau's *Memoirs* could scarcely be interpreted as merely a charitable gesture, but Richardson's agreement to print this work and to deliver it to subscribers was an act of friendship. Kelly had been committed to the Tower for life because of his complicity in the Jacobite plot of 1722. He occupied himself in making this translation, but his name did not appear on the title page. There we are told that the *Memoirs* were "done into English by a Gentleman, and publish'd for his Benefit." Another act of friendship, undertaken in quite different circumstances, was Richardson's management of a subscription edition of John Conybeare's *Sermons*, published posthumously. Conybeare at his death had been Dean of Christ Church, Oxford, and Bishop of Bristol. For his widow, Jemima Conybeare, Richardson printed a two-volume subscription edition of the late Bishop's sermons, and secured more than 4,000 subscribers. Richardson himself subscribed for six sets.

As final illustration of Richardson's kindness in undertaking editions to be published by subscription, we may note his interesting himself in behalf of the actress, Mary Porter. In 1758 she brought him the manuscript of a play by Henry Hyde, Viscount Cornbury, called *The Mistakes; or, The Happy Resentment.* Hyde himself had been dead five years at this time. The play had been written many years before his death and the manuscript presented to Mrs. Porter to be disposed of for her benefit.[30] Mrs. Porter had been the object of considerable sympathy after she had injured her hip in the 1730's, and benefit performances had been frequent. Richardson must have seen her in the role of Hermione in Ambrose Philips' *Distrest Mother*, for Pamela writes at some length of her incomparable acting in this play.[31] Hyde, who according to Lady Mary Wortley Montagu, had a good heart but not much head, gave Mrs. Porter the manuscript, but she either did not try to get it published before 1758 or was unable to find a printer. Horace Walpole wrote a preface for the play and Richardson printed it and probably managed its publication, for the imprint lists no publisher or bookseller. Again he subscribed for four copies.

Obviously all the authors who came to Richardson's press did not seek him out to manage the publication of subscription editions. Some of them were financially able to purchase the flattery of appearing in print; others were sincerely devoted to an idea or a cause which they felt was worth furthering, even though it had to be done at their own expense, or at least at their own risk. To describe all the printing that Richardson undertook for authors would prove not only supererogatory but tedious. Some of it, however, throws light on the character of his press and the nature of his relations with authors.

It would be only natural that some of the men and women

who became interested in his novels should have turned to his press with their occasional writings. Correspondence begun over the novels frequently led to printing contracts. None of this work was of much consequence to Richardson as the master of a successful printing establishment, but most of it came to him after he was well established and could afford the pleasure that such contacts brought him. I have already pointed out the printing that he did for Sarah Fielding and for Elizabeth Carter. Through Sarah Fielding he came to know Jane and Margaret Collier, daughters of the late rector of Langford Magna in Wiltshire, who grew up with the Fieldings in Salisbury after their father died in poverty in 1732.[32] Richardson printed Jane Collier's *Essay on the Art of Ingeniously Tormenting* in 1753. She had a certain independence of mind, and this essay, somewhat in the manner of Swift's ironic *Directions for Servants*, is written in an incisive style. Richardson admired her, sent a copy of her *Essay* to Lady Bradshaigh to introduce one of his friends to another, and enjoyed her disposition to maintain her opinions in the face of his.[33]

The conditions under which he printed for Charlotte Lennox are not entirely clear. Unfortunately, two letters that probably make clear the arrangements for the printing of Mrs. Lennox' *Female Quixote* seem to have disappeared. One of these was from Mrs. Lennox to Richardson, referring to some transaction with Andrew Millar; and the other was from Richardson to Millar, relative to *The Female Quixote*.[34] Richardson printed at least part of the two volumes of the first edition of this novel and the first volume of the second edition. Both editions were printed for Millar. Richardson was either helping Mrs. Lennox to make terms with Millar or was printing the work for Mrs. Lennox and seeking Millar as publisher for her book. The novel was published anonymously. Richardson wrote of it to Lady Bradshaigh: "The Female Quixote is written by a woman, a favourite of the author of *The Rambler:* Lennox, her name. Her husband and she have often visited me together. . . . The writer has genius. She is hardly twenty-four, and has been unhappy." [35] He may have printed two editions of a later novel of Charlotte Lennox, *Henrietta,* which appeared without ornaments in 1758 and in 1761. In fact, it seems likely that he owned a one-third share in this novel, for his nephew sold a share of that size to Thomas Lowndes a few years after Samuel Richardson's death.[36] That his nephew had himself bought this share after the publication of the second edition is not probable, for the popularity of the novel waned after its second appearance.

At the request of Lady Barbara Montagu, Richardson undertook the printing of *The Histories of Some of the Penitents in the Magdalen-House,* which was published anonymously in two volumes in 1760. These "histories" were written as if they had been told by the penitents themselves. Lady Barbara told Richardson that the author was a woman, but she did not reveal her name. Richardson wrote on 2 September 1759 that he was "proceeding with Dispatch in the Two Vols. of the Magdalen-House Penitents, which will be ready for Publication by the Time the Town fills." [37] On the 3rd of November he wrote her that the printing was completed and that he would advertise publication of the work in about ten days. The number printed was 750. "I put Mr. Rivington's and Mr. Dodsley's Names to the Title Pages as your Ladiship left that to me. The former will obey all the Commands that shall be transmitted to him. It is best that the Account should pass thro' one Hand." This description of the method of publication clearly indicates the difficulty of deciding, after inspection of a title page, whether a bookseller is really functioning as a bookseller, or merely serving as a publisher. The imprint in this work reads: "Printed for John Rivington . . . and J. Dodsley." These men, however, were merely publishing the book for Lady Barbara. On the 12th of December Richardson wrote Lady Barbara that he thought the sale of the book had been sufficient to satisfy his printing bill.

The Magdalen House was a charitable institution that had received Richardson's generous support. He was an annual governor of the institution and in 1761 appeared among the contributors with a gift of ten guineas.[38] Sir Charles Grandison had proposed such a scheme in 1753—"An Hospital for Female Penitents; for such unhappy women, as having been once drawn in, and betrayed by the perfidy of men, find themselves . . . unable to recover the path of virtue."[39] In the sixth edition of Defoe's *Tour Thro' Great Britain*, published a year later than the *Histories*, Richardson provided an account of this charity, stating that its purpose was "to *reclaim* and *reform* such unhappy Wretches as had *not* escaped the Snares of vile Men."[40] In recommending the stories of the Magdalens to Lady Bradshaigh, he assured her that there was "no *Shandying* in it, my dear Lady!"[41]

Though women are well represented among the authors previously discussed and though much of Richardson's preserved correspondence is with women, his acquaintance with men is much wider in extent and more catholic in nature than has previously been assumed. His printing for the literary Dr. Cheyne of Bath, for Aaron Hill and Edward Young, is described in Chapter VIII. But some evidence should be provided of the range of interest of the men who sought out his press and were numbered among his friends.

Among the first authors to employ Richardson was Archibald Hutcheson, member of Parliament for Hastings, who brought to his shop a long series of pamphlets attacking the fiscal policy of Walpole and exposing the Whig manipulation of elections. These pamphlets were published at his own expense, as a tablet to his memory in St. Clement's, Hastings, sets forth.[42] Richardson had scarcely established himself in business at this date, but he was not accepting work merely to keep his press busy. He respected Hutcheson and when he came to write *Clarissa*, he had Lord M. quote him, prefacing his remarks by saying: "I remember (*for I have it down*) what my old friend Archibald Hutcheson said; and it was a very good Saying—(to Mr. Secretary Craggs, I think, it was)." [43] Years had not altered Richardson's feelings: Craggs died in 1721, and *Clarissa* was published in 1747. That the opinions expressed in Hutcheson's pamphlets represented Richardson's own political sentiments is amply corroborated by other evidence.

That a printer can be held strictly accountable for what he prints cannot be logically maintained, but the integrity of his press was always a matter of concern to Richardson. In the 1750's, for example, he printed for Archibald Bower a group of pamphlets in a paper war that Bower was carrying on largely against the Rev. Alban Butler and the Rev. John Douglas (afterwards Bishop of Salisbury). Butler and Douglas maintained that Bower, having pretended to renounce the vows of a Jesuit, was still secretly a member of the Catholic Church. Modern scholarship sustains them, but a number of reputable Englishmen, including Richardson and his friends, William Duncombe and Lord Lyttelton, believed the statements that Bower made in the pamphlets that came from Richardson's press.

It would be absurd to contend that Richardson forthrightly espoused the position or the cause of every author for whom he printed. But it is difficult to find among the books that he printed any that were written in support of a position that he thoroughly repudiated. His dislike of Pope has been somewhat exaggerated, but it is true that he was never sympathetic with Pope's waspish satire nor with his version of Bolingbroke's philosophy. It is not surprising, therefore, to find him printing for so many of Pope's detractors and for so few of his admirers. That this situation was the result of any consciously adopted policy, it would be misleading to suggest. But among those whom Pope pilloried in the *Dunciad* are many for whom Richardson printed: Smedley, Dennis, Welsted, Cooke, Gordon, Mitchell, Popple, James Moore Smythe, Breval, Budgell, and a half-dozen others. A list even longer could be made of the enemies of deism for whom Richardson printed, but one would look in vain to find a work of a professed deist that was printed by him.

To what extent lists of books printed by other presses would prove an index to the character and opinions of their masters, it is impossible to say, for such lists are at best fragmentary and may well be atypical. But I know of only one instance in which Richardson printed works on two sides of a controversial issue. Among Richardson's friends was Richard Newton, Principal of Hart Hall before it became an Oxford college. Newton waged a long war against the opposition to the recognition of Hart Hall as one of the colleges of the university, and Richardson printed for him many of the books and pamphlets that he wrote in the conduct of this fight. One of these pamphlets was a letter addressed by Newton to William Holmes, then Vice-Chancellor of Oxford and Visitor of Hart Hall. John Conybeare, Dean of Christ Church, replied to Newton's letter in a pamphlet entitled *Calumny Refuted*. Richardson printed both the letter and the reply. It is the only time that I have found him printing for both parties to a controversy. Newton did not believe that calumny had been refuted. In fact, he came back at once in rebuttal and had Richardson print his *Grounds of the Complaint of the Principal of Hart Hall . . . In Answer to the Misrepresentations of Dr. C. . . . re, Dean of Christ Church.* That Richardson should have printed Conybeare's pamphlet is even more surprising when we learn that Richardson vigorously approved the victory that Newton finally won. In 1740 Hart Hall became Hertford College. Two years later when Richardson revised Defoe's *Tour Thro' Great Britain*, he wrote that "at last the Reverend Dr. *Richard Newton*, the worthy Principal, after an Opposition of several Years, given by some who ought to have assisted his generous View, has obtained a Point which lay very near his Heart: tho' not till several of his worthy Friends (who would have contributed largely to its Endowment, had it been effected in their Time) are demised, which must necessarily be a great Disadvantage to the good Design." [44] Richardson continued to print for Newton after he had won his fight over the recognition of Hart Hall and had turned to attack the clergy for holding simultaneously a number of livings. In January 1743, George Cheyne wrote to thank Richardson for what he called "your Book of Pluralities," which was actually Newton's *Pluralities Indefensible*, printed by Richardson in that year.[45] Richardson also sent a copy to Hill, recommending it as "a good and honest Book . . . and the rather as it is written by a good and honest Clergyman." [46]

In 1728 and 1729 Richardson printed two works for Alexander Gordon, who became a few years later the first secretary of the Society for the Encouragement of Learning and must have been largely responsible for Richardson's securing the contract as one of the three printers to that Society. Gordon printed his books at his own expense and apparently found some difficulties in meeting his obligations. Nichols prints a letter of his, dated 21 June 1726, presumably referring to Gordon's *Itinerarium Septentrionale*, in which Gordon writes of the trouble he is having in getting "the two ends of my book's expence to meet." [47] The details of the transaction are far from clear, but Gordon is planning to "lay the affair before Mr. Colvill and Mr. Richardson." Years later, when Gordon was planning to leave England to become secretary to the governor of South Carolina, he wrote Richardson, thanking him for repeated favors, and assuring him that "what remains between us unpaid by me, shall, I hope, soon be done with Honour and Gratitude." [48] The letter is undated, but it must be 1741, for Gordon is supplying Richardson with "Some Thoughts about Operas," which Richardson appropriates and attributes to Mr. B. in the fourth volume of *Pamela*.[49] Gordon had studied music in Italy, and during the travels which he describes in his *Itinerarium Septentrionale*, he was known to the countryside as "Singing Sandic." This volume is a result of a journey taken by Gordon through the north of England and parts of Scotland. It had a special interest for Richardson, because when he took over Defoe's *Tour Thro' Great Britain* in 1742 and expanded the text, it was with an expressed desire, among other things, to do further justice to Scotland, "which has generally been slightly considered by those who know little of it." [50]

Through the printing of a book for James Mauclerc, Richardson was eventually drawn into one of the various jobs of editing that he undertook from time to time. About 1737 he printed for Mauclerc a book called the *Christian's Magazine*, a kind of anthology of passages extracted from the writings of modern divines and designed to be used against a group whom Mauclerc describes on his title page as "Atheists, Deists, Socinians, Papists, and other corrupt and loose Christians." The book was published without date but was entered in Mauclerc's name in the Stationers' Register on 8 November 1737.[51] Mauclerc describes himself on the title page as "one of the oldest members of the Royal College of Physicians." The rolls of the College record the admission of a French Protestant refugee, Joseph Maucleer (or Mauclare) under date of 8 June 1689.[52] Maucleer—in all likelihood, James Mauclerc—received his M.D. at Montpellier in 1681. He was probably about eighty in 1737. The edition printed by Richardson in this year was sold by the author at his house in Orange Street near Leicester Fields and by P. Dunoyer, a bookseller in the Strand, who dealt almost entirely in foreign literature. A copy of the second edition, a very rare book, is described by McKillop.[53] This edition, dated 1748, states on the title page that it was "revis'd and corrected by Mr. S. Richardson." Mauclerc may have died between 1737 and 1748. I do not know why Richardson undertook the revision of the work. No mention is made of his editorship in advertisements for the second edition. As late as 1751 the book was still being advertised, and at that time it was said to be printed for William Sandby.[54] Sandby's shop was in Fleet Street, near the entrance to Salisbury Court.

He was the son of a prebendary of Worcester and a likely publisher for Richardson to choose, if he at that time owned any share in the work.

In an age in which religious controversy of all sorts was carried on publicly, it is not surprising that Richardson printed so many works for clergymen, from curates to bishops. The clergy constituted the largest single group for which he printed. Many of the group he probably never met; some he knew slightly; a few were among his closest friends. There is no reason to believe, for instance, that he knew George Whitefield, though he printed two of his sermons. The work that he printed for Bishop Atterbury probably reached his hands through one of the Bishop's friends, concerned with his fate when he was being tried for treason. But many of the works of the clergy were sent directly to his press and with many of the clergymen he became acquainted after having printed for them at the instigation of booksellers. Some of their writings were noncontroversial, some scholarly, some belletristic. Richardson printed an edition of Chaucer's "Prologue" and Dryden's version of his "Knight's Tale" for Thomas Morell, curate of Kew and Twickenham and a resident of Turnham Green.[55] For Thomas Spateman, vicar of Chiswick, he printed a play, *The School-Boy's Mask*. John Duncombe, curate at Sunbridge, Kent, and a close friend of Richardson's, had him print a two-volume edition of the *Works of Horace in English Verse*, by "several hands." A friend of the Duncombes, John Bunce, vicar of Hacklington, had Richardson print his translation of *St. Chrysostum of the Priesthood*.[56] Most of the writings of Richard Newton were in defense of his educational theories, or were, as I have pointed out earlier, part of his publicly conducted campaign to have Hart Hall recognized as an Oxford college.

The religious works printed by Richardson were of various sorts, though none was in defense of deism. Most of these works were by more or less orthodox members of the Church of England, though he printed for the nonconformist John Leland and for William Law, the ardent disciple of the mystic, Jacob Behmen. His printing for four or five of these clergymen will illustrate the range of these works.

William Webster represents the simple piety of the eighteenth-century clergyman who leaned toward neither deism nor dissent. Richardson's printing of his *Weekly Miscellany* has been discussed in Chapter III. When Webster was curate of St. Dunstan in the West, in Richardson's immediate neighborhood, he printed Webster's *Duty of Keeping the Whole Law,* containing his remarks on the deists. Webster said that the unfriendliness of his vicar was the cause of his remaining in this curacy for fifteen years without preferment.[57] It may have been in Webster's interest that Richardson advertised in the *Weekly Journal,* asking that any person having a presentation to a living in any of the counties adjacent to London write to him in Salisbury Court.[58] Whether or not Richardson was responsible, Webster later received a living at Ware in Bedfordshire, about twenty miles from the city, and Richardson wrote him what Webster remembered as a "kind letter." The two men became close friends in the printing and editing of the *Weekly Miscellany* and in 1758 Webster described Richardson as "absolutely the greatest Genius, the best, and the most amiable Man, that I know in the World." [59]

In the *Weekly Miscellany* in 1733 was extensively advertised an anonymous pamphlet, *The Oxford Methodists.*[60] This pamphlet, now attributed to William Law, was an apology for the movement. It was printed by Richardson for the pamphlet shopkeeper, James Roberts, and may have represented the first transaction between Law and Richardson. The first piece of evidence specifically linking the two men is in John Byrom's *Private Journal.* Byrom tells us that in 1751 Law was in London negotiating with Richardson for the printing of some of Byrom's poetry. Law had called at Richardson's shop and had advised Byrom that Richardson himself was supervising the correction of the proof of these poems.[61] In 1752 Richardson printed for Law his *Way to Divine Knowlege*. The spelling of the word *knowlege* represented Richardson's preference. He said that "in Works left to my Care, [I] omitted the *d* in *Know-lege, acknow-lege* &. and with general Approbation."[62] One of the poems of Byrom was *An Epistle to a Gentleman of the Temple,* first printed by Richardson in 1749 and reprinted in 1752. Richard-son had expressed a desire to print it when he had heard it read from the manuscript. The poem upholds William Law against the Bishop of London, Thomas Sherlock, in a controversy con-cerning the fate of man. Law's *Spirit of Prayer* expressed his position. Appended to the *Spirit of Prayer* was a quotation from Jacob Behmen that Richardson preserved among a group of miscellaneous manuscripts that were with his letters at his death. Among these manuscripts was also a passage copied from Law's *Appeal,* 1742 (p. 279).[63] The other poem of Byrom that Rich-ardson printed contains an attack on Bishop Warburton, whom Richardson's friend, Thomas Edwards, had also attacked in his *Canons of Criticism.*

Three short pieces by the Rev. Peter Peckard probably reached Richardson's press on the recommendation of William Law. Peckard, a Whig divine who later became Dean of Peterborough, was not personally acquainted with Richardson when he sent him his first manuscript, *A Dissertation on Revelations, Chap. XI. Ver. 13,* in which Peckard attempted to show that the Book of Revelations was in part completed by the Lisbon earthquake. When he sent the manuscript to Richardson, he said that Law had urged him to publish it. "If it brings any profit," Peckard wrote, "it is heartily your's, and I hope it will at least defray the expence of printing. But[,] however, if it should not . . . the deficiency I will take upon myself."[64] At Richardson's sug-gestion he modified certain remarks that he had made about Bolingbroke and Hume. Richardson had no particular admiration for either of these authors, but he felt that Peckard's adverse comments were not central to the development of his argument.[65] Martha Ferrar, Peckard's wife, had been a friend of Richardson's before her marriage.

The most popular piece of writing that Richardson printed for the clergy was James Hervey's *Meditations and Contemplations*. This work was first printed in two parts, *Meditations among the Tombs* and *Reflections on a Flower Garden*. Both were printed in quarto in 1746. Two second editions, one in octavo and the other in twelves, came out in 1748. In 1753 Richardson printed the tenth edition and would probably have continued to print for Hervey had not the Rivingtons bought the copyright of Hervey's work and turned the printing over to young Charles Rivington, who had completed his apprenticeship with Richardson in 1753.[66]

Hervey liked Richardson's printing. When Richardson found it impossible to print the third edition of his *Meditations and Contemplations* and had to turn it over to another press, Hervey commented that the "Paper is not so fair nor the Types so elegant." [67] Hervey's books of course paid for themselves. Richardson said that his profits amounted to a considerable sum but that he gave most of them away. His style he found "too flowery for prose, too affected: . . . A serious and good divine, of my acquaintance, sees him, as to his doctrines, too mystic; and I think him inclined to the enthusiastic part of Methodism." [68]

John Leland, a nonconformist minister with a D.D. from Aberdeen, brought to Richardson's press his *Reflections on the Late Lord Bolingbroke's Letters on the Study and Use of History* and his *View of the Principal Deistical Writers*. Richardson approved Leland's strictures on Bolingbroke, but he looked upon Leland's attack with mixed feelings. David Mallet's edition of Bolingbroke's *Works* had been published just before Leland's attack, but its sale had not been conspicuously successful. Richardson feared that such attacks as those of Leland and of Thomas Sherlock might revive interest in Bolingbroke. So many attacks on Bolingbroke, Richardson thought, might well "add to his [Mallet's] profits, by carrying into notice works that would have probably otherwise sunk under the weight of their dogmatical abuse and virulence." [69] Richardson had rightly estimated that nothing but controversy would stimulate the sale of Bolingbroke in 1754. Andrew Millar was said to have offered Mallet £3,000 for the copyright of his edition of Bolingbroke. Mallet refused the offer, only to discover that the work met with very little popularity.[70]

Through some intermediary Richardson's press secured a favorable recommendation to the clergy in Ireland. As early as 1721 he printed for the author Jonathan Smedley's *Poems on Several Occasions*, which went into a second edition in 1723. Smedley was successively Dean of Killala and of Clogher. He was popular in Whig circles and won the enmity of both Swift and Pope by a series of attacks on them, some of which were first printed in the *Daily Journal*, when that newspaper was being printed by Richardson. In 1728 Richardson printed Smedley's *Gulliveriana*, a volume that contains articles by Smedley that first appeared in the *Journal*. One brief essay in *Gulliveriana*, reprinted from the *Journal* and attributed inconclusively to John Dennis, is an attack on Pope in which he is unfavorably compared with both Denham and Dryden.[71] Richardson, in conversation with Nathaniel Hooke, Pope's friend, repeated this judgment of Pope, citing in comparison the same poems that Dennis (or Smedley?) had cited. He said that, as a result of this conversation, he lost Hooke's friendship.[72] His printing for Smedley and other contributors to the *Daily Journal* may have been in part responsible for the failure of his press to secure any books of Pope or Swift, except Swift's *Polite Conversations* and an abridgment of his *Gulliver's Travels*, with which Swift himself probably had no connection. For Swift's friend, Patrick Delany, however, Richardson printed books at intervals from 1732 to 1759. Delany became Dean of Down in 1744. He was well acquainted with both Swift and Thomas Sheridan; his wife, Mary Delany (née Granville), was a friend of Swift's and a correspondent of Richardson's.

For the clergyman and philanthropist, Samuel Madden, he printed a play, *Themistocles,* in 1729. In 1745 Madden again turned to Richardson's press. He had written a panegyrical poem to the memory of Hugh Boulter, Protestant Archbishop of Armagh, who had died in 1742. Boulter was strongly prejudiced against the Irish, but to Madden—and to Samuel Johnson—he was worthy of praise. Madden came to London and submitted his manuscript to Johnson for revision, paying Johnson ten guineas for this service.[73] The imprint of this poem and advertisements for the book support the inference that Madden dealt directly with Richardson and that Richardson secured a group of booksellers to publish *Boulter's Monument* for its author.

Madden is said to have edited the text of Bishop Berkeley's *Querist,* printed by Richardson in 1736–1737. He probably only saw the manuscript through the press.[74] Parts I, II, and III of the *Querist* were published in Dublin in 1735–1737. They were reprinted by Richardson for an English edition. Madden may well have been responsible for the choice of Richardson's press, but the intermediary in the transaction was Sir John Perceval, the Earl of Egmont, who noted in his diary on 27 May 1736: "I also sent Bishop Berkeley's second part of Queries to Mr. Richardson to be reprinted." [75] In Part I of the English edition is an advertisement "on occasion of re-publishing The Querist," that calls attention to particular Queries, designed to "knit both [nations] together by the firmest ties of interest." Madden may have written this advertisement. There is no evidence to show that Richardson knew Berkeley, though he later met his widow, his son, and his daughter at Cuddesden, the home of Thomas Secker, then Bishop of Oxford and later Archbishop of Canterbury.[76]

Philip Skelton, at one time curate to Samuel Madden and

student under the tutorship of Patrick Delany, had Richardson print a book for him as early as 1736 and continued to employ his press through the next two decades. If, as seems likely, much of the printing that he did for Skelton and for Delany was done at the author's expense, the commissions were of doubtful advantage to Richardson. In 1749 he asked Skelton to suggest tactfully to Delany that a printing bill was overdue.[77] In 1752 Skelton wrote Richardson that the manuscript of the first volume of his *Discourses, Controversial and Practical* was ready for the press; and he asked Richardson to dispose of the manuscript for him, when the work was completed, so as to procure for him a little profit, if that were possible. Richardson presumably professed his inability to secure a bookseller's interest for Skelton, since in the following year, after having the manuscript revised by John Leland, Skelton sent it to a London clergyman, Thomas Wilson, who tried to interest a bookseller in buying it. In February 1754, Wilson, having failed in his commission, turned the manuscript over to Richardson, who then printed it at Skelton's expense.[78] On the other hand, Richardson had been able to interest Andrew Millar in buying Skelton's *Ophiomaches: or, Deism Revealed*. Millar sought Hume's opinion before accepting the manuscript, and when Hume approved, he had Richardson print the book. A second edition was called for two years later. The author made about £200.[79]

Another member of this group of clergymen in Ireland was Thomas Wilson, who became Bishop of Sodor and Man. Wilson included among his friends both Skelton and Delany; he was also a friend of Dr. George Cheyne, one of Richardson's physicians for whom he printed during the 1730's.[80] Wilson's son, rector of St. Stephen's, Walbrook, and of St. Margaret's, Westminster, had employed Richardson's press for the printing of a pamphlet in 1736. In 1741 the elder Wilson was seeking a publisher for his essay designed to instruct the Indians in Christianity,

The Knowledge and Practice of Christianity Made Easy. His son, entrusted with the manuscript, failed to find a bookseller to sponsor the essay and took it to Richardson's press, undertaking himself to pay the costs.[81] This essay, written at the request of James Oglethorpe, carried a dedication to the Trustees of the Colony of Georgia, written by the younger Wilson. In 1757 the Bishop's son again returned to Richardson's press with his *Review of the Project for Building a New Square at Westminster*. This project had been authorized by an act of Parliament in 1755, but for want of the necessary funds to carry it to completion, it was at a standstill five years later when Richardson edited the sixth edition of Defoe's *Tour Thro' Great Britain*.[82] When the elder Wilson was succeeded by Mark Hildesley in the bishopric of Sodor and Man, Richardson wrote that "the late prelate was such a credit to religion, and kept so admirably right the people of his diocese, that I am glad so worthy a successor is given to them, and he [Hildesley] rejoices in the pleasure he shall have of finding so good order there, and that he shall have little to do, but to tread in the same path." [83]

This survey of the works that Richardson printed for the author, taken in conjunction with the list in the first part of Chapter VIII, serves to link his name with many authors and with many works that came to his attention and that may have served to shape or strengthen his opinions and prejudices. Richardson was less learned than the other three major novelists of the century and he was little influenced by his literary predecessors and contemporaries. But he was interested in manners and morals, and in his fiction he sought to realize the distress that attended a character when confronted with a choice of action. Many of the books that he printed were written by men and women who were likewise interested in the morals and manners of the century. To them we must look if we hope to find the form in which ideas reached him, for after he set up in business for himself, he did little reading that was not in line of duty. When Aaron Hill had retired to Plaistow and Richardson was supplying him with current books, he wrote, asking Hill's acceptance of several volumes, and added: "I write to have your Commands for any others, that may be agreeable to you; for I seldom read but as a Printer, having so much of that, and a Head so little able to bear it." [84]

CHAPTER VII

Law Printer to the King

IN THE year before his death Richardson attached a codicil to his will: "I have entered into partnership with Miss Cath[erine] Lintot since 24 June, 1760, and removed her printing house in the Savoy to my own in White Lyon Court, Fleet *Street*." [1] This partnership came about as a result of his purchase from Miss Lintot of a half-interest in the law patent that she had inherited from her father. Henry Lintot, son of the famous bookseller, Bernard Lintot, had died in 1758, leaving to his daughter, among other properties, his patent as law printer to the King. Richardson held his share of the patent for so short a time that perhaps any detailed discussion of this privilege is supererogatory. But in trying to find out exactly what rights he acquired by this purchase, I discovered that little was known about the law patent, or about its history. A detailed history of the patent cannot appropriately be provided in this chapter, but without a brief sketch it is not possible to see exactly what rights Richardson acquired or to understand why he should have chosen to invest in the patent almost all of his available capital.

During the year following her father's death Catherine Lintot held the patent in her name, and law books carried in the imprint the phrase, "Printed by Catherine Lintot, Law-Printer to the King's most Excellent Majesty." But she soon found it impractical to carry on her father's extensive business, and at a sale in April 1759, she disposed of much of the property that she had inherited.[2] She did not at this time sell her father's plant or his law patent. Nevertheless, she was a young girl with no desire to assume the responsibility of a business, and naturally she turned for help to Richardson, who was a friend of the family and, in particular, a friend of hers. Early in 1759 Richardson began trying to collect outstanding debts in order to get together a sum large enough to buy half of the patent. In July, when the matter had to be decided within a few weeks, he was still debating what he should or could do.[3] Uncertain about the future of his press because he had no son to inherit it and no real confidence in his nephew, William Richardson, he hesitated before concluding the deal, but finally convinced himself that this purchase would be the wisest investment he could make for his family's sake. Miss Lintot was to retain a half-interest. Richardson's decision to enter into this partnership was influenced by his feelings for Miss Lintot, illustrated in the following portion of one of his letters of 1759: "Never again, my dear Child, call me your Papa, and not treat me as such, in every particular. You must not say a word of my Time if in anything I can serve your Interest; or do you Pleasure. In either case, that will be making it, in my eyes, truly precious." [4] Shortly after Richardson's death Miss Lintot sold the half of the patent that she had retained. From the profits and from the sale of this patent, she is said to have made £45,000—a sum which gives indication of Richardson's own financial position at the end of his career.[5]

When Richardson finally consummated the deal with Catherine Lintot, what rights, precisely, had he bought a half-interest in? By the terms of Lintot's patent he had the "privilege for printing all manner of law books, which any way relate to the common or statute law of our realm of England during the term of forty years," commencing with the expiration of the previous patent, held by Edward Sayer; and "all other persons whatsoever" were forbidden "to print or cause to be printed any law books relating to the common or statute laws." [6] Edward Sayer's grant had expired in 1749; hence Lintot's grant had thirty-one years to run when it came into the possession of his daughter.[7]

No question arose over the length of time covered by this patent. Richardson and Miss Lintot could either hold or sell the right to the printing of law books for a period of about thirty years. But what law books could they print and against whom could they maintain their right? The terms of Henry Lintot's patent seem exceptionally clear, but inquiry leads to the conclusion that his patent not only fails to define these rights precisely, but that it actually misrepresents the facts. The patent adequately protected Richardson in the monopoly right to the printing of books on the common law. Consequently, after he acquired the patent, he could print such books as Bathurst's *Theory of Evidence*, Burn's *Justice of the Peace*, Gilbert's *History and Practice of Civil Actions*, Plowden's *Commentaries*, and Saint-German's *Doctor and Student*. In his right to the printing of such books, the law printer remained undisturbed. But the printing of statutory law became a point at issue as early as the sixteenth century, and a series of court decisions, continuing as late as 1758 and 1762, failed to make irrevocably certain what right the law printer had in the printing of statutory law. Disputes first arose because the law printer's rights were challenged by the King's printer, and later because his rights were challenged by the university presses. Patents granted to the law printer, to the King's printer, and to the universities of Oxford and Cambridge were all drafted with reasonable explicitness, but whether these patents were intended to reserve certain rights for one patentee against another, or whether they were intended to grant concurrent authority in some instances, were questions that had eventually to be referred to the courts. No one ever disputed the right of the King's printer to the printing of the Chronological Series of Statutes, or for that matter his right to print any proclamation of the law issuing from the King. But no patent or court decision made incontrovertibly clear what rights, if any, the King's printer had in the printing of collected statutes, or of abstracts or abridgments of statutes, made by lawyers or judges.

Presumably he had none, if Lintot's patent is to be taken at face value. But the King's printer's patent, granted to Christopher and Robert Barker on 8 August 31 Elizabeth, gave them, among other privileges, the right of the printing "omnium et singulorum statutorum, librorum, libellorum, actuum parliamenti, etc." The patent granted to George Eyre and Andrew Strahan more than two hundred years later (8 July 39 George III) gave these men the same right to print "all and singular Statutes, Books, small Books, Acts of Parliament, etc." [8] The original intention of this patent was not to conflict with that held by Richardson, in terms of which he could print "all manner of law books, which any way relate to the common or statute law." But in 1762 the Lord Chancellor, Robert Henley, expressed the opinion that the printing of Cunningham's *Digest of the Statute Law* lay solely within the patent of the King's printer.[9] This opinion was expressed incidentally to the Chancellor's decision in the case before him. Had this case come to trial in a court of law, the respective merits of the two apparently interfering patents might have been determined. At least much of the evidence for determining these merits would have been assembled. But the case was never tried, and by 1766 William Strahan had temporarily put out of question any further conflict of rights by acquiring virtual control of both the King's printer's patent and the law patent.[10] Consequently it becomes necessary to undertake the task that was not forced upon opposing counsel in the eighteenth century. The material that follows is as much of a condensation of the evidence as is consistent with a desire to make clear what rights were actually held by Samuel Richardson and Catherine Lintot.

In an appendix I have provided a list of the holders of the law patent from Richard Tottel in the sixteenth century to William

Strahan in the eighteenth. This list is a sketch of the history of the patent. At several times in the course of this history arrangements were made between law patentee and King's printer that were to affect the status of the law patentee in the eighteenth century; at times court decisions were handed down that help us in understanding an experience that Richardson had during the brief period when he held the patent.

These private arrangements and a few of these court decisions must be briefly reviewed, but before doing so, we may do well to consider a case in King's Bench that was decided in 1758, the year of Lintot's death. The decision in this case was the termination of a suit begun years earlier. In the year after he had been appointed printer at Cambridge, Joseph Bentham instituted a test case in order to find out whether the University, by right of letters patent granted by Henry VIII and Charles I, had the right to print abridgments of the statutes. Bentham printed and published, in association with Charles Corbett, *An Exact Abridgment of All the Acts of Parliament Relating to Excise on Beer, Ale, Brandy . . . with Some Few Notes and References,* 1741. The plaintiff who might have been expected to bring suit against the University was Edward Sayer, who then held the law patent, or E. and R. Nutt and R. Gosling, the lessees of Sayer; but it was actually Baskett, the King's printer, who brought an action in Chancery. Baskett secured an injunction against the sale of the book published by Bentham at Cambridge and the case was ordered to King's Bench on 24 January 1743. When the case was finally tried before King's Bench in 1758, the injunction was dissolved. Lord Mansfield, citing letters patent 20 July 26 Henry VIII, and 6 February 3 Charles I, granted concurrent authority to Cambridge.[11] Counsel for the plaintiff had a strong case, for this was the first instance in which either of the university presses, relying upon a privilege which had been neglected for more than a century, had attempted to print law books. Furthermore, an act of Charles II specifically forbade the universities to print

"Bookes of the Common Lawes or matter of State or Government," or "any Booke or Bookes the right of printing whereof doth solely and properly belong to any particular person or persons," without consent.[12] But eighteenth-century conceptions of the royal prerogative and a growing dislike of monopolies had its effect on the thinking of the judiciary. Rights granted to develop a trade in a simple economy seemed outrageously monopolistic after the economy had become complex.

In the light of Lord Mansfield's decision but not of the terms of Richardson's patent, we can understand a dispute carried on in the newspapers of 1761 between Joseph Bentham and Samuel Richardson. In that year Richardson and Miss Lintot, in association with Mark Baskett, King's printer, advertised proposals for an edition of the statutes at large, to be edited by Owen Ruffhead.[13] This edition was immediately met by the threat of another edition, to be edited by Daniel Pickering and to be printed at Cambridge for Charles Bathurst, a London bookseller. Richardson styled himself "Statute and Law-Printer to his most Excellent Majesty" in the newspaper war that was carried on in behalf of the rival editions, but it was evident that he felt, despite the terms of his patent, that he had no legal redress against the Cambridge press. Had he acquired a share in the patent before 1758, he would not have had to meet competition from Cambridge, for Bentham would not have undertaken an expensive project like an edition of the statutes at large if he had not been armed with Lord Mansfield's decision. After 1758 the only hope that Richardson and his partners had lay in printing their edition more rapidly, in underselling the Cambridge edition, and in trusting to the superior quality of their edition, if Ruffhead proved an abler editor than Pickering. The law patentees proposed a price of £5 in sheets as against the price of £6 for which the Cambridge edition was to sell, but Richardson's death in July 1761, and the subsequent delays before the law patent was finally sold to Henry Woodfall and William Strahan enabled Bentham to get along more rapidly with the Cambridge edition. Richardson fortunately did not live to discover that the Law Society subscribed for Pickering's edition and recommended it to the profession.[14]

Richardson had bought a patent that granted him exclusive right to print "all manner of law books which any way relate to the common or statute law." But as we have seen, this right was not exclusive. Both Cambridge and the King's printer had been held to have concurrent authority. Counsel for the defendant in the case of 1758 had argued that in the eighteenth century the King's printer had exercised concurrent right with the law patentee in the printing of books of statutory law, and we have seen that Richardson joined with Mark Baskett in the publication of Ruffhead's edition of the statutes at large. He had acquired a right which he could not maintain against the university presses and which he had to share jointly with the King's printer if editions or abridgments of the statutes were in question. We can again return to the question of why Baskett rather than the law patentee appeared as plaintiff against Cambridge in the 1740's and why Richardson felt compelled to print Ruffhead's edition of the statutes at large in joint partnership with Mark Baskett.

So far as can be determined, it does not seem that the King's printer had by reason of his patent any rights to the printing of an edition like Ruffhead's. The issue first arose in the reign of Elizabeth. John Cawood and Richard Jugge held jointly the patent of King's (or Queen's) printer under Elizabeth; Richard Tottel held for his lifetime the patent as law printer to the Queen. Cawood died in 1572, and Jugge and Tottel made a private agreement whereby they would share equally in the benefits of printing any abridgments of the statutes.[15] Here was the point at which much of the later confusion originated. Any agreement such as that made between Tottel and Jugge was purely voluntary and in no way binding with respect to succeeding holders of the patent. The Company of Stationers, however, held that this agreement was binding upon Jugge's successor, Christopher Barker, during the lifetime of Tottel.[16] Barker accepted the decision of the Stationers, with the proviso that his name alone appear in the imprint of such law books as had been the subject of the original agreement. In consequence of this proviso the seventh edition of William Rastell's *Collection of All the Statutes, from the Beginning of Magna Charta*, 1574, is said to be printed "by Rychard Tottel," while the eighth edition in 1579 is said to be printed "by Christopher Barker Printer to the Queenes Maiestie."

When Tottel died in 1593, this agreement terminated. His successor, Charles Yetsweirt, notified the Company of Stationers that he had been granted the privilege of printing books of the common law and the abridgments of the statutory law made by William Rastell and Ferdinando Pulton (Poulton).[17] The twelfth edition of Rastell's *Collection* (1595) therefore appeared in two impressions, the first printed by the "deputies of Christopher Barker," and the second "by Charles Yetsweirt Esq. Cum priuilegio Regiae Maiestatis." Successive patents were designed to secure to the law patentee the rights held by Yetsweirt.

Complications arose, however, because of disagreement at the time of the Restoration as to who owned the patent. By reference to the list of patentees, it can be seen that they were seldom printers. As civil servants not in the trade, the patentees either sold or leased their rights for a stipulated sum, for an annuity, for a share in the profits, or for both an annuity and a share in the profits. John More, a clerk of the signet, had been granted the patent by James I. He assigned it to Miles Fletcher and to Fletcher's partners, John Haviland and Robert Young, for an annual payment of £60 and a third of the profits.[18] More died in 1638, leaving his annuity to his daughter, Martha, the wife of Richard Atkyns.[19] In 1639, the year after More's death, Fletcher purchased from More's son, Charles, his stock and premises for £930 and sought to evade paying the annuity to More's daughter and her husband. Atkyns and his wife brought suit in Chancery, but the case was undecided when civil war broke out.

From 1643 until the Restoration no royal licenses were recognized. With the return of Charles, Fletcher sold what he thought to be his law patent to the Company of Stationers. Atkyns took his case before the King's Council, citing the specific infringement of his patent in the printing of *"Poulton's Abridgment,"* printed for the Company of Stationers and John Bill and Christopher Barker, the King's printers.[20] Atkyns contended that the joining of the King's printers in this transaction was merely a move by which Fletcher and the Company of Stationers hoped to bolster their claim against the Atkynses. Charles' Council referred the case to the Lord Chancellor, who granted Atkyns an injunction and awarded him £1,100, the estimated arrears. Less than a century later, it will be remembered, it was to be the King's printer whom Chancery was to provide with just such an injunction, when an invasion of rights was threatened by Cambridge.

An injunction of course could always be tested. King's Bench in the eighteenth century dissolved the injunction granted by Chancery in the 1740's, but the Stuart judiciary—or at least the Stuart Parliament—was not disposed to recognize the right of the King's printer, or any other printers, in books either on the common or statutory law. Abel Roper and Francis Tyton, joined by other stationers, sought to challenge Atkyns' injunction by printing Henry Rolle's *Abridgment des plusieurs cases et resolutions del Common Ley*. This printing became the subject of legal proceedings in which counsel for Atkyns cited the earlier decree in Chancery. The case was adjudged for the patentee.[21] Roper bought of the executors of Sir George Crooke the rights in *The Third Part* (*though first publish'd*) *of The Reports of Sir George Crooke* and published this book. Streator, the assignee of Atkyns, sued. The court held for Roper, but the decision was reversed in the House of Lords.[22] Atkyns or Atkyns' assignee was held to have exclusive rights. It was they and not the King's printer who defended these rights when challenged.

By 1740, as we have seen, it was Baskett, the King's printer, who defended the threatened invasion of the law patent by the University of Cambridge. This situation seems to have come about because Sir Edward Atkyns, holder of the law patent after the death of Richard Atkyns, leased his rights to George Sawbridge, William Rawlins, and Samuel Roycroft. Sawbridge and probably Roycroft as well were among the several sharers of the King's printer's patent, and thus parts of both patents fell into the same hands.[23] Imprints in abridgments of the statutes began to carry the names of both King's printers and of lessees of the law patent. A private arrangement, similar to that reached by Jugge and Tottel in the sixteenth century, was arrived at by Sir Edward Atkyns' assignees and their partners in the King's printer's patent. Once begun again, the practice continued down into and through the eighteenth century.[24] In consequence, when Charles Yorke was defending Cambridge in 1758, he could say that "in latter times, the law patentees have exercised a concurrent right with the King's printer" in the printing of statutory law.[25] He might have said more exactly that in latter times the King's printer began to exercise a concurrent right with the law printer. Perhaps the practice of sharing the profits of editions and abridgments of the statutes was the best one to follow when the phrasing of the two patents left the rights of each patentee in doubt. But wherever justice lay, the judiciary of the eighteenth century seemed disposed to challenge the monopoly rights of the law patentee, if by such action they did not forthrightly deny them.

Despite this disposition of the courts, Richardson had not made a bad bargain. It is true that he had to share profits with Mark Baskett in Ruffhead's edition of the statutes and that he had no redress against Cambridge when the competition of Pickering's edition was threatened. He had to meet this competition from Cambridge, but he must have realized that neither of the university presses was a real threat. His predecessor, Henry Lintot, had accepted a token recognition of his rights when the Oxford press desired to print Edmund Gibson's *Codex Juris*.[26] He himself was more seriously discommoded by the action of the Cambridge press. But the London book trade and the Company of Stationers were inclined to present a solid front. Booksellers were accustomed to dealing with the law printer; they had actively resented Charles Viner's attempt to print his abridgments at his own expense and were unsympathetic with his attempts to make his own arrangements for publishing this work.[27] Furthermore, the courts did not challenge the law patentee's monopoly in the printing of books of the common law. These books far outnumbered the books of statutory law. It was the right to print the common law that really induced Richardson to buy a share in the law patent when he was seeking an investment to assure his family's well-being after his death.

CHAPTER VIII

A List of Books
Printed by Richardson

PART 1. ARRANGED ALPHABETICALLY
BY AUTHORS

ALL BOOKS published anonymously have been listed under the name of the author when authorship could be discovered. Those for whom no author could be found have been grouped at the close of the list. Periodicals have been listed alphabetically under title. If Richardson printed more than one book by the same author, the titles of these books have been listed alphabetically under the name of the author, with one or two exceptions where the grouping of titles made for clarity.

Numbers in the left-hand margins have no significance except as a means of referring to titles. The same numbers appear in series in the left-hand margin of the list of books arranged chronologically (p. 229). They are also used to identify books in the list of booksellers and publishers for whom Richardson printed, and in the chapter devoted to Richardson's ornaments.

Each item in the list includes information in the following order: (a) author; (b) his dates, if known; (c) title; (d) number of edition; (e) number of volumes; (f) the date as given on the title page; (g) the numbers of the reproduced ornaments that are to be found in the book. These reproductions may be found on pp. 266–316. An asterisk following the date means that the imprint of the book states that it was printed by Richardson.

Following this information a brief note will usually be found providing some details about the author or the book, or a cross reference may refer the reader to the pages in the preceding chapters on which the book is discussed.

By referring to the chapter containing the reproductions of many of Richardson's ornaments, the reader may see most of the ornaments—in many cases, all of the ornaments—that appear in a given book. I have not, however, reproduced all of the ornaments, and in a few cases, where checking has been extremely difficult, I cannot be sure that I have given a complete list of all the reproduced ornaments that a given book contains.

For abbreviations used in this chapter, see the list of abbreviations (p. 356). The abbreviation *op. cit.* is used in this chapter only when referring to books cited more than once in the notes following the works of a given author.

49. ACHERLEY, ROGER. 1665?–1740. The Britannic constitution: or, The fundamental form of government in Britain. 1727. [1, 2, 3, 4, 5, 44, 62, 68, 70, 80, 90, 93, 95, 97]
    Acherley was a barrister and brother-in-law of Vernon, the Chancery Reporter. He worked zealously for the Hanoverians, with little reward. Richardson, among others, received orders for this book before publication; it was advertised as "printed by S. Richardson," but his name is not in the imprint (*Journal*, 17 June 1726; 3 Feb. 1727). See p. 92.

270. ——, 2nd ed. 1741.
    A second issue, with which was frequently bound a supplement, No. 271 below. This issue sold for £1/1; royal paper, £1/10. The supplement sold separately for 3s. (*Daily Advertiser*, 16 May 1741).

480. ——, 2nd ed. 1759.
    Called a "second edition," but in reality a third issue. Obviously the demand for this book had been overestimated.

93. Free parliaments: or, An argument on their constitution; proving some of their powers to be independent. 1731. [27, 43, 57]

271. Reasons for uniformity in the state, 2nd ed. 1741. [5, 53, 61, 98]
    The first edition, which I have not seen, was advertised in the *Journal*, 13 May 1729. The work was designed as a supplement for Acherley's *Britannic Constitution*, and issued with it in 1741 and 1759. The second edition may be a second issue. In 1759 the work was reissued without even a change of title page.

254. AESOP. Aesop's fables, with instructive morals and reflections, abstracted from all party considerations, adapted to all capacities; and design'd to promote religion, morality, and universal benevolence, ed. Richardson. 1740. [26]
    For a discussion of this book, see *Sale*, pp. 3–4.

404. ——, [a "new edition"]. [1753.]
    Probably a third edition.

14. ATTERBURY, FRANCIS. 1662–1732. Maxims, reflections and observations, divine, moral and political . . . To which is added, His Lordship's Latin version of Mr. Dryden's Absalom and Achitophel. 1723. [20, 25, 94]
    The *Maxims*, with preface signed "J.M.," and dated 24 May 1723, was published after Atterbury had been forced to leave England because of his connection with the Jacobite flurries in the early part of this decade. The Latin poem, with separate title page, is the second edition.

ATTIRET, JEAN DENNIS. See Spence, Joseph, No. 403.

71. BACON, PHANUEL. 1700–1783. The kite. An heroi-comical poem. 1729. [4, 43, 80]
    Bacon, a clergyman, was the author of plays and humorous verse. This poem, a tribute to Diana, will hardly bear comparison with the *Rape of the Lock*.

28. BAILEY, NATHAN. d. 1742. An universal etymological English dictionary, 2nd ed. 1724.
    Part of this dictionary was printed by Henry Woodfall and part by Richardson. Thomas Gent, as he tells us, was recommended "to the ingenious Mr. Richardson," to assist him in "his part of the Dictionary which he had from the booksellers, composed of English, Latin, Greek, and Hebrew" (*The Life of*

Mr. Thomas Gent, Printer, of York; Written by Himself, 1832, p. 143). Richardson, I believe, printed the section including the words beginning with L and continuing through S. Evidence that two printers were working on this text can be found by examining its make-up and type. A single leaf, for example, is used to conclude the words under the letter K, and the first words under L mark the beginning of a new signature. In the section that I have ascribed to Richardson, ampersands of a font different from that used in the other section are used. See p. 92.

453A. BAILEY, WILLIAM. fl. 1770.   A treatise on the better employment . . . of the poor in workhouses. 1757. [10]

Bailey was an active member of the Society for Promoting Arts and Commerce. Richardson printed this book "for the Author," who sold it at his house and through the bookshop of the Dodsleys.

134. BALGUY, JOHN. 1686–1748.   A collection of tracts moral and theological. 1734. [19, 20, 31, 35, 36, 43, 49, 52, 65, 80, 86, 103]

Balguy was a Yorkshire clergyman, prebendary of Salisbury, whose writings are anti-deistical, and ethically in the spirit of Samuel Clarke. His tracts, printed separately, are here collected for the first time.

164. BANKS, JOHN. fl. 1696.   The unhappy favourite: or, The Earl of Essex. 1735. [13, 14]

Banks, a precursor of sentimental drama, looks forward to Nicholas Rowe and away from heroic drama. This play was first produced c. September 1681. A version by James Ralph was popular during the 1730's; and a version by Henry Jones was produced in 1753, a year in which Banks' original tragedy was revived. To Banks' play, or more probably to the reworking of the theme by Jones, Richardson refers in 1753: "Will it be hereafter believed, that the Earl of Essex had a run; and that a play of the author of the Night Thoughts [Edward Young's *The Brothers*] was acted to thin houses but just eight nights?" (*Barbauld*, VI, 246). The prologue and epilogue of Banks' play are by John Dryden.

135. BARBER, MARY. 1690?–1757.   Poems on several occasions. 1734. [1, 2, 3, 41, 44, 48, 49, 52, 53, 54, 55, 56, 57, 61, 62, 63, 64, 65, 66, 67, 70, 71, 72, 78, 80, 83, 87, 90, 94, 95]

See pp. 114–115.

165. ——, 2nd ed. 1735. [7, 9, 40, 45, 46, 48, 49, 52, 58, 63, 64, 65, 66, 67, 70, 71, 72, 76, 78, 79, 80, 83, 86, 94]

    See p. 115.

186. ——, [2nd issue of 2nd ed.]. 1736.

    The new title page gives no indication of the number of the edition.

442. BARDWELL, THOMAS. d. 1780?. The practice of painting and perspective made easy. 1756.* [69, 100, 102]

    Bardwell, a minor portrait painter and copyist and perhaps a friend of Joseph Highmore (*q.v.*), undoubtedly dealt directly with Richardson. The book was sold by Bardwell at the Golden Lamp, in Lower Brook Street, Grosvenor Square, and through the bookshops of Millar, the Dodsleys, and the Rivingtons. A slender quarto (pp. vi + 64), it nevertheless sold for half a guinea, stitched, in blue paper. The text, with copperplates by François Vivares, was protected by royal license, issued 29 January 1756 ("Warrant Books," No. 371, p. 318). Ralph Straus cites an advertisement for 13 March 1756 with the price as 2s. 6d., probably an error for 10s. 6d. (*Straus*, p. 358).

376. BARNARD, SIR JOHN. 1685–1764. Considerations on the proposal for reducing the interest on the national debt. 1750. [29]

    Sir John Barnard, for many years M.P. for the City of London, was an Opposition Whig, whom Richardson supported at the polls (pp. 39; 57). Richardson owned the copyright of this pamphlet and registered the work in his name at Stationers' Hall ("Register," II, 74, 12 Feb. 1750). It was published at 6d. by John Osborn.

334. A defence of several proposals for raising of three millions for the service of the government, for the year 1746. 1746. [17]

    This pamphlet was registered at Stationers' Hall by John Osborn ("Register," I, 623, 26 July 1746). In August 1746, Richardson sent a copy to his friend, Aaron Hill (*Forster MSS.*, XIII, 3, f. 53).

242. BARTON, RICHARD. b. 1722. Farrago: or, Miscellanies in verse and prose. 1739. [8, 10, 32, 43, 45, 50, 53, 57, 60, 63, 65, 66, 67, 76, 77, 78, 80, 87]

    The imprint of this book—"Printed in the Year 1739"—implies that it was printed for the author and that probably the manuscript reached Richardson through Barton himself. I know nothing, however, of any relations between the two men.

501. BATHURST, HENRY, *2nd Earl Bathurst*. 1714–1794. The theory of evidence. 1761.*

This book was printed by Richardson as joint owner with Catherine Lintot of the law patent. See pp. 134–144.

255. BEAUFORT, LOUIS DE. 1703–1795. A dissertation upon the uncertainty of the Roman history during the first five hundred years. 1740. [12, 80]

Beaufort was associated with the *Bibliothèque britannique*, a periodical published at The Hague from 1733. The *Dissertation* was published at Utrecht, 1738; this is presumably the first English translation.

BEAUMONT, SIR HARRY. See Spence, Joseph, Nos. 402, 403, 416.

187. BENNET[T], JOHN. fl. 1736. The national merchant: or, Discourses on commerce and colonies. 1736. [14, 29, 35, 49, 66, 74]

Bennett was an agent in the West Indies of the South Sea Company, the Royal African Company, and the Society for the Propagation of the Gospel in Foreign Parts. This book, dedicated to Walpole and Sir John Barnard (*q.v.*), is rapturous in its praise of the reign of George II, whose wise policy "peopled his *American* Dominions with his superfluous and unfortunate Subjects." This is Bennett's way of saying that George encouraged the emigration of the unemployed.

188. BERKELEY, GEORGE. 1685–1753. The querist, containing several queries, proposed to the consideration of the public, Parts I, II. 1736.

See p. 130. This work was first published in Dublin. Copies of the English edition are rare. I have not been able to examine them, but a set, owned by E. H. W. Meyerstein, London, was described in the *Times Literary Supplement*, 20 May 1926, p. 339. Part III of the English edition came out in 1737. Richardson probably printed all three parts of this edition; they were advertised as a set in Mary Chandler's *Description of Bath*, 1738, a work from his press.

205A. The Querist, Part III. 1737.

365. BIRCH, THOMAS. 1705–1766. An historical view of the negoti-

ations between the courts of England, France, and Brussels, from the year 1592 to 1617. 1749. [7, 75, 103]

Birch, for many years secretary of the Royal Society, was a friend and admirer of Richardson. In 1738 a group of letters from Richardson to Birch makes clear that Richardson was printing a work for an unidentified friend of Birch (B. M. *Sloane MSS.*, 4,317, ff. 172–181). On 13 January 1749 Richardson wrote Birch, arranging for a meeting of the two men at the bookshop of Andrew Millar, who published the *Historical View* (*loc. cit.*, f. 178). I suspect that Richardson printed other works for Birch, but I have not been able to trace them to his press through ornaments.

443. BLACKLOCK, THOMAS. 1721–1791. Poems, 2nd ed. 1756. [55, 57, 59, 66, 75, 77, 86]
See p. 114.

444. ——, 3rd ed. 1756. [7, 8, 48, 73, 84, 85, 89]

59. BLACKWALL, ANTHONY. 1674–1730. An introduction to the classics, 4th ed., 1728. [11, 53, 64]
Blackwall was headmaster of Derby School and of Market Bosworth Grammar School. The book defends the Ancients against the Moderns and attempts to reduce rhetoric to "a liberal and rational Science." Richardson did not print the earlier editions. As will be seen below, its popularity outlived its author.

206. ——, 5th ed. 1737. [11, 26]

335. ——, 6th ed. 1746. [12, 37, 92]

50. The sacred classics defended and illustrated, 2nd ed. 1727. [18, 19, 20, 42, 53, 55, 71, 72, 80]
This book of Blackwall's made Clarissa ashamed of having "admired less noble and less natural beauties in Pagan authors," while knowing nothing of the "all-excelling collection of beauties, the Bible" (3rd ed., 1751–1750, VI, 394).

94. ——, Vol. II. 1731. [19, 55]
The second volume was published posthumously. With the publication of this, the first edition of Vol. II, the *Sacred Classics* became a work in two volumes.

207. ——, 3rd ed., 2 vols. 1737. [25, 30, 42, 43, 51, 72, 76, 77, 87]

351. BOLTON, ROBERT. 1697–1763.   A letter to a lady, on card-playing on the Lord's Day. 1748. [50]
    Bolton was Dean of Carlisle from 1735. This book was printed for Richardson's brother-in-law, James Leake, of Bath.
BOND, WILLIAM. See *The Plain Dealer*.

445. BOWER, ARCHIBALD. 1688–1766.   Mr. Archibald Bower's affidavit in answer to the false accusation brought against him by Papists. 1756. [16]
    Bower and Richardson were associated for a number of years in the preparation and publication of the Ancient Part of an *Universal History* (see p. 103). For the controversy of which this pamphlet and those that follow are a part, see p. 121.

454. Mr. Bower's answer to a new charge. 1757. [36, 83, 87]

455. Mr. Bower's answer to a scurrilous pamphlet. 1757. [34]

456. Mr. Bower's reply to a scurrilous libel. 1757. [50]

457. The second part of Mr. Bower's answer. 1757. [16]

256. BOWMAN, WILLIAM. d. 1744.   The imposture of Methodism display'd, In a letter to the inhabitants of the parish of Dewsbury [Yorkshire]. 1740. [19]
    BOYER, ABEL. See Fénelon François de Salignac de la Mothe.

72. BREVAL, JOHN DURANT. 1680?–1738.   Henry and Minerva. A poem. 1729. [9, 20, 22, 35, 44, 51, 54, 64, 71, 103]
    This book is catalogued under J. B. in the British Museum. For authorship, see advertisement in Mary Chandler's *Description of Bath*, 1738. Breval was particularly insulting to Pope in the prologue to his farce, *The Confederates*, and thus won a place in the *Dunciad*.

208. The rape of Helen: A mock-opera. 1737. [17]
    This somewhat crude satire on opera was first performed at Covent Garden, 19 May 1733. Minerva and Juno, disguised as country wenches, set out to thwart Venus and to prevent Menelaus from being made a cuckold.

227. Remarks on several parts of Europe, relating chiefly to their antiquities and history, 2 vols. 1738. [2, 3, 67, 70, 71, 86, 90, 97]
    See p. 98. Breval published an earlier series of *Remarks* in 1726. He probably collected most of the information while acting as a traveling tutor to the young Viscount Malpas. These volumes are handsome folios.

166. BROOKE, HENRY. 1703?–1783. Universal beauty. A poem. [Parts I–VI]. 1735. [5, 15, 16, 59, 69, 73, 81]

The six parts were published separately; consequently, when bound together, the pagination is not continuous. Each part sold for 1s. Parts II and III contain folio headpieces which I have not identified as belonging to Richardson. In 1774 the refined heroine of Brooke's novel, *Juliet Grenville*, found herself blushing at the manner in which the author of *Pamela* "undresses our sex" (III, 91–92).

95. BUDGELL, EUSTACE. 1686–1737. A letter to Cleomenes king of Sparta . . . Being an answer . . . to his Spartan majesty's royal epistle published some time since in the Daily Courant. 1731. [17, 27]

This letter is a reply to a certain R.M., an unimportant contributor to the *Daily Courant* and the author of articles in support of Walpole to which Budgell is replying (*Hanson*, pp. 110–111). Richardson knew Budgell, but held no high opinion of him (*McKillop*, pp. 143; 300). He printed nothing else for him that I have discovered. In fact, he printed only the introduction to this work. The book is in octavo, with the last leaf of the introduction a single leaf of signature M, preceded by L, four leaves, two signed. In the portion of the book not printed by Richardson are three imitations of his ornaments— Nos. 7, 48, and 57. Perhaps Richardson turned over part of the printing to some apprentice of his who had set up for himself by 1731 and had had copies made of some of his former master's equipment.

BUNCE, JOHN. See Joannes, Chrysostomus, Saint.

492. BURN, RICHARD. 1709–1785. A digest of the militia laws. 1760.*

This book was printed by Richardson as joint owner with Catherine Lintot of the law patent. See pp. 134–144. I have not been able to examine a copy, but it was advertised as printed by Richardson in the *London Chronicle*, 6–12 August 1760.

502. The justice of the peace, 5th ed. 1761.

No copy of this edition is known to me, but the seventh edition was printed for E. Richardson and C. Lintot. Elizabeth Richardson was Richardson's wife, who held her husband's share in the law patent for a short time after his death. The fifth edition was advertised in the *London Chronicle*, 24–27 January 1761, one volume, folio, selling for £1/10/0. For Richardson's share in the law patent, see pp. 134–144.

41A. BURNET[T], THOMAS. d. 1750. An essay upon government, 2nd ed. 1726. [27, 29, 36]

Burnett was rector of West Kington, Wiltshire, and a prebendary of Salisbury. This essay supports the "Happy Settlement." The first edition was published in 1716.

42. BURNET, THOMAS. 1635?–1715. The sacred theory of the earth, 6th ed., 2 vols. 1726. [18, 19, 27, 36, 55, 70]

Burnet had been Master of the Charterhouse. Richardson did not print the fifth edition, 1722. In fact, he printed only part of the second volume of the sixth edition, that portion through p. 320, which contains the last two parts of the *Theory*.

96. BURROUGHS, SAMUEL. d. 1761. An enquiry into the customary-estates and tenant-rights of those who hold lands of church and other foundations, by the tenure of three lives and twenty-one years. 1731. [24, 25]

This book was published under the pseudonym of Everard Fleetwood. It is a plea for a more intelligent dealing with lay tenantry by members of the clergy, suggesting as remedy a parliamentary measure.

395. BYROM, JOHN. 1692–1763. Enthusiasm; a poetical essay. In a letter to a friend in town. 1752. [73, 100]

See p. 127.

366. An epistle to a gentleman of the Temple. 1749. [73, 102]

See p. 127.

394. ——, [2nd ed.?]. 1752.

The title page does not indicate the number of the edition. No ornaments are used, but see p. 127.

73. BYROM, SAMUEL. An irrefragable argument fully proving, that to discharge great debts is less injury, and more reasonable, than to discharge small debts. 1729. [22, 103]

This book, "printed for the benefit of the author," was written while Byrom was in Fleet Prison for debt. Samuel Byrom was a relative of John Byrom (*q.v.*), but little is known of him. Presumably Richardson was befriending him with this printing, but Byrom's argument is so highly specious as to be amusing.

CAMPBELL, JOHN. See *An Universal History*, under title; Defoe's *Tour*, 6th. ed.; and Harris, John.

470. CARTER, ELIZABETH. 1717–1806. All the works of Epictetus, which are now extant. 1758.* [43, 69, 85, 86, 92, 100, 102]
See p. 111.

29. CASTELNAU, MICHEL DE. 1520?–1592. Memoirs of the reigns of Francis II. and Charles IX. of France . . . wherein the most remarkable passages in the reigns of King Henry VIII. of England, Queen Elizabeth, and the unfortunate Mary Queen of Scots, are set in a true light, tr. George Kelly (*q.v.*). 1724. [2, 4, 41, 44, 45, 46, 47, 53, 57, 62, 64, 65, 68, 70, 71, 97]
See pp. 39; 116. Kelly, the translator, had been committed to the Tower for life on being convicted of complicity in the Jacobite plot of 1722. Castelnau, the author, was the French Ambassador to the Court of Elizabeth.

35. CATHERALL, SAMUEL. d. 1764? Cato major. A poem. Upon the model of Tully's Essay of old age. 1725. [27, 71, 96]
Catherall, a Fellow of Oriel College, Oxford, was vicar of Ingliscomb, Somersetshire, and a prebendary of Wells.

189. CENTLIVRE, SUSANNA. 1667?–1723. The gamester, 4th ed. 1736. [69, 81]
This play—Mrs. Centlivre's experiment in sentimental comedy—is a rough adaptation of Jean François Regnard's *Le Joueur*, with the gamester's reformation at the dénouement (Ernest Bernbaum, *The Drama of Sensibility*, Cambridge, [Mass.], 1925, pp. 98–100). Another fourth edition, probably a piracy, appeared in 1736. The edition printed by Richardson has a title page in red and black, whereas the piracy is printed in black. Both are "printed for W. Feales." The piracy contains on p. 43 a crude imitation of one of Richardson's ornaments, No. 69.

432. CHAMBERLAYNE, JOHN. 1666–1723. Magnae Britanniae notitia: or, The present state of Great-Britain, 38th ed. of Southern Part, 17th ed. of Northern Part. 1755. [16, 36]
This book is one of the numerous editions of a work which Edward Chamberlayne began under the title of *Angliae No-*

titia in 1669. At the Union in 1708, the first edition of the Northern Part was published and the title was changed accordingly. John Chamberlayne carried on the work after his father's death, and his name was continued on the title pages for years after his own death in 1723. The edition of 1755 was printed for a conger, who must have employed someone to bring it up to date. Richardson printed the first part (i.e., through p. 288). See p. v.

404A. CHAMBERS, EPHRIAM. d. 1740.   Supplement to Mr. Chambers' Cyclopaedia, 2 vols. 1753.

    See pp. 99–100.

136. CHANDLER, MARY. 1687–1745.   A description of Bath, [2nd ed.?]. 1734. [2, 90]

    Mrs. Chandler was a milliner in Bath from 1705 to 1744. A copy of this poem in the Bodleian (n.d., c. 1733), probably the first edition, was not printed by Richardson. But the edition of 1734 and subsequent editions until 1755 were printed by Richardson for his brother-in-law, James Leake, of Bath. Mrs. Chandler provides in her poem a pleasant picture of Leake's bookshop (p. 15). Richardson quotes a long passage from the poem, celebrating the taste of Ralph Allen in landscape gardening, in his edition of Defoe's *Tour* (1742, II, 266; and in subsequent editions). Jerom Murch (*Biographical Sketches of Bath Celebrities*, 1893, pp. 124–125), calls the author "a worthy milliner, much respected."

190. The description of Bath . . . To which are added, Several poems by the same author, 3rd ed. 1736. [8, 10, 41, 52, 63, 67, 70, 72, 80]

228. ——, 4th ed. 1738. [8, 31, 32, 42, 51, 52, 53, 55, 63, 65, 66, 71, 79, 86, 87]

272. ——, 5th ed. 1741. [8, 10, 22, 50, 51, 53, 63, 67, 76, 78]

315. The description of Bath . . . To which is added, A true tale, by the same author, 6th ed. 1744. [8, 10, 50, 51, 53, 57, 63, 67, 76, 78, 81]

433. ——, 7th ed. 1755. [8, 10, 21, 36, 43, 46, 50, 55, 57, 66, 69, 82, 83, 85, 86]

377A. CHAPONE, SARAH KIRKHAM. 1699–1764.   Remarks on Mrs.

Muilman's Letter to the Right Honourable The Earl of Chesterfield. In a letter to Mrs. Muilman. 1750.

This pamphlet was published anonymously. Mrs. Chapone, one of Richardson's correspondents, was the mother-in-law of the bluestocking, Hester Chapone (née Mulso). I have not been able to examine this pamphlet. For Richardson's printing of it, see *McKillop*, pp. 179–180, where he cites a letter in the Forster MSS. Perhaps Richardson also printed a second edition in 1751. She refers to that edition in a letter to Richardson, 25 February 1751 (*Forster MSS.*, XII, 2, ff. 19–20).

CHAUCER, GEOFFREY. See Morell, Thomas.

229. CHEYNE, GEORGE. 1671–1743. "A catechism." 1738.

Cheyne was a physician living at Bath. A collection of his letters to Richardson is in the library of the University of Edinburgh, *Laing MSS.*, III, 356. Several years after I consulted these manuscripts, the letters were ably edited and published by Charles F. Mullett, *Letters of Doctor George Cheyne to Samuel Richardson*, Columbia, [Mo.], 1943. I am therefore citing Mullett's book rather than the manuscripts. This so-called "Catechism" I have not seen, nor do I know its title, but Cheyne wrote to Richardson, 4 January 1738, thanking him for his "ready Care in printing the Catechism" (Mullett, *op. cit.*, p. 35). On the 10th of February he wrote that he thought it "a pretty Thing for People sincerely disposed to be serious and in earnest in Religion. It will not go far with meer [*sic*] Rationalists" (Mullett, *op. cit.*, p. 36). By this date he had received a copy from Richardson.

121. The English malady. 1733. [20, 27, 31, 36, 53, 64, 67, 70, 72, 78, 103]

A manuscript letter, undated but before December 1734, refers to the printing of an edition (probably the first) of *The English Malady* (Mullett, *op. cit.*, p. 31). This essay is more readable than most of Cheyne's work, which depends for its conclusions on his physico-mathematical propositions. In 1776 when Boswell told Johnson that he had heard that Cheyne was reckoned whimsical, Johnson replied: "I would not have you read anything else of Cheyne, but his book on Health [*An Essay of Health and Long Life, q.v.*], and his

English Malady" (Boswell's *Johnson*, ed. Hill, Oxford, 1887, III, 26–27).

137. ──, 2nd ed. 1734. [20, 21, 36, 51, 53, 63, 67, 80]
    A third edition, which I have not seen, was advertised in Mary Chandler's *Description of Bath*, 3rd ed., 1736.

138. An essay of health and long life, 8th ed. 1734. [27, 51, 58, 63, 80]
    The first edition was published in 1724.

257. An essay on regimen. 1740.
    I have not reproduced the small ornaments found in this book, but they are all used in other books from Richardson's press. The stormy sessions which Cheyne and Richardson had over the printing of this book and of the *Natural Method of Cureing Diseases* are all recorded in Cheyne's letters (Mullett, *op. cit.*, p. 35, *passim*). Most of the difficulty arose because of Cheyne's exaggerated opinion of their worth, and because of the reluctance of booksellers to share this opinion. The material, finally published as the *Essay* and as the *Natural Method*, was originally designed for one book, in one or two volumes. In 1738 Cheyne decided to make two books of his material; and by 1739 he was convinced that the *Essay on Regimen* was the major work. He finally entered into an agreement with Charles Rivington and James Leake for the *Essay*. These book-sellers were to pay him 100 guineas and in addition provide him with "50 copies bound and gilt, and a Piece of Plate at £20." He agreed to protect them against loss (Mullett, *op. cit.*, p. 52). Richardson printed 3,000 copies, and the book was published on 21 September 1739 (*Gazetteer*). In 1741, Cheyne had to pay Rivington and Leake £80 to cover their loss, though an effort was made to stimulate the sale by reissuing the sheets in 1740, with a title page describing this reissue as a second edition. Sheets of the book were still available for a third issue (called a "third edition") in 1753.

257A. ──, 2nd ed. 1740.
    A second issue.

404B. ──, 3rd ed. 1753.
    A third issue. In obedience to a last-minute request of Cheyne, Richardson printed fly titles for each of the separate Discourses of the first edition of this *Essay*. In the first edition

and in the second issue, the sheet on which these fly titles were printed was cut up, and the titles were inserted in their proper places, interrupting the pagination. But in the third issue this sheet is merely folded and bound in the midst of the Table of Contents. The irascible Cheyne would have been horrified, but happily he had been dead for ten years when the third issue appeared.

230. "An historical character of the Honourable George Bailie Esq., By G.C. M.D. F.R.S." 1738.

I have not seen a copy of this single sheet, but Cheyne wrote Richardson, 23 August 1738, sending him the manuscript and asking him to print about 250 copies on a half-sheet of Imperial paper (Mullett, *op. cit.*, pp. 38, 39, 42, 66). Bailie died on 7 August 1738. The text of Cheyne's memoir was published in the *Gentleman's Magazine*, VIII (1738), 467.

291. The natural method of cureing [*sic*] the diseases of the body, and the disorders of the mind depending on the body, 3rd ed. 1742.

I have not seen a first or second edition of this book, but I feel confident that the second, third, and fourth editions were merely reissues of the sheets of the first edition. For Richardson's printing of the book, see Mullett, *op. cit.*, p. 66 ff. Cheyne wanted Richardson to accept the copyright as a gift, or at least to act as his agent in publishing the book. But Richardson persuaded him that he needed a bookseller to advance the sale of it. Cheyne therefore proposed to George Strahan that he, in conjunction with John and Paul Knapton, take the book for £125 and reimburse him for the £80 which he had lost in publishing the *Essay on Regimen*. Strahan and the Knaptons were also to receive title to all the unbound sheets of the *Essay on Regimen*. To this proposal Strahan and his partners agreed, but if the lack of success of the venture can be gauged by the number of times sheets were reissued, Cheyne's new booksellers fared no better than those who had lost £80 on the *Essay*. Strahan's title to the unbound sheets of the *Essay* proved of no value to him. After his death, however, his relative, Alexander Strahan, joined with a group of booksellers to reissue these sheets as a "third edition."

292. ——, 4th ed. 1742.

A fourth issue. It is quite clear from Cheyne's letters that this book was not reprinted in 1742. On 27 January 1743, Cheyne was still waiting word from Strahan of the success of the first edition (Mullett, *op. cit.*, p. 122). "Strahan has never had the Civility to Favour me with one Line since he had the Property of that Book," he wrote Richardson. (The date of the letter is O.S., i.e., 1742 for 1743.)

378. CHURCH, THOMAS. 1707–1756. A vindication of the miraculous powers, which subsisted in the three first centuries of the Christian church. In answer to Dr. [Conyers] Middleton's Free inquiry. 1750. [16, 45, 69, 84]

Church was a lecturer at St. Anne's, Soho, and vicar of Battersea. He wrote against both deism and Methodism. Middleton was a latitudinarian, who had been threatened with the loss of his degrees for challenging the historical accuracy of the Bible. He died in this year. See p. v.

107. CHURCHILL, AWNSHAM, ed. d. 1728. A collection of voyages and travels, 6 vols. 1732. [1, 54, 56, 61 in Vol. VI]

See p. 94.

243. THE CITIZEN: or, The weekly conversation of a society of London merchants on trade and other publick affairs. A weekly periodical, published as a single sheet from 9 February 1739 to 27 July 1739. Edited by Sir William Keith (*q.v.*). Price 2*d*.

See p. 72.

167. COCKBURN, JOHN. A journey over land, from the gulf of Honduras to the Great South-Sea. 1735. [17, 31, 36, 49, 53, 93, 103]

This work purports to be the adventures of a half-dozen Englishmen who were taken from the *John and Jane*, Edward Burt, Master, by a Spanish ship in 1731, and "set on Shoar at a Place called *Porto-Cavalo*, naked and wounded." With this is bound, continuously paged, Nicholas Withington's *Briefe Discoverye*, with a title page dated 1734. See below, under Withington.

405. COLLIER, JANE. An essay on the art of ingeniously tormenting. 1753. [12, 28, 51, 78]

See p. 118.

167A. CONYBEARE, JOHN. 1692–1755. Calumny refuted: or, An answer to the personal slanders published by Dr. Richard Newton, in his letter to Dr. Holmes. 1735. [17, 27]
See p. 122.

108. A defence of reveal'd religion. 1732. [18, 24, 31, 64, 77, 84, 103]
See p. 116.

458. Sermons, 2 vols. 1757.*
See p. 116. In October 1756, the edition was nearly finished at the press (B.M. *Add. MSS.*, 39, 311, f. 81).

43. COOKE, THOMAS. 1703–1756. The bath. A tale. 1726. [6, 42, 62]
Cooke, the son of a Braintree innkeeper, was a Whig journalist and pamphleteer, who won a place in the *Dunciad*. See p. 54.

168. COOPER, ELIZABETH. fl. 1737. The rival widows: or, Fair libertine. 1735. [7, 20, 43, 53, 73, 76]
Mrs. Cooper, an auctioneer's widow, was a very minor dramatist and poet. In 1735 this play was produced at Covent Garden, February 22, 25, 27, March 1, 4, 6. Its plot is one of doubtful intrigue, with a moral dénouement.

139. COTTON, CHARLES. 1630–1687. The genuine poetical works, 3rd ed. 1734. [49, 51, 76, 77, 79, 83, 93]
This volume contains, among other poems, "Scarronides: or Virgil Travestied," "Lucian Burlesqued," and "The Wonders of the Peake." Richardson knew Cotton's poetry: he refers to the travesty of Virgil in slurring Fielding's *Amelia* (*Barbauld*, VI, 154–155); and he quotes from "The Wonders of the Peake" in the description of Derbyshire that he revised for an edition of Defoe's *Tour* (3rd ed., 1742, III, 84).

513. CUNNINGHAM, TIMOTHY. d. 1789. The practice of a justice of peace, 2 vols. 1762.
This book was "Printed by E. Richardson and C. Lintot." For a short period after her husband's death, Elizabeth Richardson printed books as joint owner with Miss Lintot of the law patent. See pp. 134–144.

169. THE DAILY GAZETTEER. A daily newspaper, published from 30 June 1735 to 1748.
See pp. 63–68.

36. THE DAILY JOURNAL.   A daily newspaper, published from
    1720 to 1737?
       See pp. 52–63.

434. DALTON, JOHN. 1709–1763.   A descriptive poem, addressed to
    two ladies, at their return from viewing the mines near White-
    haven . . . To which are added, Some thoughts on building
    and planting, to Sir James Lowther, of Lowther-Hall, Bart.
    1755. [99]
       Dalton was rector of St. Mary-at-Hill, a canon of Worcester,
    and tutor to Lord Beauchamp, son of the Countess of Hert-
    ford. The mines about which he wrote were the famous coal
    mines, developed by Sir John Lowther and his son, Sir James,
    at Whitehaven, Cumberland. Richardson himself provided a
    detailed description of their more notable features in his sixth
    edition of Defoe's *Tour* (1762, III, 283–285). See p. v.

52. DEFOE, DANIEL. 1661?–1731.   A new family instructor; in
    familiar discourses between a father and his children, on the
    most essential points of the Christian religion. 1727. [7, 19, 42,
    55, 65, 103]
       With the tracing of this book and other works of Defoe to
    Richardson's press, speculation about his possible knowledge
    of Puritan family literature need not remain so highly conjec-
    tural. Unfortunately, we have little evidence of Richardson's
    opinion of Defoe. He praises him as the original editor of the
    Tour Thro' Great Britain (3rd ed., 1742, I, vii); and in *Clarissa*
    he refers to Defoe as "an ingenious man, tho' a *dissenter*" (3rd
    ed., 1751–1750, VII, 286–287).

109. ——, [2nd ed.]. 1732.
       A second issue, with no mention of the number of the edition
    on the title page.

294. ——, 4th ed. 1742.
       A new issue of the first edition, probably the fourth.

37. A new voyage round the world. 1725. [25]
       This book was printed at two presses. It is actually composed
    of two parts, though the parts are not numbered in the text.
    The pagination and signatures of each part begin and end in-
    dependently. Richardson printed the second half of the book,
    beginning with the text after p. 208. The pagination of his half
    of the text runs from [1]–206.

73A. Religious courtship: Being historical discourses on the necessity of marrying religious husbands and wives only . . . With an appendix of the necessity of taking none but religious servants, and a proposal for the better managing of servants, 2nd ed. 1729. [7, 44, 61, 81, 91]

Richardson printed pp. 1–176, through signature M. The preface and the remainder of the text are the work of another press.

30. A tour thro' the whole island of Great-Britain, 3 vols. 1724–1725–1727.

Richardson printed the indexes for Vols. I and II, with his ornament No. 29 in Vol. I, and Nos. 35 and 57 in Vol. II. He also printed the first and second letters in Vol. II (pp. 1–192), with ornaments No. 27, 35, and 96. The third volume is the work of another press.

232. ——, 2nd ed., 3 vols. 1738. [13, 17, 18, 26, 27, 30, 43, 53, 76]
Richardson printed only Vols. I and II.

295. ——, 3rd ed., 4 vols., ed. Richardson. 1742. [13, 14, 25, 50, 52, 53, 58, 63, 69, 71]
For a full discussion of Richardson's editorship of the *Tour*, see *Sale*, pp. 39–44.

352. ——, 4th ed., 4 vols., ed. Richardson. 1748. [7, 15, 27, 31, 38, 43, 50, 66, 69, 77, 78, 87]

406. ——, 5th ed., 4 vols., ed. Richardson. 1753. [15, 34, 50, 51, 52, 54, 57, 58, 69, 84]

514. ——, 6th ed., 4 vols., ed. Richardson. 1762–1761. [15, 31, 33, 34, 50, 85]

Richardson acknowledges in his preface to this edition (I, v), his indebtedness to John Campbell's *Political Survey of Great Britain*, advertised as in the press in 1757, but not actually published until 1774 (*London Evening Post*, 30 April–3 May 1757). He had known Campbell as early as 1744, when Campbell edited John Harris' *Voyages*, printed by Richardson. Campbell served as one of the authors of the *Universal History* (*q.v.*, under title). Richardson must have had the manuscript of Campbell's *Political Survey* in his possession and was probably planning to print it.

140. DELANY, PATRICK. 1685?–1768. The doctrine of abstinence

from blood defended. 1734. [27, 31, 36, 42, 52, 58, 67, 71]

See p. 129. A veiled reference to Richardson's printing of this book may be found in some verses of Edward Cave, addressed to Richardson in 1737 (Nichols, *Anec. of Bowyer*, p. 90).

259. An historical account of the life and reign of David, king of Israel, [Vol. I]. 1740.

This is the first edition of Vol. I of a work which later grew to three volumes. No indication is given on the title page that this is Vol. I; nor does a second edition in the same year give such indication. In November 1739, when the first volume was about ready to be published, Delany asked Richardson to tell him how well it had been received that he might know whether to be encouraged in its continuation. He said at that date that he had hopes of finishing the whole of the *Life* by Christmas (*Barbauld*, IV, 3, 8 November 1739). The first volume was published on December 11 (*Gazetteer*), but Delany's plans to finish the manuscript by Christmas went sadly awry. It was not until September 1741, that Vol. II was printed; and not until 7 January 1742 that Delany wrote Richardson that "the 3rd Book of the Life of David will, I trust in God, be finished in ten Days. The 12 first Chapters of it have been finished, & pack't up to be sent to you, for more than 3 months past; and Nine of the remaining Chapters are now finished" (*Forster MSS.*, XVI, 1, f. 65 and f. 41). While waiting for the manuscript of Vols. II and III, Richardson printed a second edition of Vol. I. Of the 750 copies of this second edition, 500 remained unsold in September 1741 (*Forster MSS.*, XVI, 1, f. 65). Richardson told Mary Barber that the sale of the work had stagnated and the curiosity of the public had been dampened by Delany's failure promptly to furnish the manuscript for Vols. II and III (*Forster MSS.*, XVI, 1, f. 65). Richardson's decision not to publish Vol. II until the manuscript of Vol. III was ready for the press was probably designed as a spur for Delany. It was not until July 1742, two years and a half after Vol. I was published, that Vols. II and III appeared (*London Evening Post*, July 24–27). In the third edition, 1745, and in the fourth edition, 1759, the text was published in two volumes.

260. ――, [Vol. I], 2nd ed. 1740.

296. ——, Vols. II and III. 1742.

325. ——, 3rd ed., 2 vols. 1745.

481. ——, 4th ed., 2 vols. 1759.*

210. Reflections upon polygamy, and the encouragement given to that practice in the scriptures of the Old Testament. 1737. [13, 55, 58, 60, 71, 87]

In 1752, Richardson, while professing not to countenance polygamy, carried on a discussion of the subject with Lady Bradshaigh in a series of letters. He is obviously drawing upon his recollections of this pamphlet of Delany's (*Barbauld*, VI, 163, 190, 207 ff.). She reminds him of how Mr. B. terrified Pamela with his arguments for polygamy (*Barbauld*, VI, 216).

245. ——, 2nd ed. 1739. [13, 30, 55, 58, 60, 65, 71, 87]

The popularity of this work did not extend beyond the first edition. In November 1739, Delany commissioned Richardson to have unsold copies ("bound, lettered, and gilded on the back") sent to a number of his friends and to every college in each university (*Barbauld*, IV, 2). The second edition has a new preface in further defense of Delany's position.

110. Revelation examin'd with candour, 2 vols. 1732. [17, 19, 36, 42, 52, 57, 58, 65, 77, 103]

This is the first English edition; an edition was published in Dublin in the same year. The work is frequently catalogued as in three volumes, but Vol. III was not added until 1763, thirty years after its original publication. Charles Rivington paid Delany £115 for the English rights (*Journals of the House of Commons*, XXII [12 March 1735], 412).

122. ——, 2nd ed., 2 vols. 1733. [19, 35, 42, 52, 55, 64, 103]

170. ——, 3rd ed., 2 vols. 1735. [17, 19, 20, 48, 53, 55, 57, 63, 64, 70, 80, 103]

326. ——, 4th ed., 2 vols. 1745. [7, 14, 15, 16, 17, 23, 31, 34, 50, 52, 53, 57, 58, 60, 66, 69, 74, 86, 87, 91]

317. Fifteen sermons upon social duties. 1744. [77]

This volume contains sermons relating to the duties of the married state, of parents to children, of children to parents, of servants to masters, and of masters to servants. For a brief discussion of its possible influence on *Clarissa*, see *McKillop*, pp. 133–136. The dedication is dated 23 February 1743.

421. Sixteen discourses upon doctrine and duties, more peculiarly Christian; and against the reigning vanities of the age. 1754.

In December 1753, Delany took exception to Richardson's use of John Locke in *Sir Charles Grandison;* he referred Richardson to the censure of Locke in one of these discourses, which was then being printed at Richardson's press (*Barbauld*, IV, 83–84; *Sir Charles Grandison*, 1754, I, 77). The book had not actually gone to press at this date, for on 22 December 1753 Richardson wrote Delany that more copy was needed, if the book were to be printed in the format agreed upon. Otherwise, Richardson argued, the amount of "leading" required and the size of the margins would suggest to the book-buying public that it was not getting its money's worth. Richardson cited a recent instance of this practice of increasing the bulk and price beyond the requirements of the text: David Mallet's edition of Bolingbroke's *Works*, 5 vols., 1754 (*Forster MSS.*, XV, 4, f. 17).

346. Twenty sermons on social duties, and their opposite vices . . . In which the five last sermons are now first printed, 2nd ed. 1747.

The second edition of *Fifteen Sermons*, 1744. See p. v.

379. Twenty sermons on social duties . . . To this edition has been added An essay towards evidencing the divine original of tythes, [3rd ed.]. 1750.

61. DENNIS, JOHN. 1657–1734. Remarks on Mr. Pope's Rape of the lock. 1728. [20, 72, 103]

This essay, written in 1714, was first published in reply to Pope's ridicule of Dennis in the *Peri Bathous*, 1728 (*Sutherland*, pp. 437–438). Dennis and Richardson became acquainted about 1725 (p. 52). He supplemented his meager earnings by serving as a sort of contributing editor to the *Daily Journal* (p. 54 and Harry G. Paul, *John Dennis*, New York, 1911, p. 96); and this paper on 11 May 1728 printed one of its many attacks on Pope, attributed to Dennis (but see p. 129) in which Pope's pastoral poetry was unfavorably compared with Ambrose Philips'. Pamela's comments on Philips' *Distrest Mother* may have been in part inspired by Dennis, but Richardson's opinions of the play seem more in the vein of Aaron Hill (*Pamela*, 1742, IV, 82–100). In his edition of Defoe's *Tour* (1762, I,

233–235), Richardson included a long passage from Dennis' *Letters Familiar, Moral, and Critical*, describing the noble prospect afforded by Leithhill in Surrey. Here he refers to to him as a "famous Critic."

74. Remarks upon several passages in the preliminaries to the Dunciad. 1729. [17, 18, 51]

See *Sutherland*, p. xli.

123. DRURY, ROBERT. fl. 1732–1735. The fancy'd queen. 1733. [50, 59, 69]

This burlesque opera was produced at Covent Garden, 14, 16 May 1733.

DRYDEN, JOHN. See Atterbury, Francis; Banks, John; Morell, Thomas.

261. DUCK, STEPHEN. 1705–1756. Alrick and Isabel: or, The unhappy marriage. 1740. [75]

See p. 113. In later life, Duck was rector of Byfleet, Surrey, the ancestral home of the Richardsons.

274. Every man in his own way: An epistle to a friend. 1741. [67, 98]

Duck's "way" was to follow the "Itch of Scribbling." Among the ways of other men, he describes those who follow Whitefield, "devoutly mad." A second edition of this epistle— or of another poem—seems to have appeared in 1742, for Duck wrote Richardson: "I have inclosed in this the last Proof of my Epistle, with some little Alteration; and should take it as a Favour if you would let Mr. Roberts know that I would not have it published till tomorrow S'ennight" (*Forster MSS.*, XVI, 1, f. 75). The letter is not dated, but it refers to Vols. III and IV of *Pamela*, which were not published until 7 December 1741. *Every Man in His Own Way* was advertised on 15 March 1741 (*Gazetteer*). Roberts and Dodsley served as publishers.

192. Poems on several occasions. 1736. [8, 10, 52, 54, 55, 56, 60, 63, 64, 67, 70, 78, 80, 87, 90, 93]

See p. 113.

211. ——, 2nd ed. 1737. [8, 10, 52, 54, 55, 63, 64, 67, 70, 78, 80, 87, 90, 93]

See p. 113.

212. The vision. A poem on the death of Her Most Gracious Majesty Queen Caroline. 1737. [70]

459. DUNCOMBE, JOHN. 1729–1786. The works of Horace in English verse. By several hands, Vol. I. 1757. [66, 71, 74, 83, 87]

Duncombe held livings at Canterbury and was one of the six preachers at Canterbury Cathedral. He was an occasional visitor at Richardson's home, married a friend of Richardson's, Susanna Highmore, and supplied Nichols with biographical information about Richardson for his *Anecdotes*. While working on this edition of Horace, he was curate at Sunbridge, Kent. He received his Canterbury living from Archbishop Thomas Herring in the year in which the first volume of the Horace was published. See p. 125.

481A. ——, Vol. II. 1759. [7, 46, 48, 53, 69, 76, 78, 82]

460. DYER, JOHN. 1700?–1758. The fleece. A poem. 1757. [46, 60, 74, 102]

Dyer was a friend of Thomas Edwards (*q.v.*) and of William Duncombe, father of John Duncombe (*Letters by Several Eminent Persons Deceased*, ed. John Duncombe, 1773, III, 56–61). For some details about the publishing of *The Fleece*, see *Straus*, pp. 108–110.

407. EDWARDS, THOMAS. 1699–1757. An account of the trial of the letter Y alias Y. 1753. [77]

Letters between Edwards and Richardson are preserved in *Forster MSS.*, XII, 1. Letters from Edwards to Richardson are in the Bodleian, *MS.* 1,011. Edwards died in Richardson's home. This pamphlet is a plea for a reform in spelling, for greater uniformity, and for a recognition of the root qualities in English words. When Edwards sent it to Richardson's press, he wrote that it was a "lean, critical Rhapsody" (*Forster MSS.*, XII, 1, f. 14). This was in February 1751; it was not until October 1752 that he furnished Richardson with a preface for the work; and not until December that Richardson advised him that he would soon begin its printing (*Forster MSS.*, XII, 1, f. 62, ff.).

408. The canons of criticism, and glossary, being a supplement to Mr. Warburton's edition of Shakespear, 5th ed. 1753. [66]

This edition was the first to come from Richardson's press. The work was first published in 1748 under the title, *A Supple-*

ment to Mr. Warburton's Edition of Shakespear. On 25 October 1752, Richardson wrote Edwards: "Mr. Bathurst [Charles Bathurst, the bookseller] has brought to me your Canons to print" (*Forster MSS.*, XII, 1, f. 64). See p. 127.

471. ——, 6th ed. 1758.

Edwards died in 1757. I have no evidence for Richardson's printing of this edition, but Bathurst may well have taken the book again to his press.

233. ELLIS, CLEMENT. 1630–1700. The scripture catechist: or, The whole religion of a Christian . . . For the use of families . . . To which is prefixed, A faithful account of the author's life and writings. By John Veneer. 1738.

This new edition of Ellis' *Catechist* cannot be traced to Richardson's press through ornaments, for none is used. But Richardson's ornaments are used in Ellis' *Self-Deceiver,* 1731, and his press was employed by John Veneer (*q.v.*) for other works. The typography and make-up of the *Catechist* suggest Richardson's presswork. Both Ellis and Veneer were published by Richardson's friend, Charles Rivington.

97. The self-deceiver plainly discover'd to himself: or, The serious Christian instructed in his duty to God, to himself, and to his neighbour. 1731. [17, 20, 35]

EMLYN, SOLLOM. See Salmon, Thomas.

EPICTETUS. See Carter, Elizabeth.

62. FÉNELON, FRANÇOIS DE SALIGNAC DE LA MOTHE. 1661–1715. The adventures of Telemachus, 12th ed., 2 vols., tr. Boyer and Littlebury. 1728. [25, 27, 29, 48, 53, 57, 71, 80, 91]

To Vol. II is added *The Adventures of Aristonous* and *A Discourse upon Epick Poetry*, the latter by A. M. Ramsay. Isaac Littlebury translated Part I of *Telemachus* in 1699; Abel Boyer, who assisted in the translation of the text for the twelfth edition, was the French tutor to William, Duke of Gloucester, and publisher of a monthly periodical, *The Political State of Great Britain*, 1711–1729. The B.M. *Catalogue* says that A. Olds also assisted in this translation. Richardson refers to *Telemachus* as a "prose epic" in both *Pamela* and *Clarissa*. Pamela used the French edition for perfecting her French (2nd ed., 1741, II, 88); and Clarissa found herself on one occasion pleasantly surrounded by a group of books, including both a French and English version of *Telemachus* (3rd ed., 1751–1750, III, 290). Fénelon's theories of government and his ideas about the training of a future leader of a great nation cause his story to bog down under the burden of his exposition, but in a remote sense *Telemachus* is a forerunner of the "novel with a purpose."

7. Instructions for the education of a daughter, 4th ed., tr. Hickes. 1721. [42, 45, 52, 63, 65, 91]

George Hickes (1642–1715) and Nathaniel Spinckes (*q.v.*) were fellow chaplains of John Maitland, Duke of Lauderdale and a staunch supporter of Charles II. Hickes' older brother, John, joined Monmouth in 1685 and was tried and executed at Taunton. Both Hickes and Spinckes were deprived of preferments on declining to take the oath of allegiance to William and Mary. Charles made Hickes "Bishop of Thetford." This translation is usually ascribed to Hickes, but John Mason says that the translation itself was made by a friend of Hickes and that Hickes merely revised the manuscript (*Gentlefolk in the Making*, Philadelphia, 1935, p. 211). At the date when this book was printed Richardson had other connections with the "Tories" (see pp. 38–41).

503. FIELDING, SIR JOHN. d. 1780.   Extracts from such of the penal laws as particularly relate to the peace and good order of this metropolis. 1761.*

This book was printed by Richardson as joint owner with Catherine Lintot of the law patent. See pp. 134–144. It includes a "Treatise on the Office of Constable," prepared by John Fielding from the manuscript notes of his half-brother, Henry (Wilbur L. Cross, *The History of Henry Fielding*, New Haven, [Conn.], 1918, III, 98–99). Cross thinks that the text was published essentially as it was left by Henry Fielding.

367. FIELDING, SARAH. 1710–1768.   The governess; or, The little female academy, 2nd ed. 1749. [30, 69, 87]

The second edition was said on its title page to be "revised and corrected," partly, it appears, at Richardson's suggestion. See p. 114.

386. ——, 3rd ed. 1751. [38]

482. The history of the Countess of Dellwyn, 2 vols. 1759. [12, 58, 77, 78, 85]

See p. 114.

461. The lives of Cleopatra and Octavia. 1757. [59, 83, 101]
See p. 113.

472. ——, 2nd ed. 1758. [12, 13]
See p. 113.

FLEETWOOD, EVERARD. See Burroughs, Samuel.

245A. FOUNDLING HOSPITAL. A copy of the royal charter, establishing an hospital for the maintenance and education of exposed and deserted young children. 1739. [10, 50]
Among the governors and guardians are Richardson's friends William Hogarth, Francis Child, John Barnard, and Archibald Hutcheson. Richardson inserts a long account of this hospital in his revision of Defoe's *Tour* (1762, II, 116–119).

FREVAL, JEAN BAPTISTE DE. See Pluche, Abbé Noël Antoine.

275. FRIEDRICH II, DER GROSSE, *King of Prussia*. Anti-Machiavel: or, An examination of Machiavel's Prince . . . Published by Mr. de Voltaire. 1741. [27]
The French edition was published at The Hague in 1740, "aux dépens de l'Editeur."

171. FROWDE, PHILIP. d. 1738. The fall of Saguntum, 3rd ed. 1735. [14, 18, 78]
This pseudo-classical tragedy, dedicated to Sir Robert Walpole, had an acting history in 1727, when the first edition was printed. The earlier edition was not from Richardson's press.

74A. GIANNONE, PIETRO. 1676–1748. The civil history of the kingdom of Naples, Vol. I, tr. Ogilvie. 1729. [1, 2, 41, 44, 47, 51, 52, 57, 61, 64, 65, 67, 68, 71, 78, 79, 81, 93, 97]
This work was first published at Naples in 1723. See p. 109.

97A. ——, Vol. II. 1731. [3, 4, 42, 48, 49, 51, 54, 56, 57, 95]

141. GIFFARD, WILLIAM. Cases in midwifry, ed. Edward Hody. 1734. [17, 35, 42, 49, 51, 78, 79, 86]
Giffard is described on the title page as surgeon and man midwife. In 1734 he was "the late Mr. William Giffard." I know nothing else about him, but Edward Hody, who revised and published the book, was a well-known London physician, a graduate of Leyden, Fellow of the Royal Society, and (in 1740) a Licentiate of the Royal College of Physicians. He was attached to the staff of St. George's Hospital (William Munk, *Roll of the Royal College of Physicians*, 2nd ed., 1878).

504. GILBERT, SIR GEOFFREY. 1674–1726.   The history and practice
    of civil actions, 2nd ed. 1761.*

     This book was printed by Richardson as joint owner with
    Catherine Lintot of the law patent. See pp. 134–144.

45. GORDON, ALEXANDER. 1692?–1754?   Itinerarium septentrion-
    ale: or, A journey thro' most of the counties of Scotland, and
    those in the north of England. 1726. [1, 2, 4, 64, 68, 70, 80, 94]
     See p. 123.

75. The lives of Pope Alexander VI. and his son Caesar Borgia.
    Comprehending . . . the chief transactions and revolutions in
    Italy, from the year 1492 to the year 1506. 1729. [2, 3, 4, 41, 45,
    67, 93, 95, 97]
     See p. 123.

276. GORDON, THOMAS. d. 1750.   The humorist. Being essays upon
    several subjects, 4th ed. 1741. [12, 26, 37, 43, 48, 51, 58, 63, 65,
    69, 71, 73]

     Gordon began his career as a journalist with the *London
    Journal,* which, in 1721, was controlled by the Independent
    Whigs. His articles at this time expressed opinions similar to
    those of Archibald Hutcheson (*q.v.*), who was writing for the
    Freeholder's Journal. But he later made his peace with Wal-
    pole; won a place as "Silenus" in the *Dunciad;* and in the
    1730's exercised a general supervision of the government press
    with which Richardson was then associated (*Hanson,* pp. 5;
    113–114). See p. 56 and Trenchard, John. Richardson did not
    print the first and third editions of *The Humorist;* the second I
    have not seen.

76. G[ORDON?] T[HOMAS?].   Two proposals for raising £1,250,-
    000 for the current service of the year 1729. 1729. [11]

     The preface is signed T.G. On p. 24 is advertised a pamphlet,
    published anonymously and entitled *Directions to Judge
    Whether a Nation Be in a Thriving Condition.* This pamphlet
    was also printed by Richardson. Both may be the work of
    Thomas Gordon.

    GREEN, JOHN, *Bishop of Lincoln.* See Weston, William.

421A. GUTHRIE, WILLIAM. 1708–1770.   The friends, 2 vols. 1754.
    [13, 28, 37, 82, 83]

     This novel was published anonymously. Richardson wrote
    Lady Bradshaigh, 14 February 1754, that Guthrie was the au-

thor. He had not read it at the time, but advised her that it was considered "tolerable" (*Forster MSS.*, XI, f. 75).

318. HARRIS, JOHN. 1667?–1719. Navigantium atque itinerantium bibliotheca. Or, A complete collection of voyages and travels, Vol. I. 1744. [88, 98, 102]

See p. 100. The "Voyages" were published weekly at 6d. apiece, beginning with No. I on 16 April 1744 (*Gazetteer*). The conger which published this work secured the protection of a royal license on 23 February 1744 ("Warrant Books," No. 367, p. 362). Richardson may not have been the only printer concerned in this large work. His ornament No. 67 is found on p. [xii] in some copies, but not in others. His ornament No. 88 is used as an inset in a large folio headpiece on p. 1 of Vol. I; and this headpiece is used with a different inset in Vol. II. Harris published this work in 1705; John Campbell revised the text for this new edition.

353. ——, Vol. II. 1748. [88, 98]

367A. HARTLEY, DAVID. 1705–1757. Observations on man, his frame, his duty, and his expectations, 2 vols. 1749.* [16, 17, 23, 36]

Edward Young urged Richardson to read this book, but his recommendation was not acted upon (*Barbauld*, II, 25–27). Hartley's was not the kind of writing that Richardson found easy to read. He knew Hartley, however; and seems to have been pleased when Hartley confirmed his belief that the "Bath waters" would be of little benefit to him (*Barbauld*, II, 46).

368. HAWKINS, WILLIAM. 1722–1801. Henry and Rosamund. A tragedy. 1749. [7, 16, 31, 53]

This play seems to have had no acting history. Its author was a Fellow of Pembroke College, Oxford, and Professor of Poetry, 1751–1756.

82. HAY, WILLIAM. 1695–1755. Mount Caburn. A poem. 1730. [80]

Hay was a barrister and M.P. for Seaford, 1734–1755.

172. HAYWOOD, ELIZA. 1693?–1756. A wife to be lett. 1735. [18, 43, 49, 64, 65, 87]

This book is, to my knowledge, the only link between Richardson and Mrs. Haywood. She certainly would have earned his disapproval, if he had known that she was the author of *Anti-Pamela, or, Feign'd Innocence Detected* (George F.

Whicher, *Life and Romances of Mrs. Eliza Haywood*, New York, 1915, pp. 22–23; *McKillop*, pp. 79–80; and *Sale*, pp. 116–117). The play had a short acting history in August 1723, with the author in the cast. Its plot is one of familiar intrigue, with a conclusion in the sentimental tradition.

409. HERVEY, JAMES. 1714–1758. The cross of Christ, the Christian's glory. [1753].

This volume contains no ornaments, but existing correspondence between Hervey and Richardson indicates clearly that Hervey was employing Richardson's press, except on those occasions when Richardson had to send Hervey's work elsewhere, because of extraordinary pressure of business (*Barbauld*, VI, facsimile of a letter from Hervey to Richardson, preceding the index). This sermon was printed, by permission of the author, for the benefit of a "poor, diseased child." A letter of Hervey indicates that 2,000 copies were printed for sale (at 6*d*.), and 150 copies for the author (*A Collection of the Letters of the Late Reverend James Hervey*, 1760, II, 95, 9 May 1753).

337. Meditations among the tombs. 1746. [13, 15, 23, 86]

See note to *Reflections on a Flower-Garden*.

338. Reflections on a flower-garden. 1746.

The ornament used in this book has not been reproduced. It can be found, among other places, in Salmon's *New Survey*, II, 842. A letter from Hervey to Richardson, 11 July 1745, probably concerned with the printing of the *Meditations* and the *Reflections*, was sold by Southgate (Catalogue of a sale, 21–22 January 1828, No. 194), but I have found no trace of it. Hervey wrote Richardson, 24 January 1747, asking that a second edition of both works be printed for spring publication. These volumes, originally printed in quarto, he now wanted in twelves (*A.L.s.*, Pierpont Morgan Library, New York City). Richardson replied that the 12mo format would be more expensive: "Small Print is dearer than large: Your Book wants Bulk, and it would be thinner, I think, in a smaller Type" (*A.L.s.*, Morgan Library). In February Hervey was distressed because Richardson was not getting forward with the second edition. He wrote to an unnamed correspondent that "if he delays the Second Edition at this rate I may possibly be able to prepare the third Letter to accompany it" (*A Collection of the Letters of the Late Reverend James Hervey*, 1760, I, 183). As the matter turned out, the edition was still in the press in November 1747 (*Barbauld*, II, 181); and Hervey had had time to write two more essays—contemplations on night and on the stars. The work was henceforth to be known by its familiar title, *Meditations and Contemplations;* and, in two volumes, to pass through edition after edition. The dispute over format was apparently resolved by Richardson's printing two second editions, one in octavo and one in twelves. For one of these editions, probably the 12mo, Hervey made an arrangement with John Rivington, whereby Rivington was to pay for the printing and to take over the impression, paying Hervey twenty-five guineas and giving him two dozen copies, bound and lettered (*Barbauld*, II, 181). After 1753, when young Charles Rivington had completed his apprenticeship with Richardson, and the Rivingtons had bought Hervey's works, Rivington did much of the printing ("Freedom Book," 4 September 1753; Septimus Rivington, *The Publishing Family of Rivington*, 1919, p. 63. He printed Hervey's *Theron and Aspasia* in 1755, I believe; and I know he printed his *Time of Danger* in 1757. See pp. v; 128.

354. Meditations and contemplations, 2nd ed., 2 vols. 8vo. 1748. [15, 23, 34]

354A. ——, 2nd ed., 2 vols., 12mo. 1748. [14, 26, 38, 92]
For the explanation of these two second editions, see note to *Reflections on a Flower-Garden*. I have seen only Vol. II of the octavo edition. Richardson did not print the third edition (p. 128).

355. ——, 4th ed., 2 vols. 1748. [12, 26, 38, 50, 78, 87, 96]

410. ——, 10th ed., 2 vols. 1753. [12, 26, 30, 43, 50, 84]
I have not been able to locate editions between the fourth and the tenth.

HICKES, GEORGE. See Fénelon, François de Salignac de la Mothe, *Instructions for the Education of a Daughter.*

422. HIGHMORE, JOSEPH. 1692–1780. A critical examination of those two paintings on the ceiling of the banqueting-house at Whitehall. 1754. [66]
Richardson knew the Highmores for years. Joseph High-

more was with him just before his death in July 1761 (*Gentleman's Magazine*, LXXXVI [Part I, Supplement, 1816], 577–578). This pamphlet was written many years before its publication.

98. HILL, AARON. 1685–1750. Advice to the poets. 1731. [90]
     Richardson knew Hill and printed his works for many years. A long correspondence between the two men, many letters of which relate to the printing of Hill's books, is preserved in the *Forster MSS.*, XIII, 2, 3.

193. Alzira. A tragedy. 1736. [51, 78]
     This is a translation of Voltaire's *Alzire*. It was acted at the Theatre Royal in Lincoln's Inn Fields in June, July, and October 1736; once in April 1737; and once at Drury Lane in April 1744. In June 1736, Hill was preparing to send the manuscript to Richardson, but was in doubt as to whether the play should be printed immediately while the town was empty, or held until winter (*Forster MSS.*, XIII, 2, f. 4). Fear of a rival translation led to its being printed during the summer; and it was published on the 17th of August (*Journal; Gazetteer*). Richardson owned a share in the copyright of the play (p. 91).

213. ——, 2nd ed. 1737. [25, 49]
     In 1744, when Hill was contemplating a revised third edition, he refers to this second edition in 12mo as one which Richardson "rather threw . . . into that Shape, as I remember, to prevent Mischief, than produce any Benefit" (*Forster MSS.*, XIII, 3, ff. 24–25). A piracy of the play had been threatened.

319. ——, 3rd ed. 1744. [79]
     This edition has the subtitle, *Spanish Insult Repented*. The text was revised for a benefit performance for Henry Giffard when he returned to acting at Drury Lane after his theater in Goodman's Fields had been closed. Hill sent the revised text to Richardson on the 22nd of March that he might reprint from it, if he felt there was demand for another edition (*Forster MSS.*, XIII, 3, ff. 24–25). Richardson decided that the revival of the play at Drury Lane, 30 April 1744, was sufficient justification for a third edition.

339. The art of acting. Part I. Deriving rules from a new principle for touching the passions in a natural manner. 1746.

The ornament used here is not reproduced. Hill wrote, 29 July 1746: "I sent the Art of Acting rather to your Eye, than Press—and leave the Time of it's Appearing wholly to your own Choice" (*Forster MSS.*, XIII, 3, f. 49). Richardson had just sent him a sheet of the proof.

234. An enquiry into the merit of assassination: With a view to the character of Caesar: and his designs on the Roman republick. 1738. [31, 71, 77, 103]

Hill suggested that this essay be printed as an eighteen-penny pamphlet rather than as a shilling one, since the pages in the more expensive size "carry a Face much more elegant, and striking," and the additional 6*d.* would, he thought, not reduce the sale (*Forster MSS.*, XIII, 2, f. 12, 14 December 1737).

306. The fanciad. An heroic poem. In six cantos. To his Grace the Duke of Marlborough, on the turn of his genius to arms. 1743. [8, 10, 54, 60, 66, 67]

Hill had an alternate title for this poem—*Go to Bed Tom.* Richardson, who said that "Printers . . . have often the Honour of being heard in the Business of Titles," disapproved of both, urging that the *Fanciad* would be thought in imitation of the *Dunciad* (*Forster MSS.*, XIII, f. 8). He was finally converted. Of the poem itself he wrote with enthusiasm when he read the manuscript, asserting that the Duke of Marlborough had always been his "favourite Hero" (*Forster MSS.*, XIII, 3, f. 6). Hill asked him to accept the copyright as an "Easter offering" (*Barbauld*, I, 89).

340. Free thoughts upon faith: or, The religion of reason. A poem. 1746. [102]

Richardson wrote Hill, 29 January 1746, that his press was always at the service of manuscripts which had the "same excellent End" as the one now before him (*Forster MSS.*, XIII, 3, f. 33). Though the manuscript is not mentioned by title, I think that Richardson is referring to this poem.

369. Gideon: or, The patriot. An epic poem: in twelve books. 1749. [55, 57, 66, 74, 102]

In spite of the title page, only three books of the poem are here published. In January 1749, while Richardson was printing the first three books, Hill wrote to him that Books IV–VI were about ready for the press (*Forster MSS.*, XIII, 3, f. 100). Hill, however, was deeply involved in the production of his play, *Merope,* during the spring of 1749; and in March he advised Richardson that he wished to publish the poem, three books at a time (*Forster MSS.*, XIII, 3, f. 109). Left to his own discretion, Richardson decided to publish *Gideon* in the spring when *Merope* was being produced at Drury Lane. He was delayed, however, for on the 16th of May he wrote: "Had it not been [that I was occupied with printing for the House of Commons] your Gideon would have been better attended to as to Time; and your Merope should not have gone to other presses" (*Forster MSS.*, XIII, 3, f. 114). No other portions of *Gideon* were ever published, except fragments that appeared in the *Prompter* and in Hill's collected works (Dorothy Brewster, *Aaron Hill,* New York, 1913, p. 124). Miss Brewster says that Hill began the poem in 1716 and completed it in 1724 (*op. cit.,* p. 166); but Hill wrote to David Mallet in 1743 that he was then "finishing the last four books" (*Works,* 2nd ed., 1754, II, 211).

320. The impartial. An address, without flattery. Being a poet's free thoughts on the situation of our public affairs. 1744. [74]

This work was dedicated to John Carteret, Earl Granville (1690–1763), who had been a parliamentary adherent of the Earl of Sunderland. Richardson's early employer, Archibald Hutcheson, had opposed Sunderland from the House of Commons; and Richardson retained a distrust of Carteret inherited from the 1720's. He was in an embarrassing situation when Hill sent him this manuscript, so flattering in its belief that Carteret was the hope of England. "I am afraid he will go to all Lengths to be Sole or Prime," Richardson wrote, "and he has formerly been said to declare, that if once more he got in, the Devil should not get him out. Lord Cowper [William Cowper, first Earl Cowper] formerly said of him, as I have heard, that he was the falsest young Man he ever knew" (*Forster MSS.*, XIII, 3, f. 17). After this blast, Richardson added: "I should be sorry, that my private Opinion, should in the least, (by inducing the Author of the charming Lines to drop the Publication) tend to obstruct so desirable and so generous an End." Carteret tried, but failed to form a ministry in February 1746.

39. The northern-star. A poem sacred to the name and memory of the immortal Czar of Russia, 3rd ed. 1725. [22, 36, 44, 45]
    The earlier editions were not printed by Richardson.

246. ——, 5th ed. 1739.
    No ornaments used. Richardson, however, was printing all of Hill's smaller pieces during these years.

83. HILL, AARON; BOND, WILLIAM; and others. The plain dealer: being select essays on several curious subjects, 2 vols. 1730. [18, 52, 57, 77, 79, 80, 103]
    See p. 48. The second volume (and perhaps the signatures following U in Vol. I) were printed by Wilde, Richardson's brother-in-law.

142. ——, 2nd ed., 2 vols. 1734.
    A second issue, with a new dedication.

84. HILL, AARON. The progress of wit. 1730. [42]

214. The tears of the muses; in a conference, between Prince Germanicus, and a male-content party. 1737.
    Hill presented this manuscript to Richardson as a "poetical present, of the satirical kind, and therefore, I am afraid, in most danger to be popular" (*Barbauld*, I, 12). He returned the final proof on 28 October 1737 (*Forster MSS.*, XIII, 2, f. 11). For once Hill correctly gauged the popularity of one of his occasional pieces: a second edition was required in the following year.

234A. ——, 2nd ed. 1738. [67]
    HODY, EDWARD. See Giffard, William.
    HOOKE, NATHANIEL. See Ramsay, Andrew Michael.
    HORACE. See Duncombe, John.

124. HOUSE OF COMMONS. "Parliamentary papers printed by order of the House of Commons." 1733–1761.
    See pp. 76–80.

297. HOUSE OF COMMONS. The journals of the House of Commons, 26 vols.
    See pp. 80–83.

15. HOUSE OF LORDS. A compleat and intire collection of the

Lords protests in the last session of Parliament; particularly touching the late horrid and detestable conspiracy . . . To which is added, The true and genuine heads of the Lord Bishop of Rochester's speech, at the bar of the Lords House, May 11th, 2nd ed. 1723.

No ornaments are used, but this work was advertised in the *Journal*, 29 May 1723, as printed for the same bookseller as the *Speech of Mr. George Kelly,* and fit to be bound up with that work. Richardson printed Kelly's *Speech* (see below).

16. HUTCHESON, ARCHIBALD. d. 1740.   An abstract of all the publick debts remaining due at Michaelmas, 1722. 1723. [5, 6, 44]
    See pp. 37; 120.

17. An abstract of an account stated by some of the clerks at the South-Sea House. 1723. [5, 6, 45, 63]

11. A collection of advertisements, letters and papers . . . relating to the last elections at Westminster and Hasting. 1722. [45, 63, 65]

5. A collection of calculations and remarks relating to the South-Sea scheme and stock. 1720. [41, 46]
    A reprinting of four pamphlets, including Nos. 3 and 4, as listed below.

2. A collection of treatises relating to the publick debts, and the discharge of the same. Publish'd at several times [i.e., from 1714 to 1720] for the service of the members of the House of Commons. 1720. [41, 46]

12. Copies of some letters from Mr. Hutcheson, to the late Earl of Sunderland. 1722. [36, 45, 46, 52, 64]
    The second, third, and fourth editions, all of 1722, are reissues of the first edition. Two states of the first edition may be distinguished by a difference in the imprint: one reads "Printed in the Year," and the other "Printed for T. Payne."

4. An estimate of the value of South-Sea stock. 1720.
    When this pamphlet was included in *A Collection of Calculations and Remarks,* 1720, it was reprinted from the same setting of type, with page numbers changed to fit the continuous pagination of the larger work. The ornament, not reproduced, does not seem to have been used by Richardson at any later date.

8. Four treatises relating to the South-Sea scheme and stock. 1721. [2, 5, 41, 46]

A reissue of four pamphlets, published in the first four months of 1721.

6. A letter to the author of the Calculations in the White-Hall Evening-Post, relating to South-Sea stock. 1720.

Ornaments not reproduced.

1. Mr. Hutcheson's answer to Mr. Crookshanks's seasonable remarks. 1719. [41, 46]

Reprinted in *A Collection of Treatises*, 1720.

9. Mr. Hutcheson's answer to the queries in the Whitehall Evening-Post. 1721. [5]

3. Some calculations relating to the proposals made by the South-Sea Company, and the Bank of England. 1720. [41]

18. Some paragraphs of Mr. Hutcheson's treatises on the South-Sea subject. 1723. [5, 6, 45, 47, 65, 96]

328. HUTCHINSON, THOMAS. 1698–1769. A sermon preached in the parish-church of Horsham, in Sussex: On Tuesday, November 5. 1745. 1745. [34]

Hutchinson edited Xenophon's *Cyropaedia* in 1727. Richardson either sent a copy to Lady Bradshaigh, or recommended it to her, for she wrote to him: "I have gone through the Cyropaedia, and was much entertained. There are noble rules and instructions for princes, and people in power; and, indeed, every body may find lessons in it worthy of imitation" (*Barbauld*, VI, 19). Richardson may have printed this work for Hutchinson; he probably read it before writing *Sir Charles Grandison*.

342. A sermon preached in the parish-church of Horsham, in Sussex, on Wednesday, December 18. 1745. Being the day appointed for a general fast. 1746. [34]

474. HYDE, HENRY, *Viscount Cornbury*. 1710–1753. The mistakes: or, The happy resentment. 1758.* [48, 53, 82, 87]

This book has been incorrectly listed among those printed at Strawberry Hill. A. T. Hazen in his *Bibliography of the Strawberry Hill Press*, New Haven, [Conn.], 1942, p. 143, presents correctly the facts of its printing. Horace Walpole wrote the preface. See p. 117. Hyde was a Jacobite M.P. for Oxford from 1732 to 1750, when he was called to the Lords as Baron Hyde.

307A. JAMES, ROBERT. 1705–1776. A medical dictionary including physic, surgery, anatomy, chymistry, and botany, in all their branches relative to medicine. Together with a history of drugs, Vol. I. 1743.

　　See pp. 97–98.

328A. ——, Vols. II, III. 1745.

424. JEFFREYS, GEORGE. 1678–1755. Miscellanies, in verse and prose. 1754. [74, 92, 100]

　　See p. 113.

483A. JOANNES, CHRYSOSTOMUS, *Saint*. St. Chrysostom of the priest-hood, tr. Bunce. 1759.*

　　See p. 125.

85. JOHNSON, ANTHONY. An historical account of the several English translations of the Bible, and the opposition they met with from the Church of Rome. 1730. [17, 24]

　　Johnson was rector of the church at Swarkston, Derby-shire.

236. KEITH, SIR WILLIAM. 1680–1749. The history of the British plantations in America. 1738.* [66]

　　See p. 72. See also *The Citizen*, under title. In spite of the pretensions of the title, the book is concerned mainly with the colony of Virginia. Richardson sent proof sheets to Hill in the summer of 1738 that he might read it before publication (*Forster MSS.*, XIII, 2, f. 18). It was printed at the expense of the Society for the Encouragement of Learning. On 20 November 1738 one thousand copies were published, selling for 4*s.* in sheets. The bill for the paper was £30/12; the printing costs were £20/8. Plates, paper for printing the plates, and advertising brought the total bill to £79/4. (B.M. *Add. MSS.*, 6,185, pp. 58–59; 85.)

19. KELLY, GEORGE. fl. 1723–1736. The speech of Mr. George Kelly. 1723.

　　Kelly was cited as the amanuensis of Francis Atterbury, Bishop of Rochester, in a treasonable correspondence with the sympathizers of the Pretender on the Continent. On 11 March 1723 the Solicitor General, asking for action against Kelly from the House of Commons, charged that he had been "a principal Agent and Instrument in the . . . detestable Conspiracy, and [had] carried on several Treasonable Correspondences to raise Insurrections and a Rebellion at Home, and to procure a foreign Force to invade these Kingdoms from Abroad" (*Political State*, XXV, 331). The House passed sentence on Kelly, and the bill went to the Lords. On 2 May 1723 Kelly appeared before the Lords to speak in his own defense (*Political State*, XXV, 437, 583–610). This speech Richardson printed in five editions during May and June. I have not seen the second edition, but the first, third, and fourth were printed from the same type-pages. Richardson had merely held the type in readiness for new impressions. In the first and third "editions" an arrangement of printers' flowers was used instead of a headpiece, but in the fourth "edition" Richardson used ornament No. 2. See p. 39 and under Castelnau, Michael, above.

20. ——, 3rd ed. 1723.

21. ——, 4th ed. 1723. [2]

22. ——, 5th ed. 1723. [25, 57]
     This edition was a *6d.* pamphlet. The earlier editions, in folio, sold for *1s.* The fifth edition was advertised for "tomorrow" in the *True Briton*, 14 June 1723.

124A. LAW, WILLIAM. 1686–1761. The Oxford Methodists: Being some account of a society of young gentlemen in that city . . . In a letter from a gentleman near Oxford, to his friend at London. 1733. [80, 91]
     The B.M. attributes this work to Law. It is an apology for the movement.

397. The way to divine knowlege. 1752. [55, 103]
     See p. 127.

388. LEAPOR, MARY. 1722–1746. Poems upon several occasions . . . The second and last volume. 1751. [8, 22, 50, 53, 76, 92, 93]
     See pp. 115–116.

111. LEDIARD, THOMAS. 1685–1743. The life of Sethos, 2 vols. 1732. [20, 24, 27, 35, 42, 43, 53, 63, 67, 71, 103]
     Lediard was attached to the staff of the Duke of Marl-

borough and spent a good portion of his life abroad. The *Life of Sethos*, a translation from the French of Jean Terrasson, was his first published work on his return to England shortly before 1732.

174. LEE, NATHANAEL. 1653?–1692. Nero, Emperor of Rome. 1735. [18, 27 (inset only), 79]
   This play, first produced in 1674, seems to have had no acting history in the eighteenth century.

412. LELAND, JOHN. 1691–1766. Reflections on the late Lord Bolingbroke's Letters on the study and use of history; especially so far as they relate to Christianity and the holy scriptures. 1753. [73]
   See pp. 128–129.

413. ——, 2nd ed. 1753. [73]

448. ——, 3rd ed. 1756. [46, 53, 60, 78]

464. ——, 4th ed. 1757. [7, 8, 48, 50]

436. A view of the principal deistical writers, 2 vols. 1754–1755. [48, 55, 71, 83, 85, 87, 103]
   Richardson did not print Vol. I. His explanation is in a letter to Philip Skelton: "But what did I not do to serve you to the utmost of my power? I parted with three pieces of work; I put out to several printers the new edition of my Grandison; took in help to the first edition of the seventh volume; I refused Dr. Leland's last piece" (*Barbauld*, V, 238). The ornaments listed are of course in Vol. II. On 30 December 1754 Richardson said that this volume, a very large octavo, would be ready for publication early in February (*Barbauld*, III, 106). In this volume Leland answers Hume and Bolingbroke.

463. ——, 3rd ed., 2 vols. 1757. [7, 8, 50, 69, 77, 85, 86, 103]
   Bound with Vol. II, continuously paged, is the fourth edition of Leland's *Reflections*. See above.

475. Serious reflections on the present state of things in these nations. Being the conclusion of Dr. Leland's View of the deistical writers, now published separately, on occasion of the general fast. 1758. [36, 50, 103]

447. A supplement to the first and second volumes of the View of the deistical writers. 1756. [43, 46, 60, 83, 85]

Bound with this supplement is the third edition of Leland's *Reflections,* continuously paged. See above.

398. LENNOX, CHARLOTTE. 1720–1804. The female Quixote, 2 vols. 1752. [37, 38, 50]
See p. 118.

399. ——, 2nd ed., 2 vols. 1752. [12]
Richardson printed only Vol. I.

475A. Henrietta, 2 vols. 1758.
See p. 119.

504A. ——, 2nd ed., 2 vols. 1761.

263. LESLIE, CHARLES. A new history of Jamaica, [2nd ed.]. 1740. [15, 27]
The first edition was published in Edinburgh, 1739, under the title, *A New and Exact Account of Jamaica.* A third edition with the same title was published in Edinburgh in 1740. I know nothing of the author.

LITTLEBURY, ISAAC. See Fénelon, François de Salignac de la Mothe, *Adventures of Telemachus.*

494. LYTTELTON, GEORGE, *1st Baron Lyttelton.* 1709–1773. Dialogues of the dead. 1760. [31, 33, 34, 50, 83, 85]
Lyttelton was a friend of Richardson's. Another state of this edition of his *Dialogues,* probably an earlier one, has ornament No. 15 on p. iii. The more common state has ornament No. 34 on this page. Ornament No. 15 had been badly damaged by 1760, and a part had been broken off. Perhaps Richardson had tried to hold the two pieces together in the chase, and then discovering that the crack was obvious, removed the ornament and substituted No. 34. A single sheet, printed as an advertisement for *Sir Charles Grandison,* 1762, quotes a passage from the *Dialogues* (p. 318) in praise of Richardson (*Sale,* p. 91).

495. ——, 2nd ed. 1760. [31, 33, 34, 50, 83, 85]

495A. ——, 3rd ed. 1760. [31, 33, 34, 50, 83, 85, 87]
These three editions were printed for William Sandby. A fourth edition, 1765, printed for Sandby's successor, John Murray, has some of Richardson's ornaments and was presumably printed at his shop by his nephew, William, who succeeded his uncle.

348. To the memory of a lady lately deceased. A monody. 1747. [59, 74, 99]

This poem was occasioned by the death of Lyttelton's wife. Richardson quotes from it in a letter to Hester Mulso in 1751: "Think you, Madam, that a certain monodist did not imagine himself possessed by this purer flame, who, mourning a dead wife of exalted qualities, could bring her to his reader's imagination, on the bridal eve, the hymeneal torch lighted up,

> Dearer to me, than when thy virgin charms
> Were yielded to my arms?

How many soft souls have been made to sigh over the images here conveyed, and to pity the sensual lover, when they should have lamented with the widower or husband!" (*Barbauld*, III, 183). Lyttelton was one of a group who were with Richardson at Tunbridge Wells in 1748. For a picture of this group, see *Barbauld*, III, frontispiece.

357. ——, 2nd ed. 1748. [59, 74, 99]

329. MADDEN, SAMUEL. 1686–1765. Boulter's monument. A panegyrical poem. 1745.* [8, 10, 49, 60, 63, 69, 71, 74, 78, 88, 89]
See p. 130.

77. Themistocles, the lover of his country. 1729. [7, 41, 70, 103]

This play was dedicated to the Prince of Wales in the hope that he might follow in the footsteps of his illustrious father. The prologue urges Englishmen to renounce their factions and revere their laws. The play was acted at Lincoln's Inn Fields in February 1729.

78. ——, 2nd ed. 1729. [7, 41, 70, 103]

79. ——, 3rd ed. 1729. [7, 41, 70, 103]

248. MAITLAND, WILLIAM. 1693?–1757. The history of London, from its foundation by the Romans, to the present time. 1739.* [44, 56]
See pp. 110–111.

63. MALLET, DAVID. 1705?–1765. The excursion. A poem. 1728. [44, 62]

Included with this poem is the ballad, "William and Margaret." Mallet was one of a group of Scots whose early work was sponsored by Aaron Hill in the *Plain Dealer*. In No. 46

Hill congratulated Scotland on the rising genius of Mallet, but unfortunately he selected for his praise "William and Margaret," which later scholarship has demonstrated to be a piece of plagiarism (*N&Q*, 7 S. II [1886], 4, 132, 410, 490). See p. 51.

40. MANLEY, MARY DE LA RIVIÈRE. 1663–1724. Mrs. Manley's history of her own life and times, 4th ed. 1725. [20]

This is a new issue of a work originally published in 1714 under the title, *The Adventures of Rivella*. It was brought out by Edmund Curll after Mrs. Manley's death, with a new preface explaining the occasion of its publication and maintaining that the *Adventures of Rivella* was in fact autobiographical. Richardson printed only this new preface. Ralph Straus in his *Unspeakable Curll*, 1928, says that the edition dated 1725 was published 10 October 1724 in two states, selling at 1*s.* 6*d.* and at 2*s.* 6*d.* For Richardson's comment on Mrs. Manley, see *McKillop*, p. 180. See also *The Ladies Miscellany* among anonymous works.

MARKLAND, JEREMIAH. See *Cythereia*, among anonymous works.

278. MARSH, CHARLES. A poetical epistle. Humbly inscrib'd to —— anybody. 1741. [4]

Charles Marsh was a London bookseller, who dabbled in writing and editing and had the reputation of an eccentric character. In 1739, when he threatened to publish a work of Hill's, the copyright of which Richardson owned, Richardson wrote him a courteous note, asking Marsh to recognize his property rights (*Forster MSS.*, XIII, 2, f. 26). Marsh was unknown to Richardson at this time. He acceded to the request and no trouble resulted.

215A. MAUCLERC, JAMES. The Christian's magazine, or treasure. [1737?].*

See p. 124 and *Sale*, xi–xii.

357A. ——, [2nd ed.?]. 1748.*

I have not seen this edition. It is described in *McKillop*, p. 315. See p. 124.

174A. MENTET [MENTEITH, MONTEITH?], ROBERT. fl. 1621–1660. The history of the troubles of Great Britain . . . from the year 1633 to 1650 . . . To which is added, D. Riordan de Muscry's True causes . . . which contributed to the restoration of King Charles II, tr. Ogilvie. 1735. [63]

See p. 109. Mentet was a Scotch minister, who fled to France during the "troubles," and was denounced as a rebel. He became secretary to de Retz and upon joining the Roman Catholic Church, was made a canon of Notre Dame. His *Histoire* was published at Paris, 1661.

236A. ——, 2nd ed. 1738. [63]
  A second issue.

125. MIDDLETON, CONYERS. 1683–1750. A letter from Rome, shewing an exact conformity between popery and paganism: or, The religion of the present Romans derived from that of their heathen ancestors, 3rd ed. 1733. [40, 62]

  Richardson thought Middleton was a "very fine writer," but he disapproved of his later work, maintaining that Middleton's disappointment in not getting a bishopric was responsible for his attack on the clergy and his flaunting of orthodoxy (*Barbauld*, V, 199; VI, 241).

99. MILLER, PHILIP. 1691–1771. The gardeners dictionary, Vol. I, fol. 1731. [5, 44, 62]
  See pp. v; 110.

126. ——, 2nd ed., Vol. I, fol. 1733. [5, 44, 55, 57, 62, 97]

216. ——, 3rd ed., Vol. I, fol. 1737. [5, 44]

249. The gardeners dictionary, Vol. II, fol. 1739. [5, 44, 56, 67, 89]

175. The gardeners dictionary, [Abridged ed. of Vol. I, fol], 2 vols., 8vo. 1735. [9, 32, 36, 65, 67, 91]

264. The gardeners dictionary, [Abridged ed. of Vol. II, fol], 8vo. 1740. [10]
  This volume completed the abridged edition, 3 vols., 8vo.

279. ——, 2nd ed. of abridgment, 3 vols. 1741. [10, 32, 59, 73]

358. ——, 3rd ed. of abridgment, 3 vols. 1748. [10, 57, 71]

399A. The gardeners dictionary, 6th ed., 2 vols. in 1, fol. 1752. [52, 60, 61, 98]

  The fourth and fifth editions in folio were published in 1743 and in 1748; and a seventh edition in folio in 1759. I have not seen copies. With the sixth edition was included *The Gardeners Kalendar*, listed below.

112. The gardeners kalendar. 1732. [18, 54, 61, 103]

127. ——, 2nd ed. 1733. [18, 54, 61, 65, 103]

144. ——, 3rd ed. 1734. [22, 53, 57, 62, 64, 65, 79, 103]

330. ——, 7th ed. 1745. [17, 66, 74, 83, 86]

I have not seen the fourth, fifth, and sixth editions.

THE MISCELLANY. See *The Weekly Miscellany*.

54. MITCHELL, JOSEPH. 1684–1738. The Totness address, versified, 3rd ed. 1727. [I, 63]

Mitchell's servility to the ministry earned him the name of "Sir Robert Walpole's poet." He was one of the many minor authors for whom Richardson printed in the 1720's who won places for themselves in the *Dunciad*. I have not found earlier editions of Mitchell's poem.

360. MONCREIF [MONCRIEF?], JOHN. Camillus. A dialogue on the navy. 1748.

The ornament is not reproduced. It may be found in Elizabeth Rowe's *Friendship in Death*, 1740, p. 152, where, because trimmed on the right side, it is easily recognizable. I know nothing of Moncreif. This pamphlet is a plea for a "wooden wall" for England.

359. Galba. A dialogue of the navy. 1748. [17, 66, 84]

A plea for the education of seamen by schoolmasters of approved morality.

217. MORELL, THOMAS, ed. d. 1784. The Canterbury tales of Chaucer, in the original, from the most authentic manuscripts; and as they are turn'd into modern language by Mr. Dryden, Mr. Pope, and other eminent hands. 1737. [17, 27, 32, 36, 43, 55, 57, 71, 103]

See p. 125. In spite of the title, this volume contains only the Prologue and Dryden's version of the Knight's Tale. It was printed for the editor by Richardson, but Morell's name is not on the title page. Morell was a friend of Hogarth, Garrick, and James Thomson—all of whom Richardson knew. It is to Dryden's version of the Knight's Tale that Mowbray refers in a letter to Belford in *Clarissa* (3rd ed., 1751–1750, VIII, 43).

265. ——, 2nd ed. 1740.

Probably a second issue. I have been unable to compare the copies of both editions, but the ornaments in both are the same.

145. MORRIS, ROBERT. Lectures on architecture. 1734. [25, 27, 29]

Morris was an architect who lived at Twickenham. These lectures were delivered between 22 October 1730 and 13 January 1735. This book is curiously printed. Richardson printed the preface and the first seven lectures, through p. 119. Page [120] is blank. The remainder is the work of another press. Lecture VIII follows Lecture VII, and then a new title page appears for the second part of the book. The pagination and signatures, however, are continuous. When the book was finally ready for publication, a dedication of two leaves was inserted between the first title page and the preface. The first part was "printed for J. Brindley," and the second part "for the author," in 1736. Apparently Richardson started printing the book while Morris was engaged in delivering his lectures. In the delay that occurred while the course of lectures was being completed, some misunderstanding between Brindley and Morris may have arisen and Morris may have taken the sheets that were printed and the remainder of his manuscript to another press; or perhaps Richardson's press became exceptionally busy and he turned over the latter part of the book to another printer.

145A. NEWTON, RICHARD. 1676–1753. The expence of university education reduced, 3rd ed. 1734. [49]

See p. 122. Richardson did not print the first and second editions.

279A. ——, 4th ed. 1741.

Ornaments not reproduced, but this is merely a reissue of forty-eight of the sixty-four pages of the third edition.

175A. The grounds of the complaint of the Principal of Hart-Hall . . . In answer to the misrepresentations of Dr. C[onybea]re, Dean of Christ Church. 1735. [3, 5, 86]

See p. 122.

175B. ——, 2nd ed. 1735. [3, 5, 86]

145B. A letter to the Revd. Dr. Holmes, Vice-Chancellor of the University of Oxford, and Visitor of Hart-Hall. 1734. [2]

See p. 122.

146. ——, 2nd ed. 1734. [2, 49]

343. The ministerial duty set forth. In an anniversary sermon

preached before the University of Oxford, 3rd ed. 1746. [17]
I have not seen earlier editions.

308. Pluralities indefensible. A treatise humbly offered to the consideration of the Parliament of Great-Britain. 1743. [15]
See p. 123.

331. ———, 3rd ed. 1745. [15, 17]
I have not seen a second edition. This edition, described as the third, may be a second issue of the second edition, for the preface (p. xv) reads: "In this Second *Edition*, it is thought. . . ." On the other hand, Newton may have merely forgotten to emend the text of the preface. To this edition is added a long appendix, with a copy of an act against pluralities prepared for the House of Lords in 1681; and a letter of the late Earl of Nottingham to Dr. Daniel Waterland "concerning the Lawfullness of a Bond to oblige to Residence."

348A. Rules and statutes for the government of Hertford College in the University of Oxford. 1747. [15, 31, 50]

249A. Rules and statutes made by Dr. R. Newton, Principal of Hart-Hall, for the government of a college intended to be incorporated by the name of . . . Hertford College, in the University of Oxford. 1739.
No ornaments, but the factotum is Richardson's. It is used in Newton's *Grounds of Complaint,* 2nd ed., 1735, p. 1.

46. University education. 1726. [25, 27, 63, 70]
This was a protest against the ease with which scholars could transfer from one college to another at Oxford. It was occasioned by what Newton called the "late irregular Admission" of a commoner of Hart Hall into Oriel College. Newton's discipline was severe.

128. ———, 2nd ed. 1733. [27, 77]

195. NICOLSON, WILLIAM. 1655–1727. The English, Scotch, and Irish historical libraries, 3rd ed. 1736. [2, 44]
Nicolson was Bishop of Carlisle from 1702 to 1718, when he was translated to Derry. The three parts of this book were published separately from 1696 to 1704, with a second edition of the English Library in 1714. They were all republished in 1732. In the edition of 1736 the parts have separate pagination.

Richardson's press was responsible for the English part. See p. 95.

OGILVIE, CAPT. JAMES. See Giannone, Pietro; and Mentet, Robert.

55. OLDMIXON, JOHN. 1673–1742. Clarendon and Whitlock compar'd. 1727. [7, 17, 18, 80]

Richardson's press was employed only once for work of this prolific Whig historian and journalist. In fact, he printed only part of this book, through signature L, p. 160. Oldmixon here attacked Clarendon, charging that his *History of the Rebellion* had been tampered with by Francis Atterbury, among others, before it went to press. Atterbury answered the charge in 1731. Oldmixon appears with Dennis among the porpoises in the *Peri Bathous*.

217A. ——, 2nd ed. 1737. [7, 17, 18, 80]

A second issue?

OLDYS, WILLIAM. See *A Collection of Epigrams*, among the anonymous works.

280. PAGET, THOMAS CATESBY, *Baron Paget*. d. 1742. Miscellanies in prose and verse. 1741. [15, 16, 50, 67, 69, 75]

Paget, the son of the first Earl of Uxbridge, was an M.P. for Staffordshire in 1715 and in 1722. Richardson printed his miscellanies in prose, through p. 284. Though the pagination is continuous throughout the book, the poetical miscellanies have a separate title page and seem to be the work of another press.

249B. PARLIAMENT. An authentic list of the knights, citizens, burgesses and commissioners for shires and burghs, of the House of Commons of Great Britain . . . To which are annexed Lists of the lords spiritual and temporal. 1739.

This was advertised in the *Gazetteer*, 19 February 1739, as "printed for S. Richardson." I have not seen a copy.

449. PECKARD, PETER. 1718?–1797. A dissertation on Revelations, Chap. XI. Ver. 13. . . . In which is attempted to be shewn, that there is some reason to believe this prophecy is completed by the late earthquake. 1756. [30]

See p. 127.

450. Observations on the doctrine of an intermediate state between death and the resurrection. 1756. [23]

On 14 May 1756 Peckard wrote that he had this manuscript ready for the press and that he would send it in a few days (*Barbauld*, V, 113).

484. Observations on Mr. Fleming's Survey. 1759. [34]

Caleb Fleming, a Presbyterian minister, had published *A Survey of the Search after Souls* in 1758. Among the contents of this *Survey* were essays by Peckard and by his friend, William Law.

309. PERRY, CHARLES. 1698–1780. A view of the Levant: particularly of Constantinople, Syria, Egypt, and Greece. 1743.

This book contains no ornaments. Richardson sent the loose printed sheets to George Cheyne at his request in November 1742. Cheyne concurred in Richardson's opinion that it was an unimportant book (Charles F. Mullett, *The Letters of Dr. George Cheyne to Samuel Richardson*, Columbia, [Mo.], 1943, pp. 116–118). Perry was a practicing physician. Time has passed a softer judgment on his work than did Richardson.

31. THE PLAIN DEALER. A semiweekly periodical, published from 23 March 1724 to 7 May 1725, ed. Hill and Bond.

See pp. 48–52.

506. PLOWDEN, EDMUND. 1518–1585. The commentaries, or Reports of Edmund Plowden, 2 pts. in 1 vol. 1761.*

This book was printed by Richardson as joint holder of the law patent (pp. 134–144). Plowden was a famous sixteenth-century jurist, who found public life closed to him after the accession of Elizabeth, because he was a Roman Catholic. His work was written in French. This edition is a translation with notes, probably by a barrister named Bromley, who, the *D.N.B.* says, translated the edition of 1779. Bound with the *Commentaries* and printed "for the translator" in 1761 is usually found the *Quaeries of Edmund Plowden*.

266. PLUCHE, ABBÉ NOËL ANTOINE. 1688–1761. The history of the heavens, 2 vols., tr. Freval. 1740.

No ornaments used. Jean Baptiste de Freval, the translator, originally planned to publish this book through the Society for the Encouragement of Learning, but finally decided to withdraw it from the Society's patronage and publish it at his own expense. He therefore "procured a discharge from Mr. Richardson, the printer, as to any further sum the society might be liable to pay on that account" (B.M. *Add. MSS.*, 6,185, p. 75, under date of 19 October 1739). A letter from Richardson to Alexander Gordon, the Society's secretary, gives his estimate of the printing costs of the book (B.M. *Add. MSS.*, 6,211, ff. 51–53). The estimate was a guinea a sheet for 1,000 sheets, octavo, without notes. Presumably this is the price that Freval finally agreed to pay Richardson when he took back his manuscript. Freval wrote one of the laudatory letters to the editor for the first edition of *Pamela*, I, vii–ix. He was still corresponding with Richardson in 1751, at which time he reminded Richardson that Pluche had always furnished him with the French text of his works, sheet by sheet, to prevent Freval's meeting with competition in his translations (*Barbauld*, V, 277–278).

281. ——, 2nd ed., 2 vols. 1741.

To this edition was added a "Revisal of the Work." Both first and second editions were in 8vo, but a so-called "second edition" in 12mo appeared in 1743, not printed by Richardson.

250. Spectacle de la nature: or, Nature display'd, Vol. IV, tr. Freval. 1739. [7, 19, 31, 49, 54, 55, 56, 60, 61, 63, 66, 70, 71, 86, 90, 94]

The fourth volume, translated by Freval, was apparently the only volume of a seven-volume work to come from Richardson's press. The *Spectacle* was designed to excite the curiosity and form the minds of youth by setting forth the relation of the several parts of the universe to the needs of man.

100. POMFRET, JOHN. 1667–1702. Poems upon several occasions, 8th ed. 1731. [50, 73]

Pomfret's "Prospect of Death" (p. 113) is quoted by Clarissa as the novel draws to its close (3rd ed., 1751–1750, VII, 168).

196. POPPLE, WILLIAM. 1701–1764. The double deceit: or, A cure for jealousy. 1736. [7, 31, 36, 43, 60, 78, 87]

Richardson undoubtedly made the acquaintance of Popple when he and Aaron Hill were coeditors of the *Prompter* and Richardson a sort of associate editor. The *Journal* (16 February 1736) elaborately announced the production of this play and in later issues defended it against a charge of plagiarism made by the Rev. James Miller, author of the *Man of Taste* (p. 60). The play was revived at Covent Garden on the 26th of February; and the text was published on the 27th (*Gazetteer*).

It had been first produced at Covent Garden on 25 April 1735. Richardson owned a one-fourth share in the copyright, with the other quarter-shares owned by Thomas Woodward, John Walthoe, Jr., and John Peele ("Register," I, 455, 26 February 1736). Robert Dodsley bought the quarter-shares owned by Woodward and Peele in 1752 (*Straus*, p. 345).

147. The lady's revenge: or, The rover reclaim'd. 1734. [17, 51, 53, 57, 61, 65, 72, 78]

For a discussion of this play and of the *Double Deceit*, see Allardyce Nicoll, *A History of Early Eighteenth Century Drama*, Cambridge, 1925, pp. 200–201. Nicoll's conclusion has a bearing on the central situation in *Pamela:* "Democracy was arising in these years; middle class drama was being produced; but the old class standards of the Restoration were too severe and too firmly implanted in the natures of the populace for any too revolutionary sentiments to be introduced." *The Lady's Revenge* ran four nights at Covent Garden, in January 1734. Aaron Hill wrote the prologue.

148. THE PROMPTER. A semiweekly periodical, published from 12 November 1734 to 2 July 1736, ed. Hill, Popple, and others.

See pp. 70–72.

PSALMANAZAR, GEORGE. See *Universal History*.

56. RAMSAY, ANDREW MICHAEL. 1686–1743. The travels of Cyrus, 2nd ed., 2 vols., tr. Hooke. 1727–1728. [17, 18, 25, 36, 57, 71]

These ornaments are in Vol. I; Richardson did not print Vol. II. Nathaniel Hooke (d. 1763), a friend of Pope's, is said to have made the translation in twenty days while at Bath for his health and to have dictated it to George Cheyne's brother (Spence's *Anecdotes*, ed. Singer, 1820, p. 36). Richardson wrote that at this time he was "a kind of Favourite" of Hooke, and that he had printed his first edition of *Cyrus;* but that having made certain remarks to the disparagement of Pope, he offended Hooke and the friendship came to an end (*Forster MSS.*, XIII, 3, f. 12). These disparaging remarks echoed an article in the *Journal*, attributed to Dennis (p. 129). I have not seen a first or a third edition of this work, but these editions were advertised in the *Country Journal*, 30 September 1727 and 9 March 1728. The second edition may be a second issue.

Ramsay's work is a kind of fiction, in imitation of Fénelon's *Télémaque*. The story provides occasions for disquisitions on the philosophy of religion.

REGNARD, JEAN FRANÇOIS. See Centlivre, Susanna.

414. RICHARDSON, SAMUEL. 1689–1761. An address to the public. 1753.

For a description of the works of Richardson, see my *Samuel Richardson*, New Haven, [Conn.], 1936, *passim*. The list which follows is by brief title, with only a few notes.

425. ——, [a variant issue]. 1754.

The first issue is dated 14 September 1753; the second is dated 1 February 1754.

148A. The apprentice's vade mecum: or, Young man's pocket-companion. 1734. [11, 58, 79]
See p. 17.

414A. The case of Samuel Richardson, of London, printer. 1753.

361. Clarissa, 7 vols. 1748. [23, 28, 50, 69, 84, 87]

372. ——, 2nd ed., Vols. I–IV only. 1749. [28, 30, 31]

The first edition was published in three installments: Vols. I, II; Vols. III, IV; Vols. V, VI, VII. When Richardson came to print the last three volumes, he anticipated the demand for a second edition by printing enough copies of these volumes for both first and second editions. Pressure of business forced him to employ two other presses to assist him with the printing of one of these volumes, but his own headpieces are used in each volume (*Forster MSS.*, XIII, 3, f. 114).

389. ——, 3rd ed., 8 vols. 1751–1750. [14, 28, 30, 45, 50, 69, 76, 82, 83]

390. ——, 4th ed., 7 vols. 1751. [8, 10, 16, 17, 69, 75, 82, 84, 96]

Richardson published the third and fourth editions in the same year, the third in twelves and the fourth in eights.

485. ——, 4th ed., 8 vols. 1759. [15, 30, 50, 77, 82, 84, 85]

The fourth edition in octavo was published in 1751; this edition is a fourth in twelves.

437. A collection of the moral and instructive sentiments, maxims, customs, and reflexions, contained in the histories of Pamela, Clarissa, and Sir Charles Grandison. 1755. [16, 50, 82]

426. Copy of a Letter to a lady . . . Answer to a Letter from a friend. 1754.

   Printed for private circulation only.

427. The history of Sir Charles Grandison, 7 vols. 1754. [23, 28, 30, 34, 87]

428. ——, 2nd ed., 6 vols. 1754. [10, 77, 78, 83, 87, 103]

   Ornament No. 78 is used only in the second issue of Vol. I. Vol. II seems to have been the work in whole, or in part, of another press. Richardson was extremely busy at this time with government contracts and was rushing three editions of this novel through the press to meet the competition of a Dublin piracy.

429. ——, 3rd ed., 7 vols. 1754. [23, 28, 77, 84, 85]

   For this edition Richardson had to secure the help of seven other printing houses (*Forster MSS.*, XI, f. 96). Vol. I, first issue, has ornaments 23, 28, 77, 85; Vol. I, second issue, has in addition, No. 84; Vol. IV has No. 28; Vol. VI has No. 84 in the final gathering, with the ornament of another press as the initial headpiece. Vol. VII has No. 28. Vols. II, III, and V have ornaments from other presses. William Strahan printed 2,500 copies of Vol. V for Richardson at a price of £23/13. (R. A. Austen-Leigh, *The Story of a Printing House*, 2nd ed., 1912, p. 49).

451. ——, 4th ed., Vol. VII only. 1756. [15]

   See *Sale*, p. 86 ff. No edition was published in 1756. This volume is made up of sheets printed for the first and third editions, and of some sheets that were reprinted for this issue. I do not believe that it was published.

515. ——, 4th ed., Vol. VII only. 1762. [15]

   See *Sale*, p. 86 ff. This volume is made up of the sheets reprinted for the issue of 1756, and of other sheets printed for the first time for this issue of 1762. It became Vol. VII of a fourth edition in 7 vols., "printed by assignment from Mr. Richardson's Executors," 1762.

391. Letters and passages restored from the original manuscripts of the history of Clarissa. 1751. [15, 28, 45, 76]

287. Letters written to and for particular friends. 1741. [13, 27, 30, 58, 69]

301. Letters written to and for particular friends, 2nd ed. 1742.
      I have not seen a copy.

344. ——, 3rd ed. 1746.
      A copy of this edition is in the Victoria Art Gallery and
      Municipal Libraries, Bath, England. I have not been able to
      check the ornaments.

381. ——, 4th ed. 1750. [14]

400. ——, 5th ed. 1752. [30]
      Two issues of this edition differ only in the imprint.

438. ——, 6th ed. 1755. [26, 37]

302. The matrimonial mirror. 1742.
      See *Sale*, p. xii. I have not seen a copy.

382. Meditations collected from the sacred books . . . Being those
      mentioned in the history of Clarissa. 1750.
      Printed, but apparently not published.

267. Pamela, Vols. I, II. 1741 [but published in 1740]. [13, 25, 30,
      50]
      Normally I have listed books by the date on the title page,
      but conflicting stories about the publication of the first edition
      of *Pamela* have led me to indicate both date of publication and
      date of imprint.

282. ——, 2nd ed. 1741. [26, 30, 37, 50]

283. ——, 3rd ed. 1741. [30, 50]
      The demand for *Pamela* required five editions in ten months.
      Richardson seems to have used the services of another shop in
      the reprinting of the text for this edition, but the introductory
      pages to Vol. I (i–xxxviii) and the last signature of this volume
      are his printing.

284. ——, 4th ed. 1741. [26, 30, 50, 58]
      These ornaments are in Vol. I; he seems to have used another
      press for all, or at least part of, Vol. II.

285. ——, 5th ed. 1741. [14, 26, 30, 50, 58, 69]

299. ——, 6th ed., 8vo. 1742.
      The first five editions are 12mo. This edition contains no
      ornaments. It was published with the third edition of Vols.
      III and IV, and this four-volume set was reissued in 1772.

344A. ——, 6th ed., 12mo. 1746. [30, 38, 50, 57, 58, 69]

I have only recently found a copy of this edition. When preparing my bibliography, I erroneously assumed that, when found, it would prove to be a reissue of sheets of the fifth edition. I had underestimated the continuing popularity of the novel. These two volumes were combined with a reissue of Vols. III and IV to make the four-volume set of the novel advertised in the *General Evening Post*, 16–18 October 1746.

430. ——, 7th ed. 1754. [26, 42, 43, 58, 84, 87]
With this edition was published a reissue of Vols. III, IV.

507. ——, 8th ed. 1762. [13, 30, 43, 83, 84]
With this edition was published a reprinting of Vols. III, IV.

286. Pamela, Vols. III, IV. 1741. [14, 58]

298. ——, 2nd ed. 1742. [14, 30, 65]

299. ——, 3rd ed., 8vo. 1742.
The first two editions are 12mo. This edition contains no ornaments. It was published with the sixth edition, 8vo, of Vols. I, II, and this four-volume set was reissued in 1772.

300. ——, 4th ed. 1742. [14, 65]
I have seen only Vol. III: this is a reissue of the second edition. The demand for Vols. III and IV was much less than that for the first two volumes.

430. ——, 5th ed. 1754.
These volumes are reissues of the second edition.

507. ——, "8th ed." 1762. [13, 30, 86]
This so-called eighth edition of Vols. III and IV is actually the fourth reprinting of the text—the only reprinting after the third edition of 1742. The two volumes were combined with the eighth edition of Vols. I and II to make a four-volume set.

268. ROE, SIR THOMAS. 1581?–1644. The negotiations of Sir Thomas Roe in his embassy to the Ottoman Porte, ed. Samuel Richardson. 1740.*
See pp. 90; 94.

251. ROWE, ELIZABETH, 1674–1737; ROWE, THOMAS, 1687–1715. The miscellaneous works in prose and verse [of Elizabeth Rowe] . . . To which are added, Poems on several occasions, by Mr. Thomas Rowe, 2 vols. 1739, 1738. [20, 36, 43, 57, 71, 84, 103]

Theophilus Rowe, the brother-in-law of Elizabeth Singer Rowe, wrote the biographical memoir and edited the material for these two volumes. Mrs. Rowe died in February 1737, and he began the task of editing in that year. But many of the "letters moral and entertaining" in these volumes are not original compositions; they are portions of Mrs. Rowe's actual correspondence. The letters to and from Cleora, for example, are severely edited versions of the letters to and from Mrs. Rowe and Frances, Countess of Hertford (Helen S. Hughes, "Elizabeth Rowe and the Countess of Hertford," *PMLA*, LIX [1944], 726–746; and Hughes, *The Gentle Hertford*, New York, 1940, *passim*). Either at his own discretion or at the request of correspondents, Theophilus Rowe had to make certain excisions. These excisions delayed publication, as did a last minute decision to include an engraved portrait of Mrs. Rowe by George Vertue. Richardson printed the second volume, dated 1738, but the first volume, dated 1739, was the work of another press. Rowe confirms this fact by referring to "my Printers" (Hughes, article cited, p. 745). He complains that his printers "have not work'd near so fast as they gave me Encouragement to hope, & the Picture [by Vertue] is not finish'd." This letter is dated 31 January 1739; the two volumes were published 8 March 1739 (*Straus*, p. 320). Richardson, as was frequently the case, may have found his press exceptionally busy in 1738–1739 and have had Rowe turn over the first volume to another press. In the following year, however, he printed an edition of Mrs. Rowe's *Friendship in Death*.

268A. ROWE, ELIZABETH. Friendship in death: in twenty letters from the dead to the living. To which are added, Letters moral and entertaining, in prose and verse. 1740. [7, 17, 19, 20, 31, 43, 46, 51, 54, 55, 56, 57, 60, 64, 65, 69, 71, 76, 77, 78, 80, 89, 103]

Earlier editions of the two works included in this volume were printed during Mrs. Rowe's lifetime. They were not from Richardson's press.

310. ——, [another edition]. 1743.

This contains the same ornaments as the edition of 1740, and is probably a reissue.

198. THE ROYAL SOCIETY. The philosophical transactions of the Royal Society.

    See pp. 73–75.

401. Diplomata et statuta Regalis Societatis. 1752.*

    The first three charters of the Society were printed in Latin.

508. SAINT-GERMAN, CHRISTOPHER. 1460?–1540. Doctor and student; or Dialogues between a Doctor of Divinity, and a student in the laws of England, 16th ed. 1761.*

    This book was printed by Richardson as joint owner with Catherine Lintot of the law patent (pp. 134–144).

SALE, GEORGE. See *Universal History*.

64. SALMON, NATHANAEL. 1675–1742. The history of Hertfordshire. 1728. [62, 63, 68, 97]

    See pp. 108–109.

65. A new survey of Great Britain, 2 vols. 1728–1729. [7, 13, 15, 16, 17, 18, 20, 21, 27, 30, 35, 39, 46, 48, 52, 54, 57, 63, 64, 65, 67, 68, 70, 73, 74, 77, 80, 86, 93, 96, 103]

    This work was published in parts, with a title page for each part but with continuous pagination. The title pages were eventually removed, usually leaving a gap in the pagination, and the text was published in two volumes. The first part was published on 18 April 1728 (*Journal*), and Parts II and III were published during this year; four more parts were published in 1729, and the remaining four parts in 1730. These parts were published "stabbed" and the marks of the stabbing may be seen in the bound volumes. In Vol. I the title page is that of Part I; in Vol. II the title page is that of Part VI as published on 2 August 1729 (*Journal*). A section of Part VI, however, is included in Vol. I. On p. 482 is an advertisement instructing subscribers for Salmon's *History of Hertfordshire* to call upon Richardson or the author for their copies.

101. ——, 2nd issue, 2 vols. 1731.

    This issue has a new title page and to the text has been added *An Examination of the British Coins Produced in Camden's Britannia*, designed to prove that these coins are not British, but that they were brought to England by the Romans and the Saxons.

86. SALMON, THOMAS, 1679–1767; and EMLYN, SOLLOM, 1697–1754, editors. A complete collection of state trials, 2nd ed., 6 vols. 1730. [5]

See pp. 92–93.

302A. ——, 3rd ed., 6 vols. 1742. [98]

See p. 93. Vols. VII and VIII had been added to this work five years after the publication of the second edition in six volumes. This third edition, however, is a reprinting of only the first six volumes. An identifiable ornament of Richardson appears only in Vol. I.

177. SAUL, EDWARD. 1677?–1754? An historical and philosophical account of the barometer, 2nd ed. 1735. [18, 58]

Saul was a former Fellow of Magdalen College, Oxford, and rector of Hartaxon, Lincolnshire, from 1706 to 1754. Richardson did not print the first edition.

80. SAVAGE, RICHARD. d. 1743. The wanderer: A poem. 1729. [7, 9, 21, 22, 32, 51, 62, 78, 90, 93, 96, 103]

Richardson and Savage perhaps became acquainted through the agency of Aaron Hill, who espoused Savage's cause in the *Plain Dealer* in 1724 and accepted his claim of being the illegitimate son of Richard Savage, fourth Earl Rivers (Hill, *Works*, 2nd ed., 1754, I, 327–328). The "Volunteer Laureate" thought this poem was his finest work. It was printed for John Walthoe and was still being advertised as late as 3 June 1735 (*Daily Courant*). In 1736 the disputatious Savage was threatening a law suit, with Walthoe and Richardson as defendants. The details of the dispute are unknown, but Aaron Hill seems to have persuaded Savage to patch up his quarrel out of court. He wrote Savage that Walthoe and Richardson had never "had the least *inclination* to injure" him; "but have often, on the contrary, express'd the kindest, and most generous sentiments" in his behalf (Hill, *Works, loc. cit.*). See also p. 51.

252. SENECA, L. ANNAEUS. Select epistles on several moral subjects. Newly translated . . . by a gentleman of Christ-Church, Oxon. 1739. [19, 51]

In some such form as this Richardson must have read Seneca. Pamela and Clarissa show a familiarity with the general position taken by Seneca in his *Morals;* and Richardson recommended him to Lady Bradshaigh (*Barbauld*, IV, 278).

415. SHEBBEARE, JOHN. 1709–1788.   A love epistle in verse. Found at Paris, in the cell of an Irish Carthusian, after his death; and sent to the Honourable R . . . . . T . . . . . , Esq. by Monsieur M. . r . . v . . x. 1753. [86, 100]

Richardson said that Shebbeare, who had lived some time in France, had been commended to him by a friend in Paris. Shebbeare seems to have gone to Paris in 1752, but he probably stayed no longer than a few months. In talking to Richardson, however, he may have left the impression that he had been longer in France; in fact, he probably told him the story that he was to circulate more widely—the story of his having obtained a medical degree in Paris and of his having been elected to the Academy of Science (James R. Foster, "Smollett's Pamphleteering Foe Shebbeare," *PMLA*, LVII [1942], 1057). Richardson wrote: "He . . . often visited me; and was fond of engaging my Ear to the Productions of his Pen. Now-and-then something seemed to be hit upon, that appeared lively; but never was Author so vain" (*Forster MSS.*, XI, f. 180, a letter to Lady Bradshaigh, 29 May 1756).

It is not likely that Shebbeare mentioned to Richardson his share in the revision of the story of Lady Vane, which appeared as the *Memoirs of a Lady of Quality* in Smollett's *Peregrine Pickle*, 1751, and was described by Richardson as "that Part of a bad Book which contains the very bad Story of a wicked Woman" (*Forster MSS.*, XII, 2, f. 11, under date of 11 January 1751; and Howard S. Buck, *A Study in Smollett*, New Haven, [Conn.], 1925, pp. 43–45). But in attributing the pseudonymously published *Letters on the English Nation* to Shebbeare, Richardson said that Shebbeare had once tried to exonerate himself from "the Charge of a very bare Imposition on a Bookseller, who accused him of selling to him, at a very high Price, as letters of the late Lord Hyde, some of his own Performances (I believe among them, some of these very Letters)" (*Forster MSS.*, XI, f. 180).

Richardson professed himself to have been glad to drop the acquaintance. He printed nothing for him but this one poem, and it, too, as Shebbeare admitted in the second issue, was a fraud. The second issue consists of the sheets of the first, with two new leaves for a new title page and a preface in which Shebbeare acknowledges his own authorship of the epistle. The publisher for the second issue was John Scott, with whom Richardson had no other relations. I think it unlikely that he was in any way concerned with the second issue.

452. ———, 2nd ed. 1756.

A second issue.

SHELVOCKE, GEORGE. See the *Universal History*.

SHIRLEY, WILLIAM. See the *Universal History*.

41. SIDNEY, SIR PHILIP. 1554–1586. The works of the Honourable Sr. Philip Sidney, 14th ed., 3 vols. 1725, 1724, 1724.

For Vol. I Richardson printed the introductory matter, exclusive of the unpaged dedication. This section contains his ornaments Nos. 29, 36, 64. He printed none of Vol. II, but all of Vol. III in which may be found Nos. 20, 25, 27, 35, 36, 52, 53, 63, 64, 68, 70, 96. Vols. I and II contain the five books of the *Arcadia;* Vol. III contains the "sixth book," the *Defense of Poesy*, poems and sonnets, and the *Lady of May*. Richardson's *Pamela* presupposes that his readers know Sidney's Pamela and her lover Musidorus (1st ed., 1742, III, 141; IV, 116, 165).

The title page of Vol. I is preceded by a title page for the three volumes. This latter title page exists in two states, which differ in imprint. One state of the title page—probably the first—contains the names of five booksellers: E. Taylor, Bettesworth, Curll, Mears, and Gosling. The other state contains only the name of W. Innys. E. Taylor is probably the wife of William Taylor, who died in 1724, naming John Osborn and William Innys his executors. For a brief period during which her husband's estate was being settled, the name of E. Taylor is associated with the bookshop in Paternoster Row, formerly owned by her husband and bought in August 1724 by Thomas Longman (Charles J. Longman, *The House of Longman*, ed. Chandler, 1936, pp. 461–462; 446. Plomer gives the date of Taylor's death as 1723). Longman also bought the copyright of books held by William Taylor, but the copyright of the works of Sidney, owned by five booksellers, was apparently bought by William Innys. While the works of Sidney were being reprinted in 1724, the title page in its first state was printed; when Innys secured the copyright, a new title page, carrying his name alone, was substituted for the original. Other hypotheses seem untenable.

322. SKELTON, PHILIP. 1707–1787. The candid reader: or, A modest, yet unanswerable apology for all books that ever were, or possibly can be wrote. 1744. [49]

See p. 131. From 1732 to 1750 Skelton was curate at Monaghan from whence he went to Pettigo, County Donegal, in the parish of Templecarn. In these poor parishes he devoted himself to the relief of his parishioners and to writing which, because of his forthright manner and ironical bent, may have been responsible for his failure to receive preferment.

431. Discourses, controversial and practical, 2 vols. 1754.

See p. 131.

373. Ophiomaches: or, Deism revealed, 2 vols. 1749. [53, 75]

See p. 131.

392. ——, 2nd ed., 2 vols. 1751. [72]

The title for this edition was simply *Deism Revealed*.

199. Some proposals for the revival of Christianity. 1736. [39, 45]

This work was first published in Dublin. It appeared anonymously.

66. SMEDLEY, JONATHAN. b. 1671. Gulliveriana . . . To which is added, Alexanderiana. 1728. [7, 17, 24, 29, 42, 48, 49, 51, 53, 57, 63, 65, 71, 77, 78, 80, 91, 96, 103]

See p. 129. In 1729, Smedley left Ireland for Madras, where his death presumably occurred.

10. Poems on several occasions. 1721.* [9, 21, 22, 32, 41, 44, 45, 46, 52, 62, 63, 64, 65, 91]

This is the earliest work that I have found with Richardson's name in the imprint. A copy in the Harvard College Library, given by Elizabeth Leake to Anna Maria Owen, has been noted by McKillop. In 1732 Elizabeth Leake became Richardson's second wife (*McKillop*, p. 288).

23. ——, [2nd ed.]. 1723. [9, 21, 22, 32, 41, 44, 45, 46, 52, 62, 64, 65, 91]

129. SMITH, JOSHUA. d. 1731. A select manual of divine meditations and prayers suited to the most necessary and solemn occasions and fitted for morning and evening service for every day in the week, 2nd ed. 1733. [11, 58, 71]

Smith was the curate of St. Mary Aldermanbury and lecturer at St. Mary le Bow. This book was his last work. The title page indicates that it was revised and corrected "by an Eminent Hand." When Richardson sent a copy of the fourth edition, 1750, to the daughter of Aaron Hill, she wrote: "Do I not, good Sir, trace in some of these beautiful Productions some fine strokes drawn by the same Masterly Hand . . . that we are so deeply indebted to . . . in Pamela and Clarissa" (*Forster MSS.*, XIII, 3, f. 132). I have not seen a first or third edition, but Richardson's hand was not "eminent" in 1733. An edition advertised in the *Gazetteer* on 24 June 1741 as sold by John Osborn was probably the third edition. See p. v.

383. ——, 4th ed. 1750. [58, 71]

SMOLLETT, TOBIAS. See *Universal History*.

SMYTHE, JAMES MOORE. See Welsted, Leonard.

303. SPATEMAN, THOMAS. d. 1761.   The school-boy's mask. 1742. [17, 31, 45, 48, 66, 71, 103]

See p. 125. This play was designed for the use of schools. Act I is at school; act II at Cambridge; acts III–V are in "life." Goodwill becomes Lord Chancellor; Bookish becomes a bishop; and Rakish and Guzzle are appropriately punished.

402. SPENCE, JOSEPH. 1699–1768.   Crito: or, A dialogue on beauty. 1752. [82, 103]

See p. 112. This work was published under the pseudonym of Sir Harry Beaumont.

218. An essay on Mr. Pope's Odyssey, 2nd ed. 1737. [11, 26, 77]

See p. 112. This edition was printed while Spence held the chair of poetry at Oxford. Richardson did not print the first edition in 1726, nor the third edition in 1747. Wilmot, an Oxford bookseller, owned the copyright of the work when the second edition was printed; he sold it to Dodsley in 1744 (*Straus*, p. 328).

416. Moralities: or, Essays, letters, fables, and translations. 1753. [16, 43, 82]

See p. 112. This book was published under the pseudonym of Sir Harry Beaumont. McKillop has called attention to a series of "Letters between a Mother, and her Daughter lately gone to Service" (pp. 54–73) which show the general influence of *Pamela* (*McKillop*, pp. 91–92). He points out that Spence, like Richardson, sponsors the notion that all men are beasts of prey.

486. A parallel; in the manner of Plutarch: between a most celebrated man of Florence; and one, scarce ever heard of, in England, 2nd ed. 1759.

See p. 113. This volume, a parallel between Antonio Maglia-
bechi and Robert Hill, a poor tailor of Buckingham, was first
printed at Strawberry Hill. Walpole published the book on
2 February 1759 and 600 copies were sold in a fortnight (A. T.
Hazen, *A Bibliography of the Strawberry Hill Press*, New
Haven, [Conn.], 1942, pp. 44–45). The second edition was
advertised in the *London Chronicle*, 8–10 February 1759.

403. A particular account of the Emperor of China's gardens near
Pekin, tr. from Jean Dennis Attiret. 1752. [23]

This book was published under the pseudonym of Sir Harry
Beaumont.

374. SPINCKES, NATHANIEL. 1653–1727. The true Church of England-Man's companion in the closet: or, A complete manual
of private devotions, 10th ed. 1749. [14, 15, 51]

Spinckes was a close friend of George Hickes (*q.v.*) and
served with him as fellow-chaplain to the first Duke of Lauderdale. Both men refused to take the oath of allegiance to William
and Mary and both became leaders among the nonjurors.
Spinckes was also a friend of the pious Robert Nelson, whose
*Companion for the Festivals and Fasts of the Church of Eng-
land*—known to the eighteenth century as Nelson's *Feasts and
Fasts*—was found by Clarissa in Mrs. Sinclair's library (3rd ed.,
1751–1750, III, 290).

149. STEBBING, HENRY. 1687–1763. An apology for the clergy of
the Church of England. 1734. [35]

Stebbing was preacher at Gray's Inn, 1731; chaplain to
George II, 1732; and in 1739 Chancellor of Salisbury.

200. A true state of the controversy with Mr. [James] Foster, on
the subject of heresy. 1736. [19]

Foster (1697–1753) was a famous Nonconformist preacher,
who indulged in controversies with both Stebbing and Tindal.

219. A reply to Mr. Foster's answer. 1737. [19]

237. STUART, ALEXANDER. 1673–1742. Dissertatio de structura et
motu musculari. 1738.*

This edition was published under the auspices of the Society

for the Encouragement of Learning. The book was first published at Leyden in 1711 under a slightly different title. Five
hundred copies of the English edition were published on 26
May 1738, and by 19 October 1739 the Society had secured the
return of its loan and revested the copyright in the author
(B.M. *Add. MSS.*, 6,185, pp. 58, 73). See p. 75.

238. SWIFT, JONATHAN. 1667–1745. A complete collection of genteel and ingenious conversations. 1738. [13, 26, 27, 30, 51, 67]
    See p. 115. The copies of this book that I have examined are
large paper ones, but Teerink in his bibliography of Swift
(1937) says that only some of the copies were on large paper.
A variant issue, in which the introduction is the work of another press, contains ornaments Nos. 13, 26, 30, 63, 79.

238A. ——, [a variant issue]. 1738.
    See note above.

57. Travels into several remote nations of the world. By Capt.
Lemuel Gulliver. Faithfully abridged, 2 vols. 1727. [25, 43,
53, 54, 63, 64, 65, 71, 83, 95]
    This abridgment contains about half the original text and
seems to follow the first Motte edition. In the preface the unknown abridger defends his right to publish another author's
text in shorter form, and urges as excuse the need to omit
immodest and indecent passages. The edition exists in two
states. One state has a "Key" of eight pages, sometimes replac-
ing the table of contents of "Lilliput" in Vol. I, and sometimes
bound at the close of Vol. II. The other state has two leaves
of advertisements for R. King at the close of Vol. II, and no
"Key." Edward Parker, a printer in Salisbury Court, printed
a serialized version of *Gulliver's Travels*, but I have been unable to compare the text printed by Parker with that printed
by Richardson.

SWINTON, JOHN. See *Universal History*.

486A. SYDENHAM, FLOYER. 1710–1787. A synopsis or general view
of the works of Plato. 1759.*
    Sydenham was a Fellow of Wadham College, Oxford, a
member of the bar, and for a time rector of Esher. This short
essay served as introduction for his translation of Plato, which
appeared in separate parts from 1759 to 1780. The *Io* and the

Greater Hippias in 1759 and the *Lesser Hippias* and the *Banquet* in 1761 were all printed by Henry Woodfall. Sydenham looked upon Plato as one of the "greatest Masters of Political Science" of ancient times. He dedicated the *Synopsis* to John Carteret, first Earl Granville, who was in 1759 President of the Council. Both Samuel Parr and Thomas Taylor, the Platonist, spoke well of his scholarship.

178. TAVERNER, WILLIAM. d. 1731. The artful husband, 4th ed. 1735. [14, 30, 49]

This play, first produced in 1717, was revived at Drury Lane with some success in 1747. Ernest Bernbaum points out the contrast between the true comedy of this play and the sentimental comedy of Mrs. Centlivre's *The Artifice*, finding the methods of each type to be well defined in the works of these two dramatists (*The Drama of Sensibility*, Cambridge, [Mass.], 1925, pp. 122–123).

TERRASSON, JEAN. See Lediard, Thomas.

81. THOMSON, JAMES. 1700–1748. Britannia. 1729. [5, 53, 68]

See p. 111. *Britannia*, generally received as an attack on Walpole's peace policy, was published anonymously with a note indicating that it was written in 1719. This note is obviously a screen behind which the author sought to protect himself from any counterthrusts of Walpole. John Edwin Wells argues that most of the text must have been written in 1728 or early in 1729 (*MP.*, XL [1942], 43–46).

87. The seasons. 1730. [1, 57]

See p. 112. This volume is the first to contain all four of the *Seasons*. With them are included Thomson's "Hymn" to the seasons and "A Poem to the Memory of Sir Isaac Newton." "Autumn" is here published for the first time, and the text of the previously published parts is extensively revised. An article by John Edwin Wells (*Library*, 4 S. XXII [1942], 223–243) throws considerable light on the problems of Thomson's bibliography. Some of these problems must be faced in determining Richardson's share in the printing of the poetry.

Surviving copies of this edition, for example, exist in several states. With some copies is bound a second edition of *Britannia*, printed (but not by Richardson) in 1730 and advertised as suitable for binding with the text from Richardson's press. Still other copies contain four leaves of minor poems, those contributed by Thomson to Ralph's *Miscellany* in 1729. These four leaves were printed by Richardson; they contain his ornament No. 59. They are, however, on different paper from that used in the remainder of the volume and are separately paged. They were printed without title page and were to be bound with sheets of the *Seasons*. The longer poem had been printed as a subscription edition. Evidently the second edition of *Britannia* and the group of four short poems were printed in an attempt to promote the sale of those copies of the subscription edition that had not been taken by subscribers. These remaining copies, considered as a trade edition, were offered for sale by Andrew Millar and James Brindley, but little success attended their efforts. A large number of copies were still unsold in 1736 when they were reissued as Vol. I of a two volume edition of Thomson's *Works* in quarto.

In the same year in which Richardson printed the *Seasons* in a subscription edition, two octavo editions of the poem were printed at other presses. John Millan owned the copyright to all parts of the poem except "Spring," which Andrew Millar had bought in 1729 for fifty guineas. Millar did not acquire all the rights to Thomson's poetry until 16 June 1738, when he bought from Millan those he did not own for £105, the price that Millan had paid Thomson in July 1729 (G. C. Macaulay, *James Thomson*, 1907, p. 25; Plomer's *Dictionary*, under Millan and Millar). Either because the text of the poems in the subscription edition had been extensively revised and that of "Autumn" added for the first time, or because some arrangement was made with Millar and Millan, the profits of the subscription edition went to Thomson. The imprint reads simply "Printed in the Year M.DCC.XXX."

179. Summer, 4th ed. 1735. [15, 73]

This new printing of "Summer" was bound with "Winter" and other poems (see below), with "Autumn" (1730) and with "Spring" (dated 1731, but actually printed in 1734) to make up *The Four Seasons and Other Poems*, printed for Millan and Millar in 1735. Wells in his article in the *Library* (*loc. cit.*) says that the copies of "Summer" dated 1735 were printed for J. Millan by N. Blandford. Either this is an error on his part, or he has not seen the edition recorded here, in which the imprint is simply "for J. Millan." Henry Woodfall printed "Spring" for *The Four Seasons* (*N&Q*, 1 S. XI [1855], 418–420); and Blandford printed the "Autumn" of 1730.

150. Winter. A poem; A hymn to the seasons; A poem to the memory of Sir Isaac Newton; and Britannia, a poem. 1734. [15, 16, 73]

See note above. No indication of the number of this edition is given, but this book is probably the second printing of the same combination of poems, originally printed for the octavo edition of 1730. It was printed for Millan.

130. THOU, JACQUES AUGUSTE DE. 1553–1617.   Jac Augusti Thuani Historiarum sui temporis ab anno Domini 1546 usque ad annum 1607, 7 vols. 1733.*

Richardson's name is in the colophon of Vol. II, the only volume that he printed. See p. 95. Other volumes were printed by Henry Woodfall, James Bettenham, Thomas Wood, James Roberts. According to Nichols (*Lit. Anec.*, II, 26), Edward Owen printed Vol. VI and much of Vol. VII, with the first eight books of Vol. VII, however, falling to William Bowyer. Ten years after publication, Andrew Millar was selling remaindered copies at five guineas, in sheets—a price four guineas cheaper than that originally charged (*St. James Evening Post*, 5–8 March 1743).

180. TRENCHARD, JOHN, 1662–1723; and GORDON, THOMAS, d. 1750. The Independent Whig, 6th ed., 3 vols. 1735. [11, 26, 58, 69, 70, 83]

This book represents a reprinting of the essays that had originally appeared in a weekly periodical of the same name, 20 January 1720 to 4 January 1721. It is the first reprinting to come from Richardson's press. Trenchard and Gordon were the two Independent Whigs that were largely responsible for the *London Journal* before it was silenced by being bought up by the government in 1722 (*Hanson*, pp. 106–108; 113–114). After Trenchard's death, Gordon made his peace with the ministry and during the 1730's exercised a general supervision over all the newspapers in the service of Walpole (p. 53).

312. ——, 7th ed., 3 vols? 1743. [12, 13, 45, 77, 78, 86, 87]

I have seen only two volumes of this edition, but probably

a third volume was printed. The title pages of volumes in both the sixth and seventh editions fail to indicate the number of volumes.

24. THE TRUE BRITON.   A semiweekly periodical, published from 3 June 1723 to 17 February 1724, edited by Philip, Duke of Wharton.

   See pp. 34–48.

25. ——. Fortnightly reprintings of the issue of this paper, in groups of four. 1723. [41, 42, 46]

   I have seen Nos. I–XVI thus reprinted; and Nos. I–IV in two states. They contain the ornaments listed above. A similar reprinting of the first thirty-two numbers was offered for sale by Birrell and Garnett, London booksellers, in 1928 in their Catalogue, No. 16. These reprintings were designed for distribution in the country.

26. ——. A reprint of all numbers of this paper in two volumes. 1723. [20, 25, 27, 35, 42, 43, 44, 48, 52, 53, 57, 62, 64, 65, 68, 70, 71, 72]

   Both volumes are dated 1723, though the second contains essays which appeared in 1724 in the original issues of the paper. At the close of Vol. II, with continuous pagination, is included *His Grace the Duke of Wharton's Speech in the House of Lords*, in defense of Bishop Atterbury (see below, under Wharton). This speech has a separate title page dated 1724.

113A. ——. A second issue of the numbers of the paper, preceded by a second issue of the *Memoirs of the Life of His Grace Philip Late Duke of Wharton* (see among anonymous works), and by a new preface to the reprint of the essays, 2 vols. 1732.

   The preface is sometimes bound before and sometimes after the Memoirs in Vol. I. A portrait of Wharton faces the title page, which reads: *The Life and Writings of Philip Late Duke of Wharton.*

185. AN UNIVERSAL HISTORY, from the earliest account of time to the present, Vol. I. 1736. [3, 5]

   See pp. 101–104.

151. VENEER, JOHN. d. 1764.   An exposition on the Thirty-Nine Articles of the Church of England, 2nd ed., 2 vols. 1734. [19, 27, 41, 54, 55, 56, 57, 64, 65, 70, 77, 78, 80, 103]

Veneer was rector of St. Andrews, Chichester. See also Ellis, Clement.

58. A new exposition on the Book of Common Prayer. 1727. [17, 27, 52, 55, 57, 80]

The argument here is that Dissenters cannot reasonably object to joining in communion with the Church of England; nor can they offer valid objection to "precomposed forms of prayer."

VOLTAIRE, FRANÇOIS MARIE AROUET DE. See Friedrich II, der Grosse, and Hill, Aaron, under *Alzira*.

88. WEBSTER, WILLIAM. 1689–1758. The duty of keeping the whole law. 1730. [7, 36, 77]

See p. 126.

113. THE WEEKLY MISCELLANY: Giving an account of the religion, morality, and learning of the present times. A weekly periodical, published from 16 December 1732 to 27 June 1741, ed. William Webster under the pseudonym of Richard Hooker of the Temple.

See pp. 68–70. The first two numbers were published as *The Miscellany*. From No. 13 on the subtitle was dropped.

201. THE WEEKLY MISCELLANY, Vol. I, a reprinting of the essays in the periodical of the same name. 1736. [17, 20, 51, 52, 65, 77, 87]

See p. 69.

114. WELSTED, LEONARD. 1688–1747. Of dulness and scandal. Occasion'd by the character of Lord Timon. In Mr. Pope's Epistle to the Earl of Burlington. 1732. [1, 41]

Welsted's attacks on Pope and the latter's retaliations are too well known to need comment.

115. ——, 2nd ed. 1732.

A second issue.

116. Of false fame. An epistle to the Right Honourable the Earl of Pembroke. 1732. [7, 78]

288. The summum bonum; or, Wisest philosophy. 1741. [5, 61]

89. WELSTED, LEONARD; and SMYTHE, JAMES MOORE, 1702–1734. One epistle to Mr. A. Pope, occasion'd by two epistles lately publish'd. 1730. [2, 4, 51, 62, 77]

For Smythe, see *Sutherland*, pp. 211–212; 455.

516. WESTON, WILLIAM. 1710?–1791. New dialogues of the dead. 1762. [16, 30, 48, 76, 78, 84, 85]

This volume was published after Richardson's death. It appeared anonymously, but can be attributed to Weston on the basis of evidence in Nichols (*Lit. Anec.*, IX, 667–668). Nichols says that John Green (1706?–1779), Bishop of Lincoln, contributed some of the dialogues (VIII, 648). Weston was vicar of Campden, Gloucestershire. The preface indicates that the favorable reception accorded Lyttelton's *Dialogues of the Dead* (*q.v.*) encouraged the author to print this volume.

27. WHARTON, PHILIP, *Duke of*. 1698–1731. His Grace the Duke of Wharton's speech in the House of Lords, on the third reading of the bill to inflict pains and penalties on Francis (late) Lord Bishop of Rochester, 2nd ed. 1723. [4, 52, 68, 70, 97]
See p. 39.

67. WHEATLY, CHARLES. 1686–1742. Bezaleel and Aholiab: or, Men's abilities and skill the gifts of God, and their professions and trades the ways of serving Him. 1728. [32]

Wheatly was the vicar of Furneaux Pelham, Sussex, near the home in Hertfordshire of Nathanael Salmon (*q.v.*). This sermon was preached on 7 December 1727 before the Merchant-Taylor's School, of which he was a graduate.

221. WHITEFIELD, GEORGE. 1714–1770. The benefits of an early piety. 1737. [27, 64]

This sermon was preached at Bow Church, London, on 28 September 1737—the year in which Whitefield gained his first great popularity as a preacher. He had received his B.A. from Pembroke College, Oxford, the year before; and in 1738 was to leave England on the first of his missionary visits to America.

222. The nature and necessity of our new birth in Christ Jesus, in order to salvation. 1737. [17]

This sermon was preached at St. Mary Radcliffe, in Bristol. It sold for 6*d.*, or two guineas per hundred to those who wished to give it away.

349. WILLIAMS, SIR CHARLES HANBURY. 1708–1759. Tar water, A ballad, inscribed to the Right Honourable Philip Earl of Chesterfield: Occasioned by reading a narrative on the success of tar water, dedicated to His Lordship by Thomas Prior, Esquire. 1747. [66, 102]

I do not know why this single piece of all the occasional verse of Williams found its way to Richardson's press. It was printed for W. Webb, with whom Richardson had no other relations. The subject of the ballad, however, was one that was near Richardson's heart. In November 1746, Young congratulated him on at last finding benefit in tar water (*Barbauld*, II, 19); and a few days later, he wrote: "[Mr. Prior] cautions us about frauds in tar, which will defeat our expectations from it. He says it must be *Norway* tar, of a *deep* brown, and pretty thin" (*Monthly Magazine*, XXXVII [1814], 140). Richardson frequently found himself prescribed for by his friends and was as frequently hard put to show his gratitude by following the advice. Prior's *Authentic Narrative of the Success of Tar Water* had been published in 1746.

289. WILSON, THOMAS, D.D. 1663–1755. The knowledge and practice of Christianity made easy to the meanest capacities: or, An essay towards an instruction for the Indians. 1741. [12, 14, 42, 43, 45, 49, 51, 57, 65, 71]
See pp. 131–132.

203. WILSON, THOMAS. 1703–1784. Distilled spirituous liquors the bane of the nation, 2nd ed. 1736. [27, 31, 48, 51, 80, 103]
The author was the son of Bishop Wilson (*q.v.*). I have not seen the first edition. See p. 131.

465. A review of the project for building a new square at Westminster; said to be for the use of Westminster-School. By a sufferer. 1757. [16, 33]
See p. 132.

153. WISEMAN, RICHARD. 1622?–1676. Eight chirurgical treatises, 6th ed., 2 vols. 1734. [27, 39, 45, 65, 71, 91]
See p. 95.

154. WITHINGTON, NICHOLAS. A briefe discoverye of some things best worth noteinge in the travells of Nicholas Withington. 1734. [93, 96, 103]
In a work published in 1735—John Cockburn's *Journey* (*q.v.*)—the *Travells* of Withington was printed as a second piece, with separate title page, dated 1734, but continuous pagination. On the title page of Cockburn's book the *Travells* are said to have been written in the reign of James I and never

before printed. They may well have been a part of the manuscripts collected by Awnsham Churchill (p. 94).

362. YORKE, CHARLES. 1722–1770.　Some considerations on the law of forfeiture, for high treason. Occasioned by a clause, in the late act, for making it treason to correspond with the Pretender's sons, or any of their agents, 3rd ed. 1748. [31, 53, 69, 76]

Charles Yorke was the son of the Lord Chancellor, Philip Yorke. His father was largely responsible for the insertion of attainder clauses in an act of 1744, making correspondence with the Young Pretender, or his brothers, punishable as an act of high treason. The pamphlet defends the position taken by the Lord Chancellor. The third edition, "corrected and enlarged," is the first that I have seen. Richardson probably did not know either Philip Yorke or his son, but he did recall after a period of twenty years the details of a case that he had heard Philip Yorke argue before the House of Lords when the latter was Attorney General (*Barbauld*, VI, 186–187). He was acquainted with Lord Royston, the elder brother of Charles Yorke. A letter from Lord Royston, thanking him for a copy of *Clarissa*, is preserved among the *Forster MSS.* (XV, 2, f. 14); and a letter from Thomas Birch, telling Lord Royston of Richardson's death, was written on the very day that he died (W. T. Whitley, *Artists and their Friends in England*, 1928, I, 50). Richardson's friend, Thomas Edwards, was probably responsible for the acquaintanceship between Richardson and Lord Royston. Edwards was a frequent visitor at Lord Royston's seat, Wrest, in Bedfordshire. In Richardson's edition of Defoe's *Tour* (6th ed., 1762–1761, III, 51), he inserts a brief description of Wrest, and prints a sonnet, written by Edwards, when he was a guest "of the noble Owner."

476. YOUNG, EDWARD. 1683–1765.　An argument drawn from the circumstances of Christ's death, for the truth of His religion. 1758.

Richardson was a friend and frequent correspondent of the author of the *Night Thoughts*, and from 1744 printed most of his work. This piece was a sermon preached before the King at Kensington in June 1758. Young was disturbed about portions of the dedication and wrote Richardson for his advice.

With the proof of the sermon Richardson sent him certain suggested emendations which were accepted (*Barbauld*, II, 49–53). Young was Chaplain in Ordinary to George II.

417. The brothers. A tragedy. 1753. [10, 82]
    This play, written before Young took orders, was left un-produced and unpublished until 1753, when it was acted by Garrick and George Anne Bellamy for eight nights at Drury Lane (Dougald MacMillan, *Drury Lane Calendar, 1747–1776*, Oxford, 1938, p. 214. The play was acted on March 3, 5, 6, 8, 10, 12, 15, 17). On the 21st of February the *Public Advertiser* announced that the profits would be turned over to charity. Richardson said that it played to "thin houses" (*Barbauld*, VI, 246). Though the profits were less than £400, Young added enough money of his own to make up a sum of £1,000 for the Society for the Propagation of the Gospel (John Doran, *Their Majesties Servants, Annals of the English Stage*, ed. Lowe, 1888, II, 161–163). Hannah Pritchard would normally have played opposite Garrick in *The Brothers*, but Doran says that the attractive Miss Bellamy persuaded Young that she should play the leading feminine role (Erixene). For Young's epilogue Garrick substituted a coarse version to be spoken by Kitty Clive. Young expressed his disgust with this attempt to aid the cause of charity.

418. ——, [a variant issue]. 1753.
    The small ornaments on the title page differ.

439. The centaur not fabulous. 1755. [34]

440. ——, 2nd ed. 1755. [34]
    This edition was "corrected."

441. ——, 3rd ed. 1755. [12, 84]
    Straus says that these three editions were published on March 4, April 18, and November 17 (*Straus*, pp. 354–357). The third edition, like the second, was "corrected." In August 1754, Young wrote to Richardson, asking him to have a copper plate of his grotesque centaur made for a frontispiece; Richardson accepted the commission (*Straus*, pp. 354–355). Straus also printed Richardson's bill for the third edition, as submitted to Andrew Millar. He charged £1/16 per sheet for 2,500 copies, twelve sheets and a half-sheet to each volume, pica type, 12mo.

The total printing costs were £22/10. The *Centaur* was printed for Millar and the Dodsleys, but apparently the Dodsleys were acting merely as publishers.

467. ——, 4th ed. 1757.
Included in Vol. IV of the *Works*, 1757. See below.

323. The complaint. Night the seventh. 1744. [1, 44, 92, 100]
This was the first of the *Nights* to be printed by Richardson. The copyright of the first five parts had been bought by Dodsley in November 1743, for 160 guineas; in January 1745, Dodsley bought the sixth part for sixty guineas (*Straus*, pp. 75–76; 326). Presumably Dodsley was not willing to continue paying for the parts at the rate established for the sixth one, and Young therefore made an arrangement with George Hawkins for the publication of Parts VII–IX. He did not sell the copyrights to Hawkins, for after the last three parts had been printed, he offered them to Dodsley for 100 guineas, and finally sold them to Andrew Millar for sixty guineas (Henry Pettit, "Preface to a Bibliography of Young's *Night-Thoughts*," in *Elizabethan Studies and other Essays in Honor of George F. Reynolds*, Boulder, [Colo.], 1945, p. 220; and Walter Thomas, *Le poète Edward Young*, Paris, 1901, p. 176*n*.). Possibly Hawkins was serving merely as publisher for the last three parts, as was Mary Cooper whose name appears with his in the imprints. If this was the arrangement that Young had made, then he would probably have been the one who chose Richardson's press for the printing. The seventh and eighth *Nights* were entered by Mary Cooper in the Stationers' Register and the ninth *Night* by Hawkins (Pettit, *loc. cit.*).

A letter from Young to Richardson is particularly pertinent to this study. Young wrote: "Mr. Cave sent me last week a specimen of a spurious copy of the Seventh Night, which, as to letter and ornaments, mimics yours" (*Monthly Magazine*, XXXVI [1815], 418). I have not seen this pirated copy, but the pirating printer was seeking to pass off his edition as genuine by using imitations of Richardson's ornaments. Cave, himself a printer, had no difficulty in recognizing the ornaments as imitations of those which he knew were a part of Richardson's equipment.

332. The complaint. Night the eighth. 1745. [100]

Young's letter to Richardson in December 1744 advised him that he would be in London after Christmas to oversee the proofreading of this part of the poem (*Monthly Magazine*, XXXVI [1813], 420). It was published 7 March 1745 (*RES*, IV [1928], 330, 414).

333. The complaint. Night the ninth. 1745. [49, 88, 102]

Though dated internally 1745, this part was registered in the Stationers' Company on 21 January 1746, and published immediately afterwards (Henry Pettit, "The Dating of Young's *Night-Thoughts*," *MLN*, LV [1940], 194–195).

363. The complaint: or, Night-Thoughts, 2 vols., 8vo. 1747–1748. [In Vol. II: 7, 10, 78]

Richardson printed only the second volume, containing the last three parts of the *Complaint* and Young's *Paraphrase of Job*. The first volume was printed for Dodsley, who owned the copyright of the first six *Nights;* the second volume for Hawkins (see above, *Night the Seventh*, 1744). In April and May 1747, Richardson and Young were discussing the proof for this corrected text of his poem; and Young pointed out that "as 'tis a time of year in which nothing can be published, the world has no cause as yet to *complain*" (*Monthly Magazine*, XXXVII [1814], 141–142). Presumably publication was delayed until autumn, with Dodsley's printer using the date 1747 and Richardson using 1748. Dodsley, with some justification, chose to consider the first six parts as a unit; consequently, the first volume of this edition is not called "Vol. I," though the second volume is labeled "Vol. II." Dodsley had issued a sixth edition of the first six parts, which Straus thinks (*op. cit.*, p. 325) probably appeared in 1746, despite conflicting testimony which dates the sixth edition 1743 in one instance and 1748 in the other (Thomas, *op. cit.*, p. 647). The year 1746 is the logical date for a sixth edition, for Dodsley calls his edition of 1747 the "seventh." Richardson's second volume, dated 1748, has no indication of the number of the edition; it is, in fact, the second edition of Parts VII–IX.

James Nichols in the preface to his edition of Young's *Complete Works*, 1854, I, iv, says that the "very accurate octavo edition of the nine Nights, which issued from Richardson's press in 1749, was the eighth of the poem in a complete form." I have not seen this edition, but from a letter of Richardson to Young, it seems clear that Richardson did not print it.

That some edition was printed in 1749 seems likely. Millar purchased the rights to the second volume on 7 April 1749 (Thomas, *op. cit.*, p. 176*n*.); and within a fortnight after the rights were sold to Millar a one-volume edition of the whole poem was advertised, published by Dodsley and Millar (*General Advertiser*, 19 April 1749; Pettit, "Preface to a Bibliography of Young's *Night-Thoughts*," *loc. cit.*). But in October 1749, when Richardson was printing an edition of the complete poem in twelves, he wrote to Young: "I never before read it in series: the first numbers [Parts I–VI] only when they came out; the second part [Parts VII–IX], as I printed it, under your inspection; and the second edition of that second [part] as I reprinted it, another printer doing Mr. Dodsley's part. But, now printing the whole, it is not possible for me to express my admiration of it" (*Monthly Magazine*, XXXVIII [1814], 430). Clearly Richardson in the autumn of 1749 is for the first time engaged in printing the poem as a whole, and the edition he is printing is not in octavo but in twelves. I have never seen an octavo edition dated 1749, and Thomas—the only person who makes it evident that he has really seen one—says that the Dyce collection at the Victoria and Albert Museum contains Vol. I only of an eighth edition, 1749. This description does not sound like that of a one-volume edition of the whole poem.

On 1 January 1750 Richardson advised Young that Andrew Millar was withholding the edition in twelves until the *octavo edition* was exhausted, but he does not make clear whether the octavo edition is in one or two volumes (*Monthly Magazine*, XXXVII [1814], 328). The earliest one-volume octavo edition of the whole poem that I have seen is dated 1750. The ornaments in that volume, however, are not Richardson's, though an imitation of his ornament No. 69 is used on the title page. That volume is said to be printed for Dodsley and Millar.

383A. ——, 12mo. 1750. [14, 15, 23, 28, 30, 50, 51, 58, 66, 69, 84]

On 9 September 1749 Richardson wrote to Young: "On re-printing your Night Thoughts, in 1 vol. 12mo. which I am desirous to put to press myself, in hopes that it will not be the less correct for it, I find that the preface to the fourth night is temporary. . . . It leaves the reader doubtful whether you will proceed with the excellent work, when the whole is before him complete" (*Monthly Magazine*, XXXVII [1814], 329). Young advised Richardson to omit the preface. On 1 January 1750 Richardson said that publication of this edition was being withheld until an earlier edition in octavo was exhausted (*Monthly Magazine*, XXXVII [1814], 328). The edition in twelves was finally published on 30 January 1750 (*Straus*, p. 340).

393. ——, 12mo. 1751. [55, 78, 84, 87]
A letter of Richardson to Young, 31 July 1750, offered for sale in 1927 by a London bookseller, Walter T. Spencer, contains details of a proposed new edition of the *Night Thoughts*. On 5 September 1750 Richardson suggested to Young that part of the preface to the earlier editions of the fourth *Night* should be used as a preface to the whole work. The edition in twelves in 1750 had appeared without any preface. Young agreed to Richardson's proposal (*Monthly Magazine*, XXXVIII [1814], 431–432). Another edition in 12mo, 1751—probably a piracy—may be distinguished from the genuine edition by its lack of any ornaments.

441B. ——, 12mo. 1755. [69, 71, 77, 84, 92]
441A. ——, 8vo. 1755.
I have not seen a copy of this edition, though I have found it advertised by booksellers. Richardson's printing bill to Andrew Millar is published by Straus. For twenty-six sheets and a half sheet, pica type, the bill was £23/17 (*Straus*, p. 355). Straus (p. 352) says that an edition dated 1755 was published on 9 November 1754, but he does not give its format.

453. ——, 8vo. 1756. [8, 50, 74, 87]
477. ——. 1758. [82, 85, 87]
496. ——. 1760. [31, 50, 69, 82, 87]
487. Conjectures on original composition. In a letter to the author of Sir Charles Grandison. 1759. [15]
Richardson made suggestions and additions for the text of this work before it was published. These have been fully described

by McKillop (*MP*, XXII [1925], 391–404. See also *Sale*, pp. 97–98). Between 500 and 1,000 copies were printed. The book was published on the 12th of May; on the 24th Richardson said that most of the copies were sold.

488. ——, 2nd ed. 1759. [30]

This edition was published on June 19; 1,000 copies were printed (*Sale*, p. 98).

509. Resignation. 1761.

This work was privately printed for Young. I have not examined a copy, but one was advertised by P. and J. Dobell, London booksellers, in their *Catalogue of Eighteenth Century Verse*, 1933, No. 3079, where it was described as in five parts, addressed to Mrs. B[oscawen], including a Funeral Epithalamium, occasioned by a New Marriage Act, 4to., (18 leaves), "Printed in the Year, 1761." In the edition which Young finally had printed for publication, he said (p. 3) that this poem had not been intended for the public, but that inasmuch as some extracts "from the few Copies which were given away" had got into the "printed Papers, it was thought necessary to publish something, lest a Copy still more imperfect than this should fall into the Press." On p. 15, when referring in the poem to Richardson's death, he wrote:

How critically tim'd the News
Which strikes me to the Heart?

And appended this note: "Whilst the Author was writing This, he received the News of Mr. *Richardson's* Death, who was then printing the former Part of the Poem."

On p. 64 is the following note: "The First Impression (from which the Printed Extracts were taken) was given only to Friends; as such they are requested to destroy it; since keeping That out of Sight is the Writer's only Apology for publishing This."

The published version is apparently shorter than the one printed for private circulation. Dobell's Catalogue offers a poem in five parts, while the published poem, despite its sixty-four pages, is entitled: *Resignation. In Two Parts, and a Postscript*, 1762. A second edition was published in 1767, still carrying one of Richardson's ornaments, No. 74. Mrs. Boscawen was the widow of Admiral Edward Boscawen, who died on 10 January 1761. Before marriage, she was Frances, daughter of William Evelyn Glanville of St. Clair, Kent. She lived until 1805.

349A. A vindication of providence: or, A true estimate of human life, [6th ed.]. 1747.

For details concerning the printing of this work, see *Monthly Magazine*, XXXVII (1814), 138, 139, letters of 17 July and 11 November 1746.

466. The works of the author of the Night-Thoughts, 4 vols., 12mo. 1757. [15, 78, 85]

This edition was published for eleven different booksellers and firms of booksellers, each of whom owned the rights in parts of Young's works. It is, I believe, the first collected edition to be published with the consent of the copyright owners. An edition in two volumes, 12mo, 1752, with Young's name on the title page, is probably a piracy. The authorship of the *Complaint* was an open secret, but Young continued to publish anonymously. I have also seen a third volume, dated 1755, containing the *Complaint*, which may be Vol. III of a piracy. At the close of the year 1756, Richardson wrote: "He [Young] is about to give the world a collection of his works, at the entreaty of booksellers, who have a property in them, in four twelves volumes" (*Barbauld*, IV, 112).

ANONYMOUS WORKS

Books published anonymously but whose authors are identifiable are not included in this list. Such books are listed under the authors to whom they have been ascribed; and the fact of their anonymous publication has been noted, when it seemed relevant.

155. An account of the Bank of Loan at Amsterdam. 1735. [50, 81]

117. An answer to the considerations, occasioned by the Craftsman upon excise, so far as it relates to the tobacco trade. 1733. [70, 76]

102. The British empire in America, consider'd. In a second letter from a gentleman of Barbadoes, to his friend in London. 1732. [77]

156. The case of the bank contract. 1735. [39, 48]

47. A collection of epigrams. 1727. [11, 25, 96]
     Lowndes (*Bibliographer's Manual*, Bohn ed., p. 746) says that this collection was probably made by William Oldys (1696–1761). The epigrams are preceded by a critical dissertation on this species of poetry.

157. ——, 2nd ed., 2 vols. 1735–1737. [13, 26, 58]
     Additional epigrams are included.

13. Cythereia: or, New poems upon love and intrigue. 1723. [9, 21, 22, 32, 40, 45, 63, 65, 78, 91, 96]
     Straus in his *Unspeakable Curll* says that this collection was edited by Jeremiah Markland (1693–1776) and published on the 6th of April (New York and London, 1928, p. 272). Nichols discusses Markland and his connection with this volume (*Lit. Anec.*, IV, 273), but the evidence for Markland's editorship seems to me far from conclusive. The volume does include Markland's version of Chaucer's Friar's Tale, and Pope's character of Addison, with Markland's answer (Nichols, *loc. cit.*). Presumably Pope's lines were reprinted from the *St. James Journal* of 15 December 1722, where a version of them had appeared.

182. The debate about the repeal of the Corporation and Test Acts. 1736. [25, 76]
     The author opposes repeal.

364. A detection of the proceedings and practices of the directors of the Royal African Company. 1749. [17]

68. Directions to judge whether a nation be in a thriving condition. 1729. [25]

223. A dissuasive from entering into Holy Orders, in a letter to a young gentleman, 3rd ed. 1738. [12, 50, 81]
     This work is a satire on the modern clergyman. I have not seen earlier editions.

204. An essay on happiness. In an epistle to the Right Honourable The Earl of Chesterfield. 1737. [5, 60, 61]
     This work was advertised in the *Gazetteer*, 6 March 1737, as by the author of *Political Justice* (see below).

69. The family companion for health. 1729. [20, 27, 64]
     See *The Practical Physician*, below.

90. The flower-piece: A collection of miscellany poems. 1731.
   [11, 49, 51, 57, 63, 64, 65, 67, 71, 72, 77, 78, 79, 80, 84, 86]

313. French faith threatening and pernicious to all Europe. 1744.
   [42]

497. A general system of the laws concerning bankrupts, by a Commissioner of Bankrupts, 2 vols. 1761.*
   This work was printed by Richardson as joint owner with Catherine Lintot of the law patent (pp. 134–144).

489. The histories of some of the penitents in the Magdalen-House, 2 vols. 1760.
   See p. 119. An edition of this work was printed in Dublin in the same year.

183. An impartial enquiry into the motives of the opposition to the ministry. 1736. [17, 77]
   The preface is signed "S.L."

269. Important considerations on the true nature of government. 1741. [17, 34]
   A plea for the return to those sentiments on which the Revolution of 1688 was grounded.

103. The ladies miscellany. Being a collection of original poems, novels, and other curious tracts, 3rd ed. 1732.
   This volume is listed because it contains the fourth edition of Mrs. Manley's *History of her own Life and Times*, for which Richardson printed a new preface in 1725 (see above, under Manley). Apparently Curll collected a number of short pieces and put them together under a new title page. There is no reason to believe that Richardson had anything to do with this book.

48. A letter from a country gentleman, to the author of the Occasional Writer [i.e., Henry St. John, Viscount Bolingbroke]. 1727. [18]
   This letter is signed "Publicola in Wiltshire." It expresses sentiments that I suspect were very close to those of Richardson himself.

304. Letter to a great man in France. 1743. [31]

104. A letter to a member of Parliament, concerning the reduction of interest. 1732. [4, 41, 52]

10A. A list of the persons who have polled for Humphrey Parsons,

Esq.; Francis Child, Esq.; . . . Richard Lockwood, Esq.; . . . or one or more of them. At the late election, for members of Parliament, for the City of London. 1722. [62]

90A. Memoirs of the life of His Grace Philip Late Duke of Wharton. By an impartial hand. 1731. [27]

Wharton died in 1731. These *Memoirs* were reissued with a second issue of the essays of the *True Briton* in 1732 (see under *True Briton*).

158. Moral reflexions on the ministry of Card. Alberoni. 1735. [17]

This pamphlet purports to be translated from the Spanish, as a kind of warning to William Stanhope, first Earl of Harrington, and former British Ambassador to Spain.

34. Musidora: A pastoral elegy, on the death of the Honourable Mrs. Bowes. 1725. [4, 68]

Elizabeth, daughter of Thomas Verney, had married George Bowes, M.P. for Durham, on 10 October 1724, at the age of fifteen. She died 14 December 1724 (The *Historical Register*, "The Chronological Diary," 1724).

159. Of power. A moral poem. 1735. [3, 94]

183A. Papers relating to the Quakers' tythe bill. 1736. [31, 43, 45, 58, 67, 86, 87]

160. The Persian strip'd of his disguise: or, Remarks on a late libel, intitled, Letters from a Persian in England to his friend at Ispahan [by George, 1st Baron Lyttelton]. 1735. [39, 74]

Lyttelton's *Letters from a Persian* went through four editions in 1735. Modeled on the *Lettres persanes*, they were considered a manifesto of the Opposition. This pamphlet is a not unintelligent answer to Lyttelton. In fact, his revision of the *Letters* for a fifth edition in 1744 shows the effect of the criticism of this anonymous pamphleteer.

184. Political justice. A poem. In a letter to the Right Hon. the Lord [Hardwicke]. 1736. [5, 90]

Philip Yorke was invested with the coif, appointed chief justice and privy councillor, and created Baron Hardwicke in 1733. This poem in somewhat fatuous praise of Yorke was written by the author of *An Essay on Happiness* (see above). For Richardson's knowledge of the Yorke family, see under Charles Yorke.

70. The practical physician for travellers, whether by sea or land. 1729. [7, 19, 27, 35, 39]

    By a member of the College of Physicians. This piece was said to be a supplement to the *Family Companion for Health* (see above).

91. The present state of the British sugar colonies, consider'd. 1731. [56, 61, 62]

    This is a protest by a gentleman from Barbadoes against sending sugar through England on its way to a final market.

161. The previous question in politics. 1735. [16, 73]

105. The principles and facts of the Lord Bishop of Chichester's sermon, and the defence of it, further examin'd and remark'd. In a letter to His Lordship from a gentleman at Durham. 1732. [35]

    The imprint in both the first and second editions reads "Printed by T. Cooper." Cooper was a printer, but his principal occupation was that of publisher. I do not know why one of Richardson's ornaments should appear in a book purporting to be printed by him. This is the only instance of such an apparent contradiction that I have found, though it seems true that issues of the *Weekly Miscellany* and of the *Gazetteer*, purporting to be printed by Cooper, were actually printed elsewhere. I can offer no adequate explanation of these facts.

106. ——, 2nd ed. 1732.

    A second issue?

384. Prologue, and epilogue, to the tragedy of Romeo and Juliet. 1751. [66, 100]

    These pieces were written for a performance of *Romeo and Juliet* by the "gentlemen of the Royal Academy at Woolwich," on 10 October 1751.

498. Proposals for a new edition of the Statutes at Large from Magna Charta to the end of the last Parliament. 1761.

    See p. 139.

132. Reasons for the neutrality of Great-Britain, deduced from her exploits for the house of Austria. 1734. [50]

224. Reflections and considerations occasioned by the petition presented to the honourable House of Commons, for taking off the drawback on foreign linens. 1738. [34]

162. The religious, rational, and moral conduct of Matthew Tindal. 1735. [19, 74]

     This pamphlet was written by a member of All Souls College, Oxford, of which Tindal was a former fellow. Tindal died in 1733.

133. Remarks upon the cases of the governor, and some of the assistants, of the York-Buildings Company. 1734. [1]

     This is not a book, nor a pamphlet. The text is printed so that it may be folded like a legal document, with the title then appearing on the outside.

163. A seasonable examination of the pleas and pretensions of the proprietors of, and subscribers to, play-houses, erected in defiance of the royal licence. 1735. [27]

119. A sequel to Britannia excisa. A new political ballad. To the tune of, Ye commons and peers. 1733. [4, 44]

 92. Some thoughts on the woolen manufactures of England. 1731. [22, 84]

120. The thoughts of an impartial man upon the present temper of the nation. 1733. [35, 51, 61]

498A. Treatise of distresses, replevins, and avowries, 4th ed. 1761.*

     This work was printed by Richardson as joint owner with Catherine Lintot of the law patent (pp. 134–144).

 70A. The true state of England, containing the particular duty, business, and salary of every officer, civil and military, in all the publick offices of Great Britain. 1729. [21]

185. An universal history. See under title, p. 212.

226. The young senator. A satyre. With an Epistle to Mr. Fielding, on his studying the law. 1738. [59, 69, 73]

     The Epistle has a separate title page, but the pagination is continuous. Wilbur Cross quotes some couplets from this poem to Fielding, pointing out that one might wish the author's skill in verse equal to his admiration for Fielding (*The History of Henry Fielding*, New Haven, [Conn.], 1918, I, 243). In 1737 Fielding enrolled as a student at the Middle Temple.

PART 2. ARRANGED CHRONOLOGICALLY
BY SHORT TITLES

LONGER titles and additional information about these books may be found in the preceding list, beginning on p. 146. In that list the books are arranged alphabetically by authors. The books have been numbered for ease of reference. A few numbers have been dropped out of the series, and a few repeated, followed by letters of the alphabet.

1719. 1. HUTCHESON, ARCHIBALD.   Mr. Hutcheson's answer.

1720. 2. HUTCHESON, ARCHIBALD.   A collection of treatises.
　　　 3. ——.   Some calculations relating to . . . the South-Sea Company.
　　　 4. ——.   An estimate of the value of South-Sea stock.
　　　 5. ——.   A collection of calculations and remarks.
　　　 6. ——.   A letter . . . relating to South-Sea stock.

1721. 7. FÉNELON, FRANÇOIS DE SALIGNAC DE LA MOTHE.   Instructions for the education of a daughter, 4th ed., tr. Hickes.
　　　 8. HUTCHESON, ARCHIBALD.   Four treatises.
　　　 9. ——.   Mr. Hutcheson's answer to the queries.
　　　 10. SMEDLEY, JONATHAN.   Poems on several occasions.

1722. 10A. ANON.   A list of the persons who have polled for Humphrey Parsons, Esq. . . .
　　　 11. HUTCHESON, ARCHIBALD.   A collection of advertisements.
　　　 12. ——.   Copies of some letters from Mr. Hutcheson.

1723. 13. ANON.   Cythereia: or, New poems upon love and intrigue.
　　　 14. ATTERBURY, FRANCIS.   Maxims, reflections and observations.
　　　 15. HOUSE OF LORDS.   A compleat and intire collection of the Lords protests in the last session of Parliament.
　　　 16. HUTCHESON, ARCHIBALD.   An abstract of all the publick debts . . . at Michaelmas, 1722.
　　　 17. ——.   An abstract of an account stated by some of the clerks at the South Sea House.

18. ——. Some paragraphs of Mr. Hutcheson's treatises.
19. Kelly, George. The speech of Mr. George Kelly.
20. ——, 3rd ed.
21. ——, 4th ed.
22. ——, 5th ed.
23. Smedley, Jonathan. Poems on several occasions, [2nd ed.].
24. The True Briton, semiweekly periodical.
25. ——. Fortnightly reprintings of this paper.
26. ——. A reprint of all numbers in 2 vols.
27. Wharton, Philip, *Duke of.* His Grace the Duke of Wharton's speech in the House of Lords, 2nd ed.

1724.
28. Bailey, Nathan. An universal etymological English dictionary, 2nd ed.
29. Castelnau, Michel de. Memoirs of the reigns of Francis II. and Charles IX. of France, tr. Kelly.
30. Defoe, Daniel. A tour thro' the whole island of Great Britain, Vol. I.
31. The Plain Dealer, semiweekly periodical.
32. Sidney, Sir Philip. See No. 41.
33. The True Briton, semiweekly periodical.

1725.
34. Anon. Musidora: A pastoral elegy.
35. Catherall, Samuel. Cato major. A poem.
36. The Daily Journal, newspaper.
37. Defoe, Daniel. A new voyage round the world.
38. ——. A tour thro' the whole island of Great Britain, Vol. II. See No. 30.
39. Hill, Aaron. The northern-star, 3rd ed.
40. Manley, Mary de la Rivière. Mrs. Manley's history of her own life and times, 4th ed. [Preface only.]
40A. The Plain Dealer, semiweekly periodical.
41. Sidney, Sir Philip. Works, 14th ed., 3 vols., 1725, 1724, 1724.

1726.
41A. Burnet, Thomas (d. 1750). An essay upon government, 2nd ed.
42. Burnet, Thomas (1635?–1715). The sacred theory of the earth, 6th ed., 2 vols.
43. Cooke, Thomas. The bath.
44. The Daily Journal, newspaper.

45. GORDON, ALEXANDER. Itinerarium septentrionale.
46. NEWTON, RICHARD. University education.

1727.
47. ANON. A collection of epigrams.
48. ——. A letter from a country gentleman.
49. ACHERLEY, ROGER. The Britannic constitution.
50. BLACKWALL, ANTHONY. The sacred classics defended, 2nd ed.
51. THE DAILY JOURNAL, newspaper.
52. DEFOE, DANIEL. A new family instructor.
54. MITCHELL, JOSEPH. The Totness address, versified, 3rd ed.
55. OLDMIXON, JOHN. Clarendon and Whitlock compared.
56. RAMSAY, ANDREW MICHAEL. The travels of Cyrus, 2nd ed., 2 vols., tr. Hooke.
57. SWIFT, JONATHAN. Travels into several remote nations of the world. By Capt. Lemuel Gulliver, 2 vols., abridged.
58. VENEER, JOHN. A new exposition on the Book of Common Prayer.

1728.
59. BLACKWALL, ANTHONY. An introduction to the classics, 4th ed.
60. THE DAILY JOURNAL, newspaper.
61. DENNIS, JOHN. Remarks on Mr. Pope's Rape of the lock.
62. FÉNELON, FRANÇOIS DE SALIGNAC DE LA MOTHE. The adventures of Telemachus, 12th ed., 2 vols., tr. Boyer and Littlebury.
63. MALLET, DAVID. The excursion.
64. SALMON, NATHANAEL. The history of Hertfordshire.
65. ——. A new survey of Great Britain, Parts I–III.
66. SMEDLEY, JONATHAN. Gulliveriana.
67. WHEATLY, CHARLES. Bezaleel and Aholiab.

1729.
68. ANON. Directions to judge whether a nation be in a thriving condition.
69. ——. The family companion for health.
70. ——. The practical physician for travellers.
70A. ——. The true state of England.
71. BACON, PHANUEL. The kite.

72. BREVAL, JOHN. Henry and Minerva.
73. BYROM, SAMUEL. An irrefragable argument.
73A. DEFOE, DANIEL. Religious courtship, 2nd ed.
74. DENNIS, JOHN. Remarks upon several passages in the preliminaries to the Dunciad.
74A. GIANNONE, PIETRO. Civil history of the kingdom of Naples, Vol. I, tr. Ogilvie. See No. 97A.
75. GORDON, ALEXANDER. The lives of Pope Alexander VI. and his son Caesar Borgia.
76. G[ORDON?], T[HOMAS?]. Two proposals for raising £1,250,000 for the . . . year 1729.
77. MADDEN, SAMUEL. Themistocles.
78. ——, 2nd ed.
79. ——, 3rd ed.
79A. SALMON, NATHANAEL. A new survey of Great Britain, Parts IV–VII. See No. 65.
80. SAVAGE, RICHARD. The wanderer.
81. THOMSON, JAMES. Britannia.

1730.
82. HAY, WILLIAM. Mount Caburn.
83. HILL, AARON; BOND, WILLIAM; and others. The plain dealer, 2 vols., a reprinting of the essays from this periodical.
84. HILL, AARON. The progress of wit.
85. JOHNSON, ANTHONY. An historical account of the several English translations of the Bible.
85A. SALMON, NATHANAEL. A new survey of Great Britain, Parts VIII–XI. See Nos. 65 and 79A.
86. SALMON, THOMAS, and EMLYN, SOLLOM, eds. A complete collection of state trials, 2nd ed., 6 vols.
87. THOMSON, JAMES. The seasons [and other poems].
88. WEBSTER, WILLIAM. The duty of keeping the whole law.
89. WELSTED, LEONARD, and SMYTHE, JAMES MOORE. One epistle to Mr. A. Pope.

1731.
90. ANON. The flower-piece.
90A. ——. Memoirs of the life of His Grace Philip late Duke of Wharton.
91. ——. The present state of the British sugar colonies.
92. ——. Some thoughts on the woolen manufactures.

93. ACHERLEY, ROGER. Free Parliaments.
94. BLACKWALL, ANTHONY. The sacred classics defended, Vol. II.
95. BUDGELL, EUSTACE. A letter to Cleomenes.
96. BURROUGHS, SAMUEL [under pseudonym of Everard Fleetwood]. An enquiry into the customary-estates and tenant-rights.
97. ELLIS, CLEMENT. The self-deceiver plainly discover'd to himself.
97A. GIANNONE, PIETRO. Civil history of the kingdom of Naples, Vol. II, tr. Ogilvie. See No. 74A.
98. HILL, AARON. Advice to the poets.
99. MILLER, PHILIP. The gardeners dictionary, Vol. I, fol.
100. POMFRET, JOHN. Poems upon several occasions, 8th ed.
101. SALMON, NATHANAEL. A new survey of Great Britain, 2 vols. [A second issue of Nos. 65, 79A, and 85A.]

1732.
102. ANON. The British empire in America, consider'd.
103. ——. The ladies miscellany.
104. ——. A letter to a member of Parliament.
105. ——. The principles . . . of the Lord Bishop of Chichester's sermon . . . examin'd.
106. ——, 2nd ed.
107. CHURCHILL, AWNSHAM, ed. A collection of voyages and travels, 6 vols. [Richardson printed Vol. VI.]
108. CONYBEARE, JOHN. A defence of reveal'd religion.
109. DEFOE, DANIEL. A new family instructor, [A second issue.]
110. DELANY, PATRICK. Revelation examin'd with candour, 2 vols.
111. LEDIARD, THOMAS. The life of Sethos, 2 vols., tr. from Jean Terrasson.
112. MILLER, PHILIP. The gardeners kalendar.
113. THE MISCELLANY [i.e., The Weekly Miscellany], weekly periodical.
113A. THE TRUE BRITON, 2 vols. [A second issue.]
114. WELSTED, LEONARD. Of dulness and scandal.
115. ——, 2nd ed. [A second issue.]
116. ——. Of false fame.

1733.
117. ANON. An answer to the . . . Craftsman upon excise.

119. ANON. A sequel to Britannia excisa.
120. ——. The thoughts of an impartial man.
121. CHEYNE, GEORGE. The English malady.
122. DELANY, PATRICK. Revelation examin'd with candour, 2nd ed., 2 vols.
123. DRURY, ROBERT. The fancy'd queen.
124. HOUSE OF COMMONS. "Parliamentary papers printed by order of the House of Commons." See pp. 76–80.
124A. LAW, WILLIAM. The Oxford Methodists.
125. MIDDLETON, CONYERS. A letter from Rome, 3rd ed.
126. MILLER, PHILIP. The gardeners dictionary, 2nd ed., Vol. I, fol.
127. ——. The gardeners kalendar, 2nd ed.
128. NEWTON, RICHARD. University education, 2nd ed.
129. SMITH, JOSHUA. A select manual of divine meditations, 2nd ed.
130. THOU, JACQUES AUGUSTE DE. Historiarum sui temporis, 7 vols. [Richardson printed Vol. II.]
131. THE WEEKLY MISCELLANY, weekly periodical.
132. ANON. Reasons for the neutrality of Great Britain.

1734.
133. ——. Remarks upon . . . the York-Buildings Company.
134. BALGUY, JOHN. A collection of tracts.
135. BARBER, MARY. Poems on several occasions.
136. CHANDLER, MARY. A description of Bath, [2nd ed?]
137. CHEYNE, GEORGE. The English malady, 2nd ed.
138. ——. An essay of health and long life, 8th ed.
139. COTTON, CHARLES. The genuine poetical works, 3rd ed.
140. DELANY, PATRICK. The doctrine of abstinence from blood defended.
141. GIFFARD, WILLIAM. Cases in midwifry, ed. Hody.
142. HILL, AARON; BOND, WILLIAM; and others. The plain dealer, 2 vols., a reprinting of the essays from this periodical. [A second issue. See No. 83.]
143. HOUSE OF COMMONS. See p. 76.
144. MILLER, PHILIP. The gardeners kalendar, 3rd ed.
145. MORRIS, ROBERT. Lectures on architecture.

145A. NEWTON, RICHARD. The expence of university education reduced, 3rd ed.

145B. ——. A letter to the Revd. Dr. Holmes.

146. ——, 2nd ed.

147. POPPLE, WILLIAM. The lady's revenge.

148. THE PROMPTER, semiweekly periodical.

148A. RICHARDSON, SAMUEL. The apprentice's vade mecum.

149. STEBBING, HENRY. An apology for the clergy of the Church of England.

150. THOMSON, JAMES. Winter [and other poems].

151. VENEER, JOHN. An exposition on the Thirty-Nine Articles, 2nd ed., 2 vols.

152. THE WEEKLY MISCELLANY, weekly periodical.

153. WISEMAN, RICHARD. Eight chirurgical treatises, 6th ed., 2 vols. [Richardson printed Vol. II.]

154. WITHINGTON, NICHOLAS. A briefe discoverye.

1735.

155. ANON. An account of the Bank of Loan at Amsterdam.

156. ——. The case of the bank contract.

157. ——. A collection of epigrams, 2nd ed., Vol. I. See No. 203A.

158. ——. Moral reflexions on the ministry of Card. Alberoni.

159. ——. Of power. A moral poem.

160. ——. The Persian strip'd of his disguise.

161. ——. The previous question in politics.

162. ——. The religious, rational, and moral conduct of Matthew Tindal.

163. ——. A seasonable examination of the pleas and pretensions of the proprietors of . . . play-houses.

164. BANKS, JOHN. The unhappy favourite.

165. BARBER, MARY. Poems on several occasions, 2nd ed.

166. BROOKE, HENRY. University beauty.

167. COCKBURN, JOHN. A journey over land.

167A. CONYBEARE, JOHN. Calumny refuted.

168. COOPER, ELIZABETH. The rival widows.

169. THE DAILY GAZETTEER, newspaper.

170. DELANY, PATRICK. Revelation examin'd with candour, 3rd ed., 2 vols.

171. FROWDE, PHILIP.   The fall of Saguntum, 3rd ed.
172. HAYWOOD, ELIZA.   A wife to be lett.
173. HOUSE OF COMMONS. See p. 76.
174. LEE, NATHANAEL.   Nero.
174A. MENTET [MENTIETH, MONTEITH], ROBERT.   The history of the troubles of Great Britain, tr. Ogilvie.
175. MILLER, PHILIP.   The gardeners dictionary, 2 vols. [Abridgment of No. 99.]
175A. NEWTON, RICHARD.   The grounds of the complaint of the Principal of Hart-Hall [i.e., Richard Newton].
175B. ——, 2nd ed.
176. THE PROMPTER, semiweekly periodical.
177. SAUL, EDWARD.   An historical . . . account of the barometer, 2nd ed.
178. TAVERNER, WILLIAM.   The artful husband, 4th ed.
179. THOMSON, JAMES.   Summer, 4th ed.
180. TRENCHARD, JOHN, and GORDON, THOMAS.   The Independent Whig, 6th ed., 3 vols.
181. THE WEEKLY MISCELLANY, weekly periodical.

1736.
182. ANON.   The debate about the repeal of the Corporation and Test Acts.
183. ——.   An impartial enquiry into the motives of the opposition to the ministry.
183A. ——.   Papers relating to the Quakers' tythe bill.
184. ——.   Political justice.
185. ——.   An universal history, [Ancient Part], Vol. I. See p. 101.
186. BARBER, MARY.   Poems on several occasions, [2nd issue of 2nd ed.]
187. BENNET[T], JOHN.   The national merchant.
188. BERKELEY, GEORGE.   The querist. Parts I, II.
189. CENTLIVRE, SUSANNA.   The gamester, 4th ed.
190. CHANDLER, MARY.   The description of Bath, 3rd ed.
191. THE DAILY GAZETTEER, newspaper.
192. DUCK, STEPHEN.   Poems on several occasions.
193. HILL, AARON.   Alzira, tr. from Voltaire.
194. HOUSE OF COMMONS. See p. 76.
195. NICOLSON, WILLIAM.   The English, Scotch, and Irish historical libraries, 3rd ed.

196. POPPLE, WILLIAM. The double deceit.

197. THE PROMPTER, semiweekly periodical.

198. THE ROYAL SOCIETY. The philosophical transactions of the Royal Society. See p. 73.

199. SKELTON, PHILIP. Some proposals for the revival of Christianity.

200. STEBBING, HENRY. A true state of the controversy with Mr. Foster.

201. WEBSTER, WILLIAM, ed. The weekly miscellany, Vol. I, a reprinting of the essays from this periodical. [Vol. II, 1738, was not printed by Richardson.]

202. THE WEEKLY MISCELLANY, weekly periodical.

203. WILSON, THOMAS. Distilled spirituous liquors the bane of the nation, 2nd ed.

1737. 203A. ANON. A collection of epigrams, 2nd. ed., Vol. II. See No. 157.

204. ———. An essay on happiness.

205. ———. An universal history, [Ancient Part], Vol. II. See p. 101.

205A. BERKELEY, GEORGE. The querist, Part III.

206. BLACKWALL, ANTHONY. An introduction to the classics, 5th ed.

207. ———. The sacred classics defended, 3rd ed., 2 vols.

208. BREVAL, JOHN. The rape of Helen.

209. THE DAILY GAZETTEER, newspaper.

210. DELANY, PATRICK. Reflections upon polygamy.

211. DUCK, STEPHEN. Poems on several occasions, 2nd ed.

212. ———. The vision.

213. HILL, AARON. Alzira, 2nd ed.

214. ———. The tears of the muses.

215. HOUSE OF COMMONS. See p. 76.

215A. MAUCLERC, JAMES. The Christian's magazine, n.d.

216. MILLER, PHILIP. The gardeners dictionary, 3rd ed., Vol. I.

217. MORELL, THOMAS, ed. The Canterbury tales of Chaucer.

217A. OLDMIXON, JOHN. Clarendon and Whitlock compared, 2nd ed. [A second issue.]

218. SPENCE, JOSEPH. An essay on Mr. Pope's Odyssey, 2nd ed.

219. STEBBING, HENRY. A reply to Mr. Foster's Answer. See No. 200.
220. THE WEEKLY MISCELLANY, weekly periodical.
221. WHITEFIELD, GEORGE. The benefits of an early piety.
222. ——. The nature and necessity of our new birth in Christ Jesus.

1738.   223. ANON. A dissuasive from entering into holy orders, 3rd ed.
224. ——. Reflections . . . occasioned by the petition . . . for taking off the drawback on foreign linens.
225. ——. An universal history, [Ancient Part], Vol. III. See p. 101.
226. ——. The young senator . . . with an Epistle to Mr. Fielding.
227. BREVAL, JOHN. Remarks on several parts of Europe, 2 vols.
228. CHANDLER, MARY. The description of Bath, 4th ed.
229. CHEYNE, GEORGE. A catechism.
230. ——. An historical character of the Honourable George Bailie, Esq.
231. THE DAILY GAZETTEER, newspaper.
232. DEFOE, DANIEL. A tour thro' the whole island of Great Britain, 2nd ed., 3 vols.
233. ELLIS, CLEMENT. The scripture catechist.
234. HILL, AARON. An enquiry into the merit of assassination.
234A. ——. The tears of the muses, 2nd ed.
235. HOUSE OF COMMONS. See p. 76.
236. KEITH, WILLIAM. The history of the British plantations in America.
236A. MENTET [MENTEITH, MONTEITH], ROBERT. The history of the troubles of Great Britain, tr. Ogilvie, 2nd ed.
237. STUART, ALEXANDER. Dissertatio de structura et motu musculari.
238. SWIFT, JONATHAN. A complete collection of genteel and ingenious conversations.
238A. ——. [A variant issue.]

1739.   241. ANON. An universal history, [Ancient Part], Vol. IV. See p. 101.

242. BARTON, RICHARD. Farrago.
243. THE CITIZEN, ed. Keith, weekly periodical.
244. THE DAILY GAZETTEER, newspaper.
245. DELANY, PATRICK. Reflections upon polygamy, 2nd ed.
245A. FOUNDLING HOSPITAL. A copy of the royal charter.
246. HILL, AARON. The northern-star, 5th ed.
247. HOUSE OF COMMONS. See p. 76.
248. MAITLAND, WILLIAM. The history of London.
249. MILLER, PHILIP. The gardeners dictionary, Vol. II. See No. 99.
249A. NEWTON, RICHARD. Rules and statutes made by Dr. R. Newton, Principal of Hart-Hall.
249B. PARLIAMENT. An authentic list . . . of the House of Commons . . . To which are annexed Lists of the Lords.
250. PLUCHE, ABBÉ NOËL ANTOINE. Spectacle de la nature, Vol. IV, tr. Freval.
251. ROWE, ELIZABETH, and ROWE, THOMAS. The miscellaneous works, 2 vols. [Richardson printed Vol. II.]
252. SENECA, L. ANNAEUS. Select epistles.

1740.   253. ANON. An universal history, [Ancient Part], Vol. V. See p. 101.
254. AESOP. Aesop's fables, ed. Richardson.
255. BEAUFORT, LOUIS DE. A dissertation upon . . . Roman history.
256. BOWMAN, WILLIAM. The imposture of Methodism display'd.
257. CHEYNE, GEORGE. An essay on regimen.
257A. ——, 2nd ed. [A second issue?]
258. THE DAILY GAZETTEER, newspaper.
259. DELANY, PATRICK. An historical account of the . . . reign of David, [Vol. I].
260. ——, 2nd ed.
261. DUCK, STEPHEN. Alrick and Isabel.
262. HOUSE OF COMMONS. See p. 76.
263. LESLIE, CHARLES. A new history of Jamaica, [2nd ed.]
264. MILLER, PHILIP. The gardeners dictionary, Vol. III. [The third volume of an abridgment. See No. 175.]

265. MORELL, THOMAS, *ed.* The Canterbury tales of Chaucer, 2nd ed.
266. PLUCHE, ABBÉ NOËL ANTOINE. The history of the heavens, 2 vols., tr. Freval.
267. RICHARDSON, SAMUEL. Pamela, 2 vols. [Dated 1741.]
268. ROE, SIR THOMAS. The negotiations of Sir Thomas Roe, ed. Richardson.
268A. ROWE, ELIZABETH. Friendship in death.

1741.   269. ANON. Important considerations on . . . government.
270. ACHERLEY, ROGER. The Britannic constitution, 2nd ed. [A second issue.]
271. ——. Reasons for uniformity in the state, 2nd ed.
272. CHANDLER, MARY. The description of Bath, 5th ed.
273. THE DAILY GAZETTEER, newspaper.
274. DUCK, STEPHEN. Every man in his own way.
275. FRIEDRICH II, DER GROSSE, *King of Prussia*. Anti-Machiavel. Published by Mr. [François Marie Arouet] de Voltaire.
276. GORDON, THOMAS. The humourist, 4th ed.
277. HOUSE OF COMMONS. See p. 76.
278. MARSH, CHARLES. A poetical epistle.
279. MILLER, PHILIP. The gardeners dictionary, 2nd ed., 3 vols.
279A. NEWTON, RICHARD. The expence of university education reduced, 4th ed.
280. PAGET, THOMAS CATESBY. Miscellanies.
281. PLUCHE, ABBÉ NOËL ANTOINE. The history of the heavens, 2nd ed., 2 vols., tr. Freval.
282. RICHARDSON, SAMUEL. Pamela, 2nd ed., 2 vols.
283. ——, 3rd ed., 2 vols.
284. ——, 4th ed., 2 vols.
285. ——, 5th ed., 2 vols.
286. ——. Pamela, Vols. III, IV.
287. ——. Letters written to and for particular friends.
288. WELSTED, LEONARD. The summum bonum.
289. WILSON, THOMAS, D.D. The knowledge . . . of Christianity made easy.

1742. 290. ANON. An universal history, [Ancient Part], Vol. VI. See p. 101.

291. CHEYNE, GEORGE. The natural method of cureing [*sic*] the diseases of the body, 3rd ed.

292. ——, 4th ed. [A fourth issue?]

293. THE DAILY GAZETTEER, newspaper.

294. DEFOE, DANIEL. A new family instructor, 4th ed. [Probably the fourth issue.]

295. ——. A tour thro' the whole island of Great Britain, 3rd ed., 4 vols., ed. Richardson.

296. DELANY, PATRICK. An historical account of the . . . reign of David, Vols. II, III. See No. 259.

297. HOUSE OF COMMONS. See p. 76.

297A. HOUSE OF COMMONS. The journals of the House of Commons. See pp. 80–83.

298. RICHARDSON, SAMUEL. Pamela, Vols. III, IV, 2nd ed.

299. ——. Pamela, Vols. I, II, 6th ed., Vols. III, IV, 3rd ed.

300. ——. Pamela, Vols. III, IV, 4th ed. [A second issue of the second edition.]

301. ——. Letters written to and for particular friends, 2nd ed.

302. ——. The matrimonial mirror.

302A. SALMON, THOMAS, and EMLYN, SOLLOM, eds. A complete collection of state trials, 3rd ed., 6 vols.

303. SPATEMAN, THOMAS. The school-boy's mask.

1743. 304. ANON. Letter to a great man in France.

305. THE DAILY GAZETTEER, newspaper.

306. HILL, AARON. The fanciad.

307. HOUSE OF COMMONS. See p. 76.

307A. JAMES, ROBERT. A medical dictionary, Vol. I.

308. NEWTON, RICHARD. Pluralities indefensible.

309. PERRY, CHARLES. A view of the Levant.

310. ROWE, ELIZABETH. Friendship in death. [A reissue?]

312. TRENCHARD, JOHN, and GORDON, THOMAS. The Independent Whig, 7th ed., 2 vols.

1744. 313. ANON. French faith threatening . . . to all Europe.

314. ——. An universal history, [Ancient Part], Vol. VII in 2 Parts, usually bound in 2 vols.

315. CHANDLER, MARY.   The description of Bath, 6th ed.
316. THE DAILY GAZETTEER, newspaper.
317. DELANY, PATRICK.   Fifteen sermons upon social duties.
318. HARRIS, JOHN.   Navigantium atque itinerantium bibliotheca, Vol. I, revised by Campbell. [Published in parts.]
319. HILL, AARON.   Alzira, 3rd ed.
320. ———.   The impartial.
321. HOUSE OF COMMONS. See p. 76.
322. SKELTON, PHILIP.   The candid reader.
323. YOUNG, EDWARD.   The complaint. Night the seventh.

1745.   324. THE DAILY GAZETTEER, newspaper.
325. DELANY, PATRICK.   An historical account of the . . . reign of David, 3rd ed., 2 vols.
326. ———.   Revelation examined with candour, 4th ed., 2 vols.
327. HOUSE OF COMMONS. See p. 76.
328. HUTCHINSON, THOMAS.   A sermon preached . . . November 5.
328A. JAMES, ROBERT.   A medical dictionary, Vols. II, III. See No. 307A.
329. MADDEN, SAMUEL.   Boulter's monument.
330. MILLER, PHILIP.   The gardeners kalendar, 7th ed.
331. NEWTON, RICHARD.   Pluralities indefensible, 3rd ed.
332. YOUNG, EDWARD.   The complaint. Night the eighth.
333. ———.   The complaint. Night the ninth.

1746.   334. BARNARD, SIR JOHN.   A defense of several proposals.
335. BLACKWALL, ANTHONY.   An introduction to the classics, 6th ed.
336. THE DAILY GAZETTEER, newspaper.
337. HERVEY, JAMES.   Meditations among the tombs.
338. ———.   Reflections on a flower-garden.
339. HILL, AARON.   The art of acting.
340. ———.   Free thoughts upon faith.
341. HOUSE OF COMMONS. See p. 76.
342. HUTCHINSON, THOMAS.   A sermon preached . . . December 18.
343. NEWTON, RICHARD.   The ministerial duty set forth, 3rd ed.

344. RICHARDSON, SAMUEL. Letters written to and for particular friends, 3rd ed.

344A. ——. Pamela, Vols. I, II, 6th ed.

1747. 345. ANON. An universal history, [Ancient Part], Vols. I–XII, 8vo. See p. 101.

346. DELANY, PATRICK. Twenty sermons on social duties, 2nd ed. [of No. 317].

347. HOUSE OF COMMONS. See p. 76.

348. LYTTELTON, GEORGE, *1st Baron Lyttelton*. To the memory of a lady lately deceased.

348A. NEWTON, RICHARD. Rules and statutes for the government of Hertford College.

349. WILLIAMS, SIR CHARLES HANBURY. Tar water.

349A. YOUNG, EDWARD. A vindication of providence.

1748. 350. ANON. An universal history, [Ancient Part], Vols. XIII–XX, 8vo. See p. 101.

351. BOLTON, ROBERT. A letter to a lady.

352. DEFOE, DANIEL. A tour thro' the whole island of Great Britain, 4th ed., 4 vols., ed. Richardson.

353. HARRIS, JOHN. Navigantium atque itinerantium bibliotheca, Vol. II, revised by Campbell. See No. 318.

354. HERVEY, JAMES. Meditations and contemplations, 2nd ed., 2 vols., 8vo.

354A. ——, 2nd ed., 2 vols., 12mo.

355. ——, 4th ed., 2 vols.

356. HOUSE OF COMMONS. See p. 76.

357. LYTTELTON, GEORGE, *1st Baron Lyttelton*. To the memory of a lady lately deceased, 2nd ed.

357A. MAUCLERC, JAMES. The Christian's magazine, [2nd ed.?].

358. MILLER, PHILIP. The gardeners dictionary, 3rd ed., 3 vols.

359. MONCREIF [MONCRIEF], JOHN. Galba.

360. ——. Camillus.

361. RICHARDSON, SAMUEL. Clarissa, 7 vols.

362. YORKE, CHARLES. Some considerations on the law of forfeiture, 3rd ed.

363. YOUNG, EDWARD. The complaint, 2 vols., 8vo. [Vol. I, 1747, was not printed by Richardson.]

1749.　364. ANON.　A detection of the proceedings . . . of the Royal African Company.

365. BIRCH, THOMAS.　An historical view of the negotiations between the courts of England, France, and Brussels.

366. BYROM, JOHN.　An epistle to a gentleman of the Temple.

367. FIELDING, SARAH.　The governess, 2nd ed.

367A. HARTLEY, DAVID.　Observations on man, 2 vols.

368. HAWKINS, WILLIAM.　Henry and Rosamond.

369. HILL, AARON.　Gideon.

370. HOUSE OF COMMONS. See p. 76.

372. RICHARDSON, SAMUEL.　Clarissa, 2nd ed., Vols. I–IV only.

373. SKELTON, PHILIP.　Ophiomaches: or, Deism revealed, 2 vols.

374. SPINCKES, NATHANIEL.　The true Church of England-Man's companion, 10th ed.

1750.　375. ANON.　An universal history, [Ancient Part], "Additions to the Universal History in Seven Volumes in Folio," 1 vol., fol. See p. 101.

376. BARNARD, SIR JOHN.　Considerations . . . on the national debt.

377A. CHAPONE, SARAH KIRKHAM.　Remarks on Mrs. Muilman's Letter to the . . . Earl of Chesterfield.

378. CHURCH, THOMAS.　A vindication of the miraculous powers . . . of the Christian church.

379. DELANY, PATRICK.　Twenty sermons on social duties. See Nos. 217, 346.

380. HOUSE OF COMMONS. See p. 76.

381. RICHARDSON, SAMUEL.　Letters written to and for particular friends, 4th ed.

382. ——.　Meditations collected from the sacred books.

383. SMITH, JOSHUA.　A select manual of divine meditations, 4th ed.

383A. YOUNG, EDWARD.　The complaint, 12mo.

1751.　384. ANON.　Prologue, and epilogue, to . . . Romeo and Juliet.

386. FIELDING, SARAH.　The governess, 3rd ed.

387. HOUSE OF COMMONS. See p. 76.

388. LEAPOR, MARY. Poems upon several occasions, Vol. II.

389. RICHARDSON, SAMUEL. Clarissa, 3rd ed., 8 vols., 12mo.

390. ——, 4th ed., 7 vols., 8 vo.

391. ——. Letters and passages restored.

392. SKELTON, PHILIP. Deism revealed, 2nd ed., 2 vols. [The second edition of *Ophiomaches*, No. 373.]

393. YOUNG, EDWARD. The complaint, 12mo.

1752.

394. BYROM, JOHN. An epistle to a gentleman of the Temple, [2nd ed.?].

395. ——. Enthusiasm.

396. HOUSE OF COMMONS. See p. 76.

397. LAW, WILLIAM. The way to divine knowlege.

398. LENNOX, CHARLOTTE. The female Quixote, 2 vols.

399. ——, 2nd ed., 2 vols.

399A. MILLER, PHILIP. The gardeners dictionary, 6th ed., 2 vols. in 1.

400. RICHARDSON, SAMUEL. Letters to and for particular friends, 5th ed.

401. THE ROYAL SOCIETY. Diplomata et statuta Regalis Societatis. See p. 73.

402. SPENCE, JOSEPH. Crito.

403. ——. A particular account of the Emperor of China's garden, tr. from Jean Dennis Attiret.

1753.

404. AESOP. Aesop's fables, ed. Richardson, [3rd ed.?].

404A. CHAMBERS, EPHRAIM. Supplement to Mr. Chambers' Cyclopaedia, 2 vols.

404B. CHEYNE, GEORGE. An essay on regimen, 3rd ed. [A third issue.]

405. COLLIER, JANE. An essay on the art of ingeniously tormenting.

406. DEFOE, DANIEL. A tour thro' the whole island of Great Britain, 5th ed., 4 vols., ed. Richardson.

407. EDWARDS, THOMAS. An account of the trial of the letter Y alias Y.

408. ——. The canons of criticism, 5th ed.

409. HERVEY, JAMES. The cross of Christ.

410. ——. Meditations and contemplations, 10th ed., 2 vols.

411. HOUSE OF COMMONS. See p. 76.

412. LELAND, JOHN. Reflections on the late Lord Boling-broke's Letters on . . . history.
413. ——, 2nd ed.
414. RICHARDSON, SAMUEL. An address to the public.
414A. ——. The case of Samuel Richardson.
415. SHEBBEARE, JOHN. A love epistle.
416. SPENCE, JOSEPH. Moralities.
417. YOUNG, EDWARD. The brothers.
418. ——. The brothers. [A variant issue.]

1754. 419. ANON. An universal history, [Ancient Part], Vol. XXI, 8vo. See p. 101.
421. DELANY, PATRICK. Sixteen discourses.
421A. GUTHRIE, WILLIAM. The friends, 2 vols.
422. HIGHMORE, JOSEPH. A critical examination of . . . two paintings . . . at Whitehall.
423. HOUSE OF COMMONS. See p. 76.
424. JEFFREYS, GEORGE. Miscellanies.
425. RICHARDSON, SAMUEL. An address to the public.
426. ——. Copy of a Letter to a lady.
427. ——. The history of Sir Charles Grandison, 7 vols., 12mo.
428. ——, 2nd ed., 6 vols., 8vo.
429. ——, 3rd ed., 7 vols., 12mo.
430. ——. Pamela, 7th ed., Vols. I, II; 5th ed., Vols. III, IV. [A third issue of the second edition.]
431. SKELTON, PHILIP. Discourses, 2 vols.

1755. 432. CHAMBERLAYNE, JOHN. Magnae Britanniae notitia, [38th ed. of Southern Part; 17th ed. of Northern Part].
433. CHANDLER, MARY. The description of Bath, 7th ed.
434. DALTON, JOHN. A descriptive poem.
435. HOUSE OF COMMONS. See p. 76.
436. LELAND, JOHN. A view of the principal deistical writers, 2 vols. [Vol. I, 1754, was not printed by Richardson.]
437. RICHARDSON, SAMUEL. A collection of . . . sentiments.
438. ——. Letters written to and for particular friends, 6th ed.
439. YOUNG, EDWARD. The centaur not fabulous.

440. ——, 2nd ed.

441. ——, 3rd ed.

441A. ——. The complaint, 8vo.

441B. ——. The complaint, 12mo.

1756. 442. BARDWELL, THOMAS. The practice of painting . . . made easy.

443. BLACKLOCK, THOMAS. Poems, 2nd ed.

444. ——, 3rd ed.

445. BOWER, ARCHIBALD. Mr. Archibald Bower's affidavit.

446. HOUSE OF COMMONS. See p. 76.

447. LELAND, JOHN. A supplement to the . . . deistical writers.

448. ——. Reflections on the late Lord Bolingbroke's Letters on . . . history, 3rd ed.

449. PECKARD, PETER. A dissertation on Revelations, Chap. XI. Ver. 13.

450. ——. Observations on the doctrine of an intermediate state.

451. RICHARDSON, SAMUEL. The history of Sir Charles Grandison, 4th ed., Vol. VII only.

452. SHEBBEARE, JOHN. A love epistle, 2nd ed. [A second issue.]

453. YOUNG, EDWARD. The complaint.

1757. 453A. BAILEY, WILLIAM. A treatise on . . . the poor in workhouses.

454. BOWER, ARCHIBALD. Mr. Bower's answer to a new charge.

455. ——. Mr. Bower's answer to a scurrilous pamphlet.

456. ——. Mr. Bower's reply to a scurrilous libel.

457. ——. The second part of Mr. Bower's answer.

458. CONYBEARE, JOHN. Sermons, 2 vols.

459. DUNCOMBE, JOHN, ed. The works of Horace, Vol. I.

460. DYER, JOHN. The fleece.

461. FIELDING, SARAH. The lives of Cleopatra and Octavia.

462. HOUSE OF COMMONS. See p. 76.

463. LELAND, JOHN. A view of the principal deistical writers, 3rd ed., 2 vols.

464. ——. Reflections on the late Lord Bolingbroke's Letters . . . on history, 4th ed.

465. WILSON, THOMAS.   A review of the project for building a new square at Westminster.
466. YOUNG, EDWARD.   Works, 4 vols.
467. ——.   The centaur not fabulous, 4th ed.

1758.   468. ANON.   An universal history, "Proposals for Publishing the Modern Part of the Universal History."
470. CARTER, ELIZABETH, ed.   All the works of Epictetus.
471. EDWARDS, THOMAS.   The canons of criticism, 6th ed.
472. FIELDING, SARAH.   The lives of Cleopatra and Octavia, 2nd ed.
473. HOUSE OF COMMONS. See p. 76.
474. HYDE, HENRY, *Viscount Cornbury*.   The mistakes.
475. LELAND, JOHN.   Serious reflections on the present state of things.
475A. LENNOX, CHARLOTTE.   Henrietta, 2 vols.
476. YOUNG, EDWARD.   An argument drawn from the circumstances of Christ's death.
477. ——.   The complaint.

1759.   478. ANON.   An universal history, [Modern Part], Vols. I–IV, fol.
479. ——, Vols. I–XIII, 8vo. See p. 103.
480. ACHERLEY, ROGER.   The Britannic constitution, 2nd ed. [A third issue.]
481. DELANY, PATRICK.   An historical account of the . . . reign of David, 4th ed., 2 vols.
481A. DUNCOMBE, JOHN, ed.   The works of Horace, Vol. II. See No. 459.
482. FIELDING, SARAH.   The history of the Countess of Dellwyn, 2 vols.
483. HOUSE OF COMMONS. See p. 76.
483A. JOANNES, CHRYSOSTOMUS, *Saint*.   St. Chrysostom of the priesthood, tr. Bunce.
484. PECKARD, PETER.   Observations on Mr. Fleming's Survey.
485. RICHARDSON, SAMUEL.   Clarissa, 4th ed., 8 vols., 12mo.
486. SPENCE, JOSEPH.   A parallel; in the manner of Plutarch, 2nd ed.

486A. SYDENHAM, FLOYER. A synopsis . . . of the works of Plato.

487. YOUNG, EDWARD. Conjectures on original composition.

488. ——, 2nd ed.

1760. 489. ANON. The histories of some of the penitents in the Magdalen-House, 2 vols.

490. ——. An universal history, [Modern Part], Vols. V–VII, fol.

491. ——, Vols. XIV–XXIV, 8vo. See p. 103.

492. BURN, RICHARD. A digest of the militia laws.

493. HOUSE OF COMMONS. See p. 76.

494. LYTTELTON, GEORGE, *1st Baron Lyttelton*. Dialogues of the dead.

495. ——, 2nd ed.

495A. ——, 3rd ed.

496. YOUNG, EDWARD. The complaint.

1761. 497. ANON. A general system of the laws concerning bankrupts, 2 vols.

498. ——. Proposals for a new edition of the Statutes at Large from Magna Charta to the end of the last Parliament.

498A. ——. Treatise of distresses, replevins, and avowries, 4th ed.

499. ——. An universal history, [Modern Part], Vols. VIII, IX, fol.

500. ——, Vols. XXV–XXXIII, 8vo. See p. 103.

501. BATHURST, HENRY, *2nd Earl Bathurst*. The theory of evidence.

502. BURN, RICHARD. The justice of the peace, 5th ed.

503. FIELDING, SIR JOHN. Extracts from . . . the penal laws.

504. GILBERT, SIR GEOFFREY. The history and practice of civil actions, 2nd ed.

504A. LENNOX, CHARLOTTE. Henrietta, 2nd ed., 2 vols.

505. HOUSE OF COMMONS. See p. 76.

506. PLOWDEN, EDMUND. The commentaries, 2 parts in 1 vol.

507. RICHARDSON, SAMUEL. Pamela, 8th ed., 4 vols. [Vols. III and IV are in reality a fourth reprinting of these volumes in 12mo. This edition was published in 1761, though dated 1762.]

508. SAINT-GERMAN, CHRISTOPHER. Doctor and student, 16th ed.

509. YOUNG, EDWARD. Resignation.

1762. 511. ANON. An universal history, [Modern Part], Vols. X–XII, fol.

512. ——,Vols. XXXIV–XXXVII, 8vo. See p. 103.

513. CUNNINGHAM, TIMOTHY. The practice of a justice of peace, 2 vols.

514. DEFOE, DANIEL. A tour thro' the whole island of Great Britain, 6th ed., 4 vols., ed. Richardson.

515. RICHARDSON, SAMUEL. The history of Sir Charles Grandison, 4th ed., Vol. VII. [A second issue.]

516. WESTON, WILLIAM. New dialogues of the dead.

CHAPTER IX

Richardson's
Printers' Ornaments

I

VERY few of the books that came from Richardson's press carried the phrase in the imprint: "Printed by S. Richardson." [1] In only one volume does his name appear in a colophon. Consequently we must seek other sorts of evidence if we are to trace his activities as a master printer. His letters and those of his friends are of some assistance; occasionally an advertisement in a newspaper provides a clue. But I soon decided that if I were to succeed in making a sizeable list of the books that he printed, I should have to resort to internal evidence. The evidence provided by printers' ornaments turned out to be the most reliable and the most generally useful.

In the first stages of my investigation I found that Richardson himself was prepared to certify that his ornaments were a means of identifying the work of his press. He was engaged in printing the first edition of his novel, *Sir Charles Grandison*, when he learned that Irish booksellers were preparing a pirated edition to be sold in Dublin and perhaps to be exported to England and Scotland. On hearing of this scheme, he wrote that "the Want of the same Ornaments, or Initial Letters [factotums], in each

Vol. will help to discover them [if exported into England], although they should put the Booksellers Names that I have affixed. I have got some Friends to write down to Scotland, to endeavour to seize their Edition, if offered to be imported." [2] Richardson believed that two of his own workmen had sent to Dublin the text of his novel in sheets. On certain of these sheets would be impressions of his ornaments, but he had no fear that Irish printers would be able to disguise the fact of piracy by using duplicates of them. He had been informed that four Irish presses were engaged in the printing of the first six volumes of *Grandison*, and that the seventh volume was being printed at a fifth press. [3] Even so, he shows no hesitancy in asserting that none of the five presses owned ornaments which were duplicates of his; and my examination of the pirated edition that was printed by these five presses bears out his conviction. Copies of printers' ornaments, sometimes made in close imitation of the originals, did exist; but such copies can be detected if the original and the imitation are placed side by side.

Richardson himself was well aware of the existence of imitations; and when he pointed out that the Irish pirated edition would not contain the same ornaments, or factotums, he did not mean that Irish printers could have no imitations of his headpieces, tailpieces, or initial letters. He merely stated that no two presses could have ornaments which would give the same impression. He knew, for example, that a London printer had pirated an edition of one of the parts of Edward Young's *Night-Thoughts*, at the time when the genuine edition had just issued from his press; and that this piratical printer had used imitations of his ornaments. Young wrote to him on the occasion: "Mr. Cave [the publisher of the *Gentleman's Magazine*] sent me last week a specimen of a spurious copy of the Seventh Night, which, as to letters and ornaments, mimics your's." [4] Edward Cave, a printer by trade, had recognized the attempt of a pirate to palm off his edition as genuine by using ornaments similar to those of

Richardson; and Cave had no doubt that Young, with no experience in the printing trade, could detect the attempt to deceive if he compared the two editions. I have not been able to locate a copy of the pirated edition of Young, but I have been able to place side by side copies of the genuine and the pirated edition of Susanna Centlivre's *The Gamester,* and to note the attempt of the pirate to deceive by putting the names of the same booksellers in the imprint and by using an ornament which is an imitation of one that Richardson used in the genuine edition.[5]

Richardson himself had copies made of some of his own ornaments when the originals showed signs of wear, or became broken or chipped. Reproductions of several of the ornaments which Richardson had copied are provided in a later section of this chapter.[6] It seems evident, therefore, that when Richardson said that the Dublin pirates could not supply themselves with the "same ornaments," he meant that no exact copies existed, and that officers instructed to seize sets of the novel exported from Ireland could walk into a bookshop, pick up a copy of *Grandison,* and by looking at the ornaments, decide whether they were confronted with a book printed by Richardson, or with one from another press. If this procedure were possible in 1753, it should be possible now.

That care should be taken in the use of printers' ornaments as evidence becomes at once apparent to anyone who has tried to draw conclusions from them. This is especially so if one is concerned with books printed in the eighteenth century, for practically all of the studies that have been made of ornaments throw light on printing practices only before 1640. In making deductions from ornaments used in the sixteenth or early seventeenth centuries, one finds comfort in the well-substantiated generalizations of such competent English bibliographers as McKerrow, Pollard, Plomer, and Morison; and one may secure illumination from a considerable number of articles concerned with the history of particular books. But only the most casual remarks have been made about printers' ornaments of the eighteenth century.

About eighteenth-century printers themselves comparatively little is known. During the first half of this century the bookseller overshadowed the printer. It is the booksellers—Lintot, Dodsley, Millar, Longman, Curll, Osborne—whose names survive in connection with the trade. "Printer Cave," as Carlyle called him, is known because of his relations with a famous magazine and a more famous lexicographer; William Bowyer lives—if he lives at all— because of the indefatigable efforts of the anecdotal John Nichols; and Richardson's press is studied because he was the author of the century's most popular novels. The latter half of the century marked the rise of presses which took a pride in their products comparable to that of some of the seventeenth-century presses. But with the development of the manufacture of English paper and of English type, bookmaking became more standardized than it had been in the previous century. Printing shops multiplied when legislative control was removed, and printing itself became a trade rather than a craft. The printer no longer had the incentive which led a proud craftsman to associate his name with a book. Therefore, unless the account books of a printer have survived, we know very little about his activities.

With the printer content with anonymity, the need for information about ornaments becomes imperative, for these ornaments constitute in many instances the only way at our disposal for identifying the work of a press. Unhappily the general information about such ornaments is fragmentary. No attempt has been made to collect and reproduce them; no history of the changes in taste reflected by the change in their character has been written. Because they are for the most part work executed to keep an engraver's pot boiling, they are usually unsigned. I have included in an appendix a list of a few signatures that I have found on eighteenth-century ornaments, but many of these are merely initials, and the names for which they stand are unknown to me. In books appearing in the first half of the century, I have noted a number of ornaments signed "F.H." and I think there can be little doubt that these are the work of Francis Hoffman. Stanley Morison, in an appendix to his *English Newspaper*, provides what little is known of Hoffman.[7] Morison reproduces some of his ornaments and indicates that they were extensively copied by other engravers. Two of these reproductions, similar in conception, seem to have suggested to the engraver the design for Richardson's ornament No. 68;[8] and *An Epistle to Mr. A. Pope*, 1732, contains an imitation of one of Hoffman's ornaments. Henry Plomer in his *English Printers' Ornaments* reproduces an ornament signed "F.H." and "M.M."; one signed "I.L."; and some of the work of Michael Burghers who worked for the Oxford press from 1680 to 1725.[9] In the main, however, Plomer is least illuminating about the ornaments of the eighteenth century.

In particular, Plomer is confusing in what he says about the physical nature of eighteenth-century headpieces and tailpieces. A reviewer of Plomer's work maintains that Plomer does not distinguish between engravings and printers' flowers:

The first is represented by the work of the engraver, where an artist cuts in relief on a block of wood or metal an individual design. There is but one such block, though it may be copied and recopied when worn out. The art antedated typographic printing and its application in book printing was very early. The second art [i.e., the making of printers' flowers] consisted in the application of punch-cutting and typefounding technique to the reproduction of decorative units, of which the printer might have at his command, not one example, but fifty or a thousand. This was a later development of particular typographic interest.[10]

The severity of this criticism does not seem to me entirely justified, but Plomer does not make it clear that he understands how ornaments were made. At one point in his book (p. 8), he cites Luckombe's *Concise History of the Origin and Progress of Printing*, 1770, to the effect that printers' flowers were "variously employed, till cutting in wood was come to perfection; when that art was eagerly encouraged, and flowers not regarded. From that time till very lately, nothing has been thought to grace the first page of a work so well as head-pieces cut in wood." At another point (pp. 28–29), Plomer says that "with the opening of the eighteenth century . . . in place of the single block woodcut head and tail pieces . . . were substituted metal blocks of a more ornate character." Plomer apparently did not find these statements inconsistent. McKerrow says that metal blocks "seem at all times to have been the exception, and that wood, in spite of its manifest inferiority from the point of view of durability, seems always to have been preferred." [11]

I think there is no doubt that Richardson's ornaments were wood blocks. Cracks develop in them, and McKerrow is positive that the presence of a crack proves that the block was made of wood. Furthermore, these cracks run up and down, and McKerrow thinks that it was "a general if not a universal rule that the grain of the blocks should run vertically," thus insuring that the cracks would not ordinarily run across the block.[12] Even if Richardson's ornaments were cut on metal instead of wood, McKerrow recognizes that they would be just as useful for the purpose to which I want to put them.[13]

In order to be doubly sure of the reliability of evidence from ornaments, I first located the ornaments in books that we know, from external evidence, came from Richardson's press. I then sought to associate an ornament with his shop over a period of years, and noted as many examples of the ornament's use as could be found. In this way, the condition of the block could be studied. The sharp lines which may be found at an early date in the ornament's history gradually become blurred; a small piece is broken off; or a border rule is removed after cracking. Vertical cracks appear and can usually be noted in successive appearances of the ornament, though sometimes a cracked block is locked up so tightly in the chase that a defect will temporarily disappear, only to reappear later. Damage to an ornament makes it more readily distinguishable from its imitations.

As a negative check to my conclusions, I have examined the work of a number of printers contemporary with Richardson, in order to be sure that the ornaments used in these books are not those found in books from Richardson's press. I have included in an appendix a selected list of the work of other presses than Richardson's. Books on this list all contain printers' ornaments. They can be used as starting points for studies similar to this one. Eventually I hope to provide more material evidence for identifying the work of the printers on this list, and of some thirty or forty other printers, many of whose names do not appear in Plomer's *Dictionary*.

Since Richardson mentioned the ornaments from *Grandison* as reliable evidence of his printing, I have chosen an ornament from this novel to serve as illustration of the method employed in this study. Two editions of this novel were published simultaneously, one in eights and one in twelves. The Dublin piracy was printed from sheets of the octavo edition.[14] On the first page of the text in the first volume of the genuine edition in eights, Richardson used an ornament which I have numbered 103. I reproduce it here:

This headpiece is obviously well worn, and as we shall soon discover, its border rule has been cut away. A portion of the left-hand upper corner is missing; and a part of the line that completed the face of the central figure has worn away. The amount of fine detail in the design is considerable, so that any attempt to copy it would make detection fairly easy. I therefore chose this ornament as a point of departure.

I first sought to find it in a book printed earlier than *Grandison* and traceable to Richardson's press through external evidence. I found it in an essay of Aaron Hill's that he had sent to Richardson's press in 1737 and that was published in 1738 under the title *An Enquiry into the Merit of Assassination: with a View to the Character of Caesar.* The ornament is used twice in this pamphlet. At this date, sixteen years before the printing of *Grandison,* the border rule is missing and the blemish in the face of the central figure has already developed.

With these dates fixed, I then began a search for the ornament in books printed earlier than 1738 and later than 1753. The vicissitudes of this search need not be described here, nor do I need to indicate the order in which I found the other books that contained the ornament in question. In the course of the search, however, I discovered certain bibliographical uses to which printers' ornaments might be put. These uses, familiar to bibliographers of early printed books, have never been widely exploited in describing books printed as late as the eighteenth century.

The earliest use which I have found of this ornament from *Grandison* is in Defoe's *New Family Instructor,* 1727. The border rule is here intact, though close examination discloses a slight crack in the upper rule, a little more than an eighth of an inch from the left-hand side. This slight defect is to become increasingly noticeable; in fact, by 1728 it can be easily detected. Examination of so-called "second" and "fourth" editions of this work of Defoe, published in 1732 and in 1742, proved momentarily embarrassing, for the condition of the ornament in these later editions was precisely as it was in 1727. These "editions," however, turned out to be merely reissues of the sheets printed in 1727, with new title pages.

This instance was not the only one in which the condition of the ornament seemed to argue against the apparent facts in the case. In Richard Savage's *Wanderer,* dated 1729 in the imprint and advertised in *Fog's Weekly Journal* on 18 January 1729, the ornament was used on p. 1, where its condition is little changed from that in Defoe's work of 1727. It is reproduced below:

The very small break, noticeable in Defoe, can be seen here in the upper left-hand corner, but the ornament shows none of its later defects. I had found, however, that in three books, dated 1728 in the imprint, a more noticeable break had developed at the point where the ornament had been slightly weakened in 1727. This discrepancy could be accounted for if a delay had occurred between the printing and the publishing of Savage's poem, and if the books dated 1728 were printed late rather than early in that year.

An advertisement in the concluding pages of *The Wanderer* for the eleventh edition of Fénelon's *Adventures of Telemachus* suggested that these pages were printed late in 1727, for the twelfth edition of Fénelon's work appeared in 1728. The reason for the delay in publication is provided by Johnson in his *Life of Savage:* "[Savage] sold the copy [of *The Wanderer*] for ten guineas, of which he afterwards returned two, that the two last sheets of the work might be reprinted, of which he had in his absence intrusted the correction to a friend, who was too indolent to perform it with accuracy." [15] Johnson is witness to the "superstitious regard" which Savage paid to the correction of proof: "[He] often altered, revised, recurred to his first reading or punctuation, and again adopted the alteration." In this instance Savage was willing to sacrifice a fifth of the sum that he had received for the poem in order to have the last two sheets—those corrected in his absence—completely reprinted. The headpiece from *Grandison* is on one of the sheets that were not reprinted. I think we may safely conclude that the poem was originally printed early in 1728, or perhaps late in 1727.

Judging from the condition of this ornament, we should infer that the three books, dated 1728 and containing it, were printed after *The Wanderer*, or in the latter half of the year. One of them, Jonathan Smedley's *Gulliveriana*, contains an article, perhaps written by Smedley, that was first printed in the *Journal* on 4 July 1728. Another—Part III of Nathanael Salmon's *New Survey of Great Britain*—was published on 19 December 1728, the second part having been published on 15 August 1728.[16] The third book of this year was John Dennis' *Remarks on Mr. Pope's Rape of the Lock*, certainly published after the *Dunciad*, which appeared on 18 May 1728. As a matter of fact, *The Progress of Dulness*, published on 11 June 1728, contains a few comments on the *Rape of the Lock*, after which its author adds: "But, I shall explain no farther, since Mr. Dennis in a short time intends to give the Publick an exact *Dissection* of this chaste *Performance*."[17] Again, I think we may conclude that this book, as well as the works of Smedley and Salmon, was printed after Savage's poem.

Richardson's further relations with Smedley, Salmon, and Dennis I have discussed elsewhere.[18] During the years between 1728 and 1738 I found the ornament of *Grandison* in works of a number of men for whom Richardson printed extensively and among whom can be found friends and acquaintances. The ornament was used in a reprint of the essays from Aaron Hill's *Plain Dealer*, printed for Richardson and his brother-in-law, Allington Wilde; in Philip Miller's *Gardeners Kalendar*; in Patrick Delany's *Revelation Examin'd with Candour*; in Dr. George Cheyne's *English Malady*; in John Conybeare's *Defence of Revealed Religion*; in Thomas Morell's edition of *The Canterbury Tales of Chaucer*. In these books and in other books of the same period the ornament was used, and with continued use

the defects become more and more apparent. To illustrate the
progress of these defects, I provide reproductions from books
published in 1729, 1734, and 1740:

From Samuel Madden's *Themistocles*.

From John Balguy's *Collection of Tracts*.

From Elizabeth Rowe's *Friendship in Death*.

In the third of these reproductions it can be seen that Richardson has removed the border rules in order to eliminate the un-
sightliness of the breaks and at the same time preserve the
ornament for further use. In this condition, however, he used it far
less frequently. I have found it in only six books that he printed
in the fourteen years between 1738 and 1743. One of them is
the work of Elizabeth Rowe from which the reproduction is

taken. It was also used in a volume of the *Miscellaneous Works* of Elizabeth and Thomas Rowe; in a play that he printed for Thomas Spateman; and in works of Thomas Birch, William Law, and Joseph Spence. Existing letters link Richardson with the last three of these authors. In the years following *Grandison* I have found the ornament used only three times, and in each case in the printing of a work of his friend, John Leland.

At least two imitations of this ornament were in existence, and were used in books published between 1744 and 1755. The imitations were made from impressions of the ornament after Richardson had removed the border rule. I have reproduced below two states of one of these imitations, and one of the other.

Imitation A. (First state)

From John Smith's *Chronicon Rusticum-Commerciale; or, Memoirs of Wool*, 2 vols., 1747.

Imitation A. (Second state)

From Colley Cibber's *Apology for the Life of Mr. Colley Cibber*, 3rd ed., 1750.

The engravers, in cutting the hind legs of the two small animals, provided a base for them to rest upon. This base in the original had been provided by the border rule. The imitation that I have labeled "A" became damaged between 1747 and 1750, as

Imitation B.

From *The Frenchman in London,* 1755. [A translation of
Louis de Boissy's *Le François à Londres,* 1727]

can be seen by an inspection of the upper right-hand corner. The
books containing "A" may have been printed by Henry Woodfall, for this ornament was used in William Havard's *Regulus,*
printed by Woodfall for Vaillant in 1744.

A history of all of Richardson's ornaments could be supplied
in the same detail as that provided for this particular headpiece.
These histories, however, would serve no useful purpose. I have
provided brief notes on the other ornaments, listing by an assigned number most of the books in which they appear, describing some of the states that make identification easier, and giving
references by short titles to books in which I have found imitations. Errors, I feel sure, have crept into these notes, but I have
tried to reduce them to a minimum. This work has of necessity
been conducted over a period of years, and has led me to many
libraries in England and America. During its early stages I was
not so familiar with Richardson's ornaments, nor so wary of
close imitations. I only hope that I have retraced most of the
steps taken during this period.

The general principles underlying this investigation are, I feel,
sound; they are applicable to studies of the work of other printers. Again and again, when external evidence had led me to
suspect that a book was printed by Richardson, I found his
ornaments in the book. Again and again, I assigned a book to
Richardson's press on the evidence of the ornaments and later
discovered external evidence to support the assignment. Practically all of the books assigned to Richardson's press by other

scholars contain his ornaments as corroboratory evidence. But there are exceptions. For reasons that I have stated elsewhere I do not believe that Richardson printed an edition of Edward Young's *Night-Thoughts* in 1749, though this work has been ascribed to his press by John Nichols.[19] W. B. Thorne attributed the six volumes of Churchill's *Collection of Voyages* to Richardson, but the first four volumes are merely reissues of the work, originally published in 1704.[20] Charles Bucke, the biographer of Mark Akenside, said that the manuscript of Akenside's *Pleasures of Imagination* was bought by Dodsley and "placed in the hands of Richardson, the celebrated author of *Pamela*, *Sir Charles Grandison*, and *Clarissa Harlowe*, to print." [21] He gives no evidence for this unsupported statement. The poem presents a bibliographical tangle,[22] and I am not sure that I have seen every state of the first edition, but those that I have seen contain ornaments belonging to John Hughs, a printer who did much of Dodsley's printing. Bucke includes in his biography a letter from Akenside to Richardson which refers to corrections in proof, but these corrections are for an article that Bucke did not identify, published by Akenside in the *Philosophical Transactions* of the Royal Society.[23] Dorothy Brewster said that Richardson did not print Aaron Hill's *Gideon*, but when I found Richardson's ornaments in *Gideon*, I checked Miss Brewster's reference in the Forster Manuscripts and found that she had made an error in transcription.[24] It was Hill's *Merope* that Richardson did not print. McKillop leaves us in some doubt as to whether Richardson printed Morgan's *History of Algiers*.[25] In 1726 Richardson had offered to transmit to Morgan any "memoirs proper to illustrate this work," but the work itself was printed by James Bettenham in 1728 and 1729.

Books other than those I have listed can undoubtedly be found; and some of my ascriptions may be successfully challenged. But I feel confident that the list which I have provided represents items thoroughly characteristic of Richardson's printing methods, and sufficiently indicative of his tastes to be illuminating, once he was enabled to escape from "the tyranny of the booksellers," and to exercise a degree of choice over the men with whom he elected to do business.

II

Reproductions of many of Richardson's ornaments are provided on the following pages. The numbers assigned to these ornaments are merely a ready means of referring to them in other sections of this book. The pair of dates that follow the number delimit the period in which I have found the ornament in use. The series of numbers below the reproductions indicate the books in which the ornament may be found. These books may be identified by referring to the list (pp. 229–250) where the books are arranged chronologically by short titles. More information about each book may be found in the list (pp. 145–228) in which the books are arranged alphabetically by authors. In the series of numbers below the reproductions the number preceded by an asterisk designates the book from which the reproduction was taken.

Following these numbers is a brief note on the condition of the ornament at various periods. The information in these notes is for the purpose of distinguishing readily between one of Richardson's ornaments and an imitation of it. I have given this information in more detail in the instances where identification is more difficult.

Finally, I have provided the short titles of some of the books in which I have found imitations of Richardson's ornaments.

These reproductions do not include all of the ornaments that I have identified as belonging to Richardson. They represent, however, a generous and characteristic sampling. In a few instances where books have proved very difficult of access, I have been unable to make a final check for this section. I believe that the ornaments reproduced appear in all the books in which I have indicated that they appeared; they may, however, appear in a few other volumes besides these noted. Though I regret this margin of error, I do not see how it can invalidate my central thesis.

No. 1 (1726–1744)

Found in nos. 45, *49, 54, 74A, 87, 107, 114, 133, 135, 323.

By 1734 the tops of the birds' heads begin to show signs of wear; by 1744 this wear is evident, and the tips of the birds' tails are failing to print.

Imitations: In *Darius's Feast*, 1734; John Dalton, *An Epistle to a Young Nobleman*, 1736 (a crude imitation, surrounded by a decorative border as integral part of the headpiece); David Mallet, *Of Verbal Criticism*, 1733 (a much closer imitation).

No. 2 (1721–1738)

Found in nos. 8, 21, 29, 45, 49, 74A, 75, 89, 135, 136, 145B, 146, *195, 227.

In 1721 this ornament is not new; by 1723 the border rule has been crushed in the lower right-hand corner, and a break has developed in the top rule, just left of center. By 1734 the inner rule at the bottom shows two definite breaks where weakening has been evident for some time. The snubbed lower right-hand corner breaks by 1738. Imitations: None found.

No. 3 (1727–1738)

Found in nos. *49, 75, 97A, 135, 159, 175A, 175B, 185, 227.

This headpiece has an elliptical opening in the center in which the printer may place any one of a number of smaller ornaments. These smaller ornaments (e.g., no. 95, below) are sometimes used as an inset in this headpiece, or in ornament no. 4; or they may be used as tailpieces.

Imitations: In *Sarah, the Quaker, to Lothario*, 2nd ed., 1728; *An Epistle to the Little Satyrist of Twickenham*, 1733 (an imitation, longer and narrower, and with no provision for a movable center).

No. 4 (1723–1741)

Found in nos. 27, 29, 34, 45, *49, 50 (the inset only), 71, 75, 89, 97A, 104, 119, 278.

This ornament, like no. 3, is designed with a removable center. It is not new in 1723; and in 1727 two slight breaks in the rule outlining the inset may be seen. By 1729 a defect in the inside rule at the upper left-hand corner is noticeable, and becomes increasingly worse. Imitations: None found.

No. 5 (1721–1741)

Found in nos. 8, 9, 16, 17, 18, 49, 81, 86, 99, 126, *166, 175A, 175B, 184, 185, 204, 205, 216, 249, 271, 288.

In 1721 this ornament, while not new, is in good condition, except for a slight break in the narrow border rule, near the lower left-hand corner. This break grows increasingly noticeable and by 1733 a part of the design in this corner shows damage. In this year a break is easily detectable in the upper inside rule, to the left of the central figure. All of these defects, including signs of bad wear on the side border rules, may be seen in the reproduction.

Imitation: In Alexander Pope, *An Essay on Man*, Part I, 1st ed., 1st issue, 1733 (an imitation with the border rule curving above the central figure).

No. 6 (1723–1726)

Found in nos. *16, 17, 18, 43.

This headpiece has a removable center. I have found few instances of its use, though the books in which it appears contain other ornaments of Richardson's which he used for a number of years. Imitations: None found.

No. 7 (1727–1759)

Found in nos. 52, 55, 65, 66, 70, 73A, 77, 78, 79, 80, 88, 116, 165, 168, 196, 217A, 250, *268A, 310, 326, 352, 363, 365, 368, 388, 444, 463, 464, 481A.

Defects develop at three points on this ornament, but Richardson continued to use it for many years. When the defects became clearly noticeable, Richardson had a copy made (no. 8), but he did not discard the damaged original. By 1735 one can detect a break beginning about one-quarter inch from the right side, which by 1739 has resulted in the disappearance of a portion of the design. A break from top to bottom, about one-half inch from the left side, develops early, but it is sometimes obscured by fitting the ornament tightly in the chase. A third break eventually results in separating the left wing of the bird from its body. All these defects show in the reproduction.

Imitations: In Stephen Duck, *Poems on Several Subjects*, 6th ed., 1730; Eustace Budgell, *A Letter to Cleomenes*, 1731. I have made no attempt to distinguish between imitations of this ornament and that of no. 8, below.

No. 8 (1736–1757)

Found in nos. 190, 192, 211, 228, 242, 272, *306, 315, 329, 388, 390, 433, 444, 453, 463, 464.

The difference between this ornament and no. 7 can clearly be seen by observing the position of the bird's head and the bird's bill. No serious defects appear until 1755 when a break is noticeable across the body of the bird. This design was popular with eighteenth century printers, and many variations upon it can be found.

Imitations: See no. 7.

No. 9 (1721–1735)

Found in nos. 10, 13, 23, 72, *80, 165, 175.

In 1721 this headpiece is not new: a defect may be easily noted in a portion of the design in the extreme upper right-hand corner. By 1723 a similar defect appears in the lower right-hand corner. In 1729 the border rule on the left side shows the dent which can be clearly seen in the reproduction.

Imitations: None found.

No. 10 (1736–1757)

Found in nos. 190, 192, 211, 242, 245A, 264, 272, 279, *306, 315, 329, 358, 363, 390, 417, 428, 433, 453A.

This ornament shows general wear throughout the years. I have noted no particular defects, because it can readily be distinguished from imitations. Richardson may have had this fact in mind when he chose to use it in his large paper edition of *Grandison*. (See p. 251.) This novel was pirated in Dublin. The presence of Richardson's ornaments in the genuine edition would make it possible to detect sets of the piracy, if these sets were exported into England.

Imitations: In William Romaine, *No Justification by the Law of Nature*, 1741; John Dalrymple, 2nd Earl of Stair, *The Memorial of the E[arl] of S[tair]*, 1744.

No. 11 (1727–1737)

Found in nos. *47, 59, 76, 90, 129, 148A, 180, 206, 218.

In 1727 a small break in the top rule, upper left-hand corner, may be found. By 1731 this break has become worse; and by 1734 the border rule is so badly damaged that Richardson removed it entirely. With the border removed, the ornament then looks much like ornament no. 12.

Imitation: In Thomas Gordon, *A Compleat History of the Late Septennial Parliament*, 3rd ed., 1722.

No. 12 (1738–1759)

Found in nos. 223, 255, 276, 289, 312, *335, 355, 399, 405, 410, 441, 472, 482.

This ornament is a copy of no. 11, which Richardson seems to have had made after he had trimmed off the border rule from no. 11. The treatment of the lines radiating outward from the figure in the center enables one to identify this headpiece without difficulty.

Imitations: None found.

No. 13 (1728–1762)

Found in nos. 65, 157, 164, 210, *232, 238, 238A, 245, 267, 287, 295, 312, 337, 421A, 472, 507.

A slight defect in a line radiating upward from the basket of fruit and to the right of center grows increasingly worse through the years. The portions of the design in the upper right-hand and left-hand corners show gradual wear until by 1740 they have both disappeared and the corners are rounded off. In 1754 a crack can be clearly seen on the right side between the bird and the winged boy.

Imitations: In *Original Letters to an Honest Sailor*, [1746]; *An Historical Account of . . . Dr. Archibald Cameron*, 1753; George Whitefield, *The Bishop of London's Pastoral Letter Answer'd*, 1739, printed by W. Trott.

No. 14 (1735–1751)

Found in nos. 164, 171, 178, 187, 285, 286, 289, 295, 298, 326, 354A, 374, 381, 383A, *389.

The reproduction shows a small break in the curving line at the bottom of this headpiece, about one-quarter inch from the left-hand corner. The stem, leading to a leaf over the head of the bird on the upper left, wears thinner and thinner at the point where it joins a blossom. This stem finally becomes completely detached from the blossom, as shown in the reproduction. These defects render the ornament identifiable among the numerous imitations.

Imitations: In Wicardel de Fleury, Marquis de Trevie, *The History of the Abdication of Victor Amedeus II*, 2nd ed., 1732; Daniel Williams, *Practical Discourses*, Vol. II, 1738; Elizabeth and Thomas Rowe, *Miscellaneous Works*, Vol. I, 1739; *A Free Apology in Behalf of the Smugglers*, 1749; *Some Observations on the National Debt*, 1752; William Hay, *Religio Philosophi*, 1753; *Advice from a Bishop*, 1759.

No. 15 (1728–1762)

Found in nos. 65, 150, 166, 179, 263, 280, 308, 326, 331, 337, 348A, 352, 354, 374, 383A, 391, 406, 451, 466, 485, 487, 494, *514, 515.

By 1745 this ornament has cracked across the right-hand side, at the beak of the bird to the extreme right; by 1747 Richardson was forced to remove this right-hand portion, for by then it had become separated from the body of the ornament and could not be held in position in the chase. Hence, an ornament, originally designed for use in octavos, had to be used after 1747 in duodecimos (as in reproduction). By 1757 a leaf in the upper left-hand corner has disappeared.

Imitations: In John Hervey, *Three Pamphlets; Entituled, Observations on the Writings of the Craftsman*, 1730; Ashley Cowper, *The Norfolk Poetical Miscellany*, Vol. II, 1744; Richard Finch, *Free and Impartial Thoughts*, 2nd ed., 1745; Caleb Fleming, *The Devout Laugh*, 1750; Charles Sackville, 2nd Duke of Dorset, *A Treatise Concerning the Militia*, 1752.

No. 16 (1728–1762)

Found in nos. 65, 150, 161, 166, 280, 326, 367A, *368, 378, 390, 416, 432, 437, 445, 457, 465, 516.

A break develops across the upper right-hand portion of the horse-shoe-shaped design in the center. This break finally extends downward across the basket of flowers, but when the ornament is fitted tightly in the chase, the break can be detected only by close observation. By 1755 a break develops in the portion of the design on which the animal to the left is perched.

Imitation: In John Hervey: *Three Pamphlets; Entituled, Observations on the Writings of the Craftsman*, 1730.

No. 17 (1727–1751)

Found in nos. *55, 56, 58, 65, 66, 74, 85, 95, 97, 110, 141, 147, 158, 167, 167A, 170, 183, 201, 208, 217, 217A, 222, 232, 265, 268A, 269, 303, 310, 326, 330, 331, 334, 343, 359, 364, 367A, 390.

The top border rule, at a point about one-half inch from the right-hand corner, shows slight signs of wear in 1727. By 1734 a definite break can be seen at this point. By 1732 a break has appeared in the right-hand side border rule. By 1736 the upper right-hand corner is snubbed. By 1746 the break across the top border rule has extended downward through the bird, located in this corner.

Imitations: In George Carleton, *The Life of Bernard Gilpin*, 5th ed., 1727, printed by W. Roberts; *An Historical View of the . . . Political Writers in Great Britain*, 1740; *A Key to the Business of the Present S[essio]n*, 1742.

No. 18 (1726–1738)

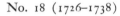

Found in nos. 42, 48, 50, *55, 56, 65, 74, 83, 108, 112, 127, 171, 172, 174, 177, 217A, 232.

By 1729 this ornament (which was not new in 1726) shows a break through the border rule in the lower left-hand corner, extending into the body of the ornament to the left of the small winged figure. A few years later a similar break develops on the right-hand side, and by 1735 Richardson had trimmed off both sides of the headpiece, so that the ornament, originally designed for use in octavos, had to be used in duodecimos. On the last occasion that I found the ornament in use, both sides had been more severely trimmed, so that the winged figures had nothing behind them.

Imitations: In *The Genuine Letters of Mary Queen of Scots to James Earl of Bothwell*, tr. Edward Simmonds, 1726, printed by A. Campbell; *Some Queries to the Author of the Enquiry into the Reasons of the Conduct of Great Britain*, 1727; Walter Aston (?), *The Restauration of King Charles II*, 1732.

No. 19 (1726–1743?)

Found in nos. 42, 50, 52, 70, 94, 110, 122, *134, 151, 162, 170, 200, 219, 250, 252, 256, 268A, 310 (a reissue of 268A?).

This ornament is not new in 1726. In 1727 a thin line, running from the center of the ornament toward the right, strikes the small figure at a point just above the knee. In the 1730's the heavy border rule on the left-hand side shows considerable wear, and by 1734 fails in part to print. These defects may be seen in the reproduction.

Imitation: In Henry Caner, *The Piety of Founding Churches for the Worship of God* (printed by and sold by J. Draper, Boston, Massachusetts), 1749.

No. 20 (1723–1743?)

Found in nos. 14, *26, 40, 41, 50, 61, 65, 69, 72, 97, 111, 121, 134, 137, 168, 170, 201, 251, 268A, 310 (a reissue of 268A?).

This ornament is not new in 1723. It shows, even at that date, slight evidence of a chip in the formal design in the lower left-hand corner. This chip is easily noticeable in the reproduction. A break across the feather which extends to the left toward the head of the left-hand figure can be seen as early as 1728. By 1734 two breaks, one in the upper and the other in the lower border rule, can be found about one and one-half inches from the left-hand side.

Imitations: None found.

No. 21 (1721–1734)

Found in nos. 10, 13, 23, 65, 70A, *80, 137.

This headpiece has a removable center: other small pieces are sometimes used in place of the lion. These removable centers are also used as tailpieces. A break in the upper border rule, one-half inch from the left, makes identification easy. Imitations: None found.

No. 22 (1721–1751)

Found in nos. 10, 13, 23, 39, 72, 73, *80, 92, 144, 272, 388.

In 1721 a break in the inner rule, lower right-hand corner, may be seen. Later breaks appear in the upper rule to the left of the eagle. Imitations: None found.

No. 23 (1745–1756)

Found in nos. 326, 337, 354, 361, 367A, 383A, 403, 427, *429, 450. No particular defects noted. Imitations: None found.

No. 24 (1728–1732)

Found in nos. 66, 85, 96, *108, 111.

Some wear is noticeable in the lower left-hand corner.

Imitations: In *War with Priestcraft*, 1732; Elizabeth Rowe, *The History of Joseph*, 4th ed., 1744; Corbyn Morris, *An Essay . . . Addressed to the Right Honourable Henry Pelham*, 1747, printed by J. Robinson.

No. 25 (1723–1742)

Found in nos. 14, 22, 26, 37, 41, 46, 47, 56, 57, 62, 68, 96, 145, 182, 207, 213, 267, *295.

By 1726 the left-hand side rule has been chipped and the upper left-hand corner snubbed. A defect in the lines forming the clouds in the upper central portion of the design (see reproduction) can be seen clearly by 1727. Signs of wear on the right-hand side rule, developing early, can be seen in an advanced state in the reproduction.

Imitations: None found.

No. 26 (1735–1755)

Found in nos. 157, 180, 206, 218, 232, 238, 238A, 254, 276, *282, 284, 285, 354A, 355, 410, 430, 438.

By 1741 a crack (see reproduction) can be seen across the tip of the animal's tail on the right side of the ornament.

Imitations: In Alexander Pope and Jonathan Swift, *Miscellanies*, 2nd ed., 3 vols., 1733, Vol. II; Antoine François Prévost, *The Life and Entertaining Adventures of Mr. Cleveland*, 5 vols., 1734–1735, Vol. I.

No. 27 (1723–1748)

Found in nos. 26, 30, 35, *41, 41A, 42, 46, 58, 62, 65, 69, 70, 90A, 93, 95, 111, 121, 128, 138, 140, 145, 151, 153, 163, 167A, 174, 203, 217, 221, 232, 238, 263, 265, 275, 287, 352.

This ornament is not new in 1723. The border rules show signs of wear. By 1729 a small horizontal break can be seen crossing the design and part of the lion's mane on the left-hand side of the ornament. The center of this headpiece is removable, and Richardson uses on occasions any one of three or four different centers.

Imitations: In Thomas Carte, *A Full Answer to the Letter from a Bystander*, 1742; James Thomson and David Mallet, *Alfred*, 1751; John Campbell, *The Rational Amusement*, 1754.

No. 28 (1748–1754)

Found in nos. 361, 372, 383A, 389, 391, 405, 421A, 427, *429. No defects noted.

Imitation: In Eliza Haywood, *Life's Progress through the Passions*, 1748, printed by T. Gardner.

No. 29 (1724–1750)

Found in nos. 30, *41, 41A, 62, 66, 187, 376.

The defects in the left-hand side rule makes this ornament readily identifiable.

Imitations: None found.

No. 30 (1728–1762)

Found in nos. 65, 178, 207, 232, 238, 238A, 245, 267, *282, 283, 284, 285, 287, 298, 344A, 367, 372, 383A, 389, 400, 410, 427, 449, 485, 488, 507, 516.

Richardson used this ornament over a long period of years. Many imitations can be found, but defects in Richardson's block make it comparatively easy to differentiate his ornament from those of other printers. A chip in the design in the lower left-hand side, about three-sixteenths of an inch from the bottom (see reproduction) can be easily detected as early as 1738. By 1753 this corner tip has broken off. A bad break can be found in the lower right-hand corner in 1750.

Imitations: In *A Collection of Papers relating to the East India Trade*, 1730; Jonathan Swift, *City Cries*, 1732; *Observations upon Mr. Budgell's Two Late Pamphlets*, 1732; *Pamela's Conduct in High Life*, 2 vols., 1741, Vol. I; *Dutch Faith*, 1745; Teresia Muilman, *A Letter . . . to . . . the Earl of Chesterfield*, 1750; *The Groans of Great-Britain*, 1753; *The Advantages of the Revolution Illustrated*, 1753.

No. 31 (1732–1762)

Found in nos. 108, 121, 134, 140, 167, 183A, 196, *203, 228, 234, 250, 268A, 303, 304, 310, 326, 348A, 352, 362, 368, 372, 494, 495, 495A, 496, 514.

As early as 1732, when this ornament appears quite new, a slight defect may be seen in the upper right-hand corner. The ornament shows little signs of wear, however, and it is not until 1748 that this defect has become noticeably worse. By 1760, a break developed across the ornament on this side, and Richardson had to trim off the right-hand side, leaving the dog with about one-quarter inch of tail. By this date the lower left-hand corner has been rounded off.

Imitations: None found.

No. 32 (1721–1741)

Found in nos. 10, 13, 23, 67, *80, 175, 217, 228, 242, 265, 279.

This ornament, not new in 1721, shows a chip in the small ball in the extreme lower left-hand corner. This may be seen in the reproduction. By 1735 a break shows across the border rule and the design itself, to the right and below the central figure.

Imitations: None found.

No. 33 (1757–1762)

Found in nos. 465, 494, 495, 495A, *514.

In 1752 this ornament was used in a pamphlet, *The Remonstrances of the Clergy of France*, said to be printed by N. Gibson, about whom nothing else seems to be known. In 1750, 1751, and 1754 the ornament was used in Robert Bolton's essay, *On the Employment of Time*, printed for John Whiston and others. In 1762, after Richardson's death, it was used in Nathaniel Lardner's *Remarks upon the Late Dr. Ward's Dissertations upon Several Passages of the Sacred Scriptures*. I cannot be sure that it was a part of Richardson's equipment, but I have included it because, during the years 1757–1761, works of three men—Defoe, Lyttelton, and Thomas Wilson (1703–1784)—contain this ornament among others which I feel certain were Richardson's.

Imitations: In Henry Baker, *Original Poems*, 2 vols., 1725–1726; Philip Doddridge, *Practical Discourses on Regeneration*, 1742; *Poetical Pieces by Several Hands*, ed. Stevens, 1752; Josiah Tucker, *A Letter to a Friend Concerning Naturalizations*, 1753; *An Essay on the Times*, 1756; Henry Stebbing, *A Discourse Concerning the Governing Providence of God*, 1757.

No. 34 (1738–1762)

Found in nos. 224, 269, 326, 328, 342, 354, 406, *427, 439, 440, 455, 484, 494, 495, 495A, 514.

No particular defects noted.

Imitations: None found.

No. 35 (1723–1736)

Found in nos. 26, 30, 41, 65, 70, 72, 97, 105, 111, 120, 122, *134, 141, 149, 187.

This ornament and No. 36 closely resemble each other, but they may be easily distinguished by the difference in the shape of the oval in the lower central portion. Both were part of Richardson's equipment, and for some years he used both, sometimes in the same volume. No. 36 seems to have been used exclusively after 1736, but I cannot be sure that this was the case. A defect in the upper border rule, an inch from the right-hand side, can be seen as early as 1728 and is easily discernible by 1734.

Imitation: In *The Gentleman's Miscellany in Verse and Prose*, 1730.

No. 36 (1722–1758)

Found in nos. 12, 39, *41, 41A, 42, 56, 88, 110, 121, 134, 137, 140, 167, 175, 196, 217, 251, 265, 367A, 432, 433, 454, 475.

A leaf, extending to the left from the lower portion of the cornucopia on the left-hand side of the ornament, becomes detached from the main portion of the design by reason of a break that starts in the 1720's. See note under No. 35, above.

Imitations: See No. 35, above.

No. 37 (1741–1755)

Found in nos. 276, *282, 335, 398, 421A, 438.

This ornament is similar to No. 38. Richardson used No. 37 in the second edition of *Pamela* and No. 38 in the sixth edition. No. 37 became badly damaged. Even so, Richardson used it in the sixth edition of his *Familiar Letters* in 1755.

Imitation: In George Lyttelton, 1st Baron Lyttelton, *Letters from a Persian in England*, 5th ed., 1744.

No. 38 (1746–1752)

Found in nos. *344A, 352, 354A, 355, 386, 398.
See note under No. 37, above.
Imitation: See No. 37, above.

No. 39 (1728–1736)

Found in nos. 65, 70, 153, 156, *160, 199.

The worn spots in the borders render this ornament easily identifiable.

Imitations: None found.

No. 40 (1723–1735)

Found in nos. 13, 125, *165.

Two scratches across the upper portion to the left serve as a ready means of identifying this headpiece.

Imitations: None found.

No. 41 (1719–1736)

Found in nos. 1, 2, 3, 5, 8, 10, 23, 25, 29, 74A, 75, *77, 78, 79, 104, 114, 135, 151, 190.

By 1729 a break may be found in the petal of a flower on the spray to the upper left. This petal is on the lowest flower of this spray and extends to the right. Examination of the reproduction will make apparent the point where the break occurred. A break in the petal of the flower at the tip of the right-hand spray may be seen by 1734.

Imitations: In Daniel Defoe (?), *The Sighs of the Church of England*, 1715; Mead (?), *The Construction of Maps and Globes*, 1717; *The True History of the Great St. Athanasius*, 1719; Samuel Bolde, *Some Thoughts Concerning Church Authority*, 1724; *The Longitude Discovered*, 1726; George Sewell, *Posthumous Works*, 1728; R. Fabian, *Trick for Trick*, 1735. Many of the imitations of this ornament are crudely conceived and executed.

No. 42 (1721–1754)

Found in nos. 7, 25, *26, 43, 50, 52, 66, 84, 97A, 110, 111, 122, 140, 141, 207, 228, 289, 313, 430.

Richardson had this ornament in his possession for a long period, but he used it only occasionally after it had begun to show signs of considerable wear. Even in 1721 it was not new: a defect had developed in the extreme right-hand part of the design, near the point where the final formalized branch extends from a pair of leaves (see reproduction).

Imitations: None found.

No. 43 (1723–1762)

Found in nos. 26, 57, 71, 93, 111, 134, 168, 172, 183A, 196, 207, 217, 232, 242, 251, 265, *268A, 276, 289, 310, 352, 410, 416, 430, 433, 447, 470, 507.

This ornament stood up well under a long period of use. By 1735, however, a break developed in the flower, dependent at the lower left. The line, moving from the stem to form the right petal of this flower, shows a slight break in 1735; this break is noticeable in 1740—the year in which the reproduction was printed.

Imitations: None found. Benjamin Griffin's *Whig and Tory*, 1720, a book which Richardson does not seem to have printed, contains this ornament. During the early 1720's Richardson was just beginning to get established and may well have turned to other shops as a source of his stock of ornaments.

No. 44 (1721–1744)

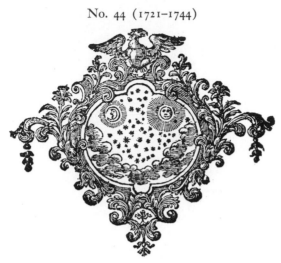

Found in nos. 10, 16, 23, 26, 29, 39, 49, 63, 72, 73A, 74A, 99, 119, 126, 135, *195, 216, 248, 249, 323.

This ornament shows little signs of wear until 1736 when the parts of the design at the extreme left and right begin to show slight defects. Its many peculiar features, however, make it easily recognizable.

Imitations: The imitations discovered are all signed "E.K.": in Edward Young, *The Revenge*, 1721; Richard Steele, *The Conscious Lovers*, 1723; Edward Young, *The Love of Fame*, 3rd ed., 1730.

No. 45 (1721–1751)

Found in nos. 7, 10, 11, 12, 13, 17, 18, 23, 29, 39, 75, 153, 165, 199, 242, 289, 303, 312, 378, *389, 391.

In its original condition this ornament had a small knob at the extreme top. By 1729 this knob has begun to show considerable wear; by 1735 it has disappeared. The fine lines extending from the pendant at the bottom gradually wear off and by 1744 are barely visible.

Imitations: None found.

No. 46 (1719–1759)

Found in nos. 1, 2, 5, 8, 10, 12, 23, 25, 29, 65, 165, 268A, 310, *433, 447, 448, 460, 481A.

Richardson used this ornament occasionally over a long period of years. It may be readily identified by a thin crack, extending to the right from the top of the flower jar in a slightly downward direction and across the formalized leaves.

Imitations: None found. The ornament itself was used in *An Essay on Study*, printed by J. L[eake?], in 1713. If this book was in fact printed by John Leake, the ornament may well have come into Richardson's possession through John Leake's son, James, who was established in business in Richardson's neighborhood until he left for Bath in 1722. Richardson took over his first three apprentices from Leake in 1722. See pp. 14–15.

No. 47 (1723–1729)

Found in nos. 18, *29, 74A.

This ornament, the largest of all the tailpieces in Richardson's stock, was either disposed of or discarded at a comparatively early date.

Imitations: Plomer reproduces an imitation in his *Printers' Ornaments*, 1924. It was taken from Truro's *History of Cornwall*, 1750.

No. 48 (1723–1762)

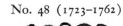

Found in nos. 26, 62, 65, 66, 97A, 135, 156, 165, 170, 183A, *203, 276, 303, 436, 444, 464, 474, 481A, 516.

The thin lines that mark the extremities of the feathers to the lower right and left of the central portion of the design gradually wear off.

Also two fine-pointed lines in the extreme lower part of the ornament disappear.

Imitations: In Eustace Budgell, *A Letter to Cleomenes*, 1731; Benjamin Robins, *An Address to the Electors*, 1739; and Sir William Keith, *A Collection of Papers and Other Tracts*, 1740, printed by J. Mechell.

No. 49 (1728–1745)

Found in nos. 66, 90, 97A, *134, 135, 139, 141, 145A, 146, 165, 167, 172, 178, 187, 213, 250, 289, 322, 329, 333.

The tip of the left wing of the eagle shows a break as early as 1734, and by 1740 the small dots in the shield beneath the eagle have become so worn that many of them fail to print.

Imitations: In Thomas Cooke, *The Eunuch*, 1737; John Campbell, *The Case of the Opposition*, 1742; Philip Dormer Stanhope, 4th Earl of Chesterfield, and Edmund Waller, *The Case of the Hanover Forces*, 1743; John Stevens, *The Modern Wife*, 1744; Richard Finch, *The Nature and Duty of Self-Defense*, 1746; John Upton, *Critical Observations on Shakespeare*, 1746.

No. 50 (1731–1762)

Found in nos. 100, 123, 132, 155, 223, 242, 245A, 267, 272, 280, 282, 283, 284, 285, 295, 315, 326, 344A, 348A, 351, 352, 355, 361, 383A, 388, *389, 398, 406, 410, 433, 437, 453, 456, 463, 464, 475, 485, 494, 495, 495A, 496, 514.

This ornament is difficult to distinguish from its many imitations, but the difference can be most readily detected by comparing the treatment of lines on the central part.

Imitations: In William Pulteney, *A Proper Reply to a Late Scurrilous Libel* [one of the two issues], 1731; Nicholas Amhurst, *A Collection of Poems on Several Occasions*, 1731; Thomas Paget, *Miscellanies*, 1741 (see p. 192); *A Satire upon Physicians*, 1755; Thomas Sherlock, *Several Discourses Preached at the Temple Church*, Vol. I, 1756.

No. 51 (1728–1753)

Found in nos. 66, 72, 74, 74A, *80, 89, 90, 97A, 120, 137, 138, 139, 147, 149, 193, 201, 203, 207, 228, 238, 252, 268A, 272, 276, 289, 310, 315, 374, 383A, 405, 406.

In the reproduction a break may be seen in the line forming the bird's right wing at a point where the wing joins the body. The thin line of the bird's tongue begins to wear away in the 1730's, and the fine point at the extreme lower center of the ornament finally disappears.

Imitation: In Arthur Murphy, *The Apprentice*, 1756.

No. 52 (1721–1753)

Found in nos. 7, 10, 12, 23, 26, 27, 41, 58, 65, 74A, 83, 104, 110, 122, 134, 135, 140, 165, 190, 192, 201, 211, 228, *295, 326, 399A, 406.

The thin lines defining the contents of the basket and projecting from the top of the ornament show gradual wear, but it is not until 1742 that a clearly defined break develops. This break is on that part of the design immediately to the right of the tip of the right wing of the central figure (see reproduction).

Imitations: None found.

No. 53 (1723–1759)

Found in nos. 26, 29, 41, 50, 57, 59, 62, 66, 81, 111, 121, 135, 137, 144, 147, 167, 168, 170, 228, 232, 242, 271, 272, *295, 315, 326, 362, 368, 373, 388, 448, 474, 481A.

The tip of the leaf in the upper right-hand section, sharply pointed in 1723, gradually wears off. By 1733 a break appears in one of the lines outlining the central figure at a point where a right angle is formed in the lower left-hand section.

Imitations: In Daniel Waterland, *Advice to a Young Student,* 1730; Richard Mead, *A Mechanical Account of Poisons,* 4th ed., 1736, printed by S. Powell, Dublin; Thomas Phillips, *Love and Glory,* 1734; Sir Richard Cox, *A Letter from Dionysius,* Dublin, 1754; George Colman, *Polly Honeycombe,* Dublin, 1761.

No. 54 (1727–1753)

Found in nos. 57, 65, 72, 97A, 107, 112, 127, 135, 151, 192, 211, 250, 268A, *306, 310, 406.

In the third volume of Sir Philip Sidney's *Works*, 1724—a book which gives every evidence of having been printed by Richardson—may be found a variant of this ornament. The reproduction seems to have been copied from a print of this variant, for the head of the bird is facing to the right in the variant and to the left in the reproduction. The three volumes of Sidney were printed at various presses, and perhaps Richardson had borrowed the ornament which he used in 1724, and had a copy made later. I have not found Richardson using either version of the ornament between 1724 and 1727, nor have I found him using the variant after 1724. Other imitations of this ornament were in use at various presses; in fact, a third variation on the design may be found in the second volume of Sidney's *Works*, a volume clearly not printed by Richardson. The leaf in the lower right-hand portion of the design is broken at an early date, and this defect soon becomes clearly noticeable, as it is in the reproduction.

Imitations: In *The Present Exigencies of the Government Consider'd*, 1719; Peter Shaw, *A New Practice of Physic*, 3rd ed., 2 vols., 1730, Vol. II; *Memoirs of the Life of Robert Wilks*, 1732, printed by William Rayner; Charlotte Lennox, *The Female Quixote*, 2nd ed., 2 vols., 1752, Vol. II.

No. 55 (1726–1756)

Found in nos. 42, 50, 52, 58, 94, 122, 126, 135, 151, 170, 192, 210, 211, 217, 228, 245, 250, 265, 268A, 310, 369, 393, 397, *433, 436, 443.

By 1734 a defect has developed in the leaf at the extreme left of the basket of fruit at the top of the ornament. The outlines of the face of the main figure have begun to wear thin by 1740.

Imitations: None found.

No. 56 (1731–1743)

Found in nos. 91, 97A, 107, 135, 151, 192, 248, 249, 250, *268A, 310.

No noticeable defects appear, but this ornament is easily distinguishable from imitations.

Imitation: In *A Collection of Voyages*, ed. Churchill, 3rd ed., 6 vols., 1746, Vol. VI.

No. 57 (1723–1756)

Found in nos. 22, *26, 29, 30, 56, 58, 62, 65, 66, 74A, 83, 87, 90, 93, 97A, 110, 126, 135, 144, 147, 151, 170, 217, 242, 251, 265, 268A, 289, 310, 315, 326, 344A, 358, 369, 406, 433, 443.

The pointed tips of the leaves projecting from the basket are gradually blunted with use, and the line which marks the inside of the scroll work to the right of center slowly wears backward from left to right. By 1743 the wear on this line is markedly noticeable. Wear also shows on the lines enclosing the crisscrossed oval in the center.

Imitations: In Daniel Defoe, *The Case of the Royal African Company*, 1730; Eustace Budgell, *A Letter to Cleomenes*, 1731; *One Thousand Seven Hundred Thirty-Nine*, 2nd ed., 1740; *The Haberdasher's Sermon*, Dublin, 1755.

No. 58 (1732–1759)

Found in nos. 110, 129, 138, 140, 148A, 157, 165, 177, 180, 183A, 210, 245, 276, 284, 285, 286, 287, 295, 326, 344A, 383, 383A, 406, *430, 482.

The portion of the design curving inward in the lower right-hand corner gradually wears at the point where it joins with the stylized branch extending toward the right. By 1742 this wear is clearly noticeable; by 1754 this portion is practically separated from the remainder of the block; and by 1759 the break is complete.

Imitations: In Samuel Clark, *Sermons*, 10 vols., 1730–1731, Vol. V, printed by W. Botham; Nathaniel Lardner, *Remarks upon the Late Dr. Ward's Dissertations*, 1762; Izrahiah Wetmore, *A Sermon, Preached before the Honourable General Assembly of the Colony of Connecticut*, [New London, Conn.], 1773, printed by T. Green.

No. 59 (1730–1757)

Found in nos. 87, 123, 166, 226, 279, 348, 357, 443, *461.

The many details in this ornament render it easily distinguishable from imitations.

Imitations: In Paul Whitehead, *Honour*, 1747; John Free, *The Danger Attending an Enlightened and Free People*, 1753, printed by R. Penny.

No. 60 (1736–1757)

Found in nos. 192, 196, 204, 210, 242, 245, 250, 268A, 306, 310, 326, 329, 399A, 447, 448, *460.

In the reproduction a slight defect may be seen in the projecting knob to the extreme left, just above center.

Imitations: *Eugenio,* 1743; Richard Gifford, *Contemplation,* 1753; Richard Owen Cambridge, *The Fakeer,* 1756; Edward Moore, *Poems, Fables, and Plays,* 1756, printed by John Hughs.

No. 61 (1729–1752)

Found in nos. 73A, 74A, 91, 107, 112, 120, 127, 135, 147, 204, 250, *271, 288, 399A.

A leaf, just above the lowest leaf and extending to the right, shows a break that is noticeable in the reproduction.

Imitations: In Thomas Pocock, *The Relief of Captives,* 1720; John Trenchard, *A Continuation of the Political Letters in the London Journal,* 1721; *An Epistle from S——o to A—a R——n,* 1724.

No. 62 (1721–1734)

Found in nos. 10, 10A, 23, 26, 29, 43, *49, 63, 64, 80, 89, 91, 99, 125, 126, 135, 144.

The narrow left end of the fold of cloth in the lower right-hand portion of the ornament is broken, and the curved line in the upper right-hand part of the design is flattened by use, as can be seen in the reproduction.

Imitations: None found.

No. 63 (1721–1745)

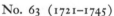

Found in nos. 7, 10, 11, 13, 17, 41, 46, 54, 57, 64, 65, 66, 90, 111, 135, 137, 138, 165, 170, 174A, 190, 192, 211, 228, 238A, 242, 250, 272, 276, *295, 315, 329.

As early as 1721 a break in the line that completes the right side of the face of the cupid can be found. The feathery tips to the right and left show constantly increasing wear.

Imitation: In Charlotte Lennox, *Poems on Several Occasions*, 1747.

No. 64 (1721–1743?)

Found in nos. 10, 12, 23, 26, 29, 41, 45, 57, 59, 65, 69, 72, 74A, 90, 108, 121, 122, 135, 144, 151, 165, 170, 172, 192, 211, 221, *268A, 310 (a reissue of 268A?).

In the reproduction a slight stemlike projection to the extreme left is all that remains of a small "knob" that had broken off by 1735. The corresponding knob to the extreme right had broken off by 1731. The ornament was abandoned when the pendantlike portion at the bottom broke off. In Book No. 268A (1740) the tailpiece is used three times. The break across the pendant is noticeable on p. 174 and can be clearly seen on p. 250 (see reproduction). On p. 285 the ornament appears with the broken piece missing.

Imitation: In Joseph Addison, *The Drummer*, Dublin, 1734, printed by Samuel Powell.

No. 65 (1721–1743?)

Found in nos. 7, 10, 11, 13, 18, 23, *26, 29, 52, 57, 65, 66, 74A, 90, 110, 127, 134, 135, 144, 147, 151, 153, 165, 172, 175, 201, 228, 242, 245, 268A, 276, 289, 298, 310 (a reissue of 268A?).

As early as 1721 a slight break may be found in the upper line of the pedestal, to the left of the burning heart which rests on it.
Imitations: None found.

No. 66 (1734–1757)

Found in nos. 135, 165, 187, 228, 236, 242, 250, 303, *306, 326, 330, 349, 352, 359, 369, 383A, 384, 408, 422, 433, 443, 459.

This ornament and the one immediately below are easily distinguishable from each other, but imitations and variants abound. The detail is sufficiently exact in both of Richardson's ornaments to make detection of imitations fairly easy.

Imitations of Nos. 66 and 67: In William Congreve, *The Double-Dealer*, Dublin, 1723, printed by George Grierson; William Congreve, *Poems upon Several Occasions*, 1735; George Lyttelton, 1st Baron Lyttelton, *Observations on the Conversion . . . of St. Paul*, 1747; Henry Jones, *Poems on Several Occasions*, 1749; Richard Owen Cambridge, *The Scribleriad*, 1751; Richard Owen Cambridge, *The Intruder*, 1754; Edward Moore, *Poems, Fables, and Plays*, 1756, printed by John Hughs.

No. 67 (1728–1744)

Found in nos. 65, 74A, 75, 90, 111, 121, 135, 137, 140, 165, 175, 183A, 190, 192, 211, 227, 234A, 238, 242, 249, 272, 274, 280, *306, 315.
See No. 66.

No. 68 (1723–1729)

Found in nos. 26, 27, 29, 34, 41, 45, *49, 64, 65, 74A, 81.

This ornament is easily distinguishable from all imitations that I have found.

Imitations: In *The Art of Beauty*, 1719 (signed "C. Gardner, sculp."); Samuel Clifford, *A Dissuasive from Perjury*, 1723 (signed "T [or J?] Bell"); Sir Constantine Phipps, *The Defence of Francis, Late Lord Bishop of Rochester*, 1723 (signed "F[rancis] H[off-man]"); *An Account of the Expedition to Carthagena*, 3rd ed., 1743.

No. 69 (1733–1760)

Found in nos. 123, 166, 180, 189, 226, 268A, 276, 280, 285, 287, 295, 326, 329, 344A, 352, 361, 362, 367, 378, 383A, *389, 390, 406, 433, 441B, 442, 463, 470, 481A, 496.

This ornament is difficult to identify, for there are several close imitations. No readily identifiable defects appear.

Imitations: In Elizabeth Thomas, *The Metamorphoses of the Town*, 3rd ed., 1731; Thomas Morell, *Poems on Divine Subjects*, 1732, printed by Edward Owen; Susanna Centlivre, *The Gamester*, 4th ed. (a pirated edition?), 1736; Joseph Spence, *An Essay on Mr. Pope's Odyssey*, 3rd ed., 1747; William Hay, *Remarks on the Laws Relating to the Poor*, 1751; Sarah Fielding and Jane Collier, *The Cry*, 3 vols., 1754, Vol. III; Edward Moore, *Poems, Fables, and Plays*, 1756, printed by John Hughs.

No. 70 (1723–1739)

Found in nos. *26, 27, 29, 41, 42, 45, 46, 49, 65, 77, 78, 79, 117, 121, 135, 151, 165, 170, 180, 190, 192, 211, 212, 227, 250.

The recognition of this ornament presents little difficulty.

Imitation: In *The Magick Glass*, 1733.

No. 71 (1723–1757)

Found in nos. 26, 29, 35, 45, 47, 50, 56, 57, 62, 66, 72, 74A, 90, 111, 129, 135, 140, 153, 165, 210, 217, 227, 228, 234, 245, 250, 251, 265, 268A, 276, 289, 295, 303, 310, 329, 358, 383, 436, *441B, 459.

In 1723 a break to the left in the inner line enclosing the central oval may be found. By 1728 a break develops near the same place in the outer line.

Imitation: In Mark Freeman (pseud.?), *The Downfal of Bribery*, [1733].

No. 72 (1723–1751)

Found in nos. *26, 50, 61, 90, 121, 135, 147, 165, 190, 207, 392.
The leaf to the extreme right-center develops a defect which shows clearly by 1735.
Imitations: None found.

No. 73 (1728–1756)

Found in nos. 65, 100, 150, 161, 166, 168, 179, 226, 276, 279, 366, 395, 412, 413, *444.
The detail is not accurately copied in the imitations that I have found.
Imitations: In Elizabeth Thomas, *The Metamorphoses of the Town*, 3rd ed., 1731; Teresia Muilman, *An Apology*, 3 vols., [1748–1749], Vol. I.

No. 74 (1728–1757)

Found in nos. 65, 160, 162, 187, 320, 326, 329, 330, 348, 357, 369, 424, 453, 459, *460.

This ornament is similar to the one below, but they can be easily distinguished from each other and from all imitations that I have found.

Imitations of Nos. 74 and 75: In *Four Original Letters*, 1739; John Stirling, *A System of Rhetoric*, 4th ed., Dublin, 1744; William P. Bath, *An Ode, Imitated from Ode XI. Book 2d. of Horace*, 1745.

No. 75 (1733–1762)

Found in nos. 261, 280, *365, 373, 390, 443.
See No. 74.

No. 76 (1733–1762)

Found in nos. 117, 139, 165, 168, 182, 207, 232, 242, *268A, 272, 310, 315, 362, 388, 389, 391, 481A, 516.

By 1738 a break develops in the line forming the left leg of the small figure on the left side of the ornament.

Imitations: In Erasmus Philips, *The State of the Nation,* 1726; William Bowman, *Poems on Several Occasions,* 1727; Elizabeth Thomas, *Life of Corina,* 1731; *An Account of the Society for Promoting Christian Knowledge,* 1755, printed by J. Oliver.

No. 77 (1721–1759)

Found in nos. 10, 65, 66, 83, 88, 89, 90, 102, 108, 110, 128, 139, 151, 183, 201, 207, 218, 234, 242, *268A, 310, 312, 317, 352, 407, 428, 429, 441B, 443, 463, 482, 485.

This ornament is easily recognizable.

Imitation: In Thomas Spence, *An Essay on Mr. Pope's Odyssey,* 3rd ed., 1747.

No. 78 (1723–1762)

Found in nos. 13, 66, 74A, *80, 90, 116, 121, 135, 141, 147, 151,

165, 171, 192, 193, 196, 211, 242, 268A, 272, 310, 312, 315, 329, 352, 355, 363, 393, 405, 428, 448, 466, 481A, 482, 516.

This ornament shows noticeable wear in the central oval as the bees nearest to the hive fail to print clearly.

Imitations: None found.

No. 79 (1729–1744)

Found in nos. 74A, 83, 90, 139, 141, 144, 145, 148A, *165, 174, 228, 238A, 319.

No noticeable defects.

Imitations: None found.

No. 80 (1726–1743?)

Found in nos. 45, 49, 50, 55, 58, 62, 65, 66, 71, 82, 83, 90, 124A, 134, 135, 137, 138, 151, 165, 170, 190, 192, *203, 211, 217A, 242, 255, 268A, 310 (a reissue of 268A?).

The line forming the top of the right wing of the bird on the left-hand side shows wear as early as 1728, and by 1735 the beak of this bird is damaged. This ornament and the one below are similar, but can be distinguished by the difference in design near the top of the vase. Imitations of both ornaments are numerous, however.

Imitations of Nos. 80 and 81: In *Advice to Sappho*, 1733; *Modern Matrimony*, 1737; *An Ode on Martial Virtue*, 1750; Richard Owen Cambridge, *The Scribleriad*, 1751; Stephen Duck, *Caesar's Camp*, 1755; Edward Moore, *Poems, Fables, and Plays*, 1756, printed by John Hughs.

No. 81 (1729–1744)

Found in nos. 73A, 74A, 137, 155, *166, 189, 223, 315.

The leaf just over the back of the head of the bird on the left-hand side of this ornament shows a slight break that may be seen in the reproduction. See No. 80.

No. 82 (1751–1760)

Found in nos. 389, 390, 402, 416, 417, 421A, *433, 437, 474, 477, 481A, 485, 496.

No special defects.

Imitations: None found.

No. 83 (1727–1762)

Found in nos. 57, 135, 139, 165, 180, 330, 389, 421A, 428, *433, 436, 447, 454, 459, 461, 494, 495, 495A, 507.

In 1727 the leaf to the right at the base of the urn is broken, and a break shows in the upper line that forms the branch extending from this leaf. By 1734 a leaf from the under side of the branch that extends to the left has broken off from the branch.

Imitations: None found.

No. 84 (1731–1762)

Found in nos. 90, 92, 108, 251, 359, 361, 378, 383A, 390, 393, 406, 410, *429, 430, 441, 441B, 444, 485, 507, 516.

No special defects.

Imitations: None found.

No. 85 (1754–1762)

Found in nos. 429, 433, 436, *444, 447, 463, 466, 470, 477, 482, 485, 494, 495, 495A, 514, 516.

Richardson presumably acquired this small tailpiece after No. 84 began to show signs of wear.

Imitations: None found.

No. 86 (1728–1762)

Found in nos. 65, 90, *134, 141, 165, 175A, 175B, 183A, 227, 228, 250, 312, 326, 330, 337, 415, 433, 443, 463, 470, 507.

In 1728 very slight breaks may be seen on the left-hand side of the central oval, and at the angle formed by the lines meeting just above and farther to the left of this break in the central oval.

Imitations: None found.

No. 87 (1734–1760)

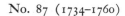

Found in nos. 135, 172, 183A, 192, 196, 201, 207, 210, 211, 228, 242, 245, 312, 326, 352, 355, 361, 367, 393, *427, 428, 430, 436, 453, 454, 459, 474, 477, 495A, 496.

No special defects noted.

Imitations: None found.

No. 88 (1745–1748)

Found in nos. *318, 329, 333, 353.

Richardson undoubtedly used this ornament more often than I have noted, but I did not decide to include it until a late date in my examination of his presswork. It illustrates the "pictorial" book ornament. A more formalized treatment of objects characterized ornaments in the first half of the century.

Imitations: None found.

No. 89 (1739–1756)

Found in nos. 249, 268A, 310, 329, *444.
This ornament, like No. 88, was used more often than I have noted.
Imitations: None found.

No. 90 (1727–1739)

Found in nos. *49, 65, 80, 98, 135, 136, 184, 192, 211, 227, 250.

The number 90 has been assigned to this enclosing design into
which can be fitted centerpieces such as the figure of justice with
the scales that appears in the reproduction. In Book No. 250, for example, ornament No. 70 is used as a centerpiece; in Book No. 49,
ornament No. 95 is used on one occasion as centerpiece; and in Book
No. 98 the word "FINIS" is set up in type in place of a centerpiece.
Ornament No. 93 is a reproduction of this same enclosing design with

a still different center. A small piece broken off the bottom of this ornament in 1738 (Book No. 227) was apparently restored by 1739 (Book No. 250).

Imitations: In *Observations on British Wool*, 1738, printed by Henry Kent; *The Farmer Restored*, 1739; *An Ode on Martial Virtue*, 1750.

No. 91 (1721–1745)

Found in nos. 7, 10, 13, 23, 62, *66, 73A, 124A, 153, 175, 326.

This small ornament was frequently used as a centerpiece in headpieces with a removable center. In Book No. 13, for example, it is used in the center of ornament No. 21, in place of the crowned lion that appears in the reproduction.

Imitations: None found.

No. 92 (1744–1758)

Found in nos. 323, 335, 354A, 388, 424, *441B, 470.

This ornament is sometimes used alone, sometimes as the center of a large headpiece. See ornament No. 100.

Imitations: None found.

No. 93 (1727–1751)

Found in nos. *49, 65, 74A, 75, 80, 139, 154, 167, 192, 211, 388.

The enclosing portion of this ornament is No. 90; the number 93 designates the centerpiece—the small cupid. This figure can be removed and is frequently used alone as a tailpiece (See Books No. 65, 139, 154, 167, 192).

Imitations: None found.

No. 94 (1723–1739)

Found in nos. 14, 45, 135, 159, *165, 250.

This ornament can be used as a tailpiece or as an inset in a large ornament.

Imitations: None found.

No. 95 (1727–1734)

Found in nos. *49, 57, 75, 97A, 135.

This ornament can be used alone or as an inset. In Book No. 49, for example, it is used as an inset in ornament No. 90.

Imitations: None found.

No. 96 (1721–1755)

Found in nos. 10, 13, 18, 30, 35, *41, 47, 65, 66, 80, 154, 355, 390, 433.

This ornament can be used alone or as an inset. In Books No. 10, 65, and 80, for example, it is used as an inset for ornament No. 21 (see reproduction of ornament No. 21).

Imitations: None found.

No. 97 (1723–1738)

Found in nos. 24, 27, 29, *49, 64, 74A, 75, 126, 227.

This factotum is damaged in the center of the left-hand border rule, and there is a chip in the inside rule, right-hand side, of the central box that encloses the initial letter.

Imitations: None found.

No. 98
(1741?–1752)

Found in nos. *271 (a second issue?), 274, 302A, 318, 353, 399A.
This large headpiece, and Nos. 99, 100, 101, and 102, show a change
in style from the headpieces numbered 1–6. Imitations: None found.

No. 99
(1747–1755)

Found in nos. *348, 357, 434. See note to ornament No. 98. Imitations: None found.

No. 100 (1744–1758)

Found in nos. *323, 332, 384, 395, 415, 424, 442, 470.

See note to ornament No. 98. In 1744 (see reproduction) two breaks can be seen across the ornament immediately to the left and below the central figure of the phoenix. In the following year two breaks develop to the right of the central figure, both below and above.

Imitations: None found.

No. 101 (1757)

Found in no. *461.

See note to ornament No. 98. Two breaks may be seen to the left of the central basket, in the upper and lower sections of the ornament.

Imitations: None found.

No. 102 (1744–1758)

Found in nos. 318, 333, 340, 349, 366, 369, 442, * 460, 470.
See note to ornament No. 98.
Imitations: None found.

No. 103 (1727–1758)

For reproductions and descriptions, see pp. 257–261.
Found in nos. 52, 61, 65, 66, 72, 73, 77, 78, 79, 80, 83, 108, 110, 111, 112, 121, 122, 127, 134, 144, 151, 154, 167, 170, 203, 217, 234, 251, 265, 268A, 303, 310, 365, 397, 402, 428, 436, 463, 475.
Imitations: See pp. 262–263.

CHAPTER X

A List of Booksellers
for Whom Richardson Printed

THIS LIST is arranged alphabetically. Following the name of the bookseller, I have given his dates, if known; and—within square brackets—the dates of the period in which he had business relations with Richardson. The series of numbers that follow the dates refer to the books themselves. These books may be identified by reference to the chronological list of Richardson's printing (pp. 229–250). If a number referring to a book is printed in italic type, the book was printed for a conger, or large group of booksellers (pp. 91–95). If a number is preceded by an asterisk, the book was probably only *published* by the bookseller. For the eighteenth-century distinction between *publishing* and *bookselling*, see pp. 86–89.

In the brief notes on these booksellers, I have sought to supply only the information that might concern a reader interested in Richardson. This information may be supplemented by that in Plomer's two *Dictionaries*, the first extending from 1668 to 1725 and the second from 1726 to 1775. To these two *Dictionaries* I am indebted for some of the facts included in my notes. On occasions, when my information does not extend beyond Plomer's, I have omitted notes.

ASTLEY, THOMAS. d. 1759. [1732–1741.] *108, *266, *281.

AUSTEN [AUSTIN], STEPHEN. d. 1750. [1740–1749.] *256, *260, *266, *270, *271, *281, *318, *353, *367A.

Austen, who dealt largely in law books and theology, was probably secured by Charles Rivington to publish certain books printed for him by Richardson. Austen himself does not seem to have employed Richardson's press.

BAKER, SAMUEL. d. 1778. [1740.] *268.

Baker was one of six booksellers appointed in 1739 by the Society for the Encouragement of Learning to act as publishers for the work that this society subsidized. He therefore acted as publisher for Richardson's edition of Sir Thomas Roe's *Negotiations*.

BALDWIN, ROBERT. d. 1810. [1759.] 481.

This book was the fourth edition of Delany's *David*, first published in 1740. By 1759 Baldwin had presumably acquired a share in this work.

BATHURST, CHARLES. d. 1786. [1738–1761.] 238, *302A*, 408, *432*, 471?, *501*.

Bathurst, the successor to Swift's bookseller, Benjamin Motte, apparently had few direct dealings with Richardson's press. Two of these books (238, 408) were printed by Richardson at the request of the owner of the copyright and not upon the order of Bathurst. Two of them (302A, 432), were printed for Bathurst as a member of a conger, and one (501) was printed by Richardson as joint patentee for the printing of all law books.

BATLEY, JEREMIAH. d. 1737. [1724–1737.] 28, *83, 86, *108, *185, 205*.

Richardson's press was not ordinarily employed by Batley. Until his death in 1737, however, Batley was a partner with Richardson in a large project—the publishing of the *Universal History*.

BATTERSBY, WILLIAM. [1730.] *86*.

A member of a large conger.

BELL, E. [1724]. *28*.

A member of a conger for Bailey's *Dictionary*.

BETTESWORTH, ARTHUR. d. 1739 [1724–1735.] *28, 37, 41, 41A, 49, 73A, *83, 86, 153, 164, 177*.

Richardson did little printing for Bettesworth, but he was frequently associated with Bettesworth's partner, Charles Hitch, who joined the firm in 1730, married Elizabeth, daughter of the founder, and carried on the business after the death of his father-in-law. See below, under Hitch.

BICKERTON, WEAVER. [1737.] 211, *217.

These books were probably printed by Richardson for the author, with Bickerton serving as publisher. His services may have been secured because he had a branch shop at Eton.

BILLINGSLEY, S. [1727.] *49*.

BIRT, SAMUEL. d. 1755. [1732–1755.] *107*, *108, *153*, 167A, *218, *232*, *260, *270, 271, 295, 318, 352, 353, 404A, 406, 432*.

Birt was a prominent bookseller, engaged in many large projects and dealing extensively in the sale of law books. Richardson printed most of these books for congers of which Birt was a member.

BONWICKE, J. and JAMES. [1734.] *153*.

BOWYER, C. [1734.] *153*.

Perhaps some relative of the bookseller, or of the famous printer, William Bowyer.

BOWYER, JONAH. [1721.] *7*.

Bowyer probably died or went out of business about 1722.

BRADLEY, JOB. d. 1798. [1731.] *97*.

Bradley was a bookseller in Chesterfield, Derbyshire, the birthplace of Charles Rivington, who undoubtedly made the arrangements with him for the joint selling of this book.

BRINDLEY, JAMES. d. 1758. [1734–1745.] 145, 147, *164*, *266, *268, *281, *329.

Brindley served in the main as publisher for books printed by Richardson for other booksellers.

BROTHERTON, JOHN. [1729–1745.] 73A, *329.

BROWNE, DANIEL. [1727–1762.] *49*, 70A, *86*, 93, *107*, *153*, *195*, 232, *270*, *271, 276, 295, 318, 352, 353, 404A, 404B, 406, 466, 504, 514*.

It seems evident that there were two Daniel Browne's at the same London address, possibly father and son; but I have not been able to learn the date of death of the elder Browne. Most of these books were published for congers of which the Brownes were members.

BUCKLAND, JAMES. d. 1790. [1761–1762.] *514*.

Buckland acquired a share in the sixth edition of Richardson's revision of Defoe's *Tour*.

BUCKLEY, SAMUEL. d. 1741. [1730–1733.] *86*, 130.

Buckley was himself a printer. These books represent ventures in which both Richardson and Buckley were interested.

BUSSEY, S. [1725.] 34.

CANTRELL, WILLIAM. d. 1727? [1727–1728.] 50, 59.

Cantrell was a bookseller in Derby, possibly the brother of Henry Cantrell, who was succeeded by Anthony Blackwall as headmaster of the Derby School. These two books printed for Cantrell were works of Blackwall.

CASLON, THOMAS. d. 1783. [1761–1762.] *514*.

Caslon acquired a share in Richardson's revision of Defoe's *Tour*. See under Lowndes, Thomas.

CHAPELLE, HENRY. d. 1764. [1740–1741.] *259, *266, *281.

John Osborn, bookseller, undoubtedly secured Chapelle's services as publisher for these books.

CHAPMAN, SAMUEL. [1724.] *30.

One of the publishers of the first edition of Defoe's *Tour*.

CLARKE, JOHN. [1730–1736.] 86, *201.

A member of a large conger, and bookseller for a reprint of William Webster's *Weekly Miscellany*. He was master of the Stationers' Company in 1760.

CLAY, F. d. 1738? [1724–1736.] 28, 86, *164, 195*.

Clay had died by 1738, for in that year the second edition of Chambers' *Cyclopaedia* was published for his executors. He had no close relations with Richardson.

CLEMENTS, RICHARD. [1741–1746.] 279A, 343.

A bookseller at Oxford, selling these books of Richard Newton, Principal of Hertford College.

COGAN, FRANCIS. [1738.] *232*.

A member of a conger concerned in the second edition of Defoe's *Tour*. He went into bankruptcy in 1754.

COOTE, JOHN. d. 1808. [1761.] 497.

A book printed by Richardson as sharer in the law patent.

COOPER, MARY. d. 1761. [1744–1755.] *320, *322, *329, *348, *351, *363, *402, *403, *432*.

Mary Cooper was the widow of Thomas Cooper. She succeeded to her husband's business about 1743. It is difficult to tell what the name of Cooper in an imprint may mean. Their shop was extensively employed as a publishing agency by authors, printers, and booksellers, with the Coopers selling books and pamphlets on commission. But Thomas Cooper seems to have done some printing; and on occasions either he or his widow seem to have been performing the services of a bookseller. Richardson frequently used the shop of the Coopers to publish the pamphlets of his friends. The copyrights of the first two books listed above, for example, were vested in their authors, Hill and Skelton; and in all likelihood it was upon Richardson's recommendation that Mary Cooper was secured to publish these works. For books of larger size, Richardson always recommended a bookseller's rather than "a mere Publisher's Management" (*Forster MSS.*, XIII, 3, f. 101–102).

COOPER, THOMAS. d. 1743? [1732–1741.] 105, 106, 114, 115, 116, 119, 156, 160, 162, 163, *196, 199, 223, 224, 234, 234A, 243, 246, 269, 288.

See above under Mary Cooper. No attempt has been made to distinguish between books and pamphlets for which Cooper was acting as publisher and those in which he may have had a bookseller's interest. I suspect, however, that most of these works were merely sold by him on commission.

CORBETT, CHARLES. d. 1752. [1733–1735.] 123, *164*.

These books are plays. Corbett's shop was known as a place where plays were sold, but he dealt less exclusively in dramatic literature than did several other booksellers.

CORBETT, SIR CHARLES. d. 1808. [1757.] 466.

Sir Charles was the son of Charles Corbett (see above). He inherited from his father a share in some of Edward Young's works. It is only for this reason that his name appears in the imprint of a book printed by Richardson—the collected works of Young.

COX, THOMAS. d. 1754? [1730.] *86*.

CREAKE, B. [1730–1735.] *86*, *178.

Creake had no direct dealings with Richardson. On one occasion he was a member of a large conger; on the other, he was publisher for a play printed for Feales.

CROKATT, JAMES. [1736–1742.] *185, 205, 225, 241, 253, 290*.

Crokatt was one of the original partners in a large project—the publication of the *Universal History*. Nichols calls him the greatest literary projector of the age. He retired from this venture, however, after the publication of the sixth volume.

CROWDER, STANLEY. d. 1798. [1759–1762.] *478, 479, 481, 490, 491, 499, 500, 507, 511, 512, 514.*

Crowder was an apprentice of James Hodges, with whom Richardson did business for a number of years. He was a partner with Richardson in the publication of the Modern Part of the *Universal History;* and he owned a share in the sixth edition of Richardson's revision of Defoe's *Tour*. In the first three books listed above—all published in 1759—Crowder's name appears as sole proprietor of a bookshop, but in the later items the imprint reads "S. Crowder & Co." Plomer says (p. 68) that the "Co." represents a partnership with Henry Woodgate, but in other places (pp. 35 and 270), he says that Samuel Brooks and Henry Woodgate were partners. These statements are of course not inconsistent, but the entries in Plomer's *Dictionary* are misleading and they do not denominate Crowder's partner in 1760. It is true that Crowder and Woodgate were partners and that Woodgate and Brooks were partners. The first partnership was dissolved, however, in 1757; and the second partnership was established in 1758 (Charles J. Longman, *The House of Longman*, ed. Chandler, 1936, p. 441). In 1759 Crowder was in business by himself; in 1760 he acquired another partner, but that partner's name is still to be discovered.

CROWNFIELD, JOHN. b. 1710. [1732.] *108.

Crownfield published this work of John Conybeare in 1732, when he was located in St. Paul's Churchyard. He probably moved in the same year to Cambridge. He was the son of Cornelius Crownfield, printer to the University of Cambridge, 1706–1740.

CRUDEN, ALEXANDER. d. 1770. [1736.] 183.

An anonymous pamphlet, pro-Hanover. Cruden was in the bookselling business for only a short time.

CURLL, EDMUND. d. 1747. [1723–1725.] 13, 40, *41.*

Obviously Richardson's relations with the unspeakable Curll would not have been extensive. These three items are a collection of poems (edited perhaps by Jeremiah Markland), a work of Mrs. Manley for which Richardson printed a new preface, and an edition of Sidney in which Curll held a share.

DARBY, JOHN. d. 1733. [1724–1730.] *28, 86, 302A, 404A.*

Darby was a printer, holding shares, as Richardson himself frequently did, in large bookselling schemes. The third and fourth of these books were printed for Darby's executors. See p. 93.

DAVEY, P. [1759–1762.] *478, 479, 481, 490, 491, 499, 500, 511, 512, 514.*

Davey was in partnership with Bedwell Law at least as early as 1756. In 1759 Davey and Law appeared as partners in the imprint of the fourth edition of Delany's *David;* and the two men were listed as partners in the proposals for the modern part of the *Universal History* and in the imprint of Vols. I–XVIII. Beginning with Vol. XIX (1760) the entries in the Stationers' Register read B. Law & Co.; and this is the style of the firm in the imprint of the sixth edition of Defoe's *Tour* (No. 514), in 1762. Perhaps Davey died in 1760. Law lived until 1798.

DAVIDSON, JOSEPH. [1740.] *259, *260.

Davidson was probably secured by John Osborn, bookseller, to assist in the publishing of the first and second editions of the first volume of Delany's *David.*

DAVIS, CHARLES. d. 1755. [1736–1743.] *195, 198, 250, *266, 270, 271, *281, 309.*

Davis and Thomas Woodward were for a long period the so-called "Printers to the Royal Society." The phrase is misleading, however, for neither of them was a printer. We know from Richardson's correspondence, for example, that No. 309 was printed by Richardson for Woodward and Davis. If Richardson printed the Royal Society's *Philosophical Transactions* from 1736, he was then printing for Davis and Woodward. Certainly from 1752 until Davis' death in 1755, he printed these transactions for Davis, and continued to print them for Davis' nephew, Lockyer Davis, who was in partnership with Charles Reymer after his uncle's death. Richardson had, however, few other relations with Charles Davis.

DAVIS, LOCKYER. d. 1791. [1755–1759.] *198, 450, 484.*

See under Charles Davis above. Lockyer Davis was in partnership with Charles Reymer, a printer. Richardson, nevertheless, continued to print the *Philosophical Transactions* for Davis and Reymer from 1755 until his death in 1761. This contract was awarded by the Royal Society rather than by Davis; otherwise, Reymer would undoubtedly have done the printing. The other two items printed by Richardson for Davis and Reymer were two tracts of the Rev. Peter Peckard.

I do not know why this bookshop was chosen for the sale of these tracts.

DICKENSON, J. [1735.] 161.
A political pamphlet.

DODD, ANNE. [1734.] *147.
Publisher for one of William Popple's plays.

DOD [DODD], BENJAMIN. d. 1764? [1744–1758.] *318, 353, 412, 413, 432, 436, 447, 448, 463, 464, 475.*
Dod was bookseller to the S.P.C.K. Most of these books were the writings of John Leland, who probably made arrangements with both Richardson and Dod for the printing and sale of his books.

DODSLEY, JAMES. [1760.] 489.
See Dodsley, Robert and James.

DODSLEY, ROBERT. d. 1764. [1739–1753.] 251, *266, 274, *281, *329, *351, 383A, 393, 402, 403, 404, 416, 417, 418.
See also Dodsley, Robert and James. Dodsley's relations with Richardson seem to have been friendly, but in the main he employed John Hughs and others to do his printing. The items printed by Richardson for Dodsley include a number of works of Duck, Spence, and Young—authors who in all likelihood requested that Richardson do the printing at the time when they made arrangements with Dodsley for the bookselling.

DODSLEY, ROBERT and JAMES. [1754–1762.] *427, *428, *429, *432, 434, *437, 439, 440, 441, 441A, 441B, *442, *443, *444, *451, 453, *453A, 459, 460, *461, 466, *470, *472, 476, 477, 481A, *486, *486A, 487, 488, 496, 516.
This printing in the main represents either Richardson's own work, for which he held the copyright, or the work of Richardson's friends to whom he undoubtedly recommended the flourishing bookshop of the Dodsleys, with its reputation for belles lettres. Included in these items are a group of books, printed by Richardson for the author, and sold by the Dodsleys.

DOWNING, JOSEPH. d. 1734. [1734.] *153.*
Downing, a printer, probably printed the first volume of this two-volume work.

FAYRAM, FRANCIS. [1724–1729.] *28, 69, 70.*
Besides Bailey's *Dictionary*, these three items include two anony-

mous medical books for home use, printed for Fayram and James Leake, the bookseller at Bath, whose sister was Richardson's second wife.

FEALES, W. [1734–1736.] *153, 164,* 171, 172, 174, 178, 189.

With the exception of the first item, all of these books are plays, for which Feales' shop was well known.

FIELD, THOMAS. [1759.] 481.

Field was merely one of a group of booksellers who acquired a share in Delany's *David,* when a fourth edition was published.

FLETCHER, JAMES. d. 1795. [1741–1746.] 279A, 343.

Fletcher's bookshop at Oxford was engaged to handle these two works of Richard Newton, Principal of Hertford College.

FLETCHER, JAMES. d. 1798, son of James Fletcher, above. See Rivington, James.

FORD, RICHARD. [1727.] *49.*

FRANKLIN, RICHARD. [1724–1739.] *30, 70A, 250.

Franklin, or Francklin, was much better known as a printer than as a bookseller, for he printed and published the antiministerial periodical, the *Craftsman,* and was frequently prosecuted for libel.

FREDERICK, WILLIAM. [1749.] 367A.

Richardson printed this work of David Hartley for James Leake and Frederick, booksellers in Bath.

FULLER, JOHN. [1748–1759.] *353,* 481.

Fuller appears only as a member of a conger for the second volume of Harris' *Voyages* and as a sharer in Delany's *David,* fourth edition.

GILLIVER, LAWTON. [1730.] *86.*

Chiefly known as one of Pope's booksellers.

GOSLING, ROBERT. d. 1741. [1725–1734.] *41, 86, 153.*

GRAVES, JOHN. [1724.] *30.

GRAY, JOHN. [1734–1738.] 136, *236, *237.

Gray was one of the booksellers for the Society for the Encouragement of Learning, and two of these items (236, 237) were printed by Richardson for this Society.

HARRIS, THOMAS. [1744.] *318.*

A member of the conger that published John Harris' *Voyages.* His name appears in the imprint of Vol. I, but when Vol. II was published in 1748, Harris was in bankruptcy.

HAWES, L. See Hitch, Charles.

HAWKINS, GEORGE. d. 1780. [1744–1755.] *323, 332, 333, 363, 432.*

When Edward Young decided to change booksellers after the publishing of the "Sixth Night" of his *Complaint*, he entered into an agreement with George Hawkins, who was to succeed Robert Dodsley. The printing was then shifted from the shop of John Hughs to that of Richardson. The first four of these items represent the printing of the last three "Nights" of the *Complaint*.

HETT, RICHARD. d. 1766? [1730–1748.] *86*, 251 (with Robert Dodsley), *259, *260, *318, 353*.

Richardson had few connections with Hett, who was looked upon as a publisher for the Dissenters. Hett's son, however, served his apprenticeship with Richardson.

HILDYARD, JOHN. d. 1757. [1740.] *256.

A bookseller in York, selling a volume written by William Bowman, a Yorkshire clergyman.

HINTON, JOHN. d. 1781. [1744–1748.] *314, 318, 353.*

Hinton secured a share in the *Universal History* (314), with the publication of Vol. VII, but he apparently sold it soon afterwards. Otherwise, he appears only as a member of the conger for Harris' *Voyages*.

HITCH, CHARLES. d. 1764. [1730–1762.] In partnership with Arthur Bettesworth, his father-in-law: *86, 153*, 177. Alone: *108, *260, *266, *270, 271*, *281, 294, *318, 353*, *367A. In partnership with L. Hawes: 400, 404, *404A, 406*, *427, *428, *429, *432*, *437, *451, 466, *478, 479*, *485, *490, 491, 499, 500, 511, 512, 514*.

Hitch and Bettesworth were listed as partners in the imprint of Salmon's *State Trials* in 1730, but Hitch's name appears alone in a volume of 1732 (108), and Bettesworth's name appears alone in a volume of 1735 (164). On the other hand, another volume of 1735 (177) was printed for Bettesworth and Hitch as partners. The exact nature of this partnership is not clear, but the two men published jointly many books, other than those printed by Richardson. Hitch served his apprenticeship with Bettesworth and he married Bettesworth's daughter. After Richardson's death, Hitch's daughter, Catherine, married Richardson's nephew, James Leake, Jr. At John

Osborn's sale in November 1751, Hitch bought a share in Richardson's *Familiar Letters*. A fifth edition of this work was printed in 1752 and Hitch's name appears alone on the first state of the title page. The title page was canceled, however, to insert in the imprint the partnership of C. Hitch and L. Hawes. This partnership must have been effected, therefore, just before the book's publication on the 30th of July (*Sale*, p. 37). The new firm also owned a share in Richardson's *Aesop* by 1753; and Richardson secured their services, among others, for the publication of *Sir Charles Grandison*, for his *Collection of Sentiments*, and for the fourth edition of *Clarissa* in 1759. The firm of Hitch and Hawes also acquired a share in Richardson's edition of Defoe's *Tour* in 1753, which they still owned when the work went into a sixth edition in 1762. Hitch was elected master of the Stationers' Company in 1758. He was one of the wardens when Richardson was master.

HODGES, SIR JAMES. [1740–1757.] *260, 263, *266, *281, *295, 318, 352, 353, 400, 404, 404*A*, 406, 430, 466.

Hodges owned a share in the fifth edition of Richardson's *Familiar Letters*, the third edition of his *Aesop*, and the seventh of *Pamela*. He probably acquired these at John Osborn's sale in November 1751. He also owned a share in the third, fourth, and fifth editions of Richardson's revision of Defoe's *Tour*. Otherwise he seems to have had few relations with Richardson's press. He had apparently disposed of these shares by 1760, and may have retired from the bookselling trade after being knighted in 1758. See p. 96.

HODGSON, JAMES. [1740.] *256.

A bookseller in Halifax, secured to publish a work of William Bowman, Yorkshire clergyman.

HOOKE, J. [1724–1726.] *28*, 42.

HOWGATE, SAMUEL. d. 1761. [1740.] *256.

A bookseller in Leeds, secured to publish a work of William Bowman, Yorkshire clergyman.

HUTTON, JAMES. d. 1795. [1737–1738.] 221, 233.

Hutton and Charles Rivington were booksellers for these two religious works. No. 221 is one of George Whitefield's sermons. Hutton became a convert of the Wesleys, and frequently held religious services at his bookshop. Later he served for many years as secretary to the Moravian Society.

INNYS, JOHN. See Innys, William.

INNYS, WILLIAM. [1725–1753.] In partnership with J. Innys: *45, *49*. Alone: 41, 74A, *75, *83, *86*, *108, 167A. In partnership with R. Manby: 125, *153*, *259. In partnership with Joseph Richardson: 394, 397, *404A*.

Innys was one of the leading booksellers in the first quarter of the century. He was elected master of the Stationers' Company in 1747, and was still in business in 1756. His relations with Richardson were never close, but they continued over a long period.

JACKSON, J. [1737–1757.] 212, 466.

Jackson's shop was largely concerned in publishing rather than in important bookselling. With Roberts, he served as the publisher of one of Stephen Duck's poems in 1737; and he must have owned the rights to one of Edward Young's poems, for his name appears in the imprint of Young's collected works, 1757.

JOHNSTON, WILLIAM. [1755–1762.] 432, 507, *514*.

Johnston was an important bookseller, but his relations with Richardson's press were negligible. He did not begin business until 1748. In the early 1760's he acquired a share in Richardson's *Pamela* and in his edition of Defoe's *Tour*.

JONES, DAVID. [1738.] 226.

Nothing is known of Jones. This pamphlet contains two anonymous poems, one of them heralding Henry Fielding's turn to the study of the law.

KEARSLEY, GEORGE. [1761–1762.] *514*.

Kearsley acquired a share in the sixth edition of Defoe's *Tour*.

KEITH, GEORGE. [1753–1759.] 404, 481.

The first of these items is the third edition of Richardson's *Aesop*, in which Keith had acquired a share.

KING, CHARLES. d. 1735. [1729–1730.] 70A, *86*.

KING, R. [1727–1729.] 57, 77, 78, 79.

An obscure bookseller. This printing consists of an abridgment of Swift's *Gulliver*, and three editions of Samuel Madden's play, *Themistocles*.

KNAPLOCK, ROBERT. d. 1737. [1730–1734.] 86, *108, *153*.

KNAPTON, JAMES. d. 1736. [1730–1735.] Alone: *83. In partnership with John Knapton: *86*, *108. In partnership with John and Paul Knapton: *153*, 167A.

Plomer gives his death date incorrectly as 1738.

KNAPTON, JOHN. d. 1770. [1730–1753.] See Knapton, James. In partnership with Paul Knapton: *260, 291, 292, *404A*.

John and Paul Knapton were brothers of James Knapton and succeeded him in business.

KNAPTON, PAUL. d. 1755. [1734–1753.] See Knapton, James, and Knapton, John.

LAW, BEDWELL. d. 1798. See Davey, P.

LEAKE, JAMES. d. 1764. [1728–1759.] 65, 69, 70, 79A, *83, 85A, 121, *129, 136, 137, 138, *148A, 190, *221, *222, 228, 257, *259, *260, *266, 272, *281, 287, 315, 337, 338, 344, 351, 354, 355, *361, 367A, *372, 381, 382, 383, 389, 390, 391, 400, *409, *427, *428, *429, 433, *437, *451, *461, *472, *485.

James Leake, the famous bookseller of Bath, was the brother of Richardson's second wife, Elizabeth Leake. He acted as publisher in Bath for many books printed for London booksellers; in more instances than I have noted, he may well have been serving merely as publisher.

LINTOT, BERNARD. d. 1736. [1730.] *86*.

Richardson had no direct dealings with this famous bookseller. See Lintot, Henry.

LINTOT, HENRY. 1709–1758. [1732–1757.] *107*, 159, 227, 268A, 276, 310, 349A, 466.

Henry Lintot was the son of Bernard Lintot, and the father of Catherine Lintot, with whom Richardson shared the patent for printing law books after Henry Lintot's death in 1758. Henry Lintot employed Richardson's press infrequently.

LITTLETON, E. [1736.] *201.

Littleton, at the Mitre against St. Dunstan's Church, was an obscure bookseller, who served as publisher for a reprinting of the essays from William Webster's *Weekly Miscellany*.

LOBB, SAMUEL. [1730.] *85.

A bookseller in Bath, acting as publisher for a book printed for Charles Rivington in London.

LONGMAN, MARY. d. 1762. [1755.] See Longman, Thomas, II.

LONGMAN, THOMAS, I. 1699–1755. [1727–1753.] In partnership with his father-in-law, John Osborn of the Oxford Arms in Lombard Street: *49,* *83, *86.* Alone: 167A, *218, *259, *260, *266, *281, 294, *318,* *329, *353,* 400. In partnership with his nephew, Thomas Longman: 404, *404A, 406.*

The elder Longman was the founder of the present house of Longman. The relationship between him and Richardson was never intimate, but it extended throughout almost all of his career as a bookseller.

LONGMAN, THOMAS, II, nephew of Thomas Longman, I. 1730–1797. [1753–1762.]

In partnership with his uncle: 404, *404A, 406.* In partnership with Mary Longman, wife of his uncle: *432.* Alone: *478, 479, 490, 491, 499, 500, 511, 512, 514.*

LORD, JOSEPH. [1740.] 256.

A bookseller of Wakefield, Yorkshire, for whom Richardson printed this attack on Methodism, written by a Yorkshire clergyman.

LOWNDES, THOMAS. 1719–1784. [1761–1762.] *514.*

Lowndes began business in Fleet Street in 1756. He bought from Caslon a 1/32 share in Richardson's revision of Defoe's *Tour,* 8 November 1760, for £5/5/0 (B.M. *Add. MSS.,* 38,730, p. 39).

MAIN, ROBERT. [1754.] *427, *428, *429.

A bookseller in Dublin, whom Richardson employed as a publisher for the first three editions of *Sir Charles Grandison.* He enlisted Main's services in carrying on his war with the Dublin pirates (*Sale,* pp. 65–69). Main's name appears for the first time on the title page of Vol. VII, first edition.

MANBY, RICHARD. d. 1769. [1733–1753.] In partnership with William Innys: 125, *153,* *259. Alone: 404B.

Manby was an important bookseller, and master of the Stationers' Company in 1765. He did little business with Richardson.

MARSH, CHARLES. [1741.] 278.

This was a poem written by Marsh. See under his name in the alphabetical list of Richardson's printing.

MATHEWS, EMANUEL. [1729.] 73A.

Charles Rivington served his apprenticeship with Mathews.

MATTHEWS, BENJAMIN. [1753.] *490.

A bookseller at Bath, secured by Leake to assist in the publication of a work of James Hervey, printed for the benefit of a poor child.

MEARS, W. [1724–1736.] *30, 37, 39, *41, 49, 86, *195*.
One of the older booksellers of London. He was succeeded by J. Nourse (*q.v.*).

MIDWINTER, DANIEL. d. 1757 [1730–1734.] *86, 153*.

MILLAN, JOHN. d. 1784. [1734–1735.] 150, 179.
These books are James Thomson's *Winter* and *Summer*. See under Thomson in the alphabetical list of Richardson's printing.

MILLAR, ANDREW. 1706–1768. [1729–1762.] *75, *153, 232*, *236, 236A, *237, *270, 271, 290, 295, 314*, *329, 345*, 348, *350, 352*, 357, *361, 365, 367, 369, *372, 373, 375*, 382, 383A, 386, 389, 390, 391, 392, 393, 398, 399, *404A, 405, 406*, 410, *419*, *427, *428, *429, 431, *432*, *437, 439, 440, 441, 441A, 441B, *442, *451, 453, *461, 466, *470, *472, 475A, 477, *478, 479*, 480, 482, *485, 487, 488, *490, 491*, 492, 496, *499*, *500*, 502, 503, 504A, *511, 512, 514*.
Though Richardson did not do all of the printing for Andrew Millar, the relations between the men were intimate, and they had respect and admiration for each other. In January 1749, Richardson wrote of him to Aaron Hill: "I think him to be a fair, honest, open Man, and one who loves to deal generously by Authors . . . none of whom, who understand their own Interests, ever leave him, after once acquainted with him. . . . He has great Business, and is in a Way of promoting the Sale of what he engages in. I have not been always so well acquainted with him, as I am of late" (*Forster MSS.*, XIII, 3, ff. 101–102). As the entries indicate, it was not until about 1747 that Millar's name as bookseller began to appear with any frequency. For most of the books before that date Millar was serving as publisher, or his name appeared in the imprint as a member of a bookselling conger. After Richardson became well acquainted with him, he employed his services for all of his own books, and continued to recommend him to friends. The intimacy of the two men was in no way disturbed by Millar's friendly relations with Henry Fielding. Millar's birth date, according to a fellow Scot, William Strahan, was 19 October 1706 (R. A. Austen-Leigh, "William Strahan and His Ledgers," *Library*, 4 S. III [1923], 279).

MOORE, A. [1723–1731.] 15, 19, 20, 21, 95.
A pamphlet shopkeeper.

MOTTE, BENJAMIN. d. 1738. [1730–1738.] *86*, 141, *153*, 238.

Motte combined the trade of printer and bookseller. He is perhaps best known as Swift's publisher. His successor was Charles Bathurst. With neither man did Richardson do much business.

NOBLE, SAMUEL. [1730.] *86*.

NOURSE, JOHN. d. 1780. [1738–1754.] *236, *237, 422, *486A.

Nourse was the successor to Mears. He was one of the booksellers appointed by the Society for the Encouragement of Learning. The first two of these books listed were printed by Richardson for this society.

NUTT, EDWARD. [1733–1734.] 117, *147.

OGLE, JOSEPH. [1740.] *256.

A bookseller at Leeds, secured by Lord (*q.v.*) to assist in the publishing of this book.

OSBORN, JOHN, SR., first of Horsley Downs, and then of the Golden Ball in Paternoster Row. [1734–1739?] See below, under John Osborn, Jr.

OSBORN, JOHN, JR., of the Golden Ball in Paternoster Row. d. 1775. [1736–1751.] For John Osborn, Sr., while his son was serving his apprenticeship to his father: 142, *153*, *157, *172, *178, *180. For father and son (probably in partnership from 1736 to 1739, though only one name—J. Osborn—appears in imprints during these years): 193, 213, *232*, 245A. For J. Osborn, Jr. (who retains the "Jr." after his name in Nos. 254 and 268, but otherwise appears as "J. Osborn"): 254, 259, 260, 265, 266, 267, *268, 279A, 281, 282, 283, 284, 285, *286, 287, *289, *290*, *295*, 296, *298, *299, *300, 306, 308, 312, *314*, 319, 325, 331, 334, 339, 340, 343, 344, 344A, *345*, 348A, *350*, *352*, *361, *372, *375*, *376*, 381, 382, 389, 390, 391.

Four men by the name of John Osborn were in the book trade during this period; consequently confusion abounds in various accounts of the Osborns. Some of this confusion can be eliminated. The John Osborns who were most closely associated with Richardson are the father and son listed here. John Osborn, Sr., published in 1726 at "the Ship at St. Saviour's Dockhead, near Horsley Downs," Southwark (*T.L.S.*, 28 August 1930, p. 684). In 1732 he published the fifth edition of the *Independent Whig*, giving his address as "the Dockhead, near Rotherhithe." This may be the same shop, but I suspect it was somewhat farther east of the address given in 1726. In any case, he moved across the river to the Golden Ball in Paternoster Row in 1733, and published the first book from Richardson's press in 1734. His son was apprenticed to him on 4 March 1729, while he was still in South-wark ("Court Book H," p. 323). In 1736, when the son completed his apprenticeship, he apparently served as partner with his father. I do not know when the latter retired, but the name "John Osborn, Jr." appears for the first time to my knowledge on Richardson's *Aesop*, published on 20 November 1739 (*Sale*, p. 3). I assumed at one time that John Osborn, Sr., died in 1739, for Nichols (*Lit. Anec.*, III, 601) records the death of a John Osborn in that year, and John Chandler, editor of *The House of Longman* (1936, p. 325), accepts this John Osborn as the bookseller, formerly of Southwark. But in a letter of Richardson in August 1741 (*Forster MSS.*, XVI, 1, ff. 55–57), he re-fers to a remark, reputedly made by "old Mr. Osborn," that he (Rich-ardson) did not have either the leisure or inclination to continue *Pamela* beyond the first two volumes. This remark was presumably made in 1741, and certainly could not have been made before No-vember 1740, when *Pamela* was first published. But old Mr. Osborn may well have withdrawn from active partnership in the business in 1739. It was he and Charles Rivington who suggested to Richardson the writing of the *Familiar Letters*, though his son may have been the actual publisher of *Pamela*. Of John Osborn, Jr., Richardson wrote in 1746: "I have a very honest and punctual Acquaintance, John Osborn in Pater-noster Row. . . . I will engage for his Exactness" (*Forster MSS.*, XIII, 3, f. 42, to Aaron Hill, 25 June 1746). Richardson's rela-tions with these Osborns extended until the retirement of John Os-born, Jr., in November 1751 (*McKillop*, p. 313*n.*).

This family of Osborn must be kept distinct from another family in which the given name of both father and son was John. John Os-born of the Oxford Arms in Lombard Street had a son, John, who was bound apprentice to William Osborne, a printer, on 7 September 1713 ("Bindings," under date). The father went into partnership with his son-in-law, Thomas Longman (*q.v.*) in 1725, and Richardson printed a few books for the firm of Osborn and Longman. Osborn, Sr., died on 13 March 1734 (*Gentleman's Magazine*, IV [1734], 164). The son completed his apprenticeship and set up as a printer. In 1724, he and Samuel Buckley received a royal license to print the Bible in Latin and to print all Latin, Greek, and Hebrew grammars for forty-one years (P.R.O., "Entry Books," No. 360, p. 326. This privilege had previously been granted to Roger Norton by letters patent during the reign of Charles II). In 1733 John Osborn, Jr., predeceased his father, leaving his share in this printing privilege to his brother-in-law,

Thomas Longman, who had married his sister, Mary (Charles J. Long-man, *The House of Longman,* ed. Chandler, 1936, p. 468). Plomer's *Dictionary* does not distinguish among these John Osborns; and the *D.N.B.* confuses John Osborn of the Golden Ball with Thomas Os-borne (*q.v.*).

OSBORN, JOHN, and T. LONGMAN. See above, and under T. Longman.

OSBORNE, THOMAS, SR. d. 1743. [1730–1737.] *86, 107,* *108, *185, 187, 195, 205.*

Thomas Osborne, according to Plomer's *Dictionary,* was succeeded by his son, Thomas, in 1738. Richardson's connections with these Osbornes were largely confined to the publishing done by these men as members of congers.

OSBORNE, THOMAS, JR. d. 1767. [1743–1762.] *225, 241, 253, 290, 307A, 314, 328A, 345, 350, 352, 375, 404A, 406, 419, 478, 479, 480, 490, 491, 499, 500, 511, 512, 514.*

OWEN, WILLIAM. d. 1793. [1749–1761.] 368, 384, 395, 407, 415, 449, 450, 484, 497, 509.

Owen's shop was at Homer's Head, near Temple Bar. Though I cannot be sure, I suspect that he was merely acting as publisher for many of these books, and that Richardson secured his services as he had sought those of Thomas Cooper before the latter's death. See p. 88.

PARKER, WILLIAM. [1740.] *260.

PAYNE, OLIVER. [1737.] *217.

Payne went into bankruptcy in 1739.

PAYNE, THOMAS. [1722–1723.] 11, 12, 13, 22, 24, 25.

This pamphlet shopkeeper should not be confused with "honest Tom Payne," the brother of Oliver Payne. For Thomas Payne's rela-tions with Richardson, see pp. 43–48.

PEELE, JOHN. d. 1770. [1727–1743.] *56, *86,* 148, 180, 196, 312.

When we consider that Nichols called Peele "a very considerable bookseller," the information about him seems surprisingly meager. In addition to the few books listed here, we must also include the newspapers, the *Daily Journal* and the *Daily Gazetteer,* in which both Peele and Richardson owned a share (see pp. 62; 65). No. 148 is also a periodical, the *Prompter;* Peele's name appears in the imprint of the first nine numbers. No. 196 is a volume in which Peele owned a quarter-share, though his name does not appear in the imprint. Peele's relations with Richardson must have been more intimate and continuous than is indicated, for he is one of the few booksellers to whom Richardson left a ring in his will. It seems evident that both men profited considerably by Walpole's subsidization of the press. For Peele's death, see Musgrave's *Obituary*.

PEMBERTON, JOHN, SR. d. 1739. [1724–1739.] For J. Pemberton, Sr.: *28*, 55, 88, 134. For J. and J. Pemberton (father and son): 200, 217A, 219, 250.

The partnership between father and son was begun in 1735. John, Jr., and his brother, Henry, formed a partnership soon after their father's death, but Richardson does not seem to have done any printing for this firm. When Henry died in 1748, he made no mention of his brother, John, in his will. The latter may have died or retired by 1748.

PEMBERTON, JOHN, JR. [1740–1741.] *266, *281. See under John Pemberton, Sr.

Since the name of J. Pemberton appears alone in these two books, presumably the partnership between John, Jr., and his brother, Henry, was not effected immediately after their father's death.

PURSER, JOHN. [1735.] 158.

Purser was a printer. He seems to have succeeded Richardson as the printer of the *Daily Journal* in 1728 (see p. 61). When he moved to Shoe Lane, near Holborn, at some date after 1730, he may have acted as publisher for some of the many pamphlets which came from his press. I do not know why this anonymous pamphlet should have been printed for him by Richardson.

REYMER [RYMER], CHARLES. See Davis, Lockyer.

RICHARDSON, JOSEPH. [1752–1761.] 394, 397, *404A*, 507.

The first three books were printed for Joseph Richardson when he was in partnership with William Innys (*q.v.*); the fourth book—the eighth edition of *Pamela*—shows Richardson's name alone. Mary Richardson, whose stock and copies were sold in 1766, was probably the widow of Joseph Richardson (*N&Q*, 7 S. IX [1890], 301).

RIVINGTON, CHARLES. 1688–1742. [1724–1741.] *28*, 50, 58, 59, *83, 85, 88, 94, 97, *99, 109, 110, *112, 122, *127, *129, 135, 140, *144, 151, 154, 165, 167, 170, *175, 186, 206, 207, *216, 221, 222, 233, 245, *249, 252, *256, 257, *259, *260, *264, *266, 267, *268, *279, 279A, *281, 282, 283, 284, 285, *286, 287.

For the relations between Richardson and Rivington, see Septimus Rivington, *The Publishing Family of Rivington*, 1919, *passim*. Charles Rivington was well established in the bookselling trade at the Bible and Crown in St. Paul's Churchyard when Richardson did his first printing for him. This volume—the second edition of Bailey's *Dictionary*—was printed in 1724 for a conger of booksellers; and it was not until 1727 that Richardson printed the first book which brought the two men into personal relationship. From then on, Richardson continued to print for Rivington; and at the latter's death on 22 February 1742, he served as executor of his will. Charles Rivington and John Osborn were the two booksellers who suggested to Richardson the writing of the *Familiar Letters;* and these two men shared the copyright of the first two volumes of *Pamela*. Rivington was succeeded by his son John, who had been bound to his father on 6 May 1735. James Rivington, another son, was bound to his father on 4 September 1739 ("Bindings," under dates). James was turned over to his brother on 6 July 1742; and in 1745 both brothers purchased their freedom of the Stationers' Company, and the firm of J. and J. Rivington began to appear in imprints of books from Richardson's press (Septimus Rivington, *op. cit.*, p. 41). Charles Rivington, Jr., served his apprenticeship as a printer to Samuel Richardson, beginning in 1746.

RIVINGTON, JOHN. 1720–1792. [1742–1762.] For John Rivington alone [1742–1745]: *298, *299, *300, 308, 317, *318*, 330. In partnership with his brother James [1745–1756]: 326, 328, 335, 337, 338, 342, 343, 344, 344A, 346, *353*, 354, 354A, 355, *358, *361, 362, *372, 374, 378, 379, 381, 382, 383, 389, 390, 391, *399A, 400, 404, *404A*, *406*, *409, 410, 421, *427, *428, *429, 430, *432*, 434, *437, *442, *451. For John Rivington alone, after the partnership between him and James had been dissolved [6 March 1756]: 466, *470, *478*, *479*, 481, *485, 489, *490*, *491*, *499*, *500*, 507, *511*, *512*, *514*. See above, under Charles Rivington.

The partnership between these two brothers was dissolved on 6 March 1756; and on the 9th of March James Rivington went into partnership with James Fletcher, the son of the Oxford bookseller (Septimus Rivington, *The Publishing Family of Rivington*, 1919, p. 42). John Rivington continued in business at his father's shop in St. Paul's Churchyard, while Rivington and Fletcher set up in business in Paternoster Row. James ultimately went to America.

RIVINGTON, JAMES. 1724–1803. [1757–1759.] In partnership with James Fletcher [from 9 March 1756]: 466, *485.

Richardson does not seem to have done any printing for the firm of Rivington and Fletcher. These two books—the collected works of Edward Young and the fourth edition of *Clarissa*—carry in the imprints the names of both John Rivington and of Rivington and Fletcher. The Rivington brothers, when partners, owned jointly a share in Young's works; and they had served as publishers for earlier editions of *Clarissa*.

ROBERTS, JAMES. d. 1754. [1724–1748.] 31, 35, 43, 48, 61, 65, 66, 72, 79A, 85A, *86*, 89, 92, 96, 113, 120, 124A, 147, 148A, 149, 155, 175A, 175B, 182, 183A, 188, 203, 205A, 210, 212, 261, 274, 303, 304, 313, 359, 360.

Roberts was a printer of some eminence and for three years (1729–1732) master of the Stationers' Company. He died at the age of 85. Most of these items are slight in nature: pamphlets, individual poems, periodicals. Roberts was probably serving only as publisher in the great majority of instances. I suspect that he served Richardson in much the same way as did Thomas and Mary Cooper and William Owen. See p. 88.

ROBINSON, JACOB. [1738–1753.] *232, 295, 318, 352, 353, 406.*

This printing represents four editions of Defoe's *Tour* in which Robinson owned a share; and two volumes of Harris' *Voyages*, published by a large conger.

ROBINSON, RANEW. [1730–1734.] *86, 153.*

ROE, JEREMIAH. [1730.] *85.

This bookseller in Derby was acting as publisher for a book printed by Richardson for Rivington.

SANDBY, WILLIAM. d. 1799. [1756–1760.] 445, 454, 455, 456, 457, *486A, 494, 495, 495A.

Sandby was a prominent bookseller, but Richardson printed for him only a series of tracts by Archibald Bower, Lyttelton's *Dialogues of the Dead*, in three editions, and Sydenham's *Synopsis of the Works of Plato*.

SANDERS, T. [1730.] *86.*

SCOTT, JOHN. [1756.] 452.

This book is the second issue of a poem of John Shebbeare. Richardson probably had nothing to do with it, but he printed the first issue for William Owen.

SENEX, MARY. [1753.] *404A.*

Plomer lists M. Senex as a man, but the license for Chambers' *Cyclopaedia* gives the name as Mary Senex ("Warrant Books," No. 368, p. 447). She may have been the wife of John Senex, who died in 1740.

SHUCKBURGH, JOHN. d. 1761. [1732–1753.] *107, 309, 404A.*

SPAVAN, R. [1749.] *366.

This bookseller may have been the son of George Spavan. His address is the same—At the Crown in Ivy Lane.

SPRINT, BENJAMIN. d. 1737. [1730.] *86.*

STAGG, JOHN. d. 1746. [1724–1745.] *30, *49, 70A, 82, 86, *329.
Stagg died in his fifty-second year.

STEVENS, JOHN. [1727.] *49.*

STONE, J. [1727.] *57.*

STRAHAN, ALEXANDER. [1753.] 404B.

Alexander Strahan was probably a son of George Strahan, who owned a share in this book. The book is, as a matter of fact, a third issue of a work first published in 1740. For George Strahan's share in the copyright, see under George Cheyne, *The Natural Method of Cureing [sic] the Diseases of the Body,* 1742.

STRAHAN, GEORGE. [1724–1746.] *30, *45, 46, *75, *97A, 121, 128, 137, 138, 145A, 174A, 175A, 175B, *195, *268, 279A, 291, 292, 343.

A number of these books were the writings or translations of Scotsmen, at least two of whom—Gordon and Cheyne—were dealing directly with Richardson. Perhaps they requested their fellow countryman, Strahan, as publisher.

SWALE, JOHN. [1740.] *256.
A bookseller in Leeds.

SYMON, EDWARD. d. 1741. [1724–1740.] *28, 62, 49, 86, 185, 205, 225, 241, 253.*

TAYLOR, E. [1725.] *41.*

E. Taylor is probably the wife of William Taylor, who died in 1724, leaving John Osborn and William Innys his executors. In the same year she was listed at the sign used by William Taylor—the

Ship and Black Swan in Paternoster Row (Charles J. Longman, *The House of Longman*, ed. Chandler, 1936, pp. 446, 461–462). For more information about her, see the alphabetical list of books printed by Richardson, under Sir Philip Sidney.

TONSON, JACOB. d. 1735. [1730.] *86*.

This is the nephew of Dryden's bookseller, Jacob Tonson. The latter retired about 1720 in favor of his nephew, and died in 1736. The nephew, who died in December 1735, predeceased his uncle by four months. He left two sons to carry on the business, Jacob III (d. 1767) and Richard (d. 1772). Richard was a quiet partner, taking little part in the conduct of the bookshop. He is not to be confused with the Richard Tonson who was the elder brother of Dryden's publisher.

TONSON, JACOB. d. 1767. [1742–1757.] In partnership with his brother, Richard: *302A*, 466.

The second book is an edition of Young's *Works*, the rights to which were held by a number of booksellers. These Tonsons were great-nephews of Dryden's bookseller.

TONSON, RICHARD. d. 1772. See under the Tonsons listed above.

VAILLANT, PAUL. d. 1802. [1740.] *268.

A book sold by Vaillant for the Society for the Encouragement of Learning.

VINCENT, ROBERT, SR. [1730.] *86*.

This bookseller describes himself as "R. Vincent, Sen." in 1730. I know nothing of his son.

WALLER, T. [1740–1754.] 255, 421A.

Waller was the proprietor of a pamphlet shop.

WALTHOE, H. [1731.] 90.

See under John Walthoe.

WALTHOE, JOHN, SR. or JR. [1727–1742.] For J. Walthoe, Sr., and J. Walthoe, Jr.: *86, 302A*. For J. Walthoe, Jr.: 196. For J. and H. Walthoe: 90. For J. Walthoe: 47, 63, 67, 71, 80, 100, 101, *107*, 111, 139, *153*, 157, 184, 187, 204, *217, 245.

Plomer's *Dictionary* makes no attempt to distinguish between the careers of two John Walthoes, who seem clearly to be father and son. In default of a death date for a John Walthoe, I can merely offer a conjecture in the light of the known facts. A John Walthoe was established as a bookseller in London as early as 1683; and on 7 March 1708,

John Walthoe, son of John, was bound apprentice to his father ("Bindings," under date). In 1730 the names of J. Walthoe, Sr., and J. Walthoe, Jr. (not as a partnership) appear in the imprint of Salmon's edition of the *State Trials*. In the edition of the *Trials* in 1742 the Walthoes appear as partners. In 1735 J. Walthoe, Jr., was listed in the *Daily Journal* (January 13) as a partner in the publication of Bayle's *Dictionary;* and in 1736 the manuscript register of the Stationers' Company lists John Walthoe, Jr., and Samuel Richardson, among others, as sharers in the copyright of Popple's play, *The Double Deceit* (I, 455, under date of February 26). In the imprint of this published play, the name of J. Walthoe appears, without the addition of the "Jr."

There is an obvious attempt in 1730, 1735, 1736, and 1742 to distinguish between a father and son, both of the same name. But with the exception of the instances which I have noted, the name of J. Walthoe, alone and without the addition of either "Sr." or "Jr." appears in imprints throughout the whole period under consideration, always with the same address in Cornhill. The John Walthoe, bound to his father in 1708, would have been freed by 1715. One would expect to find the partnership of J. and J. Walthoe, but with the one exception in the *State Trials* of 1742, the only indication of a partnership which I have found serves to make the problem more puzzling. In a book published in 1731 the names J. and H. Walthoe appear.

For two years, 1725 and 1726, a John Walthoe was master of the Stationers' Company. This Walthoe was probably the bookseller who started in business in the seventeenth century, for it is not likely that a man, freed of the company in 1715, would have been elected master in 1725. The John Walthoe who was associated with Richardson in the affairs of the *Daily Gazetteer* during the 1730's must have been a son of the master of the Stationers' Company, or, in any case, of his generation (p. 65). I am including the record of the binding of a third John Walthoe, though it is not clear what his relation is—if any—to the two Walthoes under discussion. The manuscript records of the Stationers' Company ("Bindings," under date) indicate that a John Walthoe, son of John, Citizen and Stationer, was bound to Thomas Wood, a London printer, on 5 February 1722. It does not seem possible that he was the son of either of the other John Walthoes, for his birth year could not have been later than 1707. It is scarcely credible that the John Walthoe who was bound to his father in 1708 was then married and the father of a son. Furthermore, as apprentice to a printer, the third John Walthoe would in likelihood have followed this trade rather than that of bookseller. Until more information about the Walthoes is forthcoming, I think we can safely assume that the John Walthoe most closely associated with Richardson was the one who was bound to his father in 1708.

WARD, AARON. [1730–1744.] *86, 153, 318.*

WARD, JOHN. [1748–1755.] *353, 404A, 432.*

John Ward was probably the son of Aaron. The last book which Richardson printed for Aaron Ward was Harris' *Voyages,* Vol. I, 1744; the first which he printed for John Ward was the second volume of the *Voyages,* 1748. It seems likely that Aaron Ward died in 1747; and Plomer suggests that John Ward died shortly after 1758. The Wards were merely members of congers for whom Richardson printed.

WARD, THOMAS. [1734–1737.] In partnership with E. Wicksteed: *153.* Alone: *214.*

WARE, CATHERINE. [1759–1762.] *478, 479, 490, 491, 499, 500, 511, 512.*

Catherine Ware was probably the wife of Richard Ware, who carried on the business with her son, Richard, Jr. She was a partner in the publication of the modern part of the *Universal History;* and entries in the Stationers' Register sometimes list her as C. Ware and Co., and sometimes as C. Ware and Son. Plomer suggests that she was in partnership with her husband, but there is no evidence to substantiate this assertion.

WARE, RICHARD. d. 1756. [1753.] *404A.*

Probably the husband of Catherine Ware.

WARNER, T. [1723–1749.] 27, 36, 52, 81, 98, 104, 109, 364.

No. 109 was published in 1732, and No. 364, a small pamphlet, was published in 1749. Warner was somewhat closely associated with Richardson during the days of the *Daily Journal* (p. 60). It is surprising, however, to find Warner's name reappearing in an imprint after a lapse of seventeen years.

WEBB, W. [1747.] 349.

Nothing is known of Webb. His address is given as "near St. Paul's."

WELLINGTON, RICHARD. [1735.] *164.*

This bookseller was probably the son of Richard Wellington, for both men used the same sign—the Dolphin and Crown. A share in the copyright of this book, a play of John Banks', was probably inherited by Richard Wellington from his father.

WHISTON, JOHN. 1711–1780. [1738–1754.] *232, 295,* *329, 404B.

The son of the clergyman and scholar, William Whiston, John Whiston found his shop frequented by distinguished members of the Church of England. Richardson was on one occasion at Tunbridge Wells with William Whiston, whom he described as "the noted Mr. Whiston, showing eclipses, and explaining other phaenomena of the stars, and preaching the millennium, and anabaptism (for he is now, it seems, of that persuasion) to gay people, who, if they have white teeth, hear him with open mouths, though perhaps shut hearts" (*Barbauld*, III, 318–319). Richardson's relations with John Whiston were slight.

WHITE, BENJAMIN. d. 1794. [1753.] 404B.

White was a partner of John Whiston (*q.v.*).

WHITRIDGE, HENRY. [1727–1748.] 54, 68, 74, 76, *318,* *329, *353.*

WICKSTEED, E. See Thomas Ward.

WILCOX, J. [1735.] *166.

WILDE, ALLINGTON. 1700–1770. [1730.] 83.

Wilde, Richardson's brother-in-law, was a printer. This volume, a reprint of the essays in Hill's *Plain Dealer*, was printed for Richardson and Wilde.

WILFORD, JOHN. [1730–1737.] 84, 90A, 91, 102, 132, *147, 208.

Wilford, best known as the compiler of the *Monthly Catalogue of Books*, 1723–1729, was more frequently publisher than bookseller. He may have been serving in that capacity for most of these items.

WILKIN, R. [1734.] *153.*

WILLIAMSON, RICHARD. d. 1737. [1730–1732.] *86,* *108.

WILMOT, SAMUEL. [1732–1737.] 108, 218.

Wilmot was an Oxford bookseller. The copyright of the second of these two books—Spence's essay on Pope's *Odyssey*—was owned by Wilmot. See p. 206.

WITHERS, EDWARD. [1755.] *432.*

WITHY, ROBERT. [1755.] *432.*

WOOD, JOHN. [1737–1741.] In partnership with Jeremiah Batley: *205.* Alone: *225, 241, 253.* In partnership with C. Woodward: *260, *266, *281.

Wood, who gives his address as "near St. Paul's," is not listed by Plomer. He and his partner, Jeremiah Batley, were among the original projectors of the ancient part of the *Universal History*. When Batley died in 1737, Wood remained a member of the conger until the publication of the fifth volume in 1740. In that year he entered into a partnership with C. Woodward, and this firm was secured by John Osborn to assist in the publishing of three books printed by Richardson for Osborn.

WOODFALL, HENRY. d. 1769. [1762.] 507.

This book, the eighth edition of *Pamela*, was the first to be published posthumously. Woodfall was a printer, who acquired a share in *Pamela* after Richardson's death. His death date is supplied by William Strahan, who in June 1771, wrote that Woodfall had died "about 2 yrs. ago" (R. A. Austen-Leigh, "William Strahan and his Ledgers," *Library* 4 S. III [1923], 272).

WOODMAN, JAMES. [1726.] *45.

WOODWARD, C. See under John Wood.

WOODWARD, THOMAS. [1726–1743.] *45, 49, *56, 86, 168, 195, 196, 245, *260, 275, 276, 309 (with C. Davis as "Printers to the Royal Society"), 318, 353.

Woodward, whose shop was in Fleet Street near Salisbury Court, was on friendly terms with Richardson, who borrowed copies of certain books from his shop to lend to Aaron Hill. Richardson and Woodward each owned a one-fourth share in No. 196. It is possible that Richardson was printing the *Philosophical Transactions* of the Royal Society for part of the time when Woodward and Davis were the official "printers" to this society. Neither Davis nor Woodward were actually printers. He retired in 1743 (*Forster MSS.*, XIII, 3, f. 12, Richardson to Hill). Woodward's name appears in the imprint of Nos. 318 and 353 (Harris' *Voyages*, Vols. I and II, 1744, 1748) but this was because the royal license protecting this work included his name.

WORRALL, JOHN. [1761.] 504, 508.

These books were printed by Richardson after he acquired a half-share in the patent for printing law books. Worrall dealt chiefly in books on the law.

WOTTON, THOMAS. d. 1766. [1730–1742.] 86, 107, 141, 302A.

WYAT, W. [1734.] 153.

APPENDIX A

The Location of Ornaments
Belonging to Other Printers

THE TITLES in the following list are of books that are said in their imprints to be the work of a given printer. Each book contains one or more printers' ornaments.

PRINTERS	TITLES
Ackers, Charles	Ralph, James, *Night*, 1728.
Applebee, John	*A general remonstrance to the whole people of England*, 1740.
Aris, Samuel	Abernethy, John, *A supplement to the treatise entituled, The nature, obligation, and efficacy of the Christian sacraments*, 1730.
Aris, Thomas (Red-Lyon Court, Fleet Street)	Banks, John, *Miscellaneous works*, 2 vols., 1738.
Barber, John	Higgons, Bevill, *A poem on the peace*, 1731(?).
Bettenham, James	Oldham, John, *Works*, 2 vols., 1722.
Blandford, N.	Thomson, James, *Winter*, 2nd ed., 1726.
Botham, W.	Clark, Samuel, *Sermons*, 10 vols., 1730–1731.
Bowyer, William	Brewster, Thomas, *A translation of the Second Satyr of Persius*, 1733.
Browne, T.	Masters, Mary, *Poems on several occasions*, 1733.
Buckley, Samuel	Gibson, Edmund, *The Bishop of London's third pastoral letter*, 2nd ed., 1731.
Campbell, A.	Desaguliers, John T., *The Newtonian system of the world*, 1728.

PRINTERS	TITLES
Cave, Edward	Luck, Robert, *A miscellany of new poems*, 1736.
Chrichley, Joseph	*The present government of England in church and state*, 1732.
Darby, John (and Browne, T.)	Arbuckle, James, *A collection of letters and essays*, 2 vols., 1729.
Dormer, J.	*Majesty misled*, 1734.
Downing, Joseph	*An account of several work-houses, for employing and maintaining the poor*, 2nd ed., 1732.
Downing, Mary	Maddox, Isaac, *A sermon preach'd in the parish-church of Christ-Church, London; on Thursday April the 30th.*, *1741*, 1741.
Edlin, Thomas	Boyd, Elizabeth, *The happy-unfortunate*, 1732.
Gardner, Thomas	Haywood, Eliza, *A present for a servant-maid*, 1745.
Gilbert, S.	Carey, Henry, *Dramatick works*, 1743.
Haines, Henry	Pulteney, William, *A letter from a member of Parliament to his friend in the country*, [1733].
Holt, S.	Consett, Thomas, ed. and tr., *The present state and regulations of the Church of Russia*, 1729.
Huggonson, J.	*Divine wisdom and providence*, 1736.
Hughs, John	Moore, Edward, *Poems, fables, and plays*, 1756.
Humpreys, J.	Earle, Jabez, *Verses upon several occasions*, 2nd ed., 1724.
Hunter, W.	*The Bee. A collection of choice poems.* Part II, 1715.
Ilive, T.	*The Bee. A collection of choice poems.* Part I, 1715.
Jallasson, Samuel	Rival, Pierre, *Sermon prononcé le 25 de Juin, 1727 a l'occasion de l'avenement du Roy George II a la couronne*, 1727.
Jephson, Charles	Defoe, Daniel, *Religious courtship*, 7th ed., 1743. [See colophon.]
Keimer, S.	Defoe, Daniel (?), *Burnet and Bradbury, or, The confederacy of the press and the pulpit for the blood of the last ministry*, 1715.
Kent, Henry	*Observations on British wool, and the manufacturing of it in this kingdom*, 1738.
Mathard, R.	*The life and glorious actions of His Grace James Duke of Ormond*, 1715.

PRINTERS	TITLES
Matthews, Mary	Camden, William, *Britannia*, ed. Gibson, 2nd ed., 2 vols., 1722.
Mechell, James	Keith, Sir William, *A collection of papers and other tracts*, 1740.
Mist, Nathaniel	*A collection of miscellany letters, selected out of Mist's Weekly Journal*, 2 vols., 1722.
Moore, A.	*The life and character of the late Lord Chancellor Jeffreys*, 1725. [Moore was a pamphlet shopkeeper and probably not a printer, but this book is said to have been printed *by* him.]
Oliver, John	*An account of the Society for Promoting Christian Knowledge*, 1755.
Owen, Edward	Morell, Thomas, *Poems on divine subjects*, 1732.
Palmer, Samuel (and Huggonson, J.)	Croft, R., *Remarks on the proceedings of the French court*, 2nd ed., 1731.
Pearson, W.	Behrens, Georg Henning, *The natural history of Hartz-Forest*, tr. Andree, 1730.
Penny, Robert	Free, John, *The danger attending an enlightened and free people, from a national intercourse with those, who live under an idolatrous religion*, 1753.
Powell, Samuel	Sheridan, Thomas, *A full vindication of the conduct of the manager of the Theatre-Royal*, Dublin, 1747.
Purser, John	Lyttelton, George, 1st Baron Lyttelton, *Observations on the life of Cicero*, 2nd ed., 1741.
Rayner, William	*Memoirs of the life of Robert Wilks*, 1732.
Reeve, W.	Hill, Aaron, *The insolvent*, 1758.
Reynolds, Thomas	Hare, Francis, *A letter to the Rt. Hon. Sir Richard Brocas, Lord Mayor of London*, 1730.
Rivington, Charles, Jr.	Gilpin, William, *The life of Hugh Latimer, Bishop of Worcester*, 1755.
Roberts, James	Walpole, Robert (?), *The reply of a member of Parliament to the mayor of his corporation*, 1733.
Roberts, W.	Carleton, George, *The life of Bernard Gilpin*, 5th ed., 1727.

PRINTERS	TITLES
Robinson, J.	Morris, Corbyn, *An essay . . . addressed to the Right Honourable Henry Pelham,* [1747].
Say, Edward	Carey, Henry, *Poems on several occasions,* 3rd ed., 1729.
Smith, Godefroi	Missy, Cesar de, *Les larmes du refuge,* 1736.
Towers, John	Guicciardini, Francesco, *The history of Italy,* tr. Goddard, 10 vols., 1753–1756.
Trott, W.	Whitefield, George, *The Bishop of London's pastoral letter answer'd,* 1739.
Watson, J.	Shippen, William, *A speech against Sir R—— W——'s proposal for increasing the civil list revenue,* 2nd ed., 1727.
Watts, John	Fitzgerald, Thomas, *Poems on several occasions,* 1733.
Webb, W.	*A survey of the national debts,* 1745.
Wilkins, William	Hoadly, Benjamin, *An answer to the Reverend Dr. Hare's sermon, intitul'd Church-Authority vindicated,* 1720.
Wilson, John	Williams, Daniel, *Practical discourses,* 2 vols., 1728.
Wood, Thomas	Hippisley, John, *Flora* [altered from a farce by Thomas Doggett], 3rd ed., 1729.
Woodfall, Henry	Havard, William, *Regulus, A tragedy,* 1744.
Wright, J.	Bickham, George [d. 1752], *Stowe, The gardens of the Right Honourable Richard, Lord Viscount Cobham,* 1732.

APPENDIX B

Ornaments

Signed by Engravers

IDENTIFICATION of most of these engravers cannot be supplied, and little is known about those who can be identified. For Francis Hoffman, see p. 255.

SIGNATURES	TITLES
S.A. [These may be the initials of the printer, and not those of the engraver.]	Defoe, Daniel, *The complete English tradesman*, 2nd ed., 2 vols., 1727, 1732, Vol. II.
S.A.	*The gentleman's library*, 3rd ed., 1734.
I. Bell	Thomson, James, *A poem sacred to the memory of Sir Isaac Newton*, 2nd ed., 1727.
I. B[ell?]	Massie, Joseph, *A letter to Bourchier Cleeve, Esq.*, 1757.
I. B[ell?]	Waterland, Daniel, *The nature, obligation, and efficacy of the Christian sacraments*, 2nd ed., 1730.
J. (T?) Bell	*An account of the expedition to Carthagena*, 3rd ed., 1743.
F. Hoffman	*Tale of a tub*, 1736.
F[rancis?] H[offman?]	*An argument to show the disadvantage that would accrue to the publick, from obliging the South-Sea Company to fix what capital stock they would give for the annuities*, 1720.
	Lardner, Nathaniel, *A vindication of three of our blessed Saviour's miracles*, 1729.

SIGNATURES	TITLES
	Douglas, John (?), *A letter addressed to two great men on the prospect of peace,* 1760.
	A letter from a person of distinction to the Rt. Hon. J—— E—— of Eg—t, [1749].
	Shaw, Peter, *A new practice of physic,* 3rd ed., 2 vols., 1730, Vol. I.
F[rancis?] H[offman?] and Ed. Opt.	*A letter to a certain foreign minister,* 1745.
F[rancis?] H[offman?] and M.M.	Farquhar, George, *Sir Harry Wildair,* 1728.
E. K.	Steele, Richard, *The conscious lovers,* 1723.
Ed. Opt.	Lediard, Thomas, *The naval history of England,* 2 vols. in 1, 1735, Vol. II.
S. R. [These may be the initials of the printer, Samuel Richardson.]	Chaucer, Geoffrey, *The Canterbury tales,* ed. Morell, 1740.

APPENDIX C

Richardson's Apprentices

THE FOLLOWING information is taken from manuscript records of the Stationers' Company. In volumes usually referred to as "Bindings" the most complete information about the apprentice may be found. Frequently the "Court Books" of the Company at the appropriate date record the binding of apprentices. If the apprentice took up his freedom in the Company, that fact is recorded in the "Freedom Book," and may also be recorded in the "Court Books." The data supplied usually includes the father's name, address, and trade or profession; and the monetary consideration paid to the master on the occasion of the apprentice's binding. A discussion of Richardson's apprentices has been provided on pp. 16–22.

6 August 1722   George Mitchell, Joseph Chrichley, and Thomas Gover turned over to Samuel Richardson. The entries for their bindings follow:

(1) 6 April 1719. George Mitchell, son of John, late of the Parish of St. Bartholomew the Great, London, Gentleman, deceased, to John Leake, Old 'Change printer. Freedom, 5 September 1727.

(2) 1 August 1720. Joseph Chrichley, son of John, citizen and barber surgeon, London, to Elizabeth Leake, Old 'Change printer. Consideration £10/10. Freedom, 5 September 1727.

(3) 3 October 1720. Thomas Gover, son of John of

	Gosport in Southamptonshire, bookseller, to James Leake, Salisbury Court printer. Consideration, £10. Freedom, 3 September 1728.
2 May 1727	William Price, son of William, late of the borough of Stafford in the county of Stafford, deceased, to Samuel Richardson.
5 September 1727	Samuel Jolley [bound to John Darby, 6 April 1725] turned over to Samuel Richardson. Freedom, 2 November 1742.
2 September 1729	Bethell Wellington, son of Richard, late of St. Paul's Churchyard, London, bookseller, to Samuel Richardson. Consideration £25.
5 May 1730	Halhed [Hathed] Garland, son of William Garland of Brackley in the county of Northampton, cutler, to Samuel Richardson. Consideration, £10/10. Freedom, 4 February 1752.
1 August 1732	Thomas Verren Richardson, son of William of Tower Hill, London, upholder, to Samuel Richardson. Consideration £40. Died 8 November 1732.
6 February 1733	Richard Smith, son of Richard, late of Paternoster Row, bookseller, deceased, to Samuel Richardson.
7 August 1733	Matthew Stimson, son of Thomas of Clerkenwell, staymaker, to Samuel Richardson. Consideration, £5.
7 May 1734	[Bethell Wellington, bound to Richardson in 1729, is turned over to Richardson's brother-in-law, Allington Wilde, for the remainder of his term.]
1 October 1734	Daniel Green, son of Daniel of St. Catherine's near the Tower of London, Gentleman, to Samuel Richardson. Consideration, £42.
7 August 1739	Samuel Adams, son of Samuel, late of Islington, Middlesex, mealman, deceased, to Samuel Richardson. Consideration, £36/15. Freedom, 7 February 1748.
7 August 1739	Samuel Clark, son of Samuel, late of the Parish of St. Mary Magdalen, Bermondsey, in the county of Surrey, scrivener, deceased, to Samuel Richardson. Consideration, £36/15. Freedom, 4 September 1759.
5 July 1743	James Wright, son of the Rev. John Wright, late of Great Hermitage Street in the county of Middlesex, clerk, deceased, to Samuel Richardson. Consideration, £36/15, £10 thereof paid by the Treasurer of the Sons of the Clergy, the rest by the Guardian.
3 July 1744	George Walker, son of George of Blackfriars, chair-

maker, deceased, to Samuel Richardson. Freedom, 7 October 1760.

4 December 1744   Richard Hett, son of Richard of the Poultry, London, bookseller, to Samuel Richardson. Consideration, £40. Freedom, 4 February 1752.

5 August 1746   Charles Rivington, son of Charles, late of St. Paul's Churchyard, London, bookseller, deceased, to Samuel Richardson. Consideration, £42, paid by John Rivington. Freedom, 4 September 1753. Rivington was clothed on the same day he was freed. The entry in "Court Book L," p. 73, describes him as an apprentice of Samuel Richardson "and since of Richard Reily." This entry suggests that Rivington was turned over to Reily at some date in his apprenticeship.

4 November 1746   Timothy Dicey, son of William of Northampton, printer, to Samuel Richardson. Consideration, £52/10.

5 July 1748   William Richardson, son of William of Tower Hill, London, upholder, to Samuel Richardson. Consideration, £72. Freedom, 5 August 1755.

7 August 1750   Robert Wright, son of Robert of Mill Bank, Westminster, baker, to Samuel Richardson. Consideration £42.

7 May 1751   Henry Campbell, son of John of Portsmouth, Gentleman, to Samuel Richardson. Freedom, 3 October 1758.

11 June 1754   Thomas Haward [Hayward], son of the Savoy, Esq., to Samuel Richardson. Consideration, £63.

4 October 1757   Benjamin Towne, son of John of Paunton in Lincolnshire, clerk, to Samuel Richardson. Consideration, £40. Turned over 2 March 1762 to William Richardson, White Lyon Court. Freedom, 6 August 1765.

6 February 1759   Samuel Axtell, son of William of Hampstead [Hempsted?] in Hertfordshire, butcher, to Samuel Richardson. Turned over to Joseph Gibson 2 March 1762. Freedom, 4 March 1766.

APPENDIX D

A List of the Law Patentees

RICHARD TOTTEL, printer. Tottel's patent was granted 5 May 1556 for seven years; it was renewed by Elizabeth for his lifetime on 12 January 1559. Tottel died in 1593. (*C.P.R.*, 2 and 3 Philip and Mary, III, 18; *C.P.R.*, 1 Elizabeth, I, 62–63.)

NICASIUS YETSWEIRT, clerk of the privy seal and French Secretary to Elizabeth. Yetsweirt's patent was granted 18 November 1577 for thirty years, presumably to become effective after Tottel's death. He apparently predeceased Tottel and the patent passed to his son. (Thomas C. Hansard, *Typographia*, 1825, p. 135.)

CHARLES YETSWEIRT, son of Nicasius, clerk of the privy seal and French Secretary to Elizabeth. He inherited his father's patent but held it only one year, dying early in 1595 and leaving his rights to his widow. (W. W. Greg and E. Boswell, *Records of the Court of the Stationers' Company 1576 to 1602*, for the Bibliographical Society, 1930, p. lxiv; pp. 48–49.)

JANE YETSWEIRT, widow of Charles. She published law books in her name in 1597. See, for example, Sir Robert Brooke's *Ascvns novel cases de les ans & temps le Roy, H. 8. Edw. 6. & la Roygne Mary*, and William Fleetwood's *Annalium tam regum Edwardi quinti, Richardi tertii, & Henrici septimi*. Opposed by the Stationers' Company, she complained to the Lord Keeper and the Lord Treasurer. Presumably she received no redress, for in 1598 the names of Thomas Wight and Bonham Norton appeared in law books customarily printed by the law patentee. See Hansard, *op. cit.*, p. 135.

THOMAS WIGHT and BONHAM NORTON, printers. These men were granted the patent in 1599 for thirty years. Wight's name alone appears in imprints until about 1605, when the patent seems to have been assigned to the Company of Stationers. (R. B. McKerrow, *A Dictionary of Printers and Booksellers . . . 1557–1660*, 1910, under Thomas Wight; William Dugdale, *Origines Juridiciales*, 2nd ed., 1671, p. 61, a patent of 10 March 41 Elizabeth. Hansard in his *Typographia* says (p. 174) that this patent is in Wight's name alone, but this is an error.) For imprints, see, for example, Rastell's *Collection in English of the Statutes Now in Force*, with the names of Wight and Norton, 1598. This is the thirteenth edition of Rastell; the fourteenth edition in 1603 has Wight's name alone, and the first edition of Pulton's *Kalendar* in 1606 is printed "for the Company of Stationers."

JOHN MORE, clerk of the signet. More was granted the patent by James I in 1618. His rights began after the expiration of the patent granted to Wight and Bonham Norton (10 March 1629) and extended for forty years. (Henry R. Plomer, *A Dictionary of the Booksellers and Printers Who Were at Work . . . from 1641 to 1667*, 1907, under More.) More died in 1638, leaving the income from his patent to his daughter, Martha, wife of Richard Atkyns (see pp. 141–142).

SIR EDWARD ATKYNS, nephew of Richard Atkyns and Baron of the Exchequer. Atkyns was granted the patent in November 1660. It became effective after the expiration of the patent of John More (10 March 1669) and extended for forty years. (See p. 143; *S.P. Dom.*, Charles II, November, 1660, p. 367.)

EDWARD SAYER, of St. John's College, Cambridge. Sayer was admitted to the Middle Temple in 1689, called to the bar in 1694, and migrated to the Inner Temple in 1695 (Venn's *Alumni Cantabrigiensis*; Charles H. Hopwood, *Middle Temple Records*, 1904-1905, III, 1423, 1424; F. A. Inderwick, *Calendar of the Inner Temple Records*, 1896–1901, III, 312). He first petitioned for the patent on 28 June 1701, at which time he set forth his qualifications (*S.P. Dom.*, William III, p. 391). In February 1702 William III granted the patent, to begin at the expiration of the grant to Sir Edward Atkyns (10 March 1709) and to run for forty years. It was renewed by Anne, 17 March 1702 (*S.P. Dom.*, William III, p. 515; Anne, p. 483).

Sayer assigned the patent to John Nutt, whose name last appears in the imprint of law books in 1716, to be replaced by that of his widow,

Elizabeth, and her partner, Robert Gosling. In 1722 the firm became E. and R. Nutt and R. Gosling, when Richard Nutt (probably Elizabeth's son) entered the business. In 1741 either this firm or Sayer himself leased the patent to Henry Lintot.

Another son of John Nutt, Benjamin, seems to have had some connection with the business during the 1730's, for disputes with Charles Viner, who sought to print his abridgments of law and equity at his own expense, were between Viner and the brothers Nutt. (See Strickland Gibson and Sir William Holdsworth, "Charles Viner's General Abridgment of Law and Equity," *Proceedings and Papers of the Oxford Bibliographical Society*, II [1930], Part IV, 229–325.) I have found Benjamin's name in only one imprint: Geoffrey Gilbert's *Law and Practice of Ejectments*, 2nd ed., 1741, for R. and B. Nutt and F[rancis] Gosling, the son of Robert Gosling and the founder of the famous private bank.

HENRY LINTOT, printer. Lintot was granted the patent in 1735 for forty years after the expiration of Sayer's patent (10 March 1749). Lintot died in 1758, leaving the patent to his daughter, Catherine. (P.R.O. "Warrant Books," No. 365, p. 321 and No. 366, p. 42. These entries are requisitions "to prepare a bill for our Royal Signature . . . containing His Majesty's Grant unto the said Henry Lintot." The date of the second entry is 25 July 1735.)

CATHERINE LINTOT, daughter of Henry Lintot. She held the patent in her own name until she sold a half-interest to Samuel Richardson.

SAMUEL RICHARDSON and CATHERINE LINTOT. Richardson bequeathed his share in the patent to his wife, Elizabeth.

ELIZABETH RICHARDSON and CATHERINE LINTOT. These two women held the patent for about a year, when they sold it to Henry Woodfall and William Strahan.

HENRY WOODFALL and WILLIAM STRAHAN, printers. These men bought the patent from Miss Lintot and Mrs. Richardson.

Notes

ABBREVIATIONS IN THE NOTES

I. MANUSCRIPTS

Victoria and Albert Museum, South Kensington

Forster MSS.:   The Forster Manuscripts, containing letters to and from Samuel Richardson, are in six folio volumes (XI–XVI), designated 48E5–48E10.

Stationers' Hall, London

"Register":   The manuscript registers of the Company of Stationers for the period covered by this study are in two volumes. Vol. I extends from 10 April 1710 to 25 September 1746; Vol. II from 29 September 1746 to 30 December 1776.

"Court Book":   The minutes of the monthly meetings of the master and court of assistants of the Company of Stationers are in manuscript volumes, lettered in series. For the period of this study they run from G to L.

"Bindings":   In volumes referred to by this name is the most complete information about apprentices. See p. 350.

Public Record Office, London

"Warrant Books":   These volumes, labeled variously "Entry Books" or "Warrant Books," are classified among the State Papers, Domestic.

"Money Books": These volumes are among the records of the Exchequer.

II. PRINTED BOOKS

Here, as throughout the notes, the place of publication is London, unless otherwise specified. The reference *op. cit.* is used to refer only to works previously quoted in notes to the same chapter. It is always followed by the number of the preceding note in which the full title of the work is given. Data on the acting history of plays have been taken from Allardyce Nicoll's *History of Early Eighteenth Century Drama 1700–1750*, Cambridge, 1925, if not otherwise specified. Some biographical information to be found in J. and J. A. Venn's *Alumni Cantabrigiensis*, Joseph Foster's *Alumni Oxoniensis*, and the *Dictionary of National Biography* (*D.N.B.*) has not been specifically acknowledged.

The following abbreviations are used:

Barbauld: Anna Laetitia Barbauld, *The Correspondence of Samuel Richardson*, 6 vols., 1804.

Dobson: Austin Dobson, *Samuel Richardson*, English Men of Letters Series, 1902.

Dottin: Paul Dottin, *Samuel Richardson*, Paris, 1931.

Downs: Brian W. Downs, *Richardson*, London and New York, 1928.

Hanson: Laurence Hanson, *Government and the Press*, Oxford and London, 1936.

McKillop: Alan McKillop, *Samuel Richardson*, Chapel Hill, [North Carolina], 1936.

Nichols, *Anec. of Bowyer:* John Nichols, *Biographical and Literary Anecdotes of William Bowyer, Printer*, 1782.

Nichols, *Lit. Anec.:* John Nichols, *Literary Anecdotes of the Eighteenth Century*, 9 vols., 1812–1816.

Plomer's *Dictionary:* Henry R. Plomer, G. H. Bushnell, E. R. McC. Dix, *A Dictionary of the Printers and Booksellers Who Were at Work in England Scotland and Ireland from 1726 to 1775*, Oxford, 1932 (for 1930).

Sale: William M. Sale, Jr., *Samuel Richardson: A Bibliographical Record*, New Haven, [Conn.], 1936.

Straus:	Ralph Straus, *Robert Dodsley*, London and New York, 1910.
Sutherland:	*The Poems of Alexander Pope*, Twickenham Edition, *The Dunciad* (Vol. V), ed. Sutherland, 1943.

III. PERIODICALS

Gazetteer:	*The Daily Gazetteer*
Journal:	*The Daily Journal*

Such standard abbreviations as *N&Q* for *Notes and Queries*, *MLN* for *Modern Language Notes*, etc., are usually employed.

NOTES TO CHAPTER II

1. R. A. Austen-Leigh, *The Story of a Printing House*, 2nd ed., 1912, pp. 14–16; 32.

2. No attempt has been made to indicate all points of minor disagreement between statements in this chapter and those in earlier biographical accounts of Richardson. The most accurate account is in *McKillop*, pp. 284 ff. Mr. McKillop and I consulted many of the same sources before the publication of his book and of my bibliography of Richardson. In such instances I have cited references from my own notes, but with no desire to detract from the thoroughness and accuracy of his scholarship. I have tried to give him acknowledgment for any information which I did not arrive at independently.

3. "Bindings," under date.

4. *Barbauld*, I, xli; *Universal Magazine*, LXXVIII (1786), 17–21 and 73–77; Septimus Rivington, *The Publishing Family of Rivington*, 1919, p. 37. After John Nichols' *Anecdotes of William Bowyer* had appeared in 1782 with John Duncombe's biographical notes, and after accounts of Richardson had appeared in the *Gentleman's Magazine*, LIII (1783), 924–925, and in the *New and General Biographical Dictionary*, 1784, Anne Richardson wrote to her sister, Mrs. Bridgen: "My Love, I entirely agree with you that it is necessary that my Father's own descendants should give some little account of him" (*London Mercury*, VII [1923], 385; the original of this letter, now owned by Mr. McKillop, was kindly lent to me. The manuscript text varies slightly from the printed version). The result of this agreement between the sisters was the article in the *Universal Magazine*, signed "L," but certainly written by someone who had access to papers then in the possession of the family. It is from this article, followed in its facts by Mrs. Barbauld, that we learn that Richardson "at the expiration of his apprenticeship . . . became Overseer and Corrector of a Printing-office" (p. 18). Despite the fact that the account says "*a* Printing-office," as distinct from Wilde's shop where he served his apprenticeship, later biographical accounts continued to maintain that he remained with Wilde until he set up in business for himself. Austin Dobson seems largely responsible for this unwarranted assumption.

5. C. H. Timperley in his *Encyclopaedia of Literary and Typographical*

Anecdote, 2nd ed., 1842, p. 770, says that Rivington set up in business in a house which had formerly been the residence of a Lord Mayor. In fact, it had been the residence of two Lord Mayors: Sir Thomas Bludworth, Lord Mayor during the great fire, and Sir Richard Levett (William Maitland, *The History and Survey of London,* [2nd ed.], 1756, II, 762). For Bludworth and the Levetts, father and son, see Alfred B. Beaven, *The Aldermen of the City of London,* 2 vols., 1908, 1913, index.

6. Maitland, *op. cit.* in note 5, II, 762; 1273–1274.

7. The church warden's accounts and the vestry minute books for the two parishes that might contain records of the inhabitants of Staining Lane have been examined with no results (London Guildhall, *MSS.* No. 591 and 1542). The Church of St. Mary Staining was destroyed in the London fire, but this parish continued to keep its separate accounts after the parishioners had joined with those of St. Michael, Wood Street. For Richardson's freedom, see "Court Book G," p. 229.

8. This house can be located from the rate books of St. Bride's parish (London Guildhall, *MS.* No. 78: a Constable's Ledger for 1724/25 and for 1725/26; a Rate or Assessment for the Relief of the Poor, 1727; and a Scavenger's Ledger for 1727).

9. The *Weekly Medley,* 9–16 June 1720, contains an obituary of John Wilde, who had died "last Tuesday." The record of Richardson's marriage is in the *Publications of the Harleian Society,* XVIII, 29. In Charterhouse Chapel, where Martha Wilde's father and mother had been married, she and Richardson were married on 23 November 1721.

10. *Memoirs of Mrs. Letitia Pilkington,* ed. Isaacs, New York, 1928, p. 282. Mrs. Pilkington's description of the house dates from her first visit to Richardson, probably in 1743 (*Barbauld,* II, 113).

11. This neighbor, a Miss P., contributed a letter about Richardson to Mrs. Barbauld's *Life,* I, clxxxii–cxc. She was probably the Miss Poole to whom Richardson gave a copy of the French translation of *Pamela* in 1755, and to whose mother William Strahan refers in sending regards to neighbors of Richardson (Catalogue of a sale at the Anderson Galleries, 7, 8 February 1929, No. 2318, item 376; and *Barbauld,* I, 138).

12. See note 8. For Ventris, see *Journal,* 31 October 1727.

13. *Weekly Journal; or Saturday's Post,* 26 November 1720.

14. For Senex, see the *Post Boy,* 11–13 August 1720; for Blandford, see "Court Book H," p. 192; for Purser, see the colophons of the *Journal* from 14 March 1728; for Green, see the *Post Boy,* 12–14 April 1720; for Eaton, see the *Journal,* 1 September 1731. For Mr. Dutton, see London Guildhall, *MS.* No. 78, and *Gazetteer,* 9 February 1739; for Miss Dutton, see especially *Barbauld,* I, 138, II, 106, and *European Magazine,* LV (1809), 103; for her relations with Dr. Eaton, see *London Chronicle,* 8–10 May 1759. For Mr. Grainger, see London Guildhall, *MSS.* Nos. 78 and 79, and *Journal,* 13 July 1731; for his daughter, see *N&Q,* 4 S. I (1868), 285–286, and *Catalogue of the Collection of Autograph Letters . . . Formed . . . by Alfred Morrison,* 1891, V, 252–256. For the corporation for the relief of clergymen's sons, see Maitland, *op. cit.* in note 5, II, 1292. For Richardson's binding of a deceased clergyman's son, see p. 351, James Wright.

15. *N&Q*, 12 S. XI (1922), 465–466.

16. *Forster MSS.*, XIII, 2, f. 7. The italics are mine. Hill calls this place Corney House. There was a place of that name in Chiswick, but I have found no record of its occupants during the 1730's.

17. See my article, "Samuel Richardson's House at Fulham," *N&Q*, CLXIX (1935), 133–134. A picture of this house is reproduced as the frontispiece of *Barbauld*, IV.

18. London Guildhall, *MS.* No. 79; *Forster MSS.*, XI, f. 173; XII, 1, f. 110.

19. For the fire, see *Autobiography and Correspondence of Mary Granville, Mrs. Delany*, ed. Lady Llanover, 1861, III, 163. It occurred shortly before October 14. Richardson refers to the fire in *Forster MSS.*, XII, 2, f. 88.

20. A picture of this house may be seen in *The Builder*, LXXI (18 July 1896), 48.

21. The details of his new building plans are in *Forster MSS.*, XI, ff. 163, 173. The costs are mentioned in *Forster MSS.*, XIV, 4, f. 16. For the rents, see London Guildhall, *MS.* No. 79.

22. *Forster MSS.*, XI, f. 163.

23. For details concerning the rent on the house at North-End, see *Forster MSS.*, XII, 1, f. 110.

24. For the cost of alterations on the house at Parson's Green, see *Forster MSS.*, XIV, 4, f. 16; for the date of the move, see *Autobiography of Mrs. Delany*, cited in n. 19, III, 296.

25. *Dobson*, p. 173, locates a woodcut of this house in the *Saturday Magazine*, 22 June 1839. For Richardson's description of it, see *Barbauld*, II, 298–299.

26. "Court Book H," p. 109, March 5.

27. *Ibid.*, p. 121, August 6. For the names of these apprentices, see p. 15.

28. *Daily Post*, 5 March 1720. For John Leake's address in Old 'Change, see "Bindings," 6 April 1719.

29. For the deaths of John Leake and his wife, see the registers of St. Michael le Quern and St. Vedast, cited by *McKillop*, p. 289.

30. *McKillop*, p. 289.

31. "Court Book H," p. 77, September 5. For Gover's binding, see p. 350.

32. Richardson's ornament No. 46 (see p. 288) was used by Leake in *An Essay upon Study*, printed by J. L[eake], 1713.

33. See note 27.

34. *McKillop*, p. 288.

35. See p. 351.

36. Published for the Bibliographical Society, 1947, p. 35.

37. See pp. 147–148.

38. Pages 30–32.

39. The original text of this letter to his nephew is printed in the *Imperial Review*, II (1804), 609–616. McKillop owns the only known copy of *The Apprentice's Vade Mecum*. He provides a full description of its contents in *JEGP*, XLII (1943), 40–54.

40. *Sale*, p. 110, where I have described the printed pamphlet.

41. Ellic Howe, *The London Compositor*, 1947, p. 30.

42. Howe (*op. cit.* in note 41) provides (pp. 10–41) an excellent discussion

of this problem, with a review of the various regulatory measures that were in effect at one time or another.

43. *Ibid.,* pp. 37–38.

44. *Ibid.,* p. 36.

45. See Plomer's *Dictionary* and Howe, *op. cit.* in note 41, p. 49.

46. Talbot Reed, *A History of the Old English Letter Foundries,* 1887, pp. 289–290. Reed dates the type c. 1768. It was cast for Richardson by Thomas Cottrell, who had set up for himself in Nevil's Court in 1757, following a dispute with Caslon over wages.

47. Howe, *op. cit.* in note 41, pp. 43–44.

48. *Ibid.,* p. 47.

49. *Barbauld,* I, 56–57; 62–66; 71–72.

50. "Court Book L," p. 425. On 3 March 1761 Campbell bound an apprentice. Campbell's address is given here.

51. Howe, *op. cit.* in note 41, p. 70; Austen-Leigh, *op. cit.* in note 1, p. 26.

52. Howe, *op. cit.* in note 41, pp. 69 ff.

53. Austen-Leigh, *op. cit.* in note 1, pp. 48–50. For Richardson's prices, see note 56.

54. B.M. *Add. MSS.,* 6,211, f. 51, 9 November 1738.

55. P.R.O., "Money Books," Vols. 37–47.

56. From the information in the letter to Gordon, Richardson's prices and wages can be fairly accurately computed. Other evidence of his charges may be found in B.M. *Add. MSS.,* 6,185, f. 85; *Journals of the House of Commons,* XXIV (31 May 1742), 263–265; *Straus,* p. 355; Charles Weld, *A History of the Royal Society,* 1848, I, 523; Montagu Pennington, *Memoirs of the Life of Mrs. Elizabeth Carter,* 2nd ed., 1808, I, 207–210; and the Records of the Exchequer, referred to in note 55.

57. *A.L.s.,* in Pierpont Morgan Library, New York City, 28 January 1747.

58. Howe, *op. cit.* in note 41, p. 95.

59. See *The Case of Samuel Richardson, of London, Printer,* 1753. This pamphlet is reprinted in Oxford Bibliographical Society, *Publications and Papers,* II (1930), 320–325. Tewley is identified as his foreman on p. 321. For more information about Tewley, see *N&Q,* 12 S. XI (1922), 344, 386.

60. Oxford Bibliographical Society, *loc. cit.* in note 59.

61. *Forster MSS.,* XI, f. 151, 13 August 1755.

62. See Richardson's will, P.C.C., Cheslyn 266. A good abstract is provided in *N&Q,* 12 S. XI (1922), 342–344. From a codicil to this will, dated 11 September 1759, we learn that William Richardson had set up in business for himself.

63. *Forster MSS.,* XI, f. 249, 15 July 1759; f. 257, 22 May 1759. Bailey was appointed coexecutor 5 July 1760, after Richardson had become joint owner with Miss Catherine Lintot in the law patent (*N&Q,* 12 S. XI [1922], 344, and p. 134. Bailey had been a witness at a sale of some of Miss Lintot's property in April, 1759 (B.M. *Add. MSS.,* 38,730, p. 118). A James Bailey was master of the Stationers' Company in 1768, but Plomer in his *Dictionary* records nothing but this fact.

64. *Forster MSS.,* XI, f. 259, 5 June 1759.

65. *Ibid.,* XIII, 3, f. 152, 7 November 1748.

66. R. Campbell, *The London Tradesman*, 3rd ed., 1757, pp. 134–135.

67. The press figures (press numbers, forme marks) run as high as nine in the books printed by Richardson at the end of his career. Nine presses was an exceptionally high number. Strahan, with his extraordinary business, wrote in 1771 that he had to look after the work of "7, 8, or 9 Presses, which are constantly employed" (Austen-Leigh, *op. cit.* in note 1, p. 14). For the significance of press figures, see Ronald B. McKerrow, *An Introduction to Bibliography*, Oxford, 1927, pp. 81–82.

68. See note 26.

69. "Court Book H," p. 266, 11 April 1727. Richardson accepted the office on 6 June 1727.

70. Campbell, *op. cit.* in note 66, p. 305.

71. "Court Book H," p. 393, 2 February 1730; "Court Book I," p. 87, 3 February 1736; "Court Book K," p. 285, 4 February 1746, and p. 500, 5 February 1751. In 1739 there were fifteen shares of £320, thirty shares of £160, and sixty shares of £80, some of which were divided into two £40 shares. In 1756 the £320 shares had been increased to nineteen, the £160 shares to thirty-eight, the £80 shares to forty-eight, and the £40 shares to fifty-six (William Maitland, *The History of London*, 1739, p. 611; and Maitland, *op. cit.* in note 5, II, 1251–1252).

72. Maitland, *op. cit.* in note 5, II, 1252.

73. "Court Book I," p. 412, December 1.

74. "Court Book K," p. 477, June 30.

75. "Court Book L," p. 68, June 30.

76. *Ibid.*, p. 113.

77. Sir Thomas Davies and John Barber, stationers who were elected Lord Mayor before Janssen, had been translated to the Drapers and to the Goldsmiths before their inauguration (Beaven, *op. cit.* in note 5, I, 354).

78. Janssen was the son of Sir Theodore Janssen, M.P. for London, expelled from the House because he was a director of the South Sea Company when the bubble burst. For Stephen Janssen, see Beaven, *op. cit.* in note 5, II, 130 and index; *Journals of the House of Commons*, XXII (12 March 1735), 412.

79. "Court Book L," p. 123, 1 October 1754.

80. *Ibid.*, p. 126, 8 October 1754.

81. *Ibid.*, p. 151, 18 April 1755.

82. *Ibid.*, p. 163, 25 April 1755.

83. *Ibid.*, pp. 248, 250, 11 February 1757.

NOTES TO CHAPTER III

1. Third ed., 1742, II, 153.

2. *Publications of the Sussex Archaeological Society*, XV (1863), 210; XXXV (1887), 144–149; William G. Moss, *The History and Antiquities of the Town and Port of Hastings*, 1824, pp. 114–115; Keith Grahame Feiling, *The Second Tory Party 1714–1832*, 1938, pp. 25–26.

3. Third ed., 1751–1750, IV, 241–242.

4. Justin McCarthy, *A History of the Four Georges*, New York and London, 1906, I, 191.

5. Charles B. Realey, *The Early Opposition to Sir Robert Walpole, 1720–1727,* Philadelphia, 1931, p. 83. The other fool was Thomas Coningsby.

6. David H. Stevens, *Party Politics and English Journalism, 1702–1742,* Menasha, [Wis.], 1916, p. 115.

7. Realey, *op. cit.* in note 5, p. 147, citing *Clements MSS.,* 385.

8. *Ibid.,* p. 37, citing *Hardwicke State Papers,* II, 637.

9. F. S. Oliver, *The Endless Adventure,* Boston, 1931–1934, I, 268.

10. *A Compleat and Intire Collection of the Lords Protests in the Last Session of Parliament,* 2nd ed., 1723, p. 23.

11. For Barnard, see p. 149.

12. *Daily Post,* 6 March 1724.

13. The list of those voting for Williams was published in the *Journal,* 20 March 1724. See *McKillop,* p. 297.

14. *Daily Post,* 9 and 30 March 1724.

15. 24 November 1724.

16. *Daily Post,* 7 December 1724.

17. Reginald R. Sharpe, *London and the Kingdom,* 1895, III, 28.

18. *A Letter from a Citizen to a Member of Parliament . . . Occasion'd by the Bill now Depending for Regulating Elections in the City of London,* 1725, p. 50.

19. See *A Compleat and Intire Collection,* cited in note 10.

20. *Journal,* 31 October 1727.

21. *S.P. Dom.,* George II, Bundle 8/33, cited in Plomer's *Dictionary,* p. 211.

22. Defoe's *Tour Thro' Great Britain,* ed. Richardson, 6th ed., 1762–1761, III, 271.

23. Nichols, *Anec. of Bowyer,* p. 156; Nichols, *Lit. Anec.,* IV, 584*n.,* where he says that Duncombe supplied this note on Richardson.

24. Nichols, *Anec. of Bowyer,* p. 306.

25. But Brian Downs (*Downs,* p. 8), failing to perceive the heavy irony of issue No. 6, came to the curious conclusion that this letter "voiced opinions so directly opposed to the general trend of the paper's propaganda that it is not surprizing to learn of his [Richardson's] immediate supercession in the printing."

26. One bit of evidence suggests that Thomas Sharpe was printer and Payne publisher. *Hanson,* p. 66, tells us that Sharpe disclosed under interrogation that Wharton had written five out of the first seven numbers of the paper. Since Wharton was making every effort to tempt the government into proceeding against him and openly boasting to the Keeper of the Tower that he would be his next prisoner, the authorship of the *True Briton* was an open secret. Sharpe would not have had to be its printer in order to know who was doing most of the writing for it. More important, however, is the fact that Sharpe had been frequently prosecuted as the printer of the *Freeholder's Journal* (*Hanson,* p. 65) and had been finally committed to prison for want of sureties. He was certainly known to the government, and even had he been released from jail at the time Wharton started his paper, he would have been promptly the victim of another government warrant. Delafaye had been specifically instructed "not at this time to enquire into the authors of the libels [in Wharton's paper], but to fall upon printers and publishers" (*Hanson,* p. 66). Payne freely admitted that he was both printer and publisher of the *True Briton.*

27. Feiling, *op. cit.* in note 2, pp. 13–23.

28. *Hanson*, p. 47, citing the State Papers, 25 June 1723.

29. *Ibid.*, p. 55, citing the State Papers.

30. *London Journal* and the *Weekly Journal, or Saturday's Post*, 29 February 1724; *The Political State*, XXIV (February and May 1724), 205; 532–533.

31. See, for example, the *London Journal*, 3 August 1723; the *Weekly Journal, or Saturday's Post*, 3 August 1723.

32. London Guildhall, *MS. Repertory*, Vol. 127, f. 431; and *True Briton*, 6 September 1723.

33. *Hanson*, p. 65.

34. 19 February 1724.

35. *Daily Post*, 24 February 1724.

36. See p. 313. Stanley Morison in *The English Newspaper*, Cambridge, 1932, p. 109, says that a factotum, signed by Hoffman and appearing in the *Freeholder's Journal* on 3 October 1722, was used occasionally in the *True Briton* from No. 7, 17 June 1723. The paragraph from which this statement comes is very confusing. I think he means to say that the factotum was first used in the *Universal Journal*, for he says that Payne printed both papers that used Hoffman's device, and he knows (p. 121) that Sharpe printed the *Freeholder's Journal*. On the other hand, he says that the *Universal Journal* started in January, 1723. Hence, it is difficult to see why he should say it carried a factotum in October 1722. As a matter of fact, the *Universal Journal* actually started on 11 December 1723, as a file in the B.M. shows. It ceased publication on 29 August 1724. Furthermore, the factotum in the *True Briton*, No. 7, is not signed by Hoffman or by anybody else. No. 7 of the *True Briton* was dated 24 June 1723. Morison offers no evidence for attributing the printing of either the *True Briton* or the *Universal Journal* to Payne. The colophons of the *Universal Journal*, like those of most of the issues of the *True Briton*, read "printed for T. Payne."

37. See p. 212. The edition dated 1723, "Printed: And Sold by the Booksellers of London and Westminster," contains in the second volume the essays of 1724.

38. 17 February 1724.

39. Walter Thomas, *Le poète Edward Young*, Paris, 1901, pp. 82–83. Young and Hill may have met when Young's plays, *Busiris* and *The Revenge*, were presented by Hill's friends at Drury Lane in 1719 and 1721. See Dorothy Brewster, *Aaron Hill*, New York, 1913, p. 162.

40. Brewster, *op. cit.* in note 39, p. 275.

41. *Ibid.*, p. 15.

42. *Downs*, p. 10; *Dottin*, p. 34; *McKillop*, p. 299. Downs says that there are "some grounds" for believing that Richardson printed the *Plain Dealer*, but he does not say what the grounds are, and, confusingly enough, says (p. 12) that Richardson first entered into "relations" with Hill in 1735.

43. *Barbauld*, I, 5, 2 July 1736. Mrs. Barbauld dates the first published letter of Hill to Richardson 1 June 1730, but references in this letter to Hill's essay on Caesar, printed in 1738, clearly indicate her error in transcription.

44. Theophilus Cibber (and others), *The Lives of the Poets of Great-Britain and Ireland*, 1753, V, 264.

45. 4, 8, 22 January 1725.

46. 12 October 1724; 22 January 1725.

47. Brewster, *op. cit.* in note 39, pp. 170 ff.

48. Brewster, *op. cit.* in note 39, pp. 170–172; Peter Cunningham, "James Thomson and David Mallet," in *Miscellanies of the Philobiblon Society*, IV (1857–1858), 27, a letter of Thomson to Mallet, n.d.

49. Two manuscripts of Dennis on which Richardson had written "Copies lodged by Mr. Dennis for money borrowed" came into the hands of the editor of the *Monthly Magazine* in 1817 (XLIII, 421–425). Edward Hooker in his edition of the *Critical Works of John Dennis* (Baltimore, 1943, II, x) thinks that these manuscripts were designed by Dennis for a second volume of his works to be called *Miscellaneous Tracts*. The volume was never published. The text of one of these pieces is reprinted by Hooker from the manuscript, now in the Folger Shakespeare Library. Hooker dates it c. 1725, 1726. The other piece, "Mr. Dennis to the Rev. Doctor ——," is inscribed by Richardson "Dennis on Maevius."

50. See p. 42.

51. Nichols, *Lit. Anec.*, IV, 580.

52. *Downs*, p. 9; *Dottin*, p. 34; *McKillop*, pp. 302–303.

53. Nichols, *Lit. Anec.*, I, 303; Henry R. Fox Bourne, *English Newspapers*, 1887, I, 116.

54. *Hanson*, pp. 106–108.

55. Charles B. Realey, *The London Journal and its Authors, 1720–1723*, Lawrence, [Kan.], 1935, pp. 13–17.

56. Wilkins, Toovey, Peele, and Woodward were proprietors of the *London Journal* about 1726 (*Cal. of Treas. Papers, 1720–1728*, p. 421).

57. Realey, *op. cit.* in note 5, p. 192.

58. *Ibid.*, p. 229.

59. Samuel Richardson, *Familiar Letters on Important Occasions*, ed. Downs, New York, 1928, pp. 97–98.

60. *Hanson*, pp. 113–114; Realey, *op. cit.* in note 5, p. 95; *An Historical View of the Principles, Characters, Persons, etc. of the Political Writers in Great Britain*, 1741, pp. 14–17.

61. See the Advertisment to his *Ode on the Power of Music*.

62. *Journal*, 31 October 1727; Alfred B. Beaven, *The Aldermen of the City of London*, 1908, 1913, I, 279.

63. *Weekly Miscellany*, 16, 23, 30 March 1734; 11 May 1734. *Daily Post*, 9 April 1734. For Selwin, see B. Lambert, *The History and Survey of London*, 1806, II, 139–140. For Bosworth, and his activities in connection with the Excise Bill, see *An Impartial History of the Life . . . of Mr. John Barber. . . . Written by Several Hands*, ed. Edmund Curll, 1741, p. 30.

64. See issues of 25 October 1727, 25 March 1728, 12 January 1735, 27 March 1736, 26 July 1736.

65. 18 February 1729; 13 July 1733.

66. See, for example, issues of 15 February 1734, 5 June 1736.

67. 25, 29 June 1726; 1 July 1731.

68. 27 February 1736. See James T. Hillhouse, *The Grub-Street Journal*, Durham, [N. Car.], 1928, pp. 196–204, for a detailed account of the quarrel

between Popple and the *Grub-Street Journal* and of the part played by the *Daily Journal* in his defense. For Richardson's share in the copyright of the play, see p. 194.

69. Quoted by Hillhouse, *op. cit.* in note 68, p. 150. Hillhouse says that the *Prompter* and the *Daily Journal* were published by the same printer, but he does not identify the printer.

70. *Forster MSS.*, XIII, 2, f. 9, 19 July 1736.

71. *Journal*, 15 March 1737 (*McKillop*, p. 303).

72. Morison, *op. cit.* in note 36, p. 105.

73. Plomer in his *Dictionary* (p. 205) says that an indictment of Purser appears in the Coram Rege (Rex) Roll for Michaelmas Term, 1728, for inserting false and scandalous statements, but that the charge was not pressed. He does not give the details of this indictment, but presumably Purser was in trouble with the government. This is surprising, for the columns of the *Journal* seem always to have been open to Whig supporters, and to the enemies of Pope and Swift.

74. See, for example, the issues in January 1729.

75. 1 August 1732.

76. Nichols, *Anec. of Bowyer*, p. 89.

77. Morison, *op. cit.* in note 36, p. 125. Crane and Kaye checked end dates with especial care; Morison speaks specifically of "the three-column disposition which had been originated and standardized, until its demise in 1742, by *The Daily Journal.*"

78. Hillhouse, *op. cit.* in note 68, pp. 106, 342.

79. *Barbauld*, I, 17, 6 July 1738.

80. See note 92, below.

81. *Hanson*, pp. 114–115.

82. *A Critical History of the Administration of Sir Robert Walpole*, 1743, p. 518.

83. *Hanson*, p. 111, where it is said that Barnham Gould was a principal contributor to the *Courant*. He may have written for the *Gazetteer*. Others who have been reputed to have written for it are Henry Newcomb (Newcome), master of a boarding school at Hackney (*An Historical View of the . . . Political Writers in Great Britain*, 1741, p. 53), and Theophilus Cibber, son of Colley Cibber (Wilbur Cross, *A History of Henry Fielding*, New Haven, [Conn.], 1918, I, 266).

84. Ralph, *op. cit.* in note 82, p. 518.

85. *Hanson*, p. 115. The *D.N.B.* gives Arnall's death as "1741?".

86. *An Historical View*, cited in note 83, p. 52; Ralph, *op. cit.* in note 82, p. 519; and *D.N.B.*

87. Cross, *op. cit.* in note 83, I, 269–270. On p. 266 Cross incorrectly identifies him as Thomas Pitt.

88. *Forster MSS.*, XVI, 1, f. 42v.; f. 49.

89. *Barbauld*, I, 15, where Hill congratulates Richardson on this achievement.

90. Hill, *Works*, 2nd ed., 1754, II, 68, 21 February 1739.

91. See note 56, above.

92. *Cal. of Treas. Books and Papers, 1735–1738*, pp. 55, 159, 167, 184, 193, 300, 494, 515; *Cal. of Treas. Books and Papers, 1739–1741*, pp. 3, 18, 38, 60, 218, 269, 451, 476, 492, 506. These are records of payment for the *Gazetteer*. For money

paid to Peele, see the volume for 1735–1738, pp. li, 352, and the volume for 1739–1741, p. 58.

93. *Cal. of Treas. Books and Papers, 1731–1734*, p. 210. For the *London Journal* the printer, William Wilkins, received 2d. a copy (see note 56, above).

94. *Forster MSS.*, XIII, 3, f. 41. Hill to Richardson, 13 June 1746. Morison, *op. cit.* in note 36, pp. 144–145, citing B.M. *Add. MSS.*, 38,729, 5 December 1748, gives the details of the reorganization of the *Gazetteer*. The property was to be divided into twenty shares, with each partner entitled to one share on payment of ten guineas. The printer and publisher was to be John Griffith, Green Arbour Court, Little Old Bailey. The *London Gazetteer* was to be the name of the paper arising from the ashes of the *Daily Gazetteer*. This paper, says Morison, became the *Gazetteer and London Daily Advertiser* in 1755, printed by Charles Say.

95. Nichols, *Lit. Anec.*, IV, 580; *Downs*, p. 9; *Dottin*, p. 34.

96. *Forster MSS.*, XIII, 3, ff. 14, 20, 35, 40, 41.

97. *Ibid.*, ff. 20–21, 19 May 1743.

98. *Ibid.*, f. 40, 11 April 1746.

99. *Ibid.*, f. 41, 3 June 1746.

100. "Register," I, 455.

101. Issues for 9 April, 7 June, 9 June, 24 June 1736; 19, 20 November 1737.

102. Issues for 16 December 1727, 22 March 1736, 27 February 1736, 5 July 1736, 31 March 1737. Of course these books were advertised in other newspapers. My point is that they were advertised in the *Gazetteer* with greater frequency and prominence.

103. *Downs*, pp. 9–10.

104. *McKillop*, p. 302.

105. Nichols, *Lit. Anec.*, V, 175. The brackets enclosing "Mr. Richardson" are Nichols'.

106. William Webster, *A Plain Narrative of Facts*, 1758, pp. i–ii.

107. *Forster MSS.*, XVI, 2, ff. 76, 78, 80, 82. The contributions are signed "Eusebius," a pen name used by Hill. *McKillop*, p. 301, points out that they were published in the *Miscellany* on 10, 17 February, 10 March, and 23 June 1733.

108. Charles F. Mullett, *The Letters of Doctor George Cheyne to Samuel Richardson*, Columbia, [Mo.], 1943, p. 31.

109. *Ibid.*, p. 32.

110. *McKillop*, p. 302.

111. Webster, *op. cit.* in note 106, p. 6.

112. *McKillop*, p. 301, citing the *Diary of the First Earl of Egmont*.

113. Brewster, *op. cit.* in note 39, pp. 120 ff.

114. *Forster MSS.*, XIII, 3, ff. 44–45, 10 July 1746.

115. *Loc. cit.*

116. B.M. *Add. MSS.*, 37,232, f. 137.

117. *Forster MSS.*, XIII, 2, f. 3, 6 March 1735.

118. *Ibid.*, f. 4, 30 June 1736.

119. Richardson's comments on the stage in the *Apprentice's Vade Mecum* are quoted and summarized by Alan McKillop in *JEGP*, XLII (1943), 48–52.

120. February 19.

121. *Forster MSS.*, XIII, 2, f. 22.

122. See introductory notice in Vol. XLVII.

123. Charles Weld, *A History of the Royal Society*, 1848, I, 523. The total bill for the volume was £151/7/9, the remainder, after Richardson's printing bill was paid, going to the engraver and to the paper dealer.

124. *On the Life, Writings, and Genius of Akenside*, 1832, p. 26.

125. Nichols, *Anec. of Bowyer*, pp. 306–312.

126. B.M. *Add. MSS.*, 6,185, *passim*.

NOTES TO CHAPTER IV

1. *Forster MSS.*, XIII, 3, f. 114.

2. In the newspaper room of the B.M. is a volume called *Parliamentary Papers Printed by Order of the House of Commons*, Vol. I, 1731–1748. The first bill in this volume—"A Bill for the Better Encouragement of Learning"—illustrates the kind of printing that Richardson was engaged in. Richardson printed this bill on 4 March 1737. His bill may be found in the "Money Books," in the Records of the Exchequer at the Public Record Office, Vol. XXXIX, 58. He printed 600 copies on four sheets at £2/5 per sheet, including paper. Hence his charge was £9 for the printing and paper. He added to this sum a charge for folding and stitching—£2/5, at the rate of 7s. 6d. per 100 copies. In Vol. XXXVIII, p. 349, may be found his charge for a bill "filled up and reprinted."

3. *Forster MSS.*, XIII, 3, f. 114, 16 May 1749.

4. Charles B. Realey, *The Early Opposition to Sir Robert Walpole, 1720–1727*, Philadelphia, 1931, p. 54, quoting from the *Onslow MSS.*, 512.

5. See p. 37.

6. *Gentleman's Magazine*, LIII (1783), 924.

7. The information in the following list includes the date, the volume number and page of the "Money Books" in the P.R.O., and the amount of the printing bill:

4 February 1734,	XXXVII, 218,	£124/10.
23 July 1734,	XXXVII, 338,	£ 98/10.
4 July 1735,	XXXVIII, 94,	£118/ 0.
1 July 1736,	XXXVIII, 349,	£113/12/6.
10 August 1737,	XXXIX, 58,	£171/13.
14 September 1739,	XXXIX, 468,	£ 81/17/6.
2 July 1740,	XL, 225,	£ 77/18/6.
24 November 1741,	XL, 424,	£150/ 5.
12 August 1742,	XLI, 87,	£125/18.
20 July 1743,	XLI, 259,	£ 36/16.
26 June 1745,	XLI, 491,	£118/ 8.
6 January 1746,	XLII, 297,	£587/ 3.
11 August 1747,	XLII, 428,	£ 67/10.
9 August 1748,	XLIII, 106,	£ 78/ 0.
23 January 1749,	XLIII, 341,	£287/16.
16 May 1750,	XLIII, 389,	£ 74/ 6.
31 July 1751,	XLIV, 129,	£211/18.
27 September 1752,	XLIV, 343,	£195/ 1.
15 August 1753,	XLIV, 472,	£121/18.

22 May 1754,	XLV, 194, £ 59/ 8/6.
10 October 1755,	XLV, 434, £ 53/16/6.
8 November 1756,	XLV, 576, £190/ 0/6.
[No date] 1757,	XLVI, 205, £120/10.
21 August 1758,	XLVI, 367, £304/ 9.
3 July 1759,	XLVI, 464, £149/ 1.
4 August 1760,	XLVII, 263, £ 67/ 9/6.
13 April 1761,	XLVII, 529, £ 51/15.

8. See pp. 23–24.

9. "Money Books," XXXVIII, 349.

10. *Ibid.*, XLIV, 129; XXXIX, 468; XLVI, 367.

11. *Ibid.*, XL, 424; XLIII, 244.

12. See, for example, "Money Books," XL, 424.

13. St. Bride's Institute, London, a document dated 24 September 1739.

14. *A.L.s.*, To Joseph Spence, 30 October 1749, sold by Sotheby in sale of 8 March 1939; *Monthly Magazine*, XXXVII (1814), 142; Young to Richardson, 3 May 1747; *Monthly Magazine*, XXXVII (1814), 329, Richardson to Young, 9 September 1749. The death of Grover, 1 September 1749, is recorded in the obituary notices of the *Gentleman's Magazine*, XIX, 429.

15. *Barbauld*, II, 210.

16. Information on the clerks of the House of Commons may be found in the annual issues of the *Court and City Kalendar* and of the *Court and City Register*. Richardson's will (P.C.C. Cheslyn 266) lists merely "Mr. Barwell," but this is probably Osborn Barwell, for Edward Barwell did not receive his clerkship until 1760. John Hatsell, Clerk Assistant to the House in 1761, also received a ring.

17. *Journals of the House of Commons*, XXIV (31 May 1742), 262–266, where details given in this paragraph and the following one may be found.

18. *Ibid.*, XXVII (26 May 1756), 617. Vol. XXVI extends from 17 January 1750 to 6 April 1754.

19. *Ibid.*, XXV (3 March 1749), 767; XXVI (16 Jan. 1752), 373; and XXVII (26 May 1756), 617.

20. P.R.O., "Treasury Orders and Warrants," Portfolio 247.

21. *Forster MSS.*, XIII, 3, ff. 101–102, 12 January 1749.

22. *Barbauld*, V, 195–196, 27 May 1749.

23. *Forster MSS.*, XIV, 4, f. 16; XII, 1, ff. 158, 166.

24. *Journals*, XXVII (26 May 1756), 617.

25. For Bowyer's application, see Nichols, *Lit. Anec.*, II, 353–354; for John Hughs' printing, see "Money Books," XLVIII, 405.

26. *Reports from Committees*, Session 6 December 1831 to 16 August 1832, Vol. XVIII, "Report from the Select Committee on King's Printer's Patent; with the Minutes of Evidence, and Appendix." In relation to Richardson's printing of the *Journals*, see the notation (p. 313) that a reprinting of the *Journals*, Vols. I–LVI, 1200 copies of each volume, cost £89,397/9/2. Vol. I, for example, cost £2,055/9/0. For the tabling of this report, see the *Journals*, LXXXVII (8 August 1832), 570.

27. 1771, pp. 135–136, 16 June 1755.

28. *Downs*, p. 10; Welch's article is in the *Transactions of the Bibliographical Society*, XIV, 175–241.

29. *Forster MSS.*, XIII, 1, f. 117. Letter of 27 June 1758, to Mrs. Chapone.

NOTES TO CHAPTER V

1. *Forster MSS.*, XVI, 1, f. 65, 3 September 1741.

2. See p. 112.

3. *Forster MSS.*, XIII, 3, ff. 101–102.

4. *Alexander Pope: A Bibliography*, Austin, [Tex.], 1927, I (Part II), xliv.

5. *Monthly Magazine*, XL (1815), 137. Letter of 5 August 1754.

6. See also under Castelnau, Kelly, Acherley, Giannone, and Salmon in Chapter VIII.

7. P.C.C. Cheslyn 266, abstracted in *N&Q*, 12 S. XI (1922), 342–344.

8. *N&Q*, 7 S. IX (1890), 301. Sale of Mary Richardson's stock, 1766.

9. Proposals were advertised in the *Journal*, 23 October 1730, where Richardson's name heads a list of entrepreneurs. Seven years later he offered the manuscripts to the Society for the Encouragement of Learning. See *Sale*, pp. 6–9, for a discussion of the printing and publication of Roe.

10. "Register," I, 455, 26 February 1736.

11. *Forster MSS.*, XIII, 2, f. 5; *Barbauld*, I, 6–7, 2 July 1736.

12. *Barbauld*, I, 89.

13. "Register," II, 74, 12 February 1750.

14. *Athenaeum*, 9 January 1886, p. 67*n*.

15. *Journal*, 17 June 1726.

16. *Ibid.*, 3 February 1727. The conger consisted of Bettesworth, Osborn, Longman, W. and J. Innys, Mears, Browne, Stevens, Woodward, Ford, Symon, Stagg, and Billingsley. Some of these men may have owned the major shares.

17. Sir William Holdsworth, *A History of English Law*, 1903–1938, XII, 127–130.

18. *Monthly Catalogue*, May 1729; *Journal*, 9 June 1730.

19. See Vol. I, xxiv.

20. N.S., II (1901), 404.

21. *Journal*, 13 December 1730.

22. *Ibid.*, 23 October 1730.

23. *Monthly Catalogue*, July 1729.

24. *Forster MSS.*, XIII, 3, f. 14.

25. *Ibid.*, XIII, 2, f. 4; XIII, 3, ff. 24–25.

26. *Journal*. In the issue of this paper, 17 January 1730, the work is advertised as "curiously printed in two vols. 8vo . . . printed for S. Richardson and A. Wilde."

27. Nichols, *Lit. Anec.*, I, 340, gives the names of the members of the "Old Conger," a group that called themselves about 1719 "The Printing Conger": R. Bonwicke, J. Walthoe, B. and S. Tooke, R. Wilkin, and T. Ward. In 1738, "The New Conger" was organized as a rival group; the members of the Old Conger in 1736, according to Nichols, were Bettesworth, Bonwicke, Ware, A. Ward, Osborn, and Wicksted. The New Conger, according to Nichols, was formed by Bettesworth and Charles Rivington. In 1742 its members were Daniel

Midwinter, Arthur Bettesworth, Charles Little, John Pemberton the younger, Richard Ware, Charles Rivington, John and Paul Knapton, Thomas Longman, Aaron Ward, Richard Hett, Stephen Austen, John Wood, and Thomas Bowles, who sold his one-tenth share in the conger to James Hodges, 4 June 1742. As can be seen, the membership fluctuated. In 1745, for example, an agreement among members of this conger was drawn up and signed. It reads: "We the undersigned have been concern'd in a Partnership call'd a Congor as by Articles bearing date of January 1738 now in the hands of Mr. Aaron Ward one of the said partners, among other transactions did at Auctions and other Sales purchase the Several Shares of parts of Copies of Books as above mentioned." This agreement is dated 20 March 1745 and signed by Ware, Ward, John and Paul Knapton, Thomas Longman and Co., Richard Hett, Charles Hitch, James Hodges, Stephen Austen, Henry Pemberton, John Rivington and Co. Arthur Bettesworth and Charles Rivington, the original members, were both dead in 1745, and are represented in this agreement by Charles Hitch and John Rivington. Septimus Rivington in his *Publishing Family of Rivington*, 1919, pp. 76–77, supplies some of this information. He says that in 1745 the ten members of the conger each held about a one-tenth share in eighty-five works. See also Catalogue No. 66, 1941, of Dobell's Antiquarian Bookstore, No. 2 (p. 5).

28. See note 27.

29. Page 309.

30. *McKillop*, pp. 310–311. *The Country Journal: or, The Craftsman*, 28 March 1741, prints in detail the plans of Osborne's Society.

31. *Life of Johnson*, ed. Hill, Oxford, 1887, I, 159.

32. *Gazetteer*, 29 January 1742, announced the first part for 4 February 1742.

33. See Dobell's Catalogue, cited in note 27, Item No. 32.

34. See Dobell's Catalogue, cited in note 27, Item No. 33.

35. *Forster MSS.*, XIII, 2, f. 4.

36. *Ibid.*, f. 12.

37. *Journal*, 18 November 1726; *Monthly Catalogue*, November 1726.

38. Bettenham, according to the imprint, printed Vol. II, 1729, and it was sold by Knaplock, Bettesworth, King, Pemberton, and Clarke.

39. *Forster MSS.*, XIII, 2, f. 5, 5 July 1736.

40. *Ibid.*, f. 22, 12 April 1739.

41. The date in the imprint is 1728. For the date 1727 and for other information about Chambers, see Charles J. Longman, *The House of Longman*, ed. Chandler, London, New York, Toronto, 1936, pp. 76–77; 465–468; 470–471.

42. Page 318.

43. *Forster MSS.*, XIII, 2, f. 22, 12 April 1739.

44. See p. 163.

45. For the royal license, see P.R.O., "Warrant Books," No. 367, p. 362.

46. *Journal*, October 6.

47. A copy of the Proposals, dated 30 November 1758, is in the B.M.

48. *Gazetteer*, 5 November 1744.

49. P.R.O., "Warrant Books," No. 368, p. 150.

50. "Register," II, 9.

51. Nichols, *Lit. Anec.*, II, 553–554; *Gentleman's Magazine*, LIV (1784), 892. For the comment on Psalmanazar, see *Forster MSS.*, XVI, 1, f. 26.

52. *Second Part of Mr. Bower's Answer,* 1757, pp. 17–18.

53. Edward S. Noyes, *The Letters of Tobias Smollett,* Cambridge, [Mass.], 1926, pp. 59, 65, 66, 67, 193, 194.

54. "Tobias Smollett and the *Universal History,*" MLN, LVI (1941), 1–14. On the other hand, a letter of Smollett, 8 May 1763, says that he wrote "a small part of the Modern Universal History" (Rivington, *op. cit.* in note 27, pp. 43–44).

55. *Monthly Magazine,* XLVIII (1819), 327, a letter written by Richardson's nephew, William, at his uncle's dictation, 5 April 1759.

56. Fragment of *A.L.s.,* to Benjamin Kennicott, quoted in a Catalogue of Francis Edwards, London bookseller, No. 396 (December, 1919), p. 214.

57. See under *Universal History* in Longman, *op. cit.* in note 41.

58. "Register," II, 189.

59. Rivington, *op. cit.* in note 27, p. 63; Dobell's Catalogue, cited in note 27, Item No. 31.

NOTES TO CHAPTER VI

1. See advertisement in Salmon's *Roman Stations in Britain,* 1726.

2. *McKillop,* p. 295; *Journal,* 22 July 1728; advertisement in Salmon's *New Survey of Great Britain,* Part VI, p. 482.

3. For Ogilvie's address, see *Country Journal,* 5 April 1729; for his army career, see Charles Dalton, *George the First's Army, 1714–1727,* 1910, 1912, I, 345.

4. *Journals of the House of Commons,* XXII (12 March 1735), 412.

5. *Barbauld,* I, clxix.

6. II, 167.

7. Third ed., 1742, II, 84.

8. Montagu Pennington, *Memoirs of the Life of Mrs. Elizabeth Carter,* 2nd ed., 1808, I, 207–210.

9. Dorothy Brewster, *Aaron Hill,* New York, 1913, p. 192.

10. *Dobson,* p. 96; *Forster MSS.,* XVI, 2, f. 49. Morell's poem was entitled "On his Unfinished Plan of a Poem call'd 'The Castle of Indolence.'"

11. *Country Journal,* 6 June 1730.

12. Peter Cunningham, "James Thomson and David Mallet," in *Miscellanies of the Philobiblon Society,* IV (1857–1858), 34; *Country Journal,* 6 June 1730; G. C. Macaulay, *James Thomson,* 1907, p. 31; and articles by John E. Wells in *N&Q,* CLXXX (1941), 350 and in *Library,* 4 S. XXII (1942), 223–243.

13. Wilmot sold the copyright to Robert Dodsley in 1744 (*Straus,* p. 328).

14. *An Account of the Life, Character, and Poems of Mr.* [Thomas] *Black-lock,* 1754, p. 4.

15. See p. 207. The advertisement is in the *London Chronicle,* 8–10 February 1759, and in the book itself, p. 104.

16. *Forster MSS.,* XIII, 2, f. 7.

17. *Ibid.,* XII, 1, f. 166, 24 April 1756. In later life Duck had become rector at Byfleet, the ancestral home of the Richardsons.

18. *Ibid.,* XV, 3, f. 24. William Duncombe wrote to Richardson that Jeffreys would be glad to have the bill for the printing, which he was ready to discharge.

19. *Daily Advertiser,* 24 May 1756.

20. *Barbauld*, II, 104.

21. *Cornhill Magazine*, LXXIII (1932), 474–475, 4 December [1758].

22. *Barbauld*, II, 61–64. Jane Collier took exception to one of Richardson's proposed changes in the text.

23. *Correspondence of Jonathan Swift*, ed. Ball, 1910–1914, IV, 209, 211; V, 443–444, 390–391; VI, 2n., 39.

24. *Ibid.*, VI, 67–68. The Dublin edition was called *A Treatise on Polite Conversation*, 1738.

25. *Forster MSS.*, XVI, 1, f. 53.

26. Chalmers in his Biographical Dictionary attributes to Browne the editorship of this volume.

27. *Barbauld*, II, 246.

28. *Ibid.*, II, 253.

29. *Forster MSS.*, XII, 1, f. 25.

30. See the preface by Horace Walpole.

31. First ed., 1742, IV, 92.

32. Wilbur Cross, *The History of Henry Fielding*, New Haven, [Conn.], 1918, II, 12.

33. *Barbauld*, VI, 262.

34. Offered for sale by J. W. Southgate in his Catalogue of a sale, 21–22 January 1828, Items No. 211, 239.

35. *Barbauld*, VI, 243, 24 January 1753. Can Richardson be right about her age? She is said to have been born in 1720.

36. B.M. *Add. MSS.*, 38,730, p. 148. The entry reads William and John Richardson, Salisbury Court. Richardson's brother, Benjamin, had a son John, who may have joined his cousin in the business. The date of this sale is 1769; the price, £2/5/6.

37. The manuscript of this letter and of those cited immediately below are in the Cornell University Library. They are in the handwriting of Richardson's daughter. His own handwriting had become almost illegible at this date, and he frequently dictated his letters or had his daughter or nephew make fair copies of them.

38. *An Account of the Rise, Progress, and Present State of the Magdalen Charity*, 1761, p. 151.

39. First ed., 1754, IV, 142.

40. II, 119.

41. *Forster MSS.*, XI, f. 269.

42. William G. Moss, *The History and Antiquities of the Town and Port of Hastings*, 1824, pp. 114–115.

43. Third ed., 1751–1750, IV, 241–242.

44. II, 221–222.

45. Charles F. Mullett, *The Letters of Doctor George Cheyne to Samuel Richardson*, Columbia, [Mo.], 1943, p. 121.

46. *Forster MSS.*, XIII, 3, f. 6.

47. Nichols, *Lit. Anec.*, V, 329–330.

48. *Forster MSS.*, XVI, 1, f. 11.

49. First ed., 1742, IV, 113–114.

50. Third ed., I, iv.

51. "Register," I, 476.

52. William Munk, *Roll of the Royal College of Physicians of London,* 2nd ed., 1878.

53. Page 315.

54. *Sale,* pp. xi–xii.

55. Thomas Faulkner, *The History and Antiquities of Brentford, Ealing, and Chiswick,* 1845, pp. 465–466.

56. Bunce was in all likelihood the grandson of Stephen Bunce of Deal, Kent, the home of Richardson's friend, Elizabeth Carter. He contributed a poem to the collection of the poetry of Duncombe's brother-in-law, John Hughes, edited by William Duncombe in 1735 (Thomas Milner, *The Life, Times, and Correspondence of the Rev. Isaac Watts,* 1834, p. 505*n*).

57. *Anec. of Bowyer,* p. 542.

58. 11 January 1724 and subsequent issues.

59. *A Plain Narrative of Facts,* 1758, pp. i–ii.

60. February 17 and subsequent issues.

61. *Private Journal and Literary Remains of John Byrom,* ed. for the Chetham Society by Richard Parkinson, Manchester, 1853–1857, II (Part II), 521.

62. Manuscript letters, cited in note 37, a letter to Lady Barbara Montagu, 15 October 1759.

63. *Private Journal,* cited in note 61, II (Part II), 520, 543, for the printing of *An Epistle to a Gentleman of the Temple; Forster MSS.,* XVI, 2, ff. 46–47, for the quotations from Behmen and from Law. Among these papers is also a poem of Byrom's in manuscript, apparently a rhymed review of Aaron Hill's *The Art of Acting,* 1746 (*Forster MSS.,* XVI, 2, f. 55).

64. *Barbauld,* V, 107.

65. *Ibid.,* V, 109, 112.

66. See p. 352.

67. *Barbauld,* VI, a facsimile of a letter to Richardson, 29 February 1747 [*for* 1748].

68. *Ibid.,* VI, 13.

69. *Ibid.,* III, 106.

70. Harry Ransom, *The Rewards of Authorship in the Eighteenth Century,* Austin, [Tex.], 1938, p. 62.

71. Pages 292–293. Pope attributed this article to Dennis, but Edward Hooker in his edition of the *Critical Works of John Dennis* (Baltimore, 1943, II, ix, 526) says that there is no conclusive proof that Dennis wrote it. He accepts Dennis' authorship simply because of the kind of attack that is here made on Pope. The poems compared are Pope's "Windsor Forest" with Denham's "Copper's Hill"; and Pope's "Ode for Music on St. Cecilia's Day" with Dryden's "Alexander's Feast."

72. *Forster MSS.,* XIII, 3, f. 12.

73. James Boswell, *Life of Johnson,* ed. Hill, Oxford, 1887, I, 318.

74. Ellen Leyburn, "Bishop Berkeley: *The Querist," Proc. Royal Irish Academy,* XLIV, Sec. C, No. 3 (1937), 84–85.

75. *Hist. MSS. Comm., Manuscripts of the Earl of Egmont, Diary of the first Earl of Egmont (Viscount Percival),* II, 275.

76. *Monthly Magazine,* XXXIII (1812), 541.

77. *Barbauld*, V, 194.

78. *Ibid.*, V, 217–218; 225–230; 237–238.

79. Samuel Burdy, *The Life of Philip Skelton, by Samuel Burdy*, ed. Moore, Oxford, 1914, p. 100.

80. John Keble, "The Life of . . . Thomas Wilson," being Vol. I, Parts I and II, of Wilson's *Works*, 1863, pp. xv, 923.

81. *Ibid.*, pp. 913–914.

82. 1762–1761, II, 102–103.

83. *Barbauld*, V, 44.

84. *Forster MSS.*, XIII, 3, f. 6, 2 April 1743.

NOTES TO CHAPTER VII

1. P.C.C. Cheslyn, 266. The codicil referring to this partnership is printed in *N&Q*, 12 S. XI (1922), 344. It is dated 5 July 1760.

2. B.M. *Add. MSS.*, 38,730, f. 118. At the Queen's Arms in St Paul's Churchyard, 26 April 1759.

3. *Dottin*, p. 462; *Forster MSS.*, XV, 1, a letter to Eusebius Silvester, 17 July 1759.

4. *A.L.s.*, quoted in the Catalogue of Henry Sotheran and Co., 12 November 1904, No. 646, Item No. 696.

5. R. A. Austen-Leigh, "William Strahan and his Ledgers," *Library*, 4 S. III (1923), 270.

6. P.R.O. "Warrant Books," No. 365, p. 321 and No. 366, p. 42.

7. See p. 354.

8. Thomas C. Hansard, *Typographia*, 1825, pp. 176, 184.

9. *Baskett* v. *Cunningham, et al.*, 1762, II Eden 137. See also I Wm Bl Rep. 370.

10. R. A. Austen-Leigh, *The Story of a Printing House*, 2nd ed., 1912, pp. 10–11.

11. *Basket[t]* v. *University of Cambridge*, 1758, I Wm Bl 105.

12. *Library*, 4 S. III (1922), 100–101.

13. For these newspaper charges and countercharges, see the *London Chronicle*, 4–7, 7–9 April; 26–28, 28–30 May; 11–13 June; 4–7 July; 5–8 September; 1–3 October 1761.

14. Sir William Holdsworth, *A History of English Law*, 1903–1938, XII, 75.

15. Edward Arber, *A Transcript of the Registers of the Company of Stationers*, I, 115.

16. *Ibid.*

17. W. W. Greg and E. Boswell, *Records of the Court of the Stationers' Company 1576 to 1602*, for the Bibliographical Society, 1930, p. lxiv; pp. 48–49; p. 70.

18. Henry R. Plomer, *A Dictionary of the Booksellers and Printers Who Were at Work . . . from 1641 to 1667*, 1907, under More, Fletcher, and Atkyns. The facts here are essentially correct, save in some details, but the three entries were apparently written independently and not carefully compared. Plomer consulted the documents in the case in Chancery that he cites, but he failed to consult the reports of other cases involving the same litigants.

19. Atkyns was the brother of Sir Edward Atkyns (1587–1669), and the uncle of Sir Robert Atkyns (1621–1709) and Sir Edward Atkyns (1630–1698), Baron

of the Exchequer. His great-nephew was Sir Robert Atkyns (1647–1711), who wrote the *History of Gloucestershire*.

20. Richard Atkyns, *The Original and Growth of Printing*, 1664, pp. 14–15. See also *Stationers* v. *Law Patentees*, Carter 89. Atkyns in his pamphlet says that the injunction in Chancery was granted for "*Poulton's Abridgment.*" John D. Cowley in his *Bibliography of Abridgments, Digests . . . to the Year 1800* (for the Selden Society, 1932), lists no edition of Pulton during this period. If a work of Pulton was actually reprinted at this date, it would, I think, have been called his *Kalender*, for this title was generally used in the seventeenth century for his abridgment of the statutes. Perhaps the effect of the injunction was to make copies of this edition very rare.

21. *Stationers* v. *Law Patentees*, Carter 89. The cases reported by Carter are in the main those in the Court of Common Pleas, 1664–1667. This report, however, is of the arguments of counsel before Parliament. The law book in question is called "this book of Rolls," in the pleadings of Atkyns' counsel. In the heading of the case it is called "Roll's Abridgment." The first edition of Rolle's abridgment was published for Roper, Tyton, A. Crooke, W. Leake, G. Sawbridge, T. Dring, T. Collins, J. Place, W. Place, J. Starkey, T. Basset, R. Pawlet, and S. Heyrick (Herrick), in 1668. The dispute between Atkyns and Roper had begun in 1666. Though Atkyns secured an injunction in Chancery and though he was upheld when the Stationers appealed the case to Parliament, he apparently allowed the book to be published in 1668 without mention in the imprint that it was published by assignment from him. See Cowley, *op. cit.* in note 20, pp. liv–lv.

22. *Roper* v. *Streater, cit.* 90 E.R. 107; 2 Show 258; 3 Keb 792. Roper and Tyton were also involved in printing Crooke's *Reports*, but they were joined on this occasion by only four of the group of booksellers whose names appear in the imprint of Rolle's *Abridgment*—John Starkey, Thomas Basset, Thomas Collins, and John Place. Streator sued Roper in 1670.

23. Plomer, *op. cit.* in note 18, under Sawbridge and under Roycroft. At one place, Plomer says that Richard Roycroft was a sharer in the King's printer's patent, but this seems to be an error, for I think he means Thomas Roycroft. On the other hand, he does not mention Samuel Roycroft either in his *Dictionary* of 1641–1667 or of 1668–1725. For imprints that show both King's printer and law printer linked, see, for example, Edmund Wingate's *An exact abridgment of all statutes in force and use*, 1681, and Joseph Washington's *A continuation of the abridgment of all the statutes*, 1699.

24. See, for example, three editions of *An exact abridgment of all the statutes in force and use from Magna Charta, 9 H. 3. to the beginning of the reign of King George*, printed in 1720, 1725, and 1730–1737 by his Majesty's Printers and by the assigns of Edward Sayer. John Cay's *Abridgment*, 1739, has a similar imprint. Cay's edition of the statutes at large was printed by Thomas Baskett, the son of John and his successor as King's printer, and by Catherine Lintot. Richardson joined with Mark Baskett, King's printer, in the proposals for Ruffhead's edition of the statutes at large, and this edition was finally printed by Mark Baskett and by Woodfall and Strahan, successors to the law patent of Richardson and Lintot. In the year after Richardson's death and before Woodfall and Strahan had acquired the patent, John Cay's abridgment of the statutes was

printed by Mark Baskett and by Elizabeth Richardson and Catherine Lintot.

25. *Basket[t]* v. *University of Cambridge*, I Wm Bl 105.

26. *The First Minute Book of* . . . *the Oxford University Press,* ed. Gibson and Johnson, Oxford, 1943, p. 57.

27. Strickland Gibson and Sir William Holdsworth, "Charles Viner's General Abridgment of Law and Equity," *Proceedings and Papers* of the Oxford Bibliographical Society, II (1930), Part IV, 229–325.

NOTES TO CHAPTER IX

1. These books are marked with an asterisk following the date in the list of books printed by Richardson, arranged alphabetically by authors.

2. *Forster MSS.,* XI, f. 35, To Lady Bradshaigh, 19 October 1753.

3. *The Case of Samuel Richardson,* 1753.

4. *Monthly Magazine,* XXXVI (1813), 418.

5. See pp. 155; 301.

6. See Nos. 7 and 8; Nos. 35 and 36; Nos. 37 and 38; Nos. 59 and 60; Nos. 66 and 67; and Nos. 80 and 81. Henry Plomer in his *English Printers' Ornaments,* 1924, reproduces an ornament of the year 1719 (No. 77, p. 209) that may have been the original from which Richardson's No. 26 was copied. His No. 108 (p. 227) is very similar to Richardson's No. 61; and his No. 110 (p. 227) is an ornament of the same conception as Richardson's No. 47.

7. Cambridge, 1932, pp. 321–324.

8. Morison, *op. cit.* in note 7, pp. 69, 321.

9. 1924, pp. 207, 209.

10. *Ars Typographica,* II (1926), 243.

11. *An Introduction to Bibliography,* Oxford, 1927, p. 120.

12. McKerrow, *op. cit.* in note 11, pp. 116, 119.

13. *Ibid.,* pp. 115, 120.

14. See this pirated edition, Vol. I, vii.

15. *Lives of the English Poets,* ed. Hill, Oxford, 1905, II, 367.

16. Advertisements in the *Journal.*

17. Edward N. Hooker, *The Critical Works of John Dennis,* Baltimore, 1943, II, 512.

18. See pp. 129; 108–109; 166.

19. See pp. 219–220.

20. See p. 94.

21. *On the Life, Writings, and Genius of Akenside;* 1832, p. 25.

22. Iolo A. Williams, *Seven XVIIIth Century Bibliographies,* 1924, pp. 88–89.

23. See p. 73.

24. *Aaron Hill,* New York, 1913, p. 251; *Forster MSS.,* XIII, 3, f. 114.

25. *McKillop,* p. 295.

Index

NAMES constituting the main entries in the following alphabetical lists are not indexed unless they appear in other places in the text:

A List of Books Printed by Richardson: Arranged Alphabetically by Authors, pp. 145-228.
A List of Booksellers for Whom Richardson Printed, pp. 317-343.
The Location of Ornaments Belonging to Other Printers, pp. 344–347.
Ornaments Signed by Engravers, pp. 348-349.
Names of master printers, journeyman printers, and those apprenticed to the printing trade are preceded by an asterisk; names of booksellers (other than those in the List of Booksellers, pp. 317-343) are followed by the word *bookseller*.